The Fishermen's Sourcebook
BILL WISNER

OTHER BOOKS BY AUTHOR:

Strange Sea Stories and Legends (1981)
Vanished—Without a Trace! (1977)
The Complete Guide to Salt and Fresh Water Fishing Equipment (1976)
Field & Stream New Guide to Saltwater Fishing (1973)
How to Catch Salt-Water Fish (1973)
Montauk Guide and Cook Book (1956)

BOOKS CO-AUTHORED WITH JOSEPH J. COOK:

Coastal Fishing for Beginners (1977)
Blue Whale, Vanishing Leviathan (1973)
The Nightmare World of the Shark (1968)
Warrior Whale (1966)
The Phantom World of the Octopus and Squid (1965)
Killer Whale (1963)
Your First Book of Salt Water Fishing (1961)

OTHER CO-AUTHORED BOOKS:

Sportfishing for Sharks—with Frank Mundus (1971)

THE FISHERMEN'S SOURCEBOOK

BILL WISNER

Illustrations by Victoria Blanchard, Jan Cook, and John B. Miller

MACMILLAN PUBLISHING CO., INC., New York
COLLIER MACMILLAN PUBLISHERS, London

The author acknowledges with thanks the following companies for additional illustrations used in the text:

Burke Fishing Lures for the following illustrations in Chapter 2: plug and popping plug.

Sampo Division of Rome Specialty Company, Inc. for the following illustrations in Chapter 2: barrel swivel, 3-way swivel, and snap swivel.

Mustad & Son (U.S.A.) Inc. for the following illustrations in Chapter 3: straight shank, sliced shank, curved down shank, central draught shank, humped shank, forged shank, bent-up shank, circle shank, triangular shank, round shank, ring hook eye, needle hook eye, single hook, double hook, and treble hook.

Macmillan Publishing Co., Inc.
866 Third Avenue, New York, N.Y. 10022
Collier Macmillan Canada, Inc.

Library of Congress Cataloging in Publication Data
Wisner, William L.
    The fishermen's sourcebook.
    1. Fishing. I. Title.
SH441.W58 1983   799.1   82-24940
ISBN 0-02-630570-4

10 9 8 7 6 5 4 3 2 1

Printed in the United States of America

*This book is dedicated with much affection
to my wife, Dorothy Elizabeth. Now that it's finished, maybe
she'll see enough of me to stop asking, "Who's that guy?"*

Contents

INTRODUCTION

Like many lifelong coastal residents, I cannot recall precisely when I started fishing. I know it was before I began making life miserable for my kindergarten teacher. I have been trying to match wits with finned creatures longer than I care to admit. It has been a fascinating affair. I was launched by my dad who was a product of the barefoot-boy-with-worm-on-bent-pin school of angling of the Midwest; and my maternal grandfather, a bayman and deep-water sailor-fisherman. My grandfather was a retiree from the U.S. Life Saving Service, a rugged bunch of men who launched and rowed their lifeboats in the surf.

I have been also writing about fishing for longer than I care to acknowledge. I have written about fishing for every medium except television—literally hundreds of magazine articles, my own fishing columns in two major metropolitan New York dailies and Long Island's leading newspaper, and weekly fishing programs aired by radio stations WMCA, WOR, and WCBS in Manhattan and stations on Long Island and in Connecticut. I also claim responsibility for a dozen or so fishing or sea books.

From all of my writing I originally planned to cull a king-sized harvest of nuggets of angling information and gather it together between the covers of a single volume. It was a project consuming two and a half years. The harvest was gargantuan, so enormous that even an encyclopedia format and more than one thousand pages were not enough to contain it all.

Instead of the monster originally planned, Macmillan Publishing Co. decided on the present format and size. I'm glad Macmillan made the change because I think its format makes this book unique among angling volumes. I know of no other quite like it.

What I've endeavored to do in this book is provide a sourcebook of information that will be helpful to both beginner and seasoned angler. (None of us ever learns all there is to know about fishing, and you better believe it.) I hope that *The Fishermen's Sourcebook* contributes to your stockpile of knowledge of the sport, and that by so doing it heightens your enjoyment and success as a disciple of the rod and reel.

Bill Wisner
Brightwaters, Long Island

1. Tackle & Accessories

You've heard that old saying "Fingers were invented before forks," from the times when it was still considered impolite to pick up a piece of fried chicken instead of chasing it around a plate with eating utensils. With the same reasoning we can speculate that the first fishing tackle was some equipment man is born with: two highly functional hands (the first "fishhooks," in a manner of speaking) on the ends of two quickly maneuverabie appendages, or arms (the earliest "fishing rods"). With this gear coordinated by an animal cunning, a primitive man could wade into a stream and either seize fishes with his hands or knock (or perhaps kick) them out onto the shore.

Over tens of thousands of years came improvements in his fish-catching methods. There were spears and, for mass harvests, nets and traps. Somewhere along the line, the primitive fisherman desired a better personal contact with his quarry. Perhaps it was when fishes were in water too deep to wade.

At any rate, the passage of time brought the very earliest fishing lines. On the end of this fishing line primitive man tied a device called a gorge, which subsequently was replaced by that refinement we know as a fishhook. (See "Hooks," Chapter 3.) For a long time man's fishing tackle consisted of just such a simple hand line.

The next refinement had to be a pole. You can make an angler wince by referring to a fishing rod as a "pole"; but back in the dimly lighted ages I'm talking about it *was* a pole, cut or broken from a bush or tree. Now the primitive fisherman had come upon a way to extend his reach and to better present that offering, the bait, he had learned to impale on his hook. Reels, rods made expressly for fishing, lures, fishing lines, and other goodies were still far, far in the future. Their evolvement may have started when man discovered that he could have some fun while fishing for his larder. At that moment a sport was born.

Fishing tackle has come a long, long way just since World War II, bringing a list of excellent refinements that include spinning equipment, fiberglass rods, amazingly lifelike plastic lures, improved synthetic lines, and so on.

There's more to successful fishing than just catching fish. Equally important are the relaxation and fun. And one thing is certain: to derive the most pleasure from fishing and to enjoy maximum success, you must be properly equipped. Mind you, I said "properly," not "expensively."

Anglers today can select from an enormous,

often bewildering, array of tackle. The choice is governed to a great extent by the kinds of fishing. If there are any restrictions they're imposed only by the wallet. Even with such restrictions, an angler can be well equipped without its costing him an arm and a leg.

Tips on Tackle

Although today's fishermen face an array of tackle that is awesome in its enormity and diversity, selection isn't as difficult as it might appear, and I can offer a few general tips to make things easier—I hope—for you.

1. For openers, decide on which methods—trolling, fly casting, bottom fishing or whatever—will claim your attention, at least for the time being. While you're at it, take into consideration the approximate size ranges of the fishes you'll be seeking. By rights you should also learn something about the fighting characteristics of these fishes, since those characteristics conceivably could influence your choice of gear.

2. Having decided on what angling methods and species of fish you'll start with, watch some of the action, noting the equipment used (and keeping in mind that experienced fishermen may be using lighter tackle than would be practical for you). And don't hesitate to ask questions. I've never met a seasoned fisherman yet who wouldn't share some of his knowledge with newcomers.

3. You can get additional guidance in tackle shops. Their personnel are almost invariably anglers themselves. (Such might not be the case in the sports-goods section of a department store.) Take an experienced fisherman along with you when you go to buy.

4. Set your sights on quality. Personally, I'd rather have one good rod-'n'-reel combo than two or three inferior ones. Quality isn't that much more expensive, even in inflationary times, because in the long run it always pays off in dependability, durability and performance. Cheap, junky tackle doesn't give you a good start. Its inferior performance and failures—and you can be sure there will

be failures—will not only rob you of enjoyment and fish but might discourage you entirely. Besides, that old saying still goes: the cheapest can turn out to be the most expensive.

5. Stay with name-brand, long-established tackle manufacturers. When you buy their products you buy years of research, field testing, technical advances, sound production methods and a reputation that usually is backed by warranties. Further, such manufacturers often have arrangements for repairs and worn parts replacement. In the cases of obscure manufacturers, domestic and foreign, be very wary. You could wind up with junk.

By all means take advantage of sales of name-brand tackle items. You might indeed get bargains.

6. A detail that can be overlooked when selecting tackle—and often is by beginners—is ease and comfort in handling. A person's height plays a part; so does arm length (especially important in selection of casting tackle). General build, age and strength are considerations too. Ease and comfort in handling—and I don't mean when fighting a fish, although that's important too—are considerations, because tackle that is fatiguing to use drains some pleasure from fishing.

If possible, actually fish with a rod of the type and caliber you have in mind for yourself. Maybe a friend has one you can borrow. Failing that, handle some rods in a tackle store. Note how different overall lengths, weights and butt (handle section) lengths feel to you. Maybe the salesman will mount a matching reel on a rod you're considering, then hold on to the end of the line to simulate a fish's resistance so that you can get an idea of how the outfit will feel to you in action.

Spinning vs. Conventional Tackle

One of the greatest success stories in the field of sport-fishing equipment, as I mentioned, is the enthusiastic acceptance of spinning tackle in the United States after World War II. Spinning tackle had been introduced earlier without making much of a splash; then the war came along and it was

shoved far in the background in favor of more important items like guns, tanks and aircraft.

Its introduction in the United States was resumed after World War II, but it didn't meet with popularity at first. The main reason was that conventional tackle (that with revolving-spool reels)

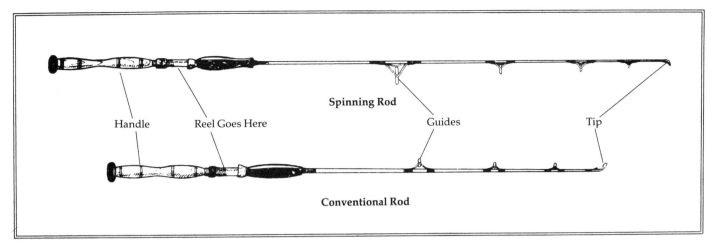

Handle   Reel Goes Here   **Spinning Rod**   Guides   Tip

Conventional Rod

had been around too long. The interloper, an alien from Europe, was too radical by comparison— "180 ° out," you might say. Its reel was mounted on the underside of the rod instead of on top, and its crank was designed for left-hand operation instead of right-hand. The long axis of its reel spool was in the long axis of the rod, not at right angles to it as in the case of a conventional reel's. Oddest of all, the spinning reel's spool was fixed, did not revolve. The spinning rod represented a radical change too. It was longer than its conventional counterpart. Its line guides were much larger than those of a regular rod, and they were on the rod's underside instead of on top.

All this took a bit of getting used to, and for a while many anglers were resistant to the change. But once spinning tackle's virtues were realized, recognition and acceptance came quickly. Today the former interloper is now every bit as popular as conventional tackle, even more so in some angling arenas. That brings up an important point:

A minute ago I mentioned spinning tackle's virtues. These lie chiefly in casting. Spinning equipment was designed originally for casting, lures and natural baits, and in this it's superior to conventional gear. It's easier for beginners to use, and they can acquire respectable casting distance sooner than with conventional tackle. Generally speaking, average anglers can cast farther with it. A cardinal virtue is that there are none of those backlashes and horrible tangles that can accompany casting with conventional equipment. And this brings up another important point:

Too many anglers look on spinning equipment as all-purpose tackle and expect it to perform equally well in all methods and under a wide assortment of conditions. Granted, spinning tackle has versatility and can be wielded in just about all fishing procedures up to a point. But to expect it to perform as well in, say, trolling or bottom fishing

—in all situations—as it does in casting is asking for disappointment and possibly lost fish. The willowy characteristic of a spinning rod that makes it superior to a conventional equivalent in casting is a detail that can work against it in trolling, causing a lure or bait to literally leap from wave to wave in the boat's wake and so be airborne more than it's in the water, where it can do its work. Similarly, a spinning rod's flexibility is such that it can pose problems in handling the fairly heavy rigs often used in bottom fishing. That combination of flexibility and heavy rigs can mask the bait nibblings of a sneaky fish, hinder setting the hook, and make it more difficult to land the fish.

Fishermen should keep it in mind that there are limits as regards the weights of lures and baited rigs that spinning tackle can handle satisfactorily. Anglers who go in for an appreciable variety of fishing might do well to be outfitted with both conventional and spinning tackle in appropriate calibers.

Some reasons for the anatomical differences in spinning tackle:

1. Generally longer, more willowy rods than the conventional equivalents: this, because it's basically casting tackle. (Ever notice the flexibility and "whippiness" of fly rods?)

2. Reel mounted underneath the rod instead of on top of it: This is a necessity because of the way line leaves (and returns) to a fixed-spool reel. For the same reason, the long axis of a spinning reel spool is in the long axis of the rod.

3. Line guides on the rod's underside instead of on top: Line leaves a fixed-spool reel in wide coils, which gravity would cause to slap against the rod if the guides were on top. With the guides underneath, gravity helps keep the coils of line clear of the rod. It's also because those wide coils that

guide on a spinning rod, notably those closest to the reel, are so much larger than those on a conventional rod. They must be large to literally gather in those loose loops of line paying out from the reel.

4. Reel crank on the left, instead of on the right, for right-handed anglers: This leaves the favored hand free for casting. For southpaws, or left-handed fishermen, there are spinning reels with their reel crank on the right. There are also "bisexual" models that can be flipped back and forth to have their crank on the right or left, as desired.

The most important difference between spinning gear and conventional tackle is that which is the very reason for the former's existence: the fixed-spool reel. It's modern fishing tackle's most revolutionary detail. After generations of fishing with reels whose spools revolved, this was the innovation hardest to accept.

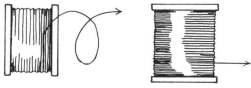

Fixed-Reel Spool   **Turning Spool**

A simple little demonstration illustrates the difference between a fixed-reel spool and one that turns. Pick up an ordinary spool of sewing thread. To simulate the revolving spool of a conventional reel, hold the spool of thread so that its long axis is parallel to your body, the loose end of the thread pointing away from you. Pull on the loose end of the thread, away from you. The spool turns, of course, to allow thread to pay out. To retrieve thread (fishing line), the spool must be turned in the opposite direction. Now hold the thread spool by one end, its other end pointing straight away from you. Hold it firmly. Seize the loose end of the thread and pull that in a straight line away from you. This is a simulation of a spinning reel's spool in operation. Note the difference in the way thread (fishing line) leaves the spool, in loose coils.

It's when line is retrieved that we find another major difference between the two types of reels. Because the spinning reel spool doesn't turn, it obviously can't retrieve line in the same fashion as a conventional reel. Instead, the spinning reel has a mechanism that is designed to gather in the line as the reel handle is cranked and evenly deposit it back on the spool. Reel manufacturers have developed a few different kinds of pickup mechanisms. Most common is the so-called bail. One bail design looks like a semicircle of heavy wire; another, des-

ignated as an automatic pickup, consists of a small metal arm, curved to gather in line. Whatever its design, the mechanism is activated when the reel crank is turned to retrieve line and is usually out of the way in casting.

Tip: Before buying reels, newcomers to spinning should compare—actually work—different types of pickup mechanisms. They may find, as many of their predecessors have, that they favor one over others.

Spinning Reels

There are two basic kinds of spinning reels. One, the more common, is the so-called open-face design. The other is called—you guessed it—closed-face. The latter type is divided into spinning and spin-casting models. All these reels have a fixed, or non-revolving, spool. And they all, like conventional reels, have an adjustable drag, or brake.

The major difference between an open-face spinning reel and a standard closed-face model is this: In the former, the spool is more or less exposed, nestled within a cuplike housing. You can see its line. In a closed-face reel the spool is concealed inside a cone-shaped housing. Line leaves and re-enters the reel via a hole in that cone's apex.

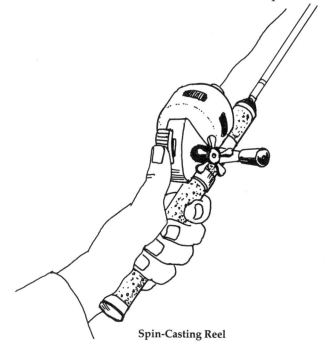

Spin-Casting Reel

The so-called spin-casting reel, also known as a push-button spinning reel, is something else again, a kind of hybrid. Its major features are the same as those of the closed-face model, and it functions in basically the same way. The two notable differences: (1) it mounts on top of the rod instead of underneath; and (2) it has a push-button lever with which the fisherman can control the outflow of line in casting. With this control lever you can slow or even stop a lure or bait in flight to drop it into a small target area. Such sharpshooting requires practice, but skilled spin casters can literally drop their rig on a dime—well, maybe on a quarter or half a buck. There's one other difference in connection with a spin-casting reel. A rod designed for it usually has an offset reel seat.

Which is better, open-face model or a closed-face type? It comes down to personal preference. I think statistics would show that more of the former are in overall use. One reason is that the cone or face on a closed-face model cuts down on casting distance by exerting friction on the line as it passes through the hole. But this is no problem if considerable casting distance isn't a major requirement. Another reason anglers might prefer the open-face type is that it's easier to check on the amount of line on the spool; and that line is more accessible if you have a problem with it. On the credit side for the closed-face type, notably the push-button model, many beginners find them easier to use.

Backlash

If ever spinning tackle earns the gratitude of anglers, especially casters, and most especially surf casters, it's for the elimination of backlashes, those quirks in conventional or revolving-spool reels that cause fierce line tangles or "birds' nests." A backlash can occur only with a revolving-spool reel. You'll see why when I explain what happens.

When you cast, your rig becomes a projectile. Its weight, propelled by the cast's force, pulls line off the reel spool, making it revolve rapidly. So long as the velocity of its turning doesn't become excessive for the rate at which line is paying out, O.K. But if the spool's turning speed becomes too great, the spool overtakes the outgoing line and begins to take it back in. This reversal occurs rudely and lasts only seconds, which is enough to create hideous tangles. These aggravating snarls consume a lot of precious fishing time to untangle (to say nothing about their wear and tear on the nervous system). Some are so hopeless that anglers simply cut them free and sacrifice the line.

There are conventional reels with built-in devices for reducing backlashes. One kind is hydraulic; another is magnetic; a third operates on an air-resistance principle, utilizing vanes. They all cost a certain amount of casting distance, which is why veteran casters prefer to use the old thumb,

judiciously applied to the reel spool as a light brake.

Tackle Weight

There's an old fishermen's saying to the effect that the lighter the tackle, the greater the sport. In the main that's true, but there's a detail or two that saying doesn't mention. The lighter the tackle, the greater the challenge—I mean, the demands on the wielder. In other words, the lighter the tackle, the more you must know what you're doing. And even if you know what you're doing, you must be prepared to lose rigs and line because there will be times when the line will part for one reason or another: the force of a fish's fight, abrasion on a rock or other obstruction, or possibly a fatigue that has developed in the line after appreciable use. Repeated losses of lures and considerable yardage of line can start to become expensive. Most important, there are losses of fish. It's up to you to decide if any extra thrills you get from playing fish on light tackle are worth those risks.

At the other extreme is tackle that is unnecessarily heavy for the assignments at hand. While this does more to assure catches (when the fish are hooked, I mean), it also shortens the playing time by fatiguing the fish more quickly, and costs the angler some action.

A beginner might better favor tackle that is just a bit too heavy over equipment that's too light. He or she can always graduate to lighter tackle as their experience dictates.

Over the years several methods of grading tackle for what I call caliber—i.e., light, medium, heavy —have been proposed. A couple of them survive in modified form. Others have been abandoned.

Today's calibration of tackle is general, simple, and has some flexibility. I suspect that it will always be that way because, when you come right down to it, grading of tackle as light, medium, heavy or whatever is a personal affair, since so many variables are involved. Everything else being equal, an outfit that is light to one angler might be medium to another, and so on.

Experience—actually fishing—is what establishes each individual's idea as to what constitutes light, medium or heavy tackle. The main criteria are that an angler select equipment that is compatible with the kinds of fishing he does, that is comfortable for him to handle, and gets results— and let calibrations fall where they may.

Grading and Line Strengths

Grading conventional salt-water tackle for caliber, or size, centers mainly around line strengths. A popular procedure, and a practical one, is to rate a rod for the maximum-strength line it can handle efficiently and safely. For example, if that ceiling is 20-lb.-test line, we speak of the gear as being 20-lb. tackle; 30-lb.-test line, 30-lb. tackle, etc. Many rods carry such a manufacturer's designation on a decal. If the user exceeds that recommended maximum, he's on his own.

Rod lengths are not a factor in that particular system of classification. Speaking broadly, fishing methods are more influential in governing rod lengths and diameters. For example, rods for casting are usually longer, and more slender and whippier proportionately, whereas those for general boat fishing are shorter than casting rods, are somewhat thicker proportionately, and consequently stiffer—meaning with more backbone to handle the heavier rigs and to bring up fishes from below.

For comparison purposes, salt-water conventional tackle can be divided into these categories: ultra-light, extra-light, light, medium, heavy and extra-heavy. There's some flexibility in each of those categories. One classification system parallels the line classes employed by the International Game Fish Association (IGFA) for its world records: *ultra-light*, 6- to 12-lb. line; *extra-light*, lines over 12-lb.-test to 20-lb.-test; *light*, 30-lb. line, 4/0 reel; *medium*, 50-lb. line, 6/0 reel; *heavy*, 80-lb.-test line, 9/0 reel; *extra-heavy*, 130-lb. line, 12/0 reel. But there are the usual variations according to fishing methods, sizes of finned game sought, and who's doing the classifying.

For practical purposes, marine spinning tackle can be divided arbitrarily into extra-light, light, medium, heavy and extra-heavy classes. Here line strengths are not the only factor. Also considered are the weights of artificials and baited rigs they can handle.

There's similar grading for fresh-water conventional and spinning tackle, but its classes are lighter simply because in fresh-water fishing everything except the sport and fun of it—and I don't mean this derogatorily at all—is on a reduced size scale: species sought, rigs, and most of the demands posed by average conditions. Fresh water has its own collection of magnificent hefties, such as king salmon, lake trout, muskellunge and the biggest catfishes; but there are no beasts in the same size league as the tunas, monstrous sharks and the biggest marlins. Some fresh-water action calls for fairly heavy rigs, but nothing like some of the monstrosities towed in salt water. Nor does fresh-water angling normally encounter tidal conditions and depths similar to those in open-sea fishing in which sinkers weighing 8, 12 or more ounces may be required to keep a rig on the ocean floor, where it can do its work.

Caliber classification of tackle is necessary for comparison purposes and general recommendations, but any quibbling over it is in my opinion a tempest in a teacup—or, if you prefer, a typhoon in a martini. Keep those classifications in mind but suit yourself. That's what counts.

Rod Construction

Over the decades many different kinds of materials have found their way into fishing rod construction: Calcutta (a cane, so named because it was shipped from that city in India), split bamboo, beryllium copper, tubular steel, Tonkin cane, and assorted woods. But it remained for the modern technology of synthetics to come up with a material approaching the ideal on all counts. That material is fiberglass.

Many fishermen, myself among them, will argue that there's no rod quite like one expertly fashioned from split bamboo, for craftsmanship and performance. But it's also a fact that such rods are expensive, and they require care. All things considered, well-made fiberglass rods are the best for the greatest number of anglers.

Fiberglass

Here, in a couple of nutshells, are the virtues of fiberglass rods: (1) Durability. Handled with reasonable care—I mean without severe abuse—they perform well for years. (2) Minimum maintenance. Unlike wooden and split-bamboo rods, they do not require periodic revarnishing for continued protection, and their color is incorporated. Assuming that the rod hardware—reel seat, line guides, etc. —is of good quality and properly protected against rust and/or salt corrosion, the only replacements that might be needed in time are badly worn or broken guides, or perhaps guide windings that have loosened. (3) Fiberglass rods are less likely than wooden rods to "take a set"—assume a permanent bend in the tip section—after long service. (A permanent bend in a rod's tip impairs its action.) (4) Inherent toughness and ability to cope with stresses and strains. One of the drawbacks of wood rods is that wood can contain hidden flaws that show up under strain, while quality fiberglass is consistent throughout. (5) Availability. There are fiberglass rods for every type of angling in every conceivable size and kind of tip action. (6) The right prices. Good fiberglass rods are within the financial grasp of everyone. And for more affluent fishermen, fiberglass lends itself readily to custom or made-to-order rods.

Recent years have brought a very interesting refinement, the so-called graphite rods. For these, manufacturers combine graphite fibers with fiberglass to produce rods of amazingly light weight and reportedly stronger than fiberglass alone.

Fiberglass rods can be divided into two broad construction categories: solid and tubular or hollow. Assuming equality of materials and workmanship, here's how they compare: solid glass rods are stronger, also heavier, for length, and there are differences in tip section action that can be important to casters. They can be less sensitive and are generally better suited to heavier lures and baited rigs. Tubular or hollow glass rods are apt to be more versatile because of their ability to handle lighter artificials, giving them a greater range of use, which can be important to a guy who must get by with one rod.

Be advised that there are fiberglass rods and fiberglass rods, if you know what I mean. They can differ greatly in quality, ratio of glass to bonding agent, type of agent, and overall construction, including hardware. All of which again underscores my advice to buy from known, reputable manufacturers, as the cheapest often turns out to be the most expensive in the long run.

You think enough of fishing to take it up as a hobby or a sport. Think enough of yourself to buy good equipment.

Taper

All fishing rods have a taper, which is to say that they're thickest in that part of their tip section closest to the handle and butt section, after which they become progressively more slender toward their far end, where the tip-top guide is located. This taper is a major detail. Taper gives rods their degree of flexibility or "bendability." By varying the nature and location of the taper, it's possible to alter rods' flexibility to suit them to general use or better adapt them to specific fishing techniques, or even specialize them for certain assignments.

What is called the tip section, remember, is all the rest of the rod beyond the handle and butt—the section which actually does the rod's work.

In connection with tip sections you'll encounter the terms slow action, moderate action or medium action, fast action, and extra-fast or ultra-fast action. Sometimes the word taper is substituted for "action" in those four terms. They all refer to the extent of bending in rods under stress. Here's an explanation of the terms, with examples:

Slow-action tip. The bending or curvature is progressive throughout, from just beyond the butt handle to the tip-top guide. In other words, the entire tip section bends to a degree, but the curvature increases out toward the end. Many fly rods have slow action, which suits their unique kind of casting.

Medium-action tip. The curvature under stress occupies the tip section's outermost half. Some fly rods have medium action, for the same reason that others have slow action. Moderate and slow actions also are favored for rods wielded in casting-accuracy tournaments.

Fast-action tip. Here the curvature is more or less confined to the tip section's outermost one-third. Fast-action tips are common among spinning rods and many casting rods. Fast action often is favored for the small fresh-water and marine sport fishes because it combines a sensitive tip-top section (to detect sneaky nibbles) with enough power to set the hook quickly. Fast-action tip sections are also seen among the longer, 8- to 9-ft. casting and spinning rods used for salmon and steelhead trout. Here a desired combination is sensitivity for light attacks on the bait and enough muscle to cope with hefty, strong opponents.

Extra-fast-action tip. The curvature under stress is confined to the outermost quarter, or slightly less, of the tip. This is a characteristic of many of the lighter (extra- or ultra-light) or shorter (6½ to 7, 7½ ft.) spinning rods, and is desirable for casting the very light lures rigged with such tackle for panfishes and trout.

Any kind of rod—spinning, conventional, fly-casting or whatever—lends itself to all those types of tip action. Sometimes fishermen building their own rods, or having them custom-made, capitalize on the opportunity to incorporate personal ideas about the nature and degree of taper.

Fiberglass rods are tough and very durable, but even the toughest rods have a limit beyond which they can meet with damage under stress. I once saw a hefty wooden big-game rod fractured just beyond the reel by a 500-lb. bluefin tuna. My point is that if a tackle shop makes a recommendation about the heaviest line that should be used with a particular rod, heed the recommendation. The line will break before the rod does. In other words your line becomes like a fuse or circuit breaker in an overloaded electrical circuit.

Rod Guides

Some pointers on rod guides: You'll find variation in the number of line guides on rods. All conventional and spinning rods are outfitted with a tip-top guide that is at the outermost end and the last guide through which line passes when leaving the rod. The number of other guides in addition to the tip-top varies according to type, model and rod length. Generally speaking, because of their line-gathering function, guides are more numerous on a spinning rod than on a conventional counterpart. A recommended minimum for the shorter spinning rods is usually four or five; on the shorter conventional rods, about three. An important point: If a rod-builder skimps on the number of guides, you can be sure he has skimped in other construction details too. Some amateur rod-makers follow a broad rule that says approximately one guide per foot of overall rod length, but it should be mentioned that there is such a thing as too many guides. This excess imposes unnecessary friction on the line.

Proper spacing can be as important as the number of guides. Guides help to distribute the strain of fighting a fish throughout a rod's length. On a conventional rod, the number and spacing of guides prevent the line from touching the rod at any point when the tip section is bent, a detail you might want to check before purchase. Line touching the rod creates unnecessary friction and wear on the line and guides. This isn't likely to be a problem with spinning rods because the guides are underneath the rod, and gravity tends to keep the line clear. Even so, the guides on a spinning rod should also be checked for a satisfactory number and proper spacing.

Another detail to check, notably on one-piece-tip conventional rods, is alignment of the guides. Poor alignment causes unnecessary wear on both line and guides and can also be indicative of poor workmanship in general. It goes without saying that rods should have quality guides—wear-resistant surfaces where contacts with the line will occur, sturdy construction, neat and adequate windings, and protection against corrosion and rust.

Most conventional and spinning rods have guides of the ring type. But models that are used a lot with wire lines have a tip-top guide of the roller type; some also have a roller guide adjacent to the tip-top. Just about all big-game conventional rods are outfitted with roller guides throughout for smoother paying-out and retrieving of heavy lines. These guides should be checked periodically to make sure their rollers turn smoothly, their frames are not cracked or broken, and their windings are secure.

Rod Joints

Fishermen have numerous topics on which they can debate ad infinitum. One such topic is the question of which is superior, a rod whose tip section is all one piece or one whose tip section consists of joints connected by ferrules. There are two schools of thought, which I'll label the OPT (for One-Piece Tip) and JTS (Jointed-Tip Section) factions.

The OPT's biggest criticism of jointed rods is that each joint is a potential breaking place when the rods are stressed. Further, they charge, each ferrule, being of metal, is more rigid than the material of the sections it joins and therefore inhibits or interrupts the overall tip section's flexibility to a certain degree. Still further, the OPT grouses, ferrules can get corroded or otherwise fouled up and become difficult to put together or disassemble, defeating their purpose. Some anglers, casters chiefly, feel so strongly about these alleged drawbacks that they stay with single-piece tip sections or at least limit the number of ferrules to one.

Before we go further, let the JTS faction point out that there's a limit to the lengths of one-piece tip sections that can be transported and stored conveniently and safely (safely for the rod, that is). Beyond those lengths are custom rods and/or special means of transporting them, usually in rod racks atop a vehicle.

The purpose of ferrules is to permit disassembly of a rod for easy transportation and storage. Each ferrule consists of two elements, a socket (called a female end or female ferrule) into which fits a plug-like end or cap (male end or male ferrule). These are on the ends of adjacent sections to be united, of course. How the two ferrule components fit each other is critical, and tolerances must be within thousandths of an inch. The fit must be only loose enough to permit ready assembly of the rod sections, yet not so loose as to allow them to turn or come apart when the stick is in use.

Standard ferrules are metal (chrome-plated, brass, aluminum, nickel-silver) and when well made have protection against rust and corrosion; but it doesn't take much foreign matter (a little sand maybe) to foul up their operation. They should be kept clean, and there's a little old stunt to lubricate them: rub the male ferrule on the side of your nose, or on your forehead or through your hair. There's usually enough of your own skin oil to keep the two ends lubricated.

A potential breaking point around ferrules used to be where the rod material joined the ferrule's sleeve. Because of differences in hardness and flex-ibility between the two materials, the rod's and the ferrule's, damaging stress was concentrated at the point where the two joined, and that's where a rod could let go. On properly made rods that problem has been corrected by a design that distributes the stress throughout the ferrule, instead of concentrating it at the point of joining.

Another ferrule refinement, among fiberglass rods, is the fiberglass ferrule. Because it's the same material as the rod, a fiberglass ferrule bends with the rod, thereby lessening chances of weakness at the joint and minimizing interruption of the rod's flexibility.

Unless the average angler is a hard-nosed casting enthusiast or purist, I think the advantages of a rod that can be taken apart for easy carrying outweigh any possible negative aspects such as those just mentioned. Besides, if rods couldn't be disassembled, can you picture the problems of metropolitan fishermen having to use mass transportation?

Tips on Reels

Some tips on reels: Conventional reels are graded for size by a number followed by a slash and a zero, thus: 1/0, 2/0, 3/0, etc. The larger the number preceding the slash, the bigger the reel. "Mills" (a nickname for reels in general) become progressively larger from 1/0 on up through 12/0, which is practically a small winch. Along with a 10/0, widely used in big-game fishing, a 12/0 is about the largest you'll see, although monstrous 14/0's and 16/0's have been made. Also extra-big are electrically powered conventional reels designed for fishing at depths of 1,000 ft. or more. I wished we'd had one of those the time a couple of us bottom-fished experimentally in 550 ft. of Atlantic Ocean with an improvised outfit that had—get this—a sash weight for a sinker. I cranked in three tilefish, the heaviest maybe 12 lbs.—which isn't big for tiles—and my back was out of whack for a week.

As reel sizes increase, so do details of their anatomy. That holds for all reels. Gears are stronger; the drag or brake is larger; reel-spool capacity increases. And the price tag gets larger. As I pointed out, progressively larger reels are basically used for progressively larger fishes. No statistics are available, but I'd say that the vast majority of conventional reels in use are no larger than 5/0, maybe 6/0, with most of those going to about 4/0, tops. Such are the sizes of far and away most of the fishes caught by rod-'n'-reelers.

There's variation—but it isn't critical—among spool capacities of reels of the same size. Again, this holds for spinning reels as well as the conventional models. Variations in capacity may be due to spool design and/or size. Also influencing capacity, of course, are the strengths or diameters of the lines used.

Sample Capacities (Approximate) for Conventional Reels of Increasing Sizes

2/0, 475 yds. of 12-lb.-test line; 3/0, 500 yds. of 20-lb. line; 4/0, 500 yds. of 30-lb. line; 6/0, 575 yds. of 50-lb. line; 9/0, 600 yds. of 80-lb. line; and 12/0, 750 yds. of 130-lb.-test line, the strongest allowed in IGFA world-record contention.

Spinning rods are produced in lengths ranging from 4- and 4½-ft. midgets weighing 2 to 3 oz. for ultra-light spinning on up to 9- to 12-ft. sticks weighing to 30 oz., for heavy-duty marine angling. They come in single-, two- and three-piece models, according to lengths and builders. Noticeable among spinning rods are their comparatively long handles. The longer, heavier models have a fore-grip for two-handed casting.

Some of the better rods may still use cork for their grips; but comfortable, durable synthetics are gradually elbowing expensive cork out of the picture. Some spinning rods have hand-contoured grips. This is a good feature. How comfortable a rod feels to the hand is important if a rod is going to be used a lot.

Spinning reels, especially the open-face type, are marketed in a long procession of sizes to handle a multitude of fresh-water and marine assignments. Weights in ounces are a common size-grading arrangement, instead of the 1/0–2/0–3/0 system employed for conventional reels. For broader cataloguing, the various sizes of spinning reels are divided into classes labeled ultra-light, light, medium, heavy, extra-heavy. It's all very flexible. Anglers do most of the grading themselves, selecting sizes that best complement their rods and best suit their purposes. The weight range goes from about 4 or 5 oz. for very light fresh-water models up to 25 and 26 oz. for heavy-caliber salt-water mills.

For general size-grading purposes we can consider marine and fresh-water spinning reels as a group; but it should be kept in mind that the salt-water models, by and large, are heavier. Therefore reels that would be called light in salt water are heavy for some fresh-water service. Line strengths, which influence rod selection also, can be a guide in choosing a reel of suitable size; and I remind you that veteran fishermen and tackle shop personnel can help.

The range of sizes in greatest general use is from about 8–10 oz. on the light side to 20 oz. on the heavy. In the lighter classes are those weighing 8–12 oz. for lines to 6- and 8-lb.-test and lures to about 1 oz. Above that, climbing through medium and heavy categories, are models from 12 to 20 oz. for 8- to 20-lb.-test lines and artificials up to about 3 oz. Beyond those are heavy-duty models to 25 and 26 oz. for lines to 30- and 40-lb.-test. There are salt-water reels for surf-casting lures up to 5 oz. and sinkers to 8 oz. and for offshore game fishing.

As in the case of conventional reels, spool capacities are in proportion to reel sizes. Again, there can be variations in spool capacities among spinning models of about the same size; but, as I said, these aren't critical. There's usually no problem, since there's latitude in selection anyway, and even in an approximate mating of reel and rod the spool capacity generally is sufficient. Fresh-water mills accommodate about 150 to 300 yds., depending upon line strength and model. Salt-water models accept anywhere from 150 yds. among the lighter ones, up to 400, 500 yds. and more among the largest.

Spinning reels can be used interchangeably in fresh water and salt water. Those designed for marine service usually have protection against salt corrosion, especially on exposed metal parts. Many fresh-water spinning reels do not have anti-corrosion protection and therefore should be cleaned as thoroughly as possible, outside and inside, after each exposure to salt water and salt air, with relubricating as needed and a complete take-apart with cleaning and oiling at intervals. (Not recommended in cleaning: hosing a reel down or dousing it under a faucet. This flushes away any protective lubricants, leaving the reel even more vulnerable to salt corrosion.)

Key Spinning Features

For practical purposes four classes of spinning tackle are considered, as follows, with their key features summarized:

Ultra-Light

For maximum action with the smallest fresh-water panfishes. Rods 4½ to 6 ft. long, weighing up to 3 oz. Reels to about 4 or 5 oz., tops. Outfits in this class are designed to cast the lightest lures, some only ⅟₃₂ oz., on hair-thin lines (3-lb.-test is "heavy" here). This featherweight tackle can be wielded for hours without fatigue; but it isn't otherwise easy to use with its extremely small artificials and lines so fine they're almost invisible.

Light

Fresh water: 6- to 7-, 7½-ft. rods, to 4, 4½ oz.; reels 5 to 7 oz. Lines of 3- to 4-lb.-test; lures to ⅜ oz. (or very small sinkers). These are versatile combos that can take trout, pickerel, small to medium basses, assorted panfishes.

Salt water: 6- to 7-, 7½-ft. rods with 8- to 10-oz. reels. Common line strengths are 6- and 8-lb.-test, going to 10- and 12-lb.-test for heavier assignments. Artificials to 1½ oz., or 2- and 3-oz. sinkers. These also are versatile outfits. They've taken blue-fish, northern weakfish, sea trout, snook, Atlantic mackerel, the smaller striped bass and red drums (channel bass), others. Also used in shallow-water bottom fishing (if tides aren't too strong) and for light trolling duty.

Medium

Fresh water: 6- to 7½-ft. rods, 4 to 6 oz.; reels about 8 oz. Lines of 4- to 6- lbs., to 8-lb.-test; ⅝-, ¾-oz. lures or small sinkers. A popular class wielded successfully for a wide range of species, larger pan-fishes to basses, trouts, walleyes, etc.

Salt water: 7- to 9-, 9½-ft. rods taking 12- to 16-oz. reels (up to 20-ounces on the longer, stouter sticks); 10- to 20-lb.-test lines; lures to 2½ oz. or 3- and 4-oz. sinkers. These too are versatile outfits. You see them on boats, piers, jetties and bridges for a variety of species—snook, bluefish and striped bass, to name but a few. Within their range they can also handle bottom rigs and light trolling duty, as well as oceanfront casting. Among the larger rods in this size class are those for two-handed casting.

Heavy

Fresh water: rods to 9 ft. long, weighing up to 10 oz.; reels to 12 oz., 8- to 20-lb.-test lines. This class's weight range of artificials is usually to about 2 oz., and the stouter outfits can handle bottom rigs of the same weight. Included are rods for two-handed casting, the so-called salmon/steelhead models, and equipment designed for rugged service generally. According to their calibers, rod-reel-line combinations in this group are fished for the largest basses, muskellunge, lake trout, hefty catfishes, husky salmon, steelheads and the like.

Salt water: rods 8½ to 9½, 10 ft.; reels up to 25, 26 oz. Lines 20- to 30-lb.-test, even 40-lb. on the heaviest outfits; lures or sinkers to 3 oz., even heavier. Collectively, this class of marine spinning tackle sees a wide range of service, from boats (its shortest rods) to surf casting (its longer sticks),

bottom fishing to trolling (the stouter rods). Its equipment is designed for the most rugged action in which spinning tackle can be employed. It includes spinning's "big guns," rod-reel combinations for offshore trolling for such battlers as sailfish, the smaller tunas and dolphins, and fishing for the smaller sharks (some fair sizes) and many other battlers. With these big guns the accent is more on backbone for strength than on flexibility for casting. Double-locking reel seats and a slotted metal cap on the rod's butt end (to fit into a fighting chair's gimbal, or socket) are among their features.

With all reels, conventional and spinning, it's of some importance to keep the spool properly filled with line. The proper degree of filling isn't so precise that it requires a ruler calibrated in millimeters, but it does have limits. It is usually suggested that the spool be filled to within about ⅛ in. of its rim.

Don't overfill or underfill a reel spool. One extreme is as bad as the other and can pose problems. With conventional reels, overfilling can load to backlashes and other snarls, and possibly a coil or two of line working its way down inside the spool's flange; and that's a real pain in the you-know-what. With spinning reels, overfilling the spool causes several coils of line to pay out, creating tangles that can be severe. Underfilling a conventional-reel spool, except to a ridiculous extent for the size of the reel, doesn't necessarily spell calamity unless you tie into an extra-long-running fish that strips your reel of line. And in that case you stand to lose line *and* fish. A more subtle problem might be a special braking effect that I'll get to in a minute. Underfilling a spinning reel will also cost you casting distance because the angle at which the line is drawn across the spool's edge impairs its smooth, uninhibited flow from the reel.

Drag or Brake Adjustment

That special braking effect I mentioned above occurs with conventional reels; and a lot of anglers are not aware of it. What happens is that as a supply of line gets low on a reel spool there is created an automatic, built-in drag effect just as though you had tightened up a bit on the reel's own brake. When this automatic drag effect is

added to the drag already in effect, it could be just enough additional braking pressure to pop the line when a fish runs. Sometimes when a fish's long runs are difficult or impossible to control and the supply of line on the spool starts to get low, it becomes necessary to adjust the reel's brake to offset that extra drag. When a line-stripping situation turns real hairy by threatening to denude a reel of its line, it may become necessary for a boat to run after the fish to give the angler a chance to crank some line back on his reel.

If you're an average angler and do not go in for extra-light tackle action or big-game fishing, chances are that the majority of the fishes you tie into will not require drag or brake adjustments of your reel during the action. However, possibilities do exist to make the drag or brake an important part of your reel's anatomy, whatever kind of reel it may be.

As the term drag hints, the function of this reel mechanism is to provide varying or adjustable degrees of resistance to a fighting fish to help tire him to the point of ultimate defeat. In other words, the drag supplements the action of your rod. In principle, the brake on your reel functions in the same manner as the brakes on your automobile: that is, through the friction of one part brought in tight contact with another. The big difference is that a reel's brake is designed to slip, except when tightened fully, if pulls on the line become excessive in strength for particular settings. This slippage is a cushion against line breakage and possible internal damage to the reel.

In an oversimplified description a reel's brake might be likened to a series of washerlike disks whose contact with each other is activated and adjusted by means of a spring-tension arrangement. Several different materials have been used in making the washers, including Teflon, metals of various kinds, asbestos, a kind of felt, and synthetics. In prolonged bouts with fish an operating drag can heat up, so its materials should be such as to keep generation of heat at a minimum. Avoid inferior reels with all-metal drag washers. The heat generated by the friction of the metal washers can cause them to expand and increase the reel's drag effect to the point that the line breaks.

Smooth drag operation is an absolute must on any reel, a cardinal quality that may not be found among the cheapies. It's easy enough to check. Load the reel with line, mount it on a rod, and feed the line through the rod's guides. Set the drag arbitrarily at some intermediate point and pull steadily on the line. It should come off the reel steadily and evenly, without "chatter," or intermittent interruptions. If there's chatter and it's a new reel,

that's bad news. Take it back. Conceivably its drag could set up or "freeze" at a critical time during an argument with a fish. If chattering develops in a reel you already own, the drag probably needs overhauling or new parts. Don't try to oil the drag. If any oil gets into the brake it will convert it into a perpetually slipping clutch.

The type and positioning of the control for drag adjustment vary according to type of reel and model. Let's look at some examples:

Conventional Reels

Far and away the most common drag adjustment here is a star-shaped wheel mounted on a shaft between the reel's end plate and crank. Turning the wheel one way tightens the drag; turning it the other way loosens it. From the shape of its control wheel this arrangement is known as a star drag. It has served generations of anglers and probably will serve generations more. Its main drawback is that it's difficult to return precisely to an earlier setting. There are no calibrations.

That's why many fishermen favor the so-called quadrant-brake control. In this arrangement the drag is adjusted by means of a lever on one side of the reel. A color-coded band alongside the lever shows how much drag is in operation and facilitates returning to a desired earlier setting with fair precision. This type of drag adjustment is available on the more expensive conventional reels.

Spinning Reels

Here drag control is by means of a knob or a wing nut, depending upon models. And the location of the control depends upon the type of drag, whether part of the line spool system or the gear housing. In the former, the control often is a wing nut right in the front in the center of the spool. In the latter, the control is a knob located in the back or on the side of the reel. Differences in accessibility of the two types are matters of personal opinion. If I can toss in my two cents' worth, I prefer a knob on the side or in back.

Presetting a drag prior to action is a subject for debate among anglers. A drag that's too loose defeats its purpose. It doesn't set up enough resistance to fighting, running fish. A drag that's unnecessarily tight, on the other hand, can cause a broken line or tire a fish too quickly, thereby robbing the angler of sport.

The importance of proper drag settings ranges from minimal, as with small fishes that are simply reeled in, to critical, as when bringing added pressure to bear on a hard-running opponent without breaking the line. This is why the range of drag adjustment is important and should be given consideration when selecting a reel, especially a spinning reel. If the drag control turns only about half a turn or so for the drag's full range, from off completely to as tight as it will go, chances are that the adjustment is much too critical to be accurate. Try another reel.

Conventional Reel Tips

Here's a handful of lesser-known facts about the spools of conventional reels:

According to manufacturers and models, and often influenced by specific sport fishing methods, the widths and depths of spools can vary even among reels in the same size class (1/0, 2/0, etc.) and is most noticeable on the smaller models. The results of these dimensional differences have varying degrees of importance, depending upon angling methods, and possibly even on situations and species of fish at times:

1. The wider a reel spool, the greater the chances that line will pile up unevenly during a retrieve. Uneven accumulations of line increase the chances of tangles on the spool and backlashes in casting. With small, light outfits it may be possible to improve distribution of line as it comes back in by guiding it back on the spool with the index finger of the rod-holding hand. It's doubtful, though, that uneven distribution of line on the reel spool will be a concern in the excitement of cranking in a catch. If it's real bad it might pay you to feed the line out afterward and distribute it more evenly.

2. In casting, a wide spool is less apt than a narrow one to gain the momentum that leads to backlashes and horrific line snarls. That's why many veteran surf fishermen favor reels with wide spools (and manufacturers make surf reels that way).

3. Line is less apt to bunch up unevenly on a narrow spool than on a wide one. However, the former's mechanical advantage changes as line goes out or comes back in, due to that built-in, automatic drag effect mentioned earlier. These changes can necessitate adjusting and readjusting of the reel's brake during the action.

In case you're asking—yes, there are conventional reels with a built-in gismo that automatically distributes the line evenly on the spool as it comes back in. Called a level wind, it's a little bobbin that shuttles back and forth on a special gear that is activated during retrieves. With it line always lies evenly and neatly on the reel spool.

The main criticism of a level-wind device (which adds to the cost of a reel, by the way) comes from casters. A level wind does cut down on casting distance by exerting friction on the line as it passes through it. But this needn't be a serious drawback unless appreciable casting distance is a factor. A more subtle drawback is that sand, corrosion, rust or other foreign matter can get into the mechanism and impair its function. It should be checked periodically for cleanliness and lubrication.

Tips on Spin Casting

You could say that spin casting has developed as an offshoot of spinning. It has earned widespread popularity, notably among inland fishermen and to a lesser extent among coastal anglers fishing protected bays and channels. A big reason for its widespread acceptance is that its tackle is just about the easiest casting equipment to use. Beginners take to it readily.

I've already mentioned the spin-casting reel and its first cousin the closed-face spinning reel earlier in this chapter. But, by way of a brief refresher, this is the deal: The reel has a fixed spool. Line leaves it in coils, which are gathered inside a cone-shaped housing and emerges through a hole in that housing's center. The mechanism for putting line back on the reel during retrieves also is internal.

But the spin-casting reel is a kind of hybrid, as I pointed out earlier, because, unlike the open-face and other closed-face spinning reels, it mounts *atop* the rod. And because it is commonly used on a bait-casting rod, it has come to be known as a spin-casting reel.

A summary of this tackle's starred features:

Reels

1. "Push-button reel" is a nickname stemming from a push lever mounted just behind the reel's

housing and conveniently next to its crank. Its purpose is to control the outflow of line in casting by engaging the reel's (pre-set) drag. Untouched, the lever lets line sail out. Pressed, the lever can lightly "feather" the outgoing line to slow it, or even stop it abruptly to drop a lure in a target area or right in front of a fish.

2. Because of a certain amount of unavoidable line friction inside, any closed-face spinning reel will not realize the casting distance of the open-face type. However, for most average anglers in average situations this is no serious drawback. Besides, the closed-face models have an advantage over the open-face type on breezy days. Since the coils of line leaving the former's spool are enclosed, there's less chance of the wind causing tangles.

3. Spin-casting reels have a drag or brake that can be adjusted to various degrees of tension. Control is usually by means of a small gnurled wheel, although there have been some models with a star wheel, like conventional reels.

4. Different builders incorporate other features such as an anti-reverse mechanism which, as on open-face reels, prevents the crank from turning backward; interchangeable spools, also on open-face reels, which make it possible to have standby spools already loaded with different strengths of line; and overall lightness, achieved through the use of aluminum alloys, sometimes in combination with high-impact plastics, the latter serving a double purpose in being non-rusting, non-corroding.

5. Since they mount atop their rods, spin-casting reels have their crank on the users' right; but there are models for left-handers.

6. Many spin-casting reels have approximately the same spool capacity, up to, say, 150 yds. of line, which generally is ample for most instances in which this gear is used. Lines—monofilament preferred—usually go to 6-, 8- and 10-lb. test for most assignments. Some have spools to accommodate lines up to 20-lb. test.

Rods

1. Because line doesn't emerge from it in coils, a spin-casting reel can be mounted on a rod whose guides are smaller than those on standard spinning rods. Some anglers combine a spin-casting reel with a standard bait-casting rod, but for the average angler the reel performs better on a spin-casting rod.

2. Spin-casting rods are generally longer and more limber than bait-casting counterparts and have somewhat larger guides. Manufacturers offer them in different lengths and tapers or actions, extra-light to heavy. The majority are in 6- to 7-ft. lengths.

3. The lighter models are intended for use with lines as light as 4-lb. test and artificials as small as ⅛ oz. (Finer lines and lighter artificials are not practical with this kind of gear.) A popular range includes 6- and 8-lb. lines and lures in the ¼- to ⅝-oz. bracket. The heavier outfits handle lines to 10-lb. test or so and 1-oz. lures. A good combination for a newcomer would be a 6½-ft. rod, 6- or 8-lb. line, and artificials weighing about ⅜ oz.

4. Although a spin-casting reel can be mounted on a rod with the usual reel-seating arrangement, the preferred setup is a rod with a recessed or offset reel seat. It's a common design for bait-casting and spin-casting mills. What it does, in effect, is lower the reel a bit on the rod so that it can be operated more easily. This is helpful with the push-button type.

So long as their weights are compatible, which is to say in fractions of ounces, any of the real small lures—or natural baits of comparable weight—can be used with a spin-casting outfit.

ABC's of Tackle Care

With reasonable care, much of it dictated by common sense, and a little affection, modern fishing tackle will reward its owner with many years of faithful service and fishing pleasure. Abuse and carelessness in handling and transport —and outright thoughtlessness—sometimes are major foes of tackle. Here are some tips on gear care:

During each fishing season all tackle items— rods, reels, lines, lures, etc.—should be checked periodically to determine their general state of health. A thorough examination should conclude the season. Interseason recesses provide opportunities to effect repairs and reconditioning, clean and lubricate reels, replace badly worn or broken parts, sharpen hooks, do a house-cleaning job on the tackle box and take an inventory of its contents, and replace or add to such items as lures, swivels, sinkers, etc. as needed. This final exam can be a pleasant chore with which to while away off-season hours. And it's very rewarding to know that you'll be all set to go when a new season is launched.

Rods

Inspect for such defects as worn or broken guides and loose or broken guide windings. Repair or replace. You can do the job yourself or take it to a local tackle shop. Grooved or otherwise badly worn guides exert unnecessary wear on lines, aging them before their time and creating potential weak spots. Check a rod's reel seat for looseness, any accumulations of salt corrosion and sand in the threads of the reel seat's locking rings.

Chances are a rod is sound if it hasn't been subjected to repeated abuse, but inspect it anyway. Fiberglass rods can be wiped clean with a damp cloth (some anglers add a mild soap to the water), then dried.

Examine a rod's ferrules for any looseness of attachment to the rod. Re-cement if necessary. There are good compounds for this. Clean the male and female ends of the ferrules and check them for excessive looseness of fit due to wear. The female socket can be cleaned with a pipe cleaner and lighter fluid. When clean, lubricate the male socket of the ferrule, as suggested earlier. Note: Do *not* use machine oil, however light. Tolerances are such that even a thin film of oil could act as a seal, creating a vacuum that could make the ferrule very difficult to pull apart when disassembling the rod.

Rods may be vulnerable to damage in transit. A rod bag affords a measure of protection. At least it protects the rod's finish; even fiberglass rods can be scratched. A rod bag also becomes a storage place when it's hung out of the way. For transporting and storing rods, especially skinny fly rods and other ultra-light sticks, many anglers prefer something more substantial than a baglike rod case and invest in tubular containers of aluminum or fiber or plastic. Lacking a container, a rod should lie flat, nothing on top of it to damage its guides. There are vertical and horizontal racks for storing rods left assembled. Personally, I think it's better to leave rods disassembled during long periods of inactivity.

Be especially careful when transporting rods. Don't lay them down where they might be sat or stepped on. Don't jam them into car trunks or pile stuff on them. And whenever possible in public transportation, take rods aboard a plane with you rather than leave them to the mercies of airline baggage manglers. Same goes for tackle boxes. On long-distance buses use the luggage rack over-

head; don't let your gear be stored below with the other baggage.

Reels

At intervals during the season, and at the end of each season before the recess until the next year, reels should be checked for general health. They should be disassembled, cleaned thoroughly, and relubricated as needed (or as recommended by the manufacturer or tackle store where bought). At such times wear-worn or otherwise defective parts can be replaced. Reels should be checked periodically for accumulations of sand or other alien matter that may have found its way inside to a gear train or the drag mechanism. Surf reels are especially subject to peppering by wind-blown sand.

Many reels today feature easy take-down (disassembly) and reassembly. The manufacturers often furnish instructions, along with a numbered list of parts for replacement ordering. Sometimes a little reel wrench is also included, and the manufacturer may throw in a tube of reel lubricant. If not, that and a wrench can usually be obtained at a tackle shop.

Other parts of reels to be given attention are (1) a conventional reel's free-spool mechanism, (2) a spinning reel's anti-reverse mechanism, and (3) the clicker buttons. Add to those such extra refinements as a level-wind mechanism, any special clutch and an anti-backlash mechanism. In short, check a reel's innards for accumulations of sand and other grit and gumminess from old lubrication.

Anodizing, baked enamel, plating, epoxy finishes and resistant metals protect modern reels against rust and corrosion, but it never does any harm to check reel exteriors every so often anyway, especially exposed metal parts. Particular attention should be given to fresh-water reels that have doubled in salt water. Rust-preventive compounds are available.

You can do your own reel servicing. Or, if you prefer to have a pro handle it, take your reel to a tackle shop or a shop specializing in reel work. If you decide to do it yourself, beware of these no-no's: (1) Don't use screwdrivers that are too big or too small, and use the right kind of driver; otherwise you can ruin that reel's screw slots for all time. (2) Don't substitute pliers for a wrench. Don't use pliers, period. (3) Don't get any lubricant on drag disks; otherwise you'll have a slipping brake. IMPORTANT: Never leave any reel with its drag on, even overnight. It could in time cause the mechanism to become sticky or chattery, or even freeze tight. Leave the brake fully off.

Tips on Accessories

Time and ever-increasing interest in sport fishing continue to bring numerous items of gear designed to contribute to angling enjoyment and success. Some of these items qualify as necessities. The value of others is an individual proposition, with each angler deciding its worth according to the kind of fishing done.

1. Tackle box. A must. Choices today can be made from among hundreds of models in a wide range of sizes to meet all needs. A major criterion is that the carrier selected have enough storage space for any extra items ordinarily carried, like a spare reel, spools of line and special lures. Another criterion is durability. Good tackle boxes satisfy this with (a) construction from high-impact plastics, (b) rust- and corrosion-resistant hardware, and (c) a resistance to gasoline and oil, which is important to outboard-boat fishermen. Easy accessibility to all contents is a highly desirable feature. Larger tackle boxes have cantilevered trays that swing outboard so that you can get at the contents without spilling or tipping the carrier. Other desirable features include latches that keep the carrier securely closed when in transit or not in use.

Jetty jockeys often favor a tackle carrier improvised from a small knapsack or shoulder bag that leaves both hands free for climbing around rocks and is easier than a standard tackle box to tote on rugged jetties. A drawback is that their contents are not as readily accessible.

2. Lure carriers. Most artificials are carried in the compartmented trays of tackle boxes. But for some fresh-water lures that are very small and easily lost, there are partitioned boxes of clear plastic. The craftsmanship and delicacy of fresh-water flies call for protection in special containers such as fly boxes and wallets.

3. Fisherman's pliers. Here's an accessory with universal application in all kinds of angling. Its jaws' grip is handy for working a deeply embedded hook out of a fish's mouth and other chores. Its cutter handles line, leader materials and wires. This tool is a must for working with wire leaders and lines. A good one should have rust and corrosion protection.

4. Clipper. Among fly and sweetwater anglers this is a standard item of equipment for cutting and trimming leaders and droppers. (Some anglers find that fingernail clippers do nicely.) Fancier and more versatile is a model that has an awl for clearing the clogged eyes of flies and a disgorger to help remove hooks.

5. Hone. A must for all fisherman. It's a small stone for sharpening hooks and takes up no space in a tackle box. It will also touch up the edge on a knife.

6. Good knife. This has so many uses that it's in the category of a must. Many anglers carry the so-called hunting-knife type that comes in a wide range of sizes and prices. I personally don't care for a pocket knife because the blades are not big enough for maximum versatility, and folding knives can get all gummed up.

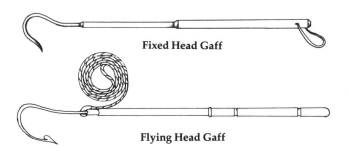

Fixed Head Gaff

Flying Head Gaff

7. Gaffs. A gaff is essentially a strong, sharp hook on a handle of suitable length. Its function is to cinch capture when a fish is brought alongside the boat. There are two types: the so-called straight or fixed-head gaff and the flying gaff. Flying gaffs are larger and heavier and are for large salt-water game. The head, which can run up to 6-plus in. across, is designed to pull free of the handle when planted in a fish, the head having been secured to the boat beforehand by a length of line rope. These gaffs come with and without a barb. The straight gaff has no barb and, as mentioned, has its head rigidly attached to the handle. This gaff comes in a wider range of sizes and meets most marine and fresh-water needs. There are short-handled straight models to hang on anglers' belts, and there are others with extra-long handles for bridge and jetty fishing. (*Tip:* Any straight gaff for boat use must have a handle long enough for that craft's cockpit freeboard.) Larger straight gaffs often are used in conjunction with flying gaffs in big-game action to subdue a fish alongside the boat. Both types have handles of wood or aluminum. Some are made to float if dropped overboard.

8. Landing net. This does the same job—cinching the capture of a fish—as a gaff but is limited to smaller fishes. Nets are more widely used in fresh-water angling than in marine fishing, although they're recommended for some salt-water scrap-

pers, notably those that can flip themselves off the hook when being reeled in. The nets are light and can be attached to the belt for stream fishing. Refinements include flotation and telescoping handles.

9. Hook disgorger. A simple tool, plastic or aluminum, it's shoved into a fish's mouth to free a deeply planted hook. It can save punctures and scratches from fishes' teeth.

10. Fishing thermometer. This is a worthwhile accessory for serious anglers. In learning more about the fishes they seek, anglers come to appreciate the effects of water temperatures on fishes' feeding habits and movements and recognize the desirability of being able to measure those temperatures. Available thermometers range from inexpensive hand-operated models for toting in a tackle box to electric-electronic instruments permanently mounted in boats.

11. Deboner. This is a specialized tool for anglers who do a lot of fishing with whole dead baits. It's merely a metal tube for removing the backbone of a dead bait in order to give it more lifelike flexibility when trolled.

12. Live-bait carrier. Much live-bait fishing involves small fishes. Keeping them alive for peak effectiveness can be a problem. A solution is a bait car or carrier, also called a killy car. It's just a small floating cage with a hatch on top for access to contents. You keep it in the water right alongside the boat. For inland fishermen there are the so-called minnow buckets that prolong bait life by protecting the fish in transit and keeping them cool and out of the sun.

13. Catch carriers. Most sweetwater fishermen use a length of stout twine, fed in through each fish's mouth and out under a gill cover, or a similar simple stringer arrangement. Some fresh-water regulars have a creel, that basketlike container that is practically the trout anglers' badge. Popular among coastal fishermen are large, tough plastic bags. These are especially useful when catches are iced for long rides home in hot weather. For small fishes a portable ice chest can do double duty. First, it's a lunch carrier and beverages cooler. On the way home, if there's ice left, it's a portable refrigerator for the catch. With cushions, it also becomes a seat.

14. Sand spike. Although it's a surf caster's accessory, a sand spike is useful to any shoreside angler. Essentially it's a rod holder mounted on a pointed leg that is thrust into sand or earth in order to hold an outfit and keep its reel out of the sand during lulls in activity.

15. Cartop rod racks. These are for long rods that do not fit well inside cars or might be damaged in transit if they did. It is also used by owners who want to leave rods assembled for ready use. Racks are easy to install, and they're padded for the protection of rod finishes. Standard model racks do not protect against theft, but you can check your tackle dealer on the present availability of a lockable model.

16. A flashlight. A must for night fishing. An excellent refinement for jetty and ocean-front regulars is a fishermen's version of the miners' head lamp. It leaves hands free for rigging, baiting, etc., in addition to lighting the way where footing is tricky.

17. Good Polaroid sunglasses. I consider these a necessity for protection against glare bouncing off water and sand and to see better below the water's surface.

18. Utility kit. This is a necessity. The contents vary from angler to angler, but here are some suggestions to include: (a) A roll of electrician's tape for emergency securing of loosened rod guides or defective reel seats. (b) Screwdrivers of the proper size and whatever other tools may be necessary, such as a reel wrench, along with lubricating oil, for on-the-scene servicing of reels. (c) A little bottle of women's clear nail lacquer to use as a shellac for temporary repair of guide wrappings that have started to unwind. (d) A small bottle of colored nail polish with which to mark lines at intervals to keep track of how much yardage is out. This is mainly a salt-water stunt used in trolling and jigging. (e) A couple of corks in which to embed loose hooks before they stick into fingers. (f) A small box of rubber bands in different sizes. (g) A few small plastic bags for odds and ends that might be misplaced in the jumble that's likely to develop in your tackle box from time to time. (h) Some strong thread and a couple of long upholsterer's needles for rigging certain baits. (i) A couple of pieces of cloth for cleaning equipment, plus a few paper towels for the hands. (j) Spare flashlight batteries.

Small items should be kept in a clear plastic box in the tackle carrier.

19. First aid kit. Every boat should carry one. Shoreside and inland fishermen will have to be guided by their own common sense. I think they should have a kit, particularly if they do any fishing at night or in remote areas where getting help could be a problem. An anti-venom kit is a good addition in places where there are poisonous snakes. The first-aid kit should also contain any special medication their owners might require.

Boat Gear

The list of boat equipment involved directly in sport fishing is lengthy. It's not within this book's scope to deal with it in detail, but there are some items that are considered necessities.

1. Fighting chair. A must for big-game fishing and sometimes for medium-size battlers. The best (and most expensive) chairs are adjustable, have a foot rest, and swing throughout 360 °. They're usually mounted so as to be removable for more cockpit room when not in use.

2. Rod holders. A must for any boat that does an appreciable amount of fishing. Cockpit-mounted, they hold rods during periods of inactivity and keep them out of the way.

3. Outriggers. These are pole-like structures from a boat at about a 45 ° angle. They are used in trolling. Outriggers are marketed in a wide range of sizes and prices for craft of all sizes, even outboards. They're installed at the factory or by boatyards. Some do-it-yourselfers buy kits and install their own.

4. Gaffs. Fishing boats carry at least a couple of straight gaffs. They add a flying gaff or two if their encounters include big game.

5. Gin pole. This is essentially a vertical boom which, in conjunction with a block and fall, is used to lift big fishes out of the sea when the fight is over. Constructed from wood or aluminum, a gin pole will handle a lot of weight but has limits. Because of the strain on it in hoisting, it's very important that a gin pole be installed properly—by professionals only.

6. Gimbal belt. This is a strong belt with a receptacle (gimbal) that accepts the rod's butt end. It's used for fighting fishes of respectable sizes while you're standing. Boats usually carry a couple of them.

7. Fighting chair harness. A wide belt that goes across the small of the back and clamps onto the reel. It lets the shoulders and back get into the act, also helps support the tackle during a fight's brief rest periods.

8. Transom door. An alternative to a gin pole. Factory-installed, it's a gate in the transom at the waterline, with rollers, for bringing large game fish (except sharks) into the boat.

9. Tuna tower. This is a skeletal structure with a railed platform rising above the flying bridge accommodating one or two observers. Its purpose is to provide better visibility, and it's used to scan the sea for signs of surfaced fishes. More elaborate towers carry duplicate boat controls so that the craft can be better maneuvered during encounters with big game.

10. Downriggers. Downriggers are "underwater outriggers" used in extra-deep trolling at levels beyond which usual trolling sinkers and planers cannot reach. They're relatively new on the saltwater scene but have been in use for years in freshwater angling. Boat owners can install them.

11. Bait carriers. There are many built-in and portable types for live baits and dead baits. One kind, known as a live-bait well, is factory installed and permits constant circulation of water. There are also portable live-bait models with pumps for circulating water.

12. Fish boxes. These are for catches up to a certain size. Some are incorporated in a fishing boat's transom, while others are portable and can be taken ashore. Good boxes are equipped with drains so that they can be hosed out and cleaned.

13. Binoculars. Every boat should carry a pair. They aid in navigation, by spotting distant buoys, shoreside landmarks, etc., can scan the sea's surface for signs of fish activity, and can spy on distant boats to see how they're doing. Also good if you happen to fish in the vicinity of a nudist colony.

14. Electronic equipment. Here boat fishermen have a selection. Most common is a depth sounder, a form of sonar, which is discussed in "Observations on Bottom Fishing," Chapter 5. There's a radiotelephone, worth its weight in gold as a communication link with shore, other boats, and in a jam, the U.S. Coast Guard. Other devices that are primarily for navigation and safety offshore and out of sight of land are loran (short for *lo*ng-*r*ange *a*id to *n*avigation), a radio direction finder (RDF for short) and radar.

15. Tackle cabinet and rod racks. Space permitting, a boat should have a permanent storage cabinet for tackle items and storage racks for rods. Both should be installed out of the weather and out of sight of thieves. They can be factory-installed, custom built, or a do-it-yourself project.

All the foregoing items are worthwhile investments, but some, like a big fighting chair, a tuna tower, radar and loran, carry hefty price tags.

2. Terminal Tackle
(Natural Baits, Lures & Rigs)

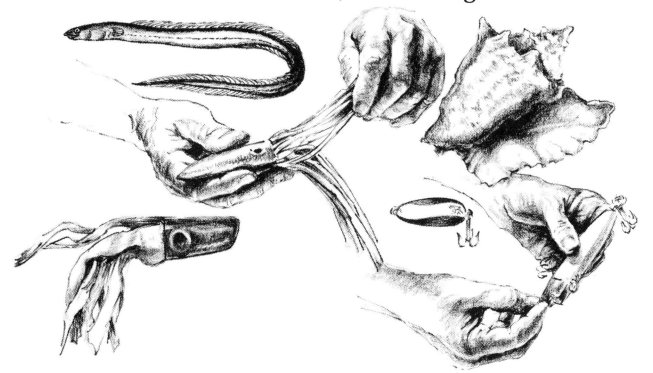

Long ago an unidentified wit, probably an angler, remarked that humans, like fish, wouldn't get into trouble if they kept their mouths shut. That's true, but the problem is that fishes, like people, have to eat to survive, and to accomplish this they must open their mouths. Unhappily for our finned friends, this plunges them into the worst kind of trouble: it gets 'em killed.

Offhand I don't know which is the stronger drive among fishes, eating for survival or sex. I'm inclined to believe it's the latter, since many species fast during spawning. No matter. What counts for angling purposes is that eating is a powerful urge, so much so that all rod-and-reeling is based

on it. One thing is for sure: If you can't get a fish to open his or her mouth, you sure aren't going to catch him or her.

We'll probably never learn when man first came up with a scheme to use some item of natural food to catch a fish. The only detail of which we can be reasonably certain is that natural baits preceded artificials or man-made imitations. And we know, too, that both kinds of attractors, natural and man-made, continue to serve sport fishing. So let's consider some pointers on terminal tackle (that, for a newcomer fisherman, is all the components at the end of a rod) by starting with a few facts on natural baits.

Natural Baits

Any item on a fish's regular menu is a potential bait for that species, and possibly for other species. Fishes, like people, share a liking for certain foods. So it's important to discover what their preferences are in their normal diets. For example, many kinds of sport fishes are fond of shrimp and squid. Many other kinds of fishes also react to shrimp or squid even though those creatures are not on their usual

menu. It appears that certain baits have an unusually widespread appeal—something special in their scent or flavor, no doubt. The fishes with the widest tastes in food, and therefore baits, are probably those that make long migrations, since they encounter the greatest variety moving through different regions.

There are literally thousands of kinds of baits,

actual or potential. Even in a lifetime we couldn't achieve a working familiarity with all of them, but there are things we can do to guide us in selections, like so:

1. Learn as much as you can about the food preferences and feeding habits of the fish you seek. Note any changes in feeding patterns from one season of the year to another. Many species feed less actively during the colder months, then become avid feeders with the warmer weather of spring. Many fast at spawning time.

2. Inquire locally about the baits currently most effective for the species you're after. This holds true in your own territory as well as in unfamiliar areas. Some fishes are fairly consistent in their diet, yet occasionally exhibit what appear to us to be erratic phases. A common procedure is to open the stomach of the first fish or two caught to see what they've been eating. That's part of an effort to match or at least approximate the fishes' current diet with baits or lures.

3. The choice of baits may be governed by availability. Baits undergo natural cycles of abundance and scarcity as a result of poor breeding years and adverse environmental conditions. At times certain baits are available only in limited supply or not at all. Your answer, of course, is to have a second team ready to go into the game. Lacking a second choice, look around for a substitute, such as an artificial that resembles the unavailable bait. Failing all that, heed No. 4, next.

4. I repeat this at intervals for emphasis: *Never be afraid to experiment,* to try baits—and lures—not on regular lists, and to test new and different ways to rig established baits. Everything in fishing has come about as the result of experimentation.

Now a look at salt-water baits. These are not necessarily in order of importance or use:

Sea Worms

Many kinds of worms are food for many different marine fishes and are therefore potential baits; but some worms are ruled out because of general unavailability, difficulty in harvesting in quantity, smallness of size, etc. The sea worms that are widely used along North American coasts are sandworms of the genus *Nereis* and bloodworms of the group Glycera. (Sandworms are known as clamworms on the West Coast.) Some do-it-yourselfers dig their own, but mostly these worms are harvested by professional diggers and distributed by local bait and tackle establishments.

On the long list of species responsive to worms are various flatfishes, striped bass, northern and southern porgies, surfperches, Atlantic Coast weakfish, black sea bass, croakers, corvinas, tautogs or blackfish. Worms can be used in all standard salt-water fishing methods from bottom fishing at anchor to trolling. According to species sought and method involved, some are cut into pieces of various sizes for fishes with small mouths; some are used whole, either small or large, hooked so part of the worm dangles or wiggles in the water. You can use sea worms by themselves, or sometimes with a couple on the same hook, or in conjunction with some sort of artificial. (One of the most successful combos on Long Island Sound is a sandworm or two trolled with a flashing spinner.) You'll find hooks on the market with tiny spikes on their shanks to keep worms extended in a lifelike manner.

The major drawback of sea worms as bait, apart from the rising cost and any periodic unavailability (there have been professional worm diggers' strikes, believe it or not), is their fragility. Worms must be hooked carefully, and even then they do not stay alive long on the hook. Once dead, or if used in pieces, they deteriorate rapidly, losing their appearance, substance, color and scent, thus becoming useless as bait. Worm baits should be checked and replaced as needed. Another pointer: Take along enough.

Clams

Number one in this group of baits is the ocean or sea clam, also known as the surf or hen clam, popularly called a skimmer. It's the biggest clam on the eastern coast of North America, with an overall distribution from about Labrador southward to North Carolina.

The pismo clam of the Pacific coast and its hardshell relatives of the U.S. Gulf Coast are also used as bait and are effective for many kinds of marine sport fishes. Ditto the soft shell—steamers, nannynose or squirt—clam. But these clams make such good eating that it seems almost sacrilegious to mention them as bait. Besides, at today's prices, who can afford them as bait?

In general, different kinds of clams—pismo, skimmer, soft-shell or whatever—are interchangeable as bait. Same thing goes for clams minced for chum or shucked and dropped overboard alongside the boat at intervals.

In northern Atlantic waters the skimmer clam is practically standard bait for cod. Skimmers also nail croakers, sea bass, flounders, porgies, tautogs, striped bass, pollock, haddock and others. Hard clams—those sold in restaurants on the half shell —will catch the same fishes. If I were opening them, though, they'd never get to the hooks. I have quite a capacity for raw clams—good as that of any codfish, I can tell you. Soft-shell clams also get a response from the same species as skimmers. The part used is the tough siphon, or neck. This has a dark, wrinkly outer skin that should be peeled off to give the bait better visibility. Pismo clams have been used on the West Coast as bait for various kinds of flatfishes, surfperches, corvinas, croakers and many others.

Crabs

The coasts of North America are home to dozens of different kinds of crabs. Depending on the sizes of fishes sought and the methods involved, crabs are rigged whole or in pieces. Those used in baiting include the lady crab, green crab, fiddler crab, calico crab, ghost crab, rock crab and northern crab. Also used—in the past, anyway— are the blue and stone crab. I say "in the past" because these two are far more in demand now as people food than as bait.

Until their growth ceases, all crabs shed their shells at intervals to develop new and larger ones. Fishermen have their own names for the molting cycle's different phases: When discarding their old, outgrown shell, the crabs are called shedders or peelers. A new and larger shell has been developing underneath the old one, but it takes a certain amount of time for this new shell to harden. During that stage its owner is a soft-shell crab, or softy, and as such is practically defenseless. As the new shell starts to harden it's like a heavy parchment, still flexible enough to bend under pressure. Nicknames for them at this time are paperback, leatherback and buckram. In due course the new shell hardens and its owner is back to normality— until the next molting. Crabs can be used in all those shell stages as bait, but the shedder and softy phases are preferred.

Crabs are morsels for many kinds of fishes. The long list includes bonefish, assorted species of snappers, blackfish or tautogs, tarpon, striped bass, bluefish, weakfish, channel bass (redfish, red drums) and croakers.

Marine Baitfishes

These are the very small to small forage species on which all larger salt- and brackish-water fishes feed. In this group are tiny minnows only a couple of inches long to the likes of mullets, menhaden, eels, herrings, young mackerels and fishes of similar sizes on the menus of larger predators. Baitfishes are rigged alive and dead, whole and in pieces as strips and fillets. They're a versatile bunch of baits. One species may excite several kinds of fishes. Some baitfishes to note:

1. Pacific California sardines are effective bait for tunas, bonitos, albacore, yellowtails, Pacific halibut, white sea bass, and barracudas.

2. Killifishes, or killies—less well known as mummichogs—are hardy and popular bait for a variety of battlers, including striped bass, northern fluke, bluefish, black sea bass and weakfish.

3. Northern or California anchovies are used as both bait and chum for Pacific barracuda, rockfishes, West Coast sculpins, yellowtails, Pacific halibut, albacore, and others.

4. Common anchovies from the Atlantic and Gulf of Mexico coasts are effective for weakfish, striped bass, bluefish, plus almost any other species that feeds a lot on herrings and their kin.

5. Spearing, also known as silverside, shiner, sperling, white bait and by other regional nicknames, is used on the East and Gulf coasts for bluefish, cod, sea bass, northern and southern flukes, Boston mackerel, striped bass, silver hake or northern whiting, and several more scrappers.

6. Sand launce, misnamed sand eel because of its slender body, is used from Labrador on down to about North Carolina for all the species mentioned for spearing, plus haddock and some others.

7. Pinfish, a deep-bodied little guy, is rigged for tarpon, amberjacks, and others. (I can testify that pinfish are very good bait for tarpon.)

8. Balao, better known as ballyhoo, belongs to a group of unusual-looking fishes known as halfbeaks, so called because of a noticeable extension of the lower jaw. Ballaos are used for sailfish and other billfishes, amberjacks, tarpon, barracudas, plus others.

9. Butterfish are found from Nova Scotia to Florida. The larger ones—4 in. or so—are rigged whole for big bluefin tuna. For smaller battlers such as bluefish and weakfish, little ones are used whole and larger ones are cut into pieces. Whole or in pieces, butterfish also serve as chum or chum fortifier for bluefin tuna, bonitos, albacore and sharks.

10. Pacific herring are found from Alaska to southern California. The smaller ones are rigged whole behind a shiny metal, bladelike artificial called a dodger, whose flash and glitter are attractions. They're usually dead because it's tough to

keep them alive. Pacific herring are plug-cut; that is, the head is cut off on an angle, giving the body a pluglike appearance for Pacific salmon bait. These herring also attract yellowtails, Pacific halibut and several other species.

11. Mullet baits are best known by two varieties: common or striped mullet, used on the Atlantic and Pacific coasts, and a silver or white mullet on the Atlantic seaboard. Mullets are difficult to impossible to keep alive, especially on hooks, and so are rigged dead. The bait is rigged whole or in various-sized pieces. Mullet will take channel bass (red drums, redfish), striped bass, snook, dolphins, tunas, marlins, tarpon, bluefish, groupers, northern fluke and weakfish, among other scrappers.

12. Menhaden, commonly called mossbunker or 'bunker, plus such better forgotten aliases as fatback, pogy and razorbelly, serves as bait from Nova Scotia to Florida. Because of their oily flesh, menhaden are used for a wide variety of salt-water sport fishes, among which are striped bass, various mackerels, sharks, bluefins and other tunas, channel bass (redfish, red drum), bluefish and weakfish. Small menhaden are used whole and larger ones in pieces. Mossbunkers are also ground into a mushy, oily, blood-streaked pulp that makes an excellent chum for sharks, Boston mackerel, bluefish, giant bluefin tuna, and any other species calling for chumming.

Note: Having oily flesh, mossbunkers spoil quickly unless placed under refrigeration promptly; and when they start to spoil, the smell will tear holes in your shirt. (I once worked on fishing docks, and part of my job was to run a couple of tons of 'bunkers through a big meat grinder to create chum. Exposed to a hot summer sun for a few hours in open trucks, they were real fragrant by the time I got them. Anyone who has been downwind of a 'bunker boat, as they call the vessels netting these fish commercially, in the summer knows what I mean.) A drawback to menhaden as bait is the softness of the flesh. It doesn't stay on a hook too well, and it may have to be secured with some turns of thread, especially for any casting. Mossbunkers are difficult to keep alive and, for bait, are sold in frozen form. Some fishermen buy packages of them and run them through a home meat grinder for chum as needed. This is more trouble than it's worth, and if done at home it goes over like a brick airplane. It's much easier to buy the stuff in big cans all ready to go.

Mussels

These mollusks, cousins of clams, serve anglers well as bait and as chum. Among the better known is the Atlantic mussel or sea mussel, found along the Atlantic seaboard from the Arctic down to North Carolina. This species was introduced many years ago to Pacific coast waters where a breed of mussel known variously as sea mussel and big mussel is found. Mussels are good bait for tautogs (blackfish), flounders, corvinas, Pacific Coast rockfishes, croakers and many other species. But they present a couple of problems. They're difficult to keep on a hook; the amount of meat in each shell is often small, maybe too small for certain gamesters. A solution to both problems: Fashion a gob of bait from two or more mussels, impale it on the hook, and secure it with a few loops of coarse thread. Mussels also make an effective chum presented in different ways: (1) their meat minced and placed in a chumpot (see "Chumming," Chapter 6), (2) with their shells on, but cracked, in a chumpot, or (3) with their shells cracked just enough to let body juices escape and dropped overboard right alongside the boat in clusters of three or four at intervals. Mussels, with their shells cracked, can also be put to good service as a magnet in traps that catch baitfishes such as spearing.

Squid

Squid are attractive to many different kinds of fishes. Offhand I'd say that just about any marine fish with a mouth big enough to accommodate squid will feed on them whenever possible. There are several species of squid along the Pacific and Atlantic seaboards. I can't remember ever seeing squid used alive, probably because keeping them that way in captivity is a lot of trouble and the only alternative is to catch them yourself and rig them right away, a highly unlikely opportunity. Squid are sold in packages, frozen. Rigged whole, they are trolled for white marlin, swordfish, tunas, bluefish, striped bass and other game. Used in combination with another bait or alone, whole squid are also effective in drift-chumming for sharks. Long strips of squid—an end left dangling and sometimes split up the middle for eye-catching flutter—are effective for a long parade of fishes in bottom fishing and surf casting: black sea bass, northern and southern porgies, weakfish, northen kingfish, cod, striped bass, fluke or summer flounder, channel bass, pollock, all the West Coast rockfishes, and any other species that go for a strip bait. Squid bait is tough, durable and stays on a hook well.

Shrimps

Used as bait, some species are lumped together under the label sand shrimp. They have representatives on the Pacific coast from Alaska to southern California and along the Atlantic Coast from Labrador to the Carolinas. Sand shrimps are found in sandy bottoms, rocky areas and seaweed gardens. They rate as food and bait for a whole flock of salt-water fishes on both coasts. Other bait shrimps are the so-called grass shrimps, the larger specimens of which are sometimes called common prawns and are found along Gulf of Mexico and Atlantic shores, and the Pacific Coast's ghost shrimp, three species of which have a collective distribution from Alaska to Baja California. Shrimps can be used as bait for all marine sport fishes that do not require a large bait. Dropped overboard a couple at a time at regular intervals, they're also a good chum. Those species victimized by shrimp include weakfish, assorted mackerels, porgies (scup), striped bass, flatfishes such as fluke and flounders, croakers, sculpins, white sea bass, bluefish and northern kingfish.

Other Marine Baits

North American coastal anglers also use as baits (1) moon snails and periwinkles, (2) whelks, (3) conches, (4) octopus, (5) sand bugs, also called beach bugs, sand crabs and mole shrimp, (6) small herrings such as the Atlantic herring and glut herring, (7) alewives, and (8) shad. Eels can be effective baits in trolling and surf casting either alive or dead, but mostly dead because they're too hard to handle when alive. Whole or in chunks, eels have accounted for sharks, cobias, striped bass, bluefish, marlins, weakfish and broadbill swordfish, among other species. In certain trolling and casting rigs just the skin is used, sometimes in combination with a metal squid. When water inflates the skin, it gives it a lifelike fullness and wiggle. Finally, as baits, in a pinch there are strips, fillets and chunks cut from fishes already caught. These have been known to catch more of the same species plus other kinds. That goes for just about any kind of salt-water fish you can name. Fortunately for anglers, most fishes are cannibalistic to a degree.

Here are some pointers on fresh-water baits and not necessarily in order of importance or frequency of use:

Minnows

Technically, the fishes we refer to as minnows are members of the Cyprinidae, the minnow and carp family. With approximately 192 species, it's the largest family of fresh-water fishes, both in numbers and for sheer quantity, on the North American continent. Because of their universal distribution and numbers, minnows are the single most important source of food for all larger fresh-water fishes. They're encountered in every conceivable kind of aquatic environment: little ponds to large lakes, brooks to rivers, quiet streams to fast water, warm waters to cold. The vast majority of minnows are little fellows, attaining average lengths of 2 to 4 or 5 in. They serve as bait for large-mouths, smallmouths and other fresh-water basses, for the widespread crappies and other popular panfishes, for pickerel, pike, lake trout, and in ice fishing (see Chapter 12). Minnows are rigged alive and dead, in graduated sizes according to the finned game sought.

Frogs

These amphibians are great bait for basses, and the kinds used include the so-called pickerel frog, leopard frog, green frog and junior-size bullfrog. They're rigged alive because their swimming actions in the water make a bass's mouth water. (Artificial frogs are worked with the rod tip to simulate this action.) Frogs are rigged alive by hooking carefully through the lips, like a minnow, or through the skin of the back of one leg near the crotch. There's also a store-bought harness you can get. *Tip:* In clear water a leg-hooked frog on low-visibility monofilament, with no terminal-tackle hardware to impair the bait's action or look unnatural, will often induce bass strikes when other come-ons fail. Dead frogs are also rigged as bait for basses, catfishes and other sweetwater scrappers. Used dead, they must be flexible (anglers break their bones if necessary) and must be worked with the rod to give them action.

Unless anglers can go out and capture their own, the serious drawback to frogs is their availability.

Worms

Someone has speculated that earthworms have been used by more fresh-water fishermen than just about all other natural baits put together. It wouldn't surprise me. From kids on up, fishermen have impaled worms on hooks in small pieces—to fit into little fishes' mouths—singly and in writhing gobs of two or more to entice a great variety of sport fishes, including breams, trouts, basses, pickerels, walleyes, catfishes and all kinds of panfishes. Worms are also trolled, cast, drifted and bottom-fished. One of the greatest testimonials to earthworms' effectiveness as bait is that they're imitated by dozens of soft plastic versions.

City dwellers can buy their worms in tackle shops. Their suburban and rural brethren are more fortunate in that they can obtain theirs for nothing if willing to put in a little effort. In spring and summer, anglers dig them and capture the so-called night crawlers by hand on the surface if they're quick enough. Another method of capturing earthworms, according to a veteran fresh-water fishing friend of mine, is called "grunting." A wooden stake is driven into the ground, leaving a few inches exposed, whereupon the top of the stake is rubbed vigorously with a coarse file. It's claimed that the resulting vibrations drive earthworms out of hiding (presumably with their hands to their ears). If you don't drive any to the surface, my friend says, you're either not grunting right or maybe you just don't have any worms.

Crayfish and Shrimp

In various sizes crayfish, or crawfish, are rigged alive, hooked carefully in the back or through the tail, for a variety of fresh-water sportsters, including trout, largemouth and smallmouth basses, channel catfish, bream and other species. Some anglers break off the large claws to make the crayfish more "swallowable." The tail section only of large crayfish may also be used.

There are species of shrimp, commonly called grass shrimp, that inhabit fresh waters. They're small, so much so that two or three may be needed to make a respectable mouthful for a fish, but they catch crappies, bluegills and other panfishes.

Crickets and Grasshoppers

Although they're terrestrial insects, crickets and grasshoppers jump or fall into brooks, streams and ponds in numbers, a windfall that doesn't go unnoticed by trouts, basses and other hungry fishes. Enterprising fishermen can gather their own crickets and grasshoppers. The former are collected by looking under fallen tree limbs and other debris that have lain on the ground for a long time. An old stunt is to leave a piece of discarded carpet on the ground in the backyard for crickets to hide under. Grasshoppers can be gathered in summer by spreading an old fuzzy blanket out in a field and stomping through the grass to drive them onto the blanket, where their legs get caught in the fuzz. Since crickets and grasshoppers can be kept alive for a while without difficulty, it's suggested that a

supply of them for bait be gathered beforehand rather than wait until the day you go fishing, when you might not be able to collect enough.

Other Fresh-Water Baits

Among other come-ons: (1) Caterpillars and grubs (the larval stage of beetles). (2) The larvae of aquatic insects such as the hellgrammite, which is the large larva of the dobsonfly. (3) Salmon eggs. These are widely used as bait and sold in jars for that purpose. The bait hooks are very small, but the biggest eggs can be impaled individually. Adding some red yarn to the hook is said to heighten the eggs' effectiveness. They can also go on the hook in a cluster. Trout are prime targets, but other species like the eggs as well. (4) Fresh-water mussels and clams. If you can get 'em, they're baits that will take panfishes, carp, catfishes, other species.

Then there are some odd lots: (5) Marshmallows have taken trout, bullheads, carp and assorted panfishes when impaled on hooks in pieces of suitable size. No, they don't have to be toasted. (6) Doughballs. There are several recipes for these. Simplest is to knead and press a piece of white bread to form a ball on a hook. Another is created by mixing equal parts of flour and peanut butter with hot water to moisten, then pressing and kneading it on the hooks. Carp, catfishes and bullheads, trouts and sunfishes have been taken on this bait. You can also substitute a cheese, such as cheddar, for the white bread. (7) Newts, or salamanders. These are a natural bait that is effective for basses. (8) Beef liver. In pieces of graduated sizes for smaller to medium fishes and in fluttering strips for the larger ones, liver will attract several kinds of fresh-water species. (9) Canned corn, the whole-kernel type, no cream sauce. One or more kernels are impaled on a hook, according to species sought, and will attract panfishes, carp, bullheads and others—even trout on occasion. (10) Long-timers tell me that in a pinch a piece of salami, ham, bologna or frankfurter will serve as bait and has accounted for various panfishes and bullheads.

In sum, a few general pointers concerning natural baits, salt-water and fresh-water:
1. If there's an order of priority, position No. 1 would probably go to live baits, since their freshness is obvious and any movements they make are likely to add to their attraction. Many anglers like

to procure their own, using small seines for the likes of little baitfishes and shrimp, traps for crabs, and so on. Larger fishes destined to become live bait—whiting, mackerels, etc.—are hook-and-line caught beforehand.

In addition to the efforts involved, the problem often is in transporting and keeping baitfishes, either caught or bought, alive and in good condition until time to use them. Devices such as a killy car (a floating cage) and a minnow bucket can solve the problem. Some boats designed for fishing have a built-in live-bait well. Keeping larger fishes alive for any length of time is a real problem. Without a holding container of suitable size with circulating water and suitable protection against the sun, the fishes can die from oxygen starvation or water that's too warm for them. Some baits—worms, crabs and insects—require only a little care to keep alive.

2. Live baits are not absolutely necessary. This is fortunate because the vast majority of anglers today have neither the opportunity nor the inclination to go out and get their own, and they may not be able to buy live baits. The only alternative, of course, is dead baits. These come in two forms, fresh and frozen.

Ideally, dead bait should be as fresh-caught as possible. You'll have to do as many fishermen do, rely on frozen baits, age unknown. Many marine baits are sold frozen in packages. They do a job, but should be thawed before use so they'll have the flexibility for a more natural appearance. Believe it or not, a minnow stiff as a board doesn't look right to a fish. For the same reason, anglers remove the backbone of larger baitfishes.

Chum that has been under refrigeration is likely to contain ice crystals that make the material buoyant and impair its distribution. And if the stuff floats near the surface you'll provide a buffet for sea birds. Thaw it well beforehand.

3. It goes without saying that live baits should be hooked as carefully as possible, which means minimum handling and inserting the hook in such a way as not to badly injure the bait or kill it outright, defeating the purpose of a live attractor. Even with maximum care, many baits won't stay alive on a hook for any length of time. Some die very quickly. There's nothing you can do about that, but at least you'll know you have the freshest possible dead bait.

One school of thought advocates minimum handling of any bait, live or dead, on the theory that handling imparts a human scent that may repel certain fishes. Years ago a Midwestern fresh-water angler recommended dipping the fingers in bourbon before handling bait, thus masking any human scent. He was serious (but he may have been doing more with the Old Grand-Dad than dipping his fingers in it). He didn't say if it helped him catch more fish, but presumably his bass died the happiest of any in those parts.

4. There are a few exceptions when freshness isn't a major consideration. These include such specialized cases as the gosh-awful-smelling baits prepared for catfishes and the ripe chunks of fish placed in crab traps and eelpots.

5. Even with experience it isn't easy to predict how much bait you'll need on a given day. Tackle shop personnel and fishing station—or rowboat livery—operators usually can advise. If there must be an extreme, I'd rather wind up with too much bait than too little.

6. You can't cover all bases when it comes to baits, but for fickle species it's wise to carry a couple of different kinds the species fancies. No guarantee for that suggestion, but it could spell the difference between a catch and a skunking (going home empty-handed.)

7. By way of another backup system, you might also take along any lures simulating the desired sport fish's favorite food.

Artificial Baits or Lures

While there are occasions when lures seem to nail more fish than natural baits, nothing tops the real thing in the overall picture. And it must be remembered that artificial, man-made baits—lures—are designed to simulate items of fishes' natural food. At least the vast majority of them are. But there are some lures for which imagination must be stretched to discern even a passing resemblance to anything in nature; yet they catch fish. These lures obviously work because of certain attractive features—such as forms, movements, colors, sound effects, or whatever—that they possess. Or conceivably these lures arouse fishes' curiosity or spirit of competition enough to provoke strikes. And here and there, I suspect, are lures designed (unwittingly or otherwise) to catch more fishermen than fish.

The subject "natural baits vs. artificials" can stir

up spirited discussions, but serious anglers are prepared to use both—not necessarily at the same time, but as occasions demand. Lures have a number of advantages over their real-life counterparts. (1) There's no availability problem as there is with natural baits. (2) They're easily transported and there's no worry about spoilage in hot weather. (3) A lure's service life is a lot longer than that of its natural counterpart (barring a popped line or getting hung up on something). With a little luck a lure can last for years, with an occasional change of a component—hook or skirt—owing to general wear. All that adds up to economy.

Don't misunderstand. I'm not talking down naturals in favor of artificials. I'm just trying to provide you with reasons why you should amass a personal inventory of lures.

With the different types, with the different models of each type, and a range of sizes for each model, plus differences in manufacturers' versions, there are thousands of artificials. And I'm not talking about mass-production quantities. Nor am I including artificial flies (see the Chapters 8 and 9 fly-fishing).

Still, all of today's lures can be subdivided according to basic types, with a special division for hybrids—combinations of features of basic types. I catalogue them like this: 1) plugs, 2) spoons, 3) jigs, 4) feathers, 5) spinners, 6) soft-plastic lures and 7) miscellaneous types.

Plugs

"Plugs" is the collective term for all man-made artificial baits designed to simulate some kind of small fish or item of natural food fancied by finned game. For example, there are plugs designed to simulate mullet, frogs and mice—all items devoured by fishes. Imitation comes in many forms. There are models that zigzag or have the darting movements of forage fishes and models that behave erratically like an injured creature. Body materials are wood and, more commonly, plastics. They come in every hue of the rainbow and with blotches, bands, and even polka dots. Some have one treble hook for armament; others carry two or three.

The upshot of all this is that manufacturers market a staggering and bewildering number of different plug models. It's obvious that there can be no simple formula with which only a handful of plugs will handle many and varied assignments. However, certain guidelines can assist in selection:

1. Your first consideration should focus on the species sought. Knowledge of feeding habits is essential. (What items are on the species' diet?) Its manner of feeding is equally important. Is it aggressive or slow? Does it feed on the bottom or on the surface or in between?

2. Plug weights are another important consideration. Yesteryear's heavier plugs can't be handled satisfactorily by today's light equipment. Some of the lightest-caliber tackle demands fractional-ounce plugs as light as 1/16th oz., even lighter. Plug weights, sizes and shapes also depend on weather and light conditions. For example, in very clear water or on bright days a smaller plug is indicated; whereas in cloudy water or in poor light a bigger, more visible plug is more effective.

3. Plug colors and finishes are other vital considerations. Manufacturers have paid much attention to detail in recent years, aided by the development of plastics and refined production techniques. To what extent fishes discern colors is still debated, but it appears that certain hues or combinations are more effective with some species than others. There's no question but that brightness of color can be an eye-catching attraction. By the same token, solid, mottled and polka dot patterns seem to have varying degrees of effectiveness according to species. And often anglers use different colors depending on water and light conditions. Logically, bright colors are better suited to dirty water and poor light, while less bright colors are more suited to clear water and bright sunlight. As for plug finishes, technology has produced such innovations as plugs with lifelike eyes and plastic plugs with realistic finishes undreamed of in the days of wooden plugs. Plastics, too, can handle the dental assaults of toothy battlers better.

4. Plug action is still a consideration. I'll go into this later, but you must consider the level at which a plug is designed to function at its best. For example, there are surface and near-surface riders and plugs, for intermediate planes as well as those designed to travel very deep.

5. The hook armament of plugs is also of prime importance. It's often dictated by the model of plug. Fishermen develop their own ideas as to what constitutes the proper armament for the fishes they hunt. They may remove a set of treble hooks or add one or change their positioning, and so on.

In sum, plugs vary widely in their anatomical details and performance, and all of the above features are to be considered in your selection. Now I'll divide all plugs into basic groups, for some additional pointers.

Underwater Plugs

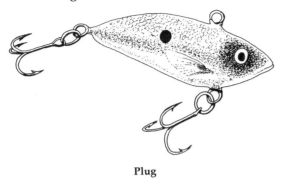

Plug

1. Floaters and Divers. As the names imply, these plugs float when lying inactive on the surface, and dive when they are retrieved. They achieve different depths through design details such as an adjustable metal lip, head cut at an angle or grooved, etc. Those with a metal lip in front can be adjusted to travel many feet down and aid the plug's action. Many underwater models have a built-in wobble or dart when retrieved. Some are designed with pointed front ends and do not have a built-in action. For effectiveness they rely on the angler's working them with his rod tip in retrieves. Here he can experiment in creating erratic dart-and-pause movements. Related to these plugs are darters. Most darters float in horizontal fashion but some float almost vertically, head end up. Their main claim to success is based on a wiggling action, and because of it they're rigged for a sizable collection of fish. They have another advantage over floating-diving models in that they respond well to varied-speed retrieving at the surface. Basically they're shallow-water lures because of their buoyancy and are not as suited to deeper water.

2. Sinking Plugs. These sink as soon as they land on water. The rate of descent varies among models, but the majority sink slowly. This is a plus, because the sinkers can be held at a desired depth by retrieving with the rod tip, and thus they permit probing at different levels—an added advantage over the floating-diving type of plug. The longer the pause after the plug hits the water, the deeper it will go. By timing (counting to oneself), it's possible to return a plug to approximately the same depth repeatedly.

3. Deep Divers. The name of these plugs describes their function, although there are some models that will float when at rest before boring into the depths on retrieves. For deep submersion these plugs depend upon a wide metal lip which functions like the diving planes of a submarine. As a result, the more line between a deep diver and the rod tip the farther down it will go. This plug comes

into its own in salt water when the targets are cruising well below surface. In fresh water they star during the hot days of summer when fishes shift to deeper, cooler water.

Surface Runners

Popping Plug

This group is distinguished from others by popping plugs and other sound-producing models and by those designed to create a fuss when worked.

1. Typical poppers are characterized by a concavity at their head end. When worked with a rod tip, they duck just under the surface, where the concavity produces a popping sound and lots of bubbles, which fishes find (fatally) alluring. Alterations of the concavity's size, shape and depth change the nature and intensity of the pops. Fishes can hear poppers before they see them. This is understandably an added advantage at night or in murky water. Popping plugs float when at rest, "vocalize" when they start to move. They can be cast or trolled and are basically shallower-water lures. Varying their traveling speed naturally intensifies or lessens their sonic effects and bubbly wake. In fresh water they're useful for enticing bass and other loners out from the cover under which they're lurking. In general, poppers are retrieved slowly to give a fish time to notice the sounds and a chance to locate the source and investigate. One technique is to slowly retrieve the plug a short distance, pause, twitch it with the rod tip, resume the wind-in, pause, jerk it, and so on. In both fresh and salt water poppers can do a job when raiders are clobbering a school of baitfish and are likely to hit anything that moves.

2. Other kinds of surface plugs—swimmers, torpedo shapes, etc.—rely for effectiveness on generating some kind of commotion on the top of the water when they are retrieved or towed. Depending upon the models, their fuss may be ripples, splashes, threshing or whatever. This is achieved by little devices that include flaps, propellers, and arm- or leglike appendages. Surface-commotion plugs stay on top most of the time when in motion. Their intention is to simulate a baitfish or another creature such as a frog trying to get the hell out of there. So they're best suited to gamesters that either normally feed at the surface

or will rise to seize a tidbit. It's among salt-water surface riders that we find the giants of the plug family, like the 12-in.-long jointed eel. Surface plugs are made to imitate a wide range of food items for both fresh- and salt-water service: frogs, minnows, herring, menhaden, spearing, etc. Some imitate the antics of a crippled fish. Depending upon size, they may be armed with one to three treble hooks.

Many old-timers argue that color patterns are not important. Nevertheless, bright colors such as all-white, red and white, all-yellow, and silver-flashing finishes will do good before they do harm.

Surface-commotion plugs are fished at different speeds, according to the natural actions of the types of creatures they're trying to imitate. Thus some are worked fast so that they skitter across the surface like a baitfish, even leaping clear at intervals. Others are given slow or moderate-speed swimming action. Still other models are left more or less stationary, but twitched with the rod tip at intervals. Surface plugs see a wide range of uses in fresh water and salt water. In the latter they're often rigged in surf fishing and boat casting.

Developing a Plug Assortment

Plugs are among the most valuable lures. Every serious fisherman should develop his own assortment. The nucleus of your plug inventory should consist of basic versatile types. Here are some guidelines to consider: (1) items that will lure the kinds of fishes you seek; (2) entwined with No. 1, the most frequent fishing methods, personal and general, in that area. These two guidelines should help you determine how many different models— underwater, surface, etc.—you'll need. An important factor in No. 1 is the selection of plug colors and finishes. Some of the standards in fresh water are silvery, red and white frog pattern, all-yellow and yellow polka dot, and black scale. In salt water, popular finishes include blue mullet, silver-flash, mackerel scale, gold flashing, all-yellow, red and white and all-white. (3) The type and caliber of tackle wielded. Spinning gear and light bait-casting equipment are limited as to the weights of artificials and natural baits they can handle satisfactorily. For such weapons there are frac-tional-ounce mini-models. Heavier plugs point to conventional-type tackle. Fishing conditions enter the picture too. Casting on a quiet lake is one thing, while flinging a plug from a windswept ocean strand, where there can be considerable strain on the lure, is quite another.

You won't go wrong in your selection if you visit a local tackle shop, outline your requirements, and ask for guidance. Usually tackle shop personnel are anglers themselves. In any case, their cash register's jangling tells them what lures are currently most effective. Once you've established the nucleus of a collection suited to the area fished, you can build a personal inventory gradually, adding plugs as experience dictates. A wise angler always carries spares of the models he rigs most often.

Spoons

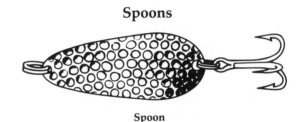

Spoon

A spoon is a metal lure, usually more or less of an elongated oval shape. It derives its name from its resemblance to a teaspoon's bowl section. Attachment to a line or leader is made simply by means of a hole at the lure's leading end. Its trailing end is its business section, for this carries its armament, commonly a swinging treble hook.

Spoons are believed to be among the senior artificials, have been traced back to about 5,000 years ago. The origin of modern spoons in America began with an incident involving an ardent young Vermont fisherman named Julio Buell, who, it is said, accidentally dropped a teaspoon overboard, while eating lunch. He was helplessly watching the spoon disappear into the depths when he noticed that its flash and action drew a response from a fish or two. He returned to the lake several days later with a broken-handled teaspoon on which he had soldered a hook and which he tied to his line at the handle end. His crude invention was so successful that in 1834 he received what is believed to be the first U.S. patent for a trolling lure. Today there are spoons by the hundreds. They come in fresh- and salt-water models, in a multitude of sizes, weights, materials and finishes. Most of them still retain that traditional spoon shape, with modifications of the bowl to form concave and convex sides. Deviations include models with shapes intended to resemble small baitfishes in profile. Others are contorted in an S-curve or are bent in various ways. Spoons are stamped out of brass, stainless steel, copper or an alloy, and may have a natural silvery or even golden polished finish, or they can be plated or enameled. Many are left shiny for glitter. This effect has been enhanced in some, such as the Hopkins No-Eql series, by a kind of rippled surface that reflects like a lot of little mirrors. Many spoons are painted in bright colors—red, white, yellow, etc.—to achieve a (fish) eye-catching effect. The Dardevle series, created by luremaker Lou Eppinger and his company, is a case in point.

Like any man-made baits, spoons are intended to imitate, through their shape, finish and action in the water, some item of natural fish food. In addition to eye-catching shapes, spoons have such actions as side-to-side sashaying and erratic darting to make them attractive when worked. There are all sorts of combinations.

Spoons are marketed in a wide range of lengths and weights. At one length are little fellows with bodies 1–1½ in. long, and at the other are the huge mossbunker spoons up to 12 in. long and 4 in. wide. If you can't hook a striper with a 'bunker spoon, you can club him to death. Then there are featherweight models as light as ¹⁄₁₆ oz. for duty with ultralight tackle. Some of the very lightest are even cast with fly rods.

In fresh-water service, small spoons to ¼ oz. or so are used for panfishes. Heavier models to ¾ oz. will nail bass, pickerel, good-sized trout, smaller pike and muskellunge. In the heavier caliber are spoons to 2 oz. that are better for heavyweight bass, muskies, lake trout, salmon and big pike. Spoons can be cast or trolled. When cast they are usually retrieved slowly but erratically, alternating spurts with pauses, during which the artificials are allowed to sink, flutter and show their flash. As in retrieves, trolled spoons can be worked at various depths.

Salt-water spoons are trolled, cast from boats, and used in the surf and worked as spoons are in fresh-water use. Keep in mind that spoons, being of solid metal, are relatively heavy for their size and will sink if not activated by the rod. Spoons have nailed an impressive list of salt-water battlers including bluefish, striped bass, barracuda and channel bass.

The most common hook arrangement for spoons is one treble, dangling free at the tail end. Small spoons may carry a swinging double hook instead of a treble. At the other end some of the large spoons, like the 'bunker spoon, often have a single fixed hook. But their hook sizes range up to 12/0 and are husky. Some spoons are left with their hooks unadorned. But there are models with dressings of feather or bucktail. The choice provides a good opportunity for fishermen to experiment with both types. Every tackle box should contain at least a basic assortment of spoons. Again, tackle shop personnel are usually able to offer recommendations.

Jigs

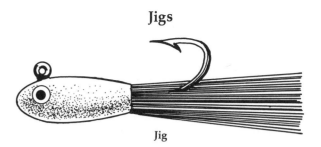

Jig

Years ago this term applied to a small group of artificials such as the cedar jig, a torpedo-shaped lure with a wooden body (usually cedar), a weighted and streamlined head end, and a hook rigidly embedded in its trailing section. Cedar jigs were—and still are—killers for bluefish, tunas and other gamesters, but they're hard to find nowadays. When artificials underwent a population explosion in models and sizes, jigs were part of it and now constitute an army of lures ranging in weight from a fraction of an ounce to 6 oz. or more.

In general, jigs today are of two basic types. One is characterized by a stubby, short but heavy head of solid metal to which is affixed a skirt of nylon threads or other material, including feathers, a fringe of rubber bands or animal hairs. Those with a skirt of animal hairs are often called bucktails, from the time when the hairs used were from the tail of a buck deer. Attachment is made directly to a loop atop the head; the hook is embedded in the body and surrounded by the skirt. These lures are often spoken of as "leadheads" or "leadheaded jigs." The other basic jig type is the time-honored trolling feather, used for generations to nail tunas, dolphins, bluefish, king mackerel and many other kinds of finned game.

Collectively, all jigs can be used interchangeably in salt and fresh water, although some types are traditionally associated more with salt than with fresh and vice versa.

A classic type commonly associated with salt water is the diamond jig, so called because its body shape is that of a long, skinny diamond in one end of which a hook is embedded. Being molded from lead gives these jigs mass in small sizes, and many are chrome-plated for brightness. The unplated ones must be rubbed periodically with sandpaper or emery cloth, or scraped with a knife, to restore an attractive luster. It's better to buy plated models. A first cousin of the diamond jig is a variation whose lead body is in the wiggly shape of a small eel. All these metal jigs can be trolled, cast or jigged for a variety of fishes that include sea bass, bluefish and Atlantic mackerel. *Tip:* Because of their design, behavior in water, and the way fishes hit these jigs, it's important that their hooks be always needle-sharp; otherwise it may be almost impossible to set the hooks.

Among leadhead models, variety in design and weight is achieved by the shape of the head and the nature and color of the skirts. Some are egg-shaped; others are roundish. Some heads are bullet-shaped; others have a flat but beveled leading end, and so on. The colors of the heads differ with models, and commonly the head has eyes for added effect. Skirt colors vary too. A jig with a skirt streaming behind it is intended to simulate a small baitfish in flight.

With the exception of the feather types used in trolling, jigs are also characterized by their weight. Being molded from lead, they're heavy for their size. This, coupled with the minimal air resistance of their shape, makes them easy to cast. They're like little projectiles.

In the family of fresh-water jigs for light spinning tackle and small game, there are models going as light as 1/32 oz. to 1/4 oz. For general all-round light-tackle service, there are those in the 1/4 to 1/2 oz. range. A step upward are jigs in weights from 5/8 oz. to 1 oz.-plus for heavier tackle and larger game. Hooks are in proportion, of course. Jigs have accounted for many sweetwater fishes, including walleyes, largemouth and smallmouth basses, and assorted panfishes.

Salt-water jigs are heavier. Here weights go from about 1/8 oz. for a small feather type up to 4 oz. and more among the leadheads. On the larger models hook sizes go up to 8/0. Here again weights are gauged to equipment, the smaller and lighter models being rigged for light or spinning tackle. As in fresh-water service, these artificials are cast from shores and boats and are also trolled, as well as fished from piers and bridges. Leadheads have racked up an impressive list of victims, including striped bass, mackerels and school-size tunas. Feather types have taken tunas, marlins, bonitos, barracudas and numerous other battlers.

Leadheads can be combined effectively with other artificials. One combo, proven effective for bluefish, striped bass and other battlers, is a double-lure arrangement that marries a leadhead jig with a plug. Two rod-'n'-reel outfits are used so that each lure can be adjusted independently. On one line, riding higher, is the plug, often a popper, but it can be another shallow- or deeper-riding model, depending upon water depths. On the other line, a bit lower and just astern of the plug, is a leadhead jig or bucktail. The theory is that the plug attracts and the jig catches, but sometimes fish hit the plug too.

A two-jig setup is also used for fresh-water basses. Here a single rod and line are used. One jig goes on the leader, while its mate is connected via a dropper, created by an extension blood knot. When the knot is tied, an extra length of line is left extended for a dropper. You can experiment with two models of jigs or different weights of the same model, perhaps in different colors too. When weights differ, the heavier one is attached to the leader for balance. In the sweetwater procedure the double-jig rig is cast from a boat, allowed to hit bottom, then retrieved at varying speeds, with pauses and spurts, to suggest fleeing baitfish.

Jigs are useful lures. Every angler's bag of tricks should contain a selection.

Feather Lures

Feather Lure

Artificial baits referred to as feather lures, or just "feathers," have been the stock-in-trade of offshore trollers for generations. Often they're lumped with the huge jig family, but I prefer to keep feathers in a group by themselves. The basic components of a feather lure are a bullet-shaped head, 3/4 in. to 1 in. long and chromed to make it shiny, and a skirt of natural feathers about 3 or 4 in. long. Usually the head carries fake red eyes for added realism and attraction. Feathers may be all white or in two-color combinations such as red and white or green and yellow. Most of the lure's weight is in its head. It can range as light as 1/8 oz. up to 8 oz. and heavier, depending upon size and manufacturer.

A feather doesn't come with a hook unless it's marketed as a complete assembly. This is to allow a choice of hook pattern and size. Fishermen often have their own ideas as to which designs and calibers work best. It also gives latitude in determining the length and strength of the wire leader on which the attractor will go.

A feather lure is easily rigged. The desired length of leader—wire, monofilament or whatever —is fed through a lengthwise hole in the lure's head. On that free end of the leader is attached the chosen hook, usually a ring-eye type. A small loop or a few twists—if the leader is wire—is needed to secure it. The metal head points in the direction the lure will be trolled, of course, and the hook is drawn up inside the skirt of feathers. At the leader's remaining free end is fashioned another loop.

This will connect with a snap swivel on the end of the line.

Some skirts are fashioned from natural feathers. At one time feathers from a certain kind of Japanese chicken were favored because of their length. Subsequently the lures came to be known as Jap feathers, and are still known as such. Other skirts are made of nylon and similar synthetics. Skirts come in white, yellow, red, blue, green and color combinations. Many anglers favor the synthetics over natural feathers because they better withstand the toothy assaults of some game fishes.

The natural-feather models are still in a class by themselves and very much in the picture. They're good artificials, accounting for tunas, bonitos, bluefish, wahoo, barracudas and other battlers in surface and near-surface action. Every offshore troller should carry an assortment of colors and color combos, with spares of those proved most effective. A couple of red-and-whites are a must: this color combination is one of the most universally lethal of all.

Spinners

Spinner

Spinners constitute a large group of fresh- and salt-water lures. There are some differences among the many models, but they all share one anatomical detail in common: one or more blades that spin when the artificial moves through the water. The lure's attraction centers about a blade's motion, glitter or flash, and the vibrations it sets up. The spinners' ability to produce underwater sounds is an important detail. Fishes can hear them, even if they can't see them, at night or in murky water. Spinners are used in casting and trolling.

A spinner's chief feature, its blade, may be oval, shaped like an elongated leaf, nearly round, or teardrop- or kidney-shaped. Blade lengths range from ½ in. to 1¼ in. Blade finishes come in silver, chrome, gold, copper, brass and enamel, the latter in colors such as white, yellow and red.

In addition to the blade, the basic spinner consists of a short wire shaft on which the blade is mounted on a revolving arm, called a clevis, which permits it to rotate freely. Some models incorporate a swivel for attachment to the line. Some carry

a connector at the lower end of the shaft for attachment of hooks. Others have both. Red plastic beads are often added to the shaft for added attraction. There are also models consisting of two barrel swivels connected by a ring on which the blade rotates. Variations include models that carry two, three or more blades.

Spinners can be rigged in many ways, in accordance with fishing method and species sought. And they can be lethal in combination with natural and artificial baits. For example, marine trollers often use spinners of the Willow Leaf, June Bug and Cape Cod designs, baited with sandworms, to score handsomely with striped bass. Fresh-water anglers use spinners armed with hooks carrying worms or minnows to catch basses.

Some spinners carry additional adornment such as skirts of bucktail or feathers or of plastic or rubber in bright colors, with hooks left bare or baited. Spinners in combination with plastic worms are popular for bass on big impoundments in the South.

You can purchase blades in assorted shapes and sizes separately, to incorporate in rigs ahead of a lure or baited hook as an added attraction.

Hook arrangements on spinners are left up to you. Single, double and treble hooks are interchangeable on many models. Sometimes two single hooks are rigged in tandem. As a general rule, multibladed spinners are used in trolling, while weighted models are used in casting. Small metal beads on the shaft, or a small metal body, provide the weight. Spinners for trolling average up to about 5 in. long, and those used in casting range to 3 in.

Small spinners are used in fly-fishing to supplement a streamer or wet fly. In salt water, spinner blades often are an effective addition to bottom rigs in drifting. They can be trolled slowly or cast from boats, piers and bridges and retrieved slowly.

In short, spinners provide many opportunities for interesting experimentation.

Soft-Plastic Lures

In the 1950s plastics invaded the lure field and have since produced a mass of artificials for fresh-water and salt-water fishing.

I can't list them all here. To give you an idea of their scope, marine anglers now have plastic squids, eels, bloodworms, mackerel, shrimp, sandworms and mullet. Many of these fakes are reproduced with amazing fidelity to shape, color, "skin" (finish) and action. For fresh-water fishermen there are plastic minnows, frogs, crickets, hellgrammites, grasshoppers, crayfish, worms and you-name-it. Some of these soft-plastic lures even ingeniously incorporate the bait's natural scent.

These imitations may be used alone or in tandem with spinners, spoons, jigs and other artificials, often according to ideas or theories entertained by the users. That they catch fish either way is testimony to their effectiveness.

Miscellaneous Artificials

Here are some lures to consider:

1. Surgical tubes or just tubes. These came on the marine fishing scene in the 1950s and resemble plastic tubing used in blood transfusions and other medical procedures, hence the name. They're rigged for trolling. I can speculate as to why surgical tubes are effective. I figure it's because they suggest small baitfishes and tasty young eels, and when being trolled the rush of water past them generates an enticing wiggling-fluttering action. Plastic tubing for adaptation as fishing lures comes in various diameters and in bulk for cutting to lengths from about 2½ or 3 in. up to 12-plus, the latter if the tubes are intended to simulate adult eels. The tubing also comes in a variety of colors such as red, white, green, amber, black and brown. Do-it-yourselfers buy the tubing in bulk and cut their own lures to desired lengths. Surgical tubes are rigged singly or in multiple-unit rigs that incorporate up to nine or more small tubes strung out by short lengths of wire from a spreader. Variously nicknamed "umbrella rig," "coat hanger," and "Christmas tree," these multiple-tube rigs

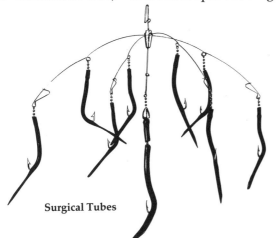

Surgical Tubes

suggest a group of baitfish hustling through the water. I've seen umbrella rigs take two and three striped bass at once when a school is worked, for which reason I join other conservation-minded anglers in disliking them.

Surgical tubes have found their way along the

U.S. East Coast to Florida, where they have been used successfully on the flats. But they're still new enough that their full potential is yet to be determined. I believe that tube lures will become much more widespread in salt water as time goes on. They might just invade fresh-water angling too if they haven't done so already.

2. Metal squids. These are really a part of the jig family. Metal squids are manufactured from the so-called block tin and other metals and have been in marine anglers' tackle boxes for generations, ready for casting, trolling and jigging. They're made in several shapes to suggest such forage fishes as silversides, killies, sand eels, young mullet, etc. Many models are chrome- or nickle-

Metal Squid

plated for eye-catching flash and glitter. Usually they carry a single hook, which may be embedded in the body or swing at the stern end. On some, the dangling hook is a treble. They can be fished with nude hooks, but many users decorate the hook with a piece of pork rind or some other bait, or with a bit of bucktail or pieces of bright-colored feather. In weight they range from fractional-ounce midgets to fish destroyers of 4 and 5 oz.

Originally metal squids were intended as shore-side casting lures, a fact that gave rise to the surf-casting term squidding. Victims include channel bass (redfish or red drum), weakfish, striped bass and bluefish. Each model has its own set of recommendations regarding the way it should be fished. Lacking those, different retrieve and trolling speeds should be tried to determine which depths and actions get the best results.

3. Bait Tails. Relative newcomers in the angling arena, Bait Tails are the brainchild of the late Al Reinfelder, prominent U.S. East Coast angler-writer, and his fishing buddy Lou Palma. It took

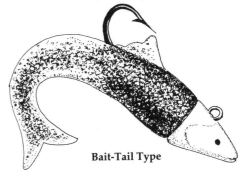

Bait-Tail Type

them five years to perfect the Bait Tail, which was introduced in 1965. It's a simple lure consisting of a metal head, for weight in casting, and a flexible plastic body for lifelike action in water. Its head and body are continuous in form, suggesting in profile a typical baitfish. A single hook of appropriate size is embedded in the metal head and rides with its point on top. An offset eye atop the head is for attachment.

Judging by claims made for Bait Tails, they're among the most versatile of all lures. They can be fished in salt and fresh water, and they come in a gradation of sizes and a wide variety of colors to handle a range of scrappers. They can be cast, trolled and jigged from all kinds of locations and boats. Used with spinning and conventional tackle, Bait Tails have racked up an angling score that includes northern pike, sea trout, bluegills, snook, black bass, bluefish, walleyes, barracuda, crappies, tarpon and Spanish mackerel.

4. Chicken-bone and turkey-bone lures. Way back, fishermen salvaged the leg bones of chickens and turkeys demolished at the family dinner table, bleached 'em white, and strung them on short lengths of wire with a hook. The resulting lures were primarily for trolling, and reportedly were effective for bluefish, striped bass and large weakfish. Chicken- and turkey-bone artificials have long since faded from the scene, which is why I mention them here. I think they're worth reviving. They're easy to fashion.

5. Weirdos that have caught fish: (a) A shiny beer can opener to which a hook was soldered. (b) A worn-out shaving brush with a hook hidden among its bristles—an improvised bucktail. (c) A shiny beer bottle cap fashioned into a spinner (it was a promotion gimmick for a brand of beer). I saw a coho salmon—a beer drinker, no doubt—caught on it. (d) A mermaid lure, a kind of jig, an obvious novelty whose plastic body had a swinging treble hook dangling from her tail. If a fish tried to grab a piece of tail, he got a mouthful of lethal hardware.

Lines

Prior to World War II there was mainly only one kind of line: linen. True, silk was exclusively used in fly-fishing lines, and at one time there were lines of horsehair and cotton sewing thread, but linen was it.

Today's lines come in far greater variety to better suit a much wider range of assignments. They come in braided and single-strand (monofilament) types, round, oval or flattish in cross section. They're made from tough, water-resistant, rot-resistant synthetic materials carrying labels such as nylon, Micron (Cortland Line Company's), Perlon (a German product) and Terelyne (England). They're marketed in every conceivable practical strength. One manufacturer, for example, produces monofilament in strengths from 4-lb. test, up through the heaviest line most commonly used in big-game angling, 130-lb. test, to a heavy-duty mono rated at 200 lbs. There are lines with degrees of limpness or stiffness, and there are colored lines for reduced visibility in water. There are also solid wire lines of steel and Monel, and lines that have synthetic material on the outside and a metal core inside, all for deeper trolling.

The Synthetics

Nylon was the first synthetic to be used extensively in fishing-line manufacture. It's tough stuff and has a high tensile strength. The early nylon lines possessed excessive stretch, but that problem has been largely eliminated now, although nylon still has more give than some of the other synthetics.

Ultimately other materials found their way into line manufacture. One that has really made it big is Dacron. In addition to durability, Dacron has a high imperviousness to water that prevents swelling or rotting. Furthermore, it offers two big bonuses. It has less stretch than nylon. Decreased stretch means added sensitivity at the rod end, an asset with small or delicately biting fishes and in detecting nibbles in deep-water sinker bouncing. Dacron also incorporates greater strength in finer diameter, which permits more line of a given strength to be spooled on a reel. Further, Dacron undergoes less water drag, and has less wind resistance in casting. Keep in mind that minimal water drag means less strain on line and rod in trolling, which can be appreciable when a lot of yardage is out. Another advantage of decreased water drag is in sinker bouncing, where it allows use of a somewhat lighter sinker in order to hold bottom.

Synthetic lines come in two basic types: braided and monofilament. In the former the braiding can be likened to the twisting of strands on each other to form rope. Monofilament, in contrast, is a single strand of line. It's created by an extrusion process in which the material is forced under pressure through fine holes in the manner of extruding pasta for spaghetti.

Monofilament lines are enormously popular, and personal preference is more of a factor than equipment in choosing between mono and braided types. Both line types are used interchangeably in all fresh- and salt-water methods, but here are some points to consider: (1) Mono lines are usually less visible in water than braided ones. So if jittery fish in clear water are a problem, mono is a better choice. (2) Monofilament lines are overall more durable than braided types. And they're more resistant to abrasion, which is important when fishing around rocks, coral, barnacle-encrusted wrecks, etc. (If you use braided lines in such areas, check them at intervals for signs of abrasion damage throughout several yards at their rig end and remove any frayed portions. (3) Limper, softer-finish lines usually cast better and are not as hot to a braking thumb, but they fray more readily and are not as abrasion-resistant as the harder finishes. Many braided lines do provide a harder and stiffer finish if you should prefer them.

Every angler has criteria for an ideal line: strength per diameter, minimum stretch, durability, etc. Manufacturing methods cause variations. I suggest trying different brands and types of the same brand name until you find the lines that best fit your personal blueprint.

Wire and Metal-Core Lines

Wire and metal-core lines are designed for deep trolling. Ordinary line has a certain amount of buoyancy that prevents getting a lure or bait down deep enough to cruising fishes at lower planes. There's also an upward thrust on a rig as it's being towed. These factors can be offset in ordinary line by incorporating a drail, or trolling sinker, in the terminal tackle or by addition of a trolling planer, which looks like a short-winged airplane and works on the principle of a submarine's diving planes. But it's better to do without these extra weights if possible.

Metal lines do a job up to a point. Their metal makes them heavier, so they ride deeper than ordinary lines without extra hardware. They're not always the complete solution. For in very deep trolling—as for lake trout—metal lines may not be enough, and trolling sinkers, or even downriggers, may be required. But for much subsurface action the lines alone are enough.

As mentioned, there are two major types: those with metal cores and those made of solid metal. There are two kinds of cored lines. One has a center of metal that is surrounded by some other material, usually a synthetic; the other type is just the reverse of that and has metal wire braided over a monofilament core. The wire, or solid-metal lines, in contrast to the cored ones, are just that. They have no outer covering of any kind. Metals used in their construction include stainless steel, Monel (a nickel alloy), copper and bronze. There are also types in which strands of metal are braided together like cable.

A cored line's or a solid line's sinking coefficient —how deep it will go—is important and differs according to construction and materials. Cored lines do not sink as far or as fast as all-metal types, and among the latter, the twisted or braided kinds do not sink as far or as fast as solid types. All have maximum depths to which they will go by themselves under the usual range of conditions. But it's always useful to know how much line is out. To aid in this, some lines incorporate color changes at set intervals, or fishermen can mark their lines every 5 to 10 fathoms (30–60 ft.) with ladies' bright-colored nail polish or pieces of electrician's tape or adhesive tape.

The most popular wire lines are the solid type in stainless steel or Monel. They do their job admirably and are the best all-round choice. But there are some things about solid wire lines that beginners should know:

1. They're harder to handle than regular lines, since they're stiffer. This stiffness can cause fearsome snarls if wire is payed out too fast or wound back on the reel carelessly. Braided wire handles a bit more easily than the solid type, but it is also bulkier.

2. Kinking is the big headache with all metal lines. Each kink is a potential weak spot. The solid wire type is the worst offender in this respect, but all wire lines should be checked before a trip and any kinked portions removed. More often than not, trying to straighten kinks increases their weakening effect.

3. It should be kept in mind that braided and twisted metal lines do not sink as far as solid wire, but also to be considered are trolling speed and the weight of the rig. Solid Monel goes about as deep as any wire, 50 ft. being an average maximum at usual trolling rates.

4. A reel isn't filled entirely with wire line. The standard procedure is to fill the spool approximately two-thirds with the synthetic line ordinarily used. This serves as backing. Then add the desired yardage of wire. One reason for backing wire line is economy. To begin with, wire isn't exactly cheap. More important, it undergoes fatigue after extensive use, turning brittle, and must be

replaced. When backing is used, only the working section of wire need be discarded. Most chores can be handled with 100 to 150 yds. of wire line plus its backing. In no case should the amount of wire cause overloading of the reel spool (if necessary, decrease the backing). An overload of wire can cause tangles you wouldn't believe. Wire lines are available in greater strengths, but the average range is from about 20-lb. test to 40- and 50-lb. test.

5. Wire line has no real give. This can be an advantage when an appreciable amount of line is out. It means that most of the jigging or other lure-working action by the rod tip reaches the rig and isn't absorbed or lessened by stretch in the line, which could occur with standard synthetic lines.

6. Tackle notes: (a) A rod for use with wire line should have at least one roller guide, the tip-top. And any ring-type guides must be of tough material, such as Carboloy, to resist grooving by wire. (b) There are conventional-type reels designed for wire line. They have wide, comparatively shallow spools.

Author-angler Frank Moss, once a professional sport-fishing skipper himself, worked out some interesting comparisons between systems using wire line and those involving trolling sinkers. With 50-lb. mono at a trolling speed of 3 knots, it requires a 6-oz. sinker to take a 1-oz. lure down 12 ft. with 100 ft. of line out. The length-depth ratio here is approximately 8:1. At the same speed, with the same amount of yardage out, Monel wire of roughly equal strength also will carry a 1-oz. artificial to a depth of 12 ft., same 8:1 ratio. However, 100 ft. of Monel in that strength weighs about 3 oz., which is half as much weight as required in a sinker to achieve the same depth. Since that 8:1 ratio holds under average conditions, we can use it as a yardstick to figure how much wire line should go on a reel for different depths.

Frank Moss's Table		
Water Depth (in feet)	Best Lure Depth (in feet)	Length of Wire (in feet)
10	8	64
20	17	136
30	26	208
40	35	280
50	44	352

Leaders

A leader, also called a trace, is that component of terminal tackle between the line and a lure or a baited hook. Leaders are involved in just about all fishing methods.

Leaders serve several purposes:

1. For decreased visibility. Mono line in certain colors is less noticeable to fishes than braided line and so is used as a leader with braided line when jittery fish or clear water is involved. By the same token, a leader of mono or other material may be tied into the main line of a bottom-fishing rig to get a baited hook away from such fish-distractors as sinkers and swivels. In fresh-water fishing with braided line, a somewhat decreased visibility is achieved by 3 to 6 ft. of mono leader, secured to the line by a blood knot.

2. As added protection against abrasion by a fish's rough skin or body projections. In shark fishing, for instance, you must have the protection of metal leaders against their sandpaper hide.

3. As protection against fishes' dental equipment. Leaders here must be made of wire to guard against dental damage by toothy species such as bluefish, barracuda, muskellunge and walleyes.

4. For added strength or abrasion protection when fishing with braided lines around submerged objects such as rocks, wrecks, coral and barnacle-encrusted bridges, jetties and pilings. Braided lines, as mentioned earlier, are more prone to abrasion damage than monofilament.

5. In trolling. One purpose of the leader here is to lessen line twist with artificials or baits that tend to spin when towed. Another leader use is to lessen strain when heavy rigs are involved.

6. In surf casting with heavy rigs. Some fishermen rig a relatively short length of leader as a kind of shock absorber to protect the line, figuring it's better to lose a couple of feet of leader than maybe several yards of broken line.

7. For presentation of a lure in fly-fishing. See Chapters 8 and 9 devoted to fly-fishing.

Except in the aforementioned situations, users of mono lines can dispense with leaders for most assignments. Mono possesses an inherent lower visibility in combination with strength. If desired, any line twist can be lessened by connecting a lure with a swivel. About the only time a mono leader might be used with mono line is when greater diameter or strength is desired at the rig end. Greater diameter gives an added measure of abrasion protection among rocks, etc., while greater strength may be desirable for handling sizable, rambunctious opponents alongside the boat. But here the leader would have to be fairly long, since its greater strength is of no consequence in landing operations until at least a few turns are on the reel. Until then the maximum strength of the line-leader system is that of its weaker component, the line.

Wire and Cable

As leader material, wire is getting increasing competition from monofilament, and for good reasons: mono is easier to handle and rig, it doesn't undergo metal fatigue, nor does it rust or develop weakening kinks. Minor kinks can be straightened —once, maybe—but this is chancy and requires bending, which weakens the wire.

Situations demanding wire leaders are more numerous in salt water than in fresh water, where about the only gamesters that require them are those with damaging teeth such as muskellunge, walleyes and large pikes.

Two kinds of wire are used in leaders. One is stainless steel; the other is carbon steel, popularly named piano wire. Piano wire is a bit stronger than stainless, but the difference isn't that great for most situations. Any strength advantage is nullified, in my opinion, by the fact that piano wire rusts, thereby becoming weaker, and the shininess of its tinning or plating can scare some fishes. (For those jittery species there are wire leaders colored a shade of brown.)

Also in use is a hybrid that could be called a best-of-two-worlds leader. It combines monofilament (users' choice of length and strength) with 1½ or 2 ft. of wire (users' choice of strength) for protection against teeth and abrasive areas about a fish's head. That short length of wire also facilitates the rigging of certain baits that are difficult to rig with an all-mono leader. The mono-wire combo is rigged in big-game fishing, and usually a few of the short wire sections, with or without baits, are readied in advance to facilitate changing as desired.

As a broad guide to strength classes, you might note the following:

1. Extra-light: Nos. 2 4 to 8 in. or so up to 3 ft., with light gear for protection against teeth, scales or sharp gill covers. Used with tackle up to 12-20-lb. test.

2. Light: Nos. 5 through 7. Used in varying lengths to 6 ft., alone or with mono leaders for protection against teeth, etc., for 20- and 30-lb.-class tackle. Rigged for such marine species as sailfish,

the biggest bluefish, lunker-sized striped bass, young tunas, California yellowtails, etc. Also used for muskellunge, northern pike, salmons, lake trout, others.

3. Medium: Nos. 8 through 10. Rigged in desired lengths to 10 ft. and more with tackle in the 40- and 50-lb. class for Pacific sailfish, alligator gars, the smaller marlins, swordfish and sharks in the 200–300-lb. range. No. 9 is a useful size for 40- and 50-lb. lines.

4. Light-heavy: Nos. 11 through 13. In lengths up to 30 ft. with 80- and 130-lb. tackle for marlins, sharks, tuna, swordfish up to about 500 lbs. or so.

5. Heavy-duty: Nos. 14 and 15. Also rigged in lengths to 30 ft. Designed for 130-lb. tackle and the largest game fishes. These are tough leaders to handle; most big-game anglers ride with lighter sizes.

Here's a guide to wire diameters and strength. The larger the figure, the thicker and stronger the wire.

	Guide to Wire Diameters & Strengths		
Wire Size	Diameter (in inches)	Strength in Pounds-Test Stainless rigged in short lengths, tackle and salt-water fly-fishing Steel	Piano Wire
No. 2	0.011	27	28
3	.012	32	34
4	.013	37	39
5	.014	44	46
6	.016	56	60
7	.018	69	76
8	.020	86	93
9	.022	104	114
10	.024	128	136
11	.026	148	156
12	.028	176	184
13	.030	202	212
14	.032	232	240
15	.034	272	282

It must be remembered that a wire's strength does not determine the overall unit strength of a line-leader system. The system's maximum strength is only that of its weaker component. An exception occurs when a few turns of a stronger leader are on the reel spool. Then you have full benefit of a leader that is stronger than a line.

If there's any rule for leader lengths, it advises not to rig any more than is necessary to satisfy a situation's requirements. Most lighter-tackle fishermen using artificials prefer to dispense with wire, since its stiffness can impair lure action. Many use wire only when sharp-toothed species are involved, and then rig the finest wire they can get away with and restrict it to very short lengths, just enough to keep the line beyond a quarry's bite.

Cable leaders are made from strands of wire twisted on each other in the manner of the strands in rope. In contrast, wire leaders are single-strand in construction. Because it's fashioned from strands of finer wire, cable tends to be more supple than a wire leader, which retains some of its metal's inherent stiffness and isn't as vulnerable to kinks, but in comparable strengths it's more bulky. The rigging of cable leader is largely confined now to big-game fishing for the likes of giant tuna and big marlins, for which service it's plastic-coated to protect the hands. But here again there's competi-

tion from monofilament, since mono is made in strengths of 200-lb. test and better. There's also competition from heavy wire. Cable leaders come already made up, but many big-game regulars create their own. Making cable leaders requires metal sleeves and a crimping tool.

World-record hopefuls must heed International Game Fish Association regulations or their catches will be disqualified. IGFA rules do not specify materials and strengths, *but they do limit lengths.* Also limited by IGFA regulations: *(1)* maximum length of any double line used; *(2)* maximum combined length of a leader and a double line. These restrictions apply in both marine and fresh-water record contention and are influenced by line classes (i.e., 2-lb. test, etc., through 130-lb. test). For fly fishing, the IGFA has a separate list of rules.

Swivels

A swivel is a connector, and it can be used in the following ways: 1) to connect leader, line, and bait or lure; 2) to simply connect leader with bait or lure; or 3) to connect the snell of a hook to a line. The swivel's purpose is to provide strength at the connection and to lessen the twisting of line, leader or snell caused by any rotation of a bait or artificial. Swivels are particularly useful in trolling, but they are used in all angling techniques. The only fishermen who don't use swivels are veterans who consider them extra hardware and fish spookers.

Swivels come in three basic types and one combination. The types are:

1. Barrel swivel, also called a "two-loop" and "two-way." It consists of an eye at each end connected by a stout pin on which the swivel can turn freely.

2. Three-way swivel. This design has three eyes of wire that are united by a metal collar in which the eyes are free to revolve.

3. Snap swivel. This type combines a barrel swivel with a safety snap that works on the same principle as a safety pin. A snap swivel is a must with any lure whose actions include spinning, in order to prevent line twisting.

Snap Swivel

Swivels and snaps are manufactured from various metals, including brass, plain or nickel-plated, and stainless steel, plain or nickel-plated. Some have black or tobacco-colored finishes to make them less conspicuous.

Swivels are marketed in a wide range of sizes and strengths, the latter according to the diameter of the wire involved. You'll find that one manufacturer produces barrel swivels in tests from 20 lbs. (0.021 in. in diameter) to 250 (0.08-in. wire). Another manufacturer will produce snap swivels in strengths ranging from 60-lb. test (0.026 in. wire) to 350-lb. test (wire diameter: 0.080).

Barrel Swivel

3-Way Swivel

Gradations for size follow designations like those used for hooks—4/0, 1/0, No. 5, etc. The only trouble, as with hooks, is that strengths for a given-size swivel may vary among manufacturers. When you need appreciable strength, it's wise to specify that rather than a size.

Floats

Floats are small, buoyant devices whose main function is to suspend a baited rig at a desired level. Sometimes floats are called bobs, or bobbers, since their second function is to notify anglers when there are nibbles at the bait, which they do by their bobbing response. Floats were originally made of cork, with a wooden centerpost for attachment to the rig; but today tackle makers offer fancier models in various forms. You'll find them egg-shaped, with a plastic body now replacing the cork and the centerpost of wood or aluminum.

part of a casting rig, thought must be given to their weight and minimal wind resistance. In general, floats are rigged for species that move in upper water levels near the surface in both fresh and salt water.

There are specialized floats for shark fishing that are easily made. They can be fashioned from blocks of cork or Styrofoam. I favor cork because the whiteness of Styrofoam can distract a shark from the bait. Each block need be only inches in all dimensions, just enough to suspend a baited rig. (See "Big-Game Fishing," Chapter 11.) With either material, a slit is made in one side of the block to receive the line and just deep enough to hold the float in place. This arrangement permits easy adjustment on the line so that the rig's depth can be regulated and allows the float to be flipped free if a shark is attracted to it. Toy balloons also are rigged as floats in shark fishing, but I advise against them because they are not easily adjustable and they can't be flipped off. Those plastic containers in which household bleach is sold are also used as floats, but like balloons, they're not readily adjusted and they can't be flipped free when they attract a shark.

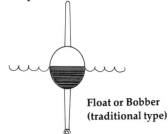

**Float or Bobber
(traditional type)**

You'll also find plastic ones that are round and don't require a centerpost. In addition there are elongated, cigar-shaped floats. The plastics come in all-red or all-white colors or, like most cork models half-'n'-half.

In selecting floats, you must consider their ability to support the baited rig involved. When they're

Sinkers

Sinkers are among the items of angling gear the least changed over the decades. Sinkers are still made from lead, ideal because of its small mass weight, easy molding into different shapes, and durability. And they're still made in the same basic shapes as they were many years ago, as well as in a wide range of sizes and weights. This tells us that they've been doing something right for a long time.

Here's a quick summary of the different kinds rigged in salt and fresh waters.

1. Split-shot and clamp-on sinkers. These are fractional-ounce sinkers used when only a very small amount of weight is required, such as when you only need enough sinker weight to counteract the

upward thrust of a gently flowing tide or current to keep the rig at a desired depth. They're easily attached to a leader or line by squeezing the split shot shut with fisherman's pliers, or by folding over the earlike tabs of the clamp-on sinkers.

2. Bank type. This sinker is the most common type rigged in salt-water bottom fishing. It is sold in sizes from 1 oz. to 5 oz. and more. Bank sinkers often carry a raised figure indicating their weight.

3. Bass swivel, or dipsey design. A built-in swivel in this sinker enables it to roll along the bottom, making it a good type for bottom fishing while drifting. Because of its shape and mobility it's theoretically less likely to get snagged than a bank sinker.

Some Types of Sinkers

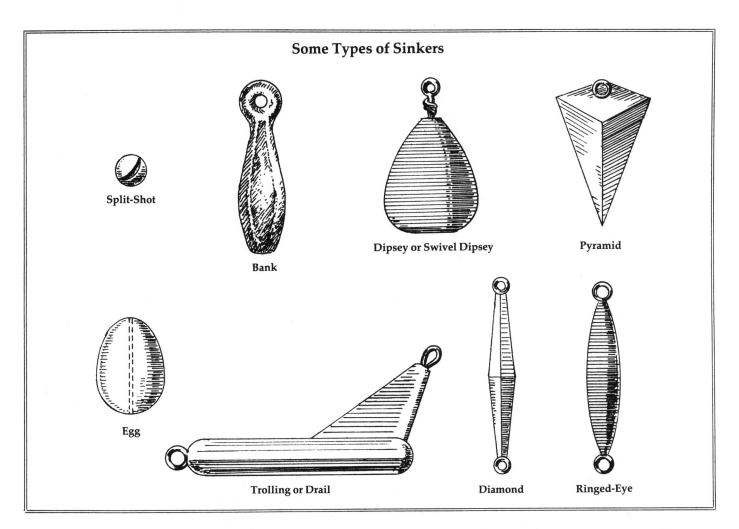

Split-Shot

Bank

Dipsey or Swivel Dipsey

Pyramid

Egg

Trolling or Drail

Diamond

Ringed-Eye

4. Pyramid sinker. This sinker has long been a standard item in surf casters' tackle boxes because it holds well in sand. It's often used in conjunction with a fish-finder rig. For greater holding power against currents, like an undertow, there are double and treble pyramids.

5. Egg (oval) and ball (round) types. These sinkers are similar. They're both attached by feeding the line or leader through a channel in their center, leaving them free to move up or down or roll along sea bottom. They're often rigged for bottom fishing, or with a fish-finder setup with live bait because they allow the bait a more natural freedom.

6. Trolling sinkers. These are of drail and keeled designs for incorporation between line and leader or wherever desired in terminal rigs. They're used in deep trolling at levels beyond the reach of wire lines and ordinary rigs. For extra-deep trolling, there are trolling planers, essentially an adjustable streamlined sinker with diving planes. Some of these can take a rig down to more than 200 ft.

7. Flat diamonds. They are old-timers on the scene, roughly diamond-shaped but flat in front and back. They are among the heaviest sinkers and are used in ocean bottom fishing in deep water.

8. Ringed-eye sinkers. These come in two general designs: a diamond and cigar shape, both of which are elongated, or skinny and streamlined. There are ring eyes at both ends to enable incorporation anywhere in a system. These sinkers are used primarily for trolling and casting, but like most sinkers, they're adaptable to other procedures.

9. Pencil sinkers. These are similar to a pencil in shape and are sold in various lengths and weights for casting or trolling. Pencils are easily rigged by feeding right onto a leader or line.

I don't care how much you spend for your rods and reels or how many artificials you amass, you'll never catch a single fish without that simple, most inexpensive item of gear, a hook. Wander into the hook section and browse around. You might learn some things you never knew about fishhooks.

How to Rig a Whole Squid for White Marlin and Swordfish

1. Get 12–15 ft. of wire (No. 7 to No. 9) or monofilament leader. Mono is easier to handle, but wire gives better protection against the roughness of a white marlin's bill. Accordingly, if mono is rigged it should be in a heavier strength than the line.

2. Attach a 6/0 to 9/0 hook—it must have a needle-sharp point to penetrate the marlin's bony jaw—to the leader so that it can swing. Do not make a loop on the leader's other end yet.

3. Now you will need a small cork, about 3/4 in. long, ½ in. wide at its greater diameter, and a pinch-on sinker. A 6- to 8-oz. squid is fine.

4. With a needle run a hole lengthwise through the cork at its center. Feed the cork on the leader, its wider end toward the hook, down to within a few inches of the hook. Leave it there for the time being. Add the pinch-on sinker to the leader between cork and hook. Squeeze it shut only enough to keep it on the leader, not enough to prevent its adjusting.

5. Stretch out the squid alongside the rig, pointed end of the body aimed away from the hook. The squid's eyes should be opposite your hook's bend. Shift the cork so that its smaller end is about ½ in. farther down on the leader than the squid's pointed end. (The cork will be inside the squid, so you must allow for it.) Adjust the pinch-on sinker until it's snug against the cork's wider end. Pinch it tight.

6. Feed the leader's free end up inside the squid's skirtlike mantle, bring it out approximately in the center of the bait's pointed end (which should be aimed in the direction of the rod so that the tentacles will trail). Wire usually can be guided all the way through. With mono you may need a very long needle, or may have to make a tiny slit where the leader is to emerge.

7. Your leader now is lying inside the squid's mantle in its long axis. Pull it on out until the cork is drawn up as far as it will go inside. Thrust your hook through the squid's head between the eyes. The hook's point and part of its bend will be exposed.

8. Complete the rig with a couple of turns of heavy thread or light twine around the bait's head just above the eyes. This securing and that cork inside the body will keep the squid extended in lifelike fashion instead of bunching up at the hook.

9. Finally, make a loop on the leader's free end for attachment to the line. Recommended for connection is a snap swivel—on the line. This permits easy changing of rigs. White marlin often mutilate a bait beyond further use.

3. Hooks

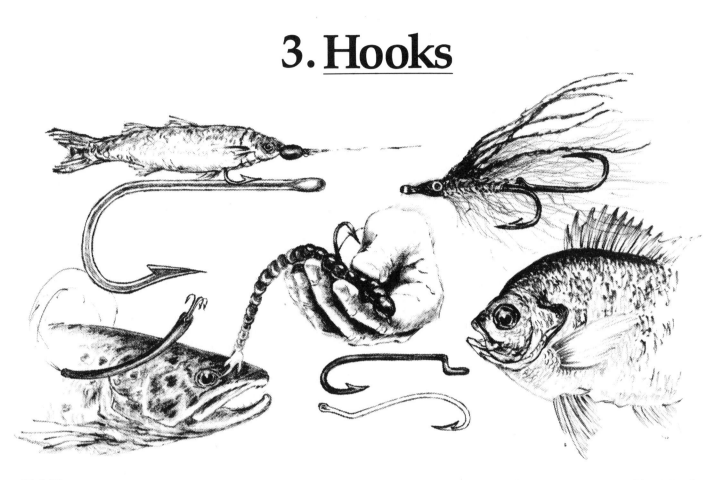

We shall never know precisely when man broadened his largely plant diet by becoming a fisheater. But somewhere along the line one of those hairy, beetle-browed ancestors of ours looked into a pool, saw something swimming, and decided it might be good to eat. Having arrived at that monumental decision, he then had to figure out how to capture the thing swimming around. At that moment was born the first fisherman.

The earliest fish hunters probably used spears. It was a simple advance in logic to try the same weapons that had proved effective on land animals. But spearing fishes has its obvious shortcomings, what with the optical tricks played by water, and after early man had gone hungry a few times, it finally dawned on him that there had to be something better.

He still wasn't bright enough to invent a fishhook, however. His brain child was a simple device called a gorge. A gorge is a short sticklike shaft of some material—bone, wood, horn or shell—sharpened on both ends and secured to fish line at its middle. It was shoved into a bait lengthwise. When a fish gulped a bait, a pull on the line brought the pointed gorge crosswise in the quarry's mouth or throat.

Gorges worked, were fished for tens of thou-

sands of years thereafter, and were used by North American Indians when the New World began receiving visitors. But they too had a drawback. A victim had to swallow the bait before a gorge could function. Too many fishes merely nibbled at the bait. There had to be a better way.

It turned out that the better way was a hook. It occurred to someone that if a gorge were curved, it might be more effective. The result of this reasoning was a primitive double-pointed hook, probably made from bone or horn. Encouraged by the improvement, fishermen experimented further and discovered that a single-point hook worked better than a double. A barb on the point was a refinement yet to come, but the first ancestor of the modern fishhook had come into being. This is believed to have occurred sometime before the dawn of the Neolithic Age, which began in Europe circa 10,000 B.C., spreading from the east.

Over the next 10,000 years man experimented with many different materials in fashioning hooks—stone, copper, bronze and iron. From iron eventually came steel—iron mixed with carbon—to make it hard, strong and tough. And from this new metal evolved our present-day steel fishhooks.

Modern steel fishhook manufacture had its

beginnings in Europe during the 14th and 15th centuries, but as an industry did not take form until the 1600s, when it became an offshoot of the manufacture of needles in England. It was there that a man named Charles Kirby began producing hooks in quantity, employing some of the basic techniques still in use. Among his contributions were the tempering and hardening of steel in hooks and the invention of the Kirby hook pattern. Kirby is but one in a long parade of designs out of England still around today. Others are Pennell, Sneck, Sproat, O'Shaughnessy, Carlisle and Limerick. The U.S. has made contributions too, with such patterns as the Siwash (a salmon pattern named for the Pacific Northwest Siwash Indians), Cincinnati bass, California bass, Indiana bass and the codfish hook. In addition, Norway has made sizable contributions. It was there in 1832 that O. Mustad & Son was established and subsequently grew to become the world's greatest maker of hooks. Among them are Mustad Vikings, Pacific Bass, Sea Haw, Sea Demon, Chestertown, etc.

Today's machines, for my money, produce excellent hooks at modest prices. Each manufacturer may have its own formula for composition and treatment, but tempered carbon steel is a prime material. (It's hard, strong and durable.) This brings up one question about steel itself. If it has a drawback, it lies in its tendency to rust. But a little care on the part of hook owners will add more rust prevention. And if worse comes to worse and a hook does rust enough to be discarded, a hook is still inexpensive to replace.

There are a number of hook finishes to stave off rust. Among those devised are a "blued" finish, tinning, nickel plating, bronzed finish, cadmium plating and—at one time—gold plating. You'll find that cheaper hooks have blued or lacquered finishes that are perishable and deteriorate rapidly in salt water. One of the superior finishes is the cadmium plating applied to salt-water hooks. Mustad has some hooks that are further protected by being both cadmium-plated and tinned.

A fisherman may have to weigh hook strength against rust and corrosion protection. For marine hooks, strength is the more important asset, with a high degree of corrosion-and-rust prevention as a bonus. In many kinds of fresh-water fishing, especially for small game, it may be the other way around. It depends upon the kind of angling done and the sizes of the fishes involved. Panfishes, for example, do not require strong hooks. ("Panfish" refers to size. A fresh-water angling term, it can be applied to any fish small enough to fit in a frying pan.) In contrast, a striped bass of moderate size

can straighten out a "soft" hook.

To combat the headaches caused by rust or corrosion from salt, hooks of stainless steel and others of nickel alloy (you may have heard the name Z-Nickel) were devised. Years ago the protection offered by stainless steel and nickel was offset by the metals' softness. Hooks could straighten under stress; their points became bent and would no longer penetrate. Time has brought improvements and hardening in both stainless steel and nickel hooks.

In addition, manufacturers have added other improvements. Not long ago Wright & McGill, a leading U.S. tackle manufacturer, came out with their Keel Hook for fly fishermen, in both regular steel and stainless, which features a special offset shank to prevent snagging.

Still another refinement in hook design is the so-called sliced shank among some bait-fishing types. Here the shank carries one, two or more tiny, pointed spikes to keep a worm or other bait extended in lifelike fashion. Then there are fine-wire hooks designed for live-bait fishing—fine to minimize damage to the bait, light to give it maximum freedom.

Whatever its pattern, the essential qualities of a good hook are ready penetration, strength and holding ability. Various physical features contribute to these assets, and the degree to which each contributes differs among patterns. As a random example, one type of hook point will penetrate a bony jaw better than others. Or a particular hook's bend may be better suited to the way a certain species takes a bait. Because variables are involved, there can be no one pattern that will handle all assignments with equal facility. And that, of course, is why there are so many styles.

In rebuttal, though, let it be added hastily that hook selection is not as involved as it might sound, and it's not difficult to find a versatile pattern that will take several different species. The Sproat and O'Shaughnessy are among cases in point.

It always will help in hook selection to know something about the mouth and jaw anatomy of the species sought. Some, like the salt-water tautog and the brook trout, have tough mouths. Others, like the weakfish, have delicate, easily torn mouths. Still others, like the billfishes, have bony jaws. It also helps to know how a species approaches a bait, whether it nibbles or toys with it, or grabs it one-two-three. And some considera-tion has to be given to the caliber of tackle involved. Obviously it is more difficult to strike a fish (set the hook) with a light rod than with a stur-dier one.

The Anatomy of a Hook

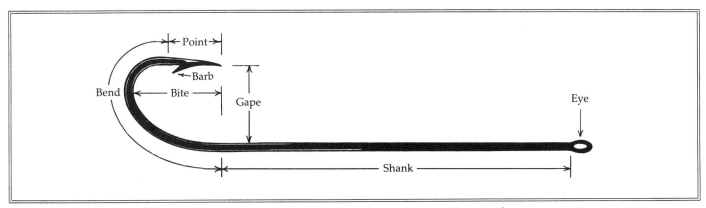

Hooks are made from wire. Most of them are round in cross section, but among some marine patterns, notably the larger sizes rigged for bigger game, the sides are flattened for added strength. Manufacturers use designations such as "X," alone or preceded by a number, and the terms "fine" and "stout" to indicate different diameters. Diame-ters enter the picture when it comes to penetration and holding ability. For instance, a light-wire hook may penetrate a certain species' mouth better than the same pattern in a heavier gauge, but it also is springier and more liable to straighten out if strain becomes great enough. On the other hand, a heavier-gauge hook is better suited to driving home in a tough mouth and is less likely to bend once it has been planted. Sometimes it's necessary to make a compromise. There are patterns for that too.

Hook Points

A hook's business end is its point. Without that it is nothing. There are these basic types of points, each with its own penetrating characteristics:

Hollow. The hollowing is a rounding out between the point's tip, the actual point, and the tip of its barb. This type is designed for fast penetration. On large-caliber hooks, however, it's impractical because it reduces their point strength.

Needle. Slender in its tip section, the point also is designed for fast penetration, but its slenderness is a drawback because it renders the hook vulnerable to bending and blunting, especially when it hits bone.

Spear. A classic and common form, it is an all-pur-pose hook—not as fast in penetration as the hollow and needle points, but with good holding power.

Arrow. Point is shaped like an arrowhead. It has poor penetration because of its design, but by the same token it holds rather well when it does pene-trate.

Barbless. Early hooks had points of this type. Years ago, before they went to nets, commercial tuna fishermen wielded stout rods and rigged arti-ficials with barbless hooks to facilitate unhooking their catches. The only places you might see barb-less hooks in the sport fishery are in release tour-naments—fishing contests in which catches are released (for conservation) instead of being kept—and possibly in fish tag-and-release projects.

And there have been other types of points desig-nated as spade, knife-edge and twin barb.

Point Tip

Additionally, hook makers have done some other things to points in an effort to aid penetration. These involve the point's very tip. (Forget the barb for now.) There are four basic ideas; any others are variations: (1) straight point, in which the tip's axis is in line with the shank's, or at least parallel to it; (2) rolled point, whose tip curves inward toward the shank; (3) bent-in point, whose idea is the same as the rolled point's, but with a fine difference in that the entire point, not just its tip, bends inward toward the shank, giving it a shape suggestive of a cat's claw; (4) bent-out point, which is the opposite of No. 3 in having its tip bent outward, away from the shank. You'll find all four among today's hooks.

Various degrees of penetration and holding power are claimed for the different types of points and the straightness or curvature of their tips. The length of a point (i.e., from its outermost tip to the tip of its barb) is a factor. Generally speaking, a long or medium point has good penetration, holds well, and is serviceable for just about all species, with the possible exception of those with thin, delicate mouth parts. Longer points are not only unnecessary for those fishes; they might even be a disadvantage. Better for those is a short point. With a short point, however, a hook can be more difficult to set—and easier for the fish to throw—because of the angle between its tip and the tip of its barb.

It must be remembered, though, that the foregoing are just some of the mechanical factors contributing to hooks' efficiency. The type of bend, shank length, etc., also are at work, and the possible combinations of physical factors in hook design are practically infinite.

Shank

The shank could be called a hook's shaft. Among most hooks it is straight, but there are alterations in certain patterns.

Unfortunately, there's no standardization of shank lengths among hooks of the same overall size, owing to variations among patterns and manufacturers. For practical purposes we can designate them as average or regular, and longer

and shorter than average. Those are vague, flexible terms at best, but there's no alternative. When shanks are longer or shorter than average for a given hook style and size, the letter "X" and a number, together with the terms "long" and "short," are used. Thus the designation "1X long" signifies a shank as long as that of a hook one size larger; "2X long," the shank length of a hook two sizes larger; and so on. Conversely, "1X short" indicates a shank length equal to that of the next size smaller hook; "2X short," two sizes smaller; etc. For general purposes these variations are of no great moment to users. Overall hook size is more important for the average angler.

Mechanically, the action of a hook's shank is that of a lever, helping to bring the point forward so it will bite in better. Everything else being equal, longer- and shorter-than-average shanks have their own advantages, as follows:

Long Shank. Protects against sharp teeth, and with small sharp-toothed species eliminates the need for a wire leader. A long shank also facilitates unhooking fishes that have a habit of taking a bait well back in the throat. Additionally, long shanks often are favored for fashioning streamers and bucktails in fly-fishing. But long shanks have a couple of drawbacks. At times their greater leverage actually aids in working a hook loose. Too, the longer the shank, the shallower a hook's bite, so that the weapon loses a certain amount of its hooking talent. When appreciably longer shanks are involved, it may be necessary to select a pattern with a wide gap and bent-out point to compensate for the shallow bite.

Short Shank. One advantage is that more of the hook, if not all of it, can be hidden in a bait, thereby lessening the bait's unnatural appearance to a fish. (Make no mistake, some fishes become suspicious and wary if there's anything peculiar-looking about a bait.) This hiding becomes important when small baits are involved. A short-shank hook usually means a good setting when a fish gulps the bait, which a fish can do more readily than with a longer-shank type. A short shank also means less hook weight, an advantage in small artificial flies where flotation is essential. Further, a short-shank hook is less likely than one with a long shank to hamper a bait's actions. On the debit side, there is less of that leverage afforded by longer shanks, so a short-shank hook is more suited to soft-mouth species.

Memo: The firmness of fishes' mouth parts varies widely according to species. It ranges from soft and delicate, as in the case of the northern weakfish (and is what gave the species its name, along with a nickname, "papermouth"), to leathery and tough, as in the case of the tautog or blackfish. Such details influence selection of hooks for good holding power, fast penetration, etc.

We're most familiar with hook shanks that are straight, but there are numerous variations, each with certain advantages:

Straight. Far and away, this is the most popular because of its proven effectiveness.

Sliced. Described earlier. It is usually straight but with tiny spikes.

Curved-Down. The shank curves away from the point, the idea being to more closely correlate line of pull with line of penetration. A drawback is that it has a shallow bite, a disadvantage in setting the hook.

Central Draught. About opposite the point, the shank bends inward in a kind of offset. The advantage claimed is quicker penetration.

Humped. One or more humps is incorporated in the shank. This type is employed in the manufacture of artificials. The purpose of the humps is to better secure the lure body material(s) to the shank.

Forged. The shank and bend are both flattened on the sides for greater strength. Forged shanks are a characteristic of some of the larger hooks rigged in marine big-game fishing.

Turned or Bent-Up. The upper section of the shank is bent outward. The claimed advantage is a raking action for penetration. This style is suited to soft-mouth species.

Circle. The shank is so curved that, with the bend and a curved-in point, the appearance is that of a circular hook. Mustad makes this type for tuna. A claimed advantage is great holding power.

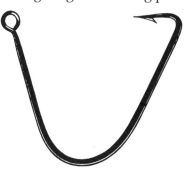

Triangular. The shank is bent at about a 45 ° angle, and the point aims upward and inward, giving the effect of a triangle. The angle may be achieved by a curve or be more angular. Originally this shank was created for bait fishing at anchor because the hook drives its point upward into the roof of the fish's mouth. It has proved lethal on pike and wall-eyes. Mustad incorporates this type of shank in its pike hooks.

Bends

There are three basic types of bends, many others merely being variations in degrees of curvature:

Round Bend

Round. The bend is U-shaped. It is the most common type.

Square. The bend style is a continuous curve, but has a more flattish appearance at its deepest part.

Flat-Round. That half of the bend nearest the shank has the usual U-curvature, but then it turns more abruptly upward at the point.

These and their variations are incorporated in various hook patterns in compatibility with other details. Accordingly, anglers need not concern themselves.

Bends may also be "straight," "kirbed," or "reversed." A straight bend is one in which the spear (point and barb) is aligned with the shank. In kirbed and reversed types the spear is bent slightly to the right or left of the shank's axis. The straight bend is the all-round type and most common, and also the most recommended. The offset afforded by kirbing or reversing is believed to be an advantage in that it is less apt than the straight type to slip free of a fish's mouth without digging in, and is farily common among hooks used for natural baits. Kirbed and reversed hooks, however, may require more force to set. They also may spin when trolled or cast and therefore are less desirable for artificials.

The nature of a hook's bend determines its gap, or the distance between the point's tip and the shank. The gap, in turn, determines its holding ability. In general, the wider the gap, the better the penetration and the larger the bite when the hook digs in. A drawback is that wider-gap hooks can work loose more readily. With a narrow-gap hook you have the reverse of the foregoing details, including

less tendency to work loose and an advantage of being better hidden in a bait.

Eyes

As you would suspect by now, there are even several types of hook eyes. Two of the most common are the ring and the needle eye.

Ring Hook Eye   **Needle Hook Eye**   **Eyeless**

In the ring type the end of the shank is bent in a small circle to form an eye or loop for attachment to the line or leader. Usually the eye is at right angles to the plane of the hook, but there are some ring patterns where it is in the same plane. Commonly the wire forming the eye is of uniform diameter throughout, and it may be open (that is, the end of the wire forming the eye bends around to the shank but isn't connected with it) or it may be closed. A closed-ring eye is tempered with the hook, and therefore is stronger. But the open-ring eye type is sometimes preferred because it can be pried open for placing on the bend of another hook in a tandem arrangement, then squeezed shut with pliers. Among certain types of ring hooks the upper end of the shank and the wire forming the eye are tapered. This model is used primarily when it is desirable to reduce a hook's weight, as in floating flies. In still another type of ring eye, called looped, the eye's wire, which may be tapered or uniform, extends a short distance down on the shank alongside it, and can be opened. Looped-eye hooks have long been used in fashioning wet flies for salmon. In another kind of eye, the brazed type, the ring is brazed to the shank for maximum strength. Some big-game hooks, like one of Mustad's tuna patterns, have brazed eyes.

As its name implies, the eye in a needle-eye hook is like that of a needle. This kind of eye is preferred over a ring type when it's necessary to draw the shank up into a bait, as when rigging whole mullet, eels, etc.

Then there are eyeless hooks. These are designed for use with snells or for embedding in the body of a metal lure. In the former instance, with snells, the hooks usually come with a short length of nylon, gut, tarred line or other material already secured to the shank's upper end. Attachment to line or leader is made via a loop in this snood. Some anglers cast their own metal squids, and for embedding in these artificials there are eyeless hooks with long shanks.

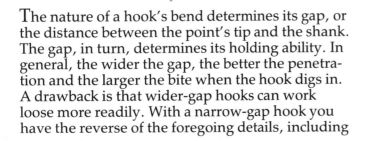

Among the majority of fresh- and salt-water hooks in popular service, neither that upper segment of the shank bearing the eye nor the eye itself is bent one way or the other. In certain designs, though, their mechanics are such that penetrability is improved by bending the eye, or a short section of shank adjacent to the eye, at an angle to the shank proper. The bending may be in the direction of the point, "turned down," or away from the point, "turned up."

Single-Double-Treble Hooks

Except when plugs and certain other artificials are involved, most marine and fresh-water angling assignments call for a single-type hook. In this instance the single- means a standard form, with one shank, bend and point, and is used to set it apart from double and treble hooks. More than one single-type hook can be rigged. Singles see widespread service in bait fishing, whatever the method; but many lures, such as flies, streamers, spoons and jigs, carry them.

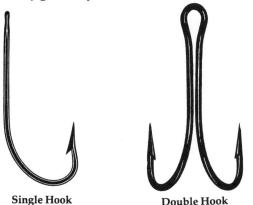

Single Hook   **Double Hook**

There are also double and treble hooks for arming plugs, spoons and other lures.

A double hook is essentially two hooks in one. Each component has its own shank, bend and point. The shanks parallel each other, and the bends are back to back, so to speak. They are from the same piece of wire, their shanks being contin-

uous at the top to form an eye for attachment. Some doubles are open between the two parallel shanks to facilitate attachment to a ring or other connector. On others the shanks are brazed together for added strength. Double hooks come in various patterns, just as though they were single.

Treble Hook

A treble hook, of course, is three hooks in one, its trio of bends and points curving away from one another and equally spaced. At the top their shanks share a common eye for attachment. Trebles also come in different patterns—Eagle Claw (Wright & McGill's), Sproat bend, etc.

Singles, doubles and trebles are sold separately and plain for replacement service and for use in fashioning rigs at home, rearming of lures, etc. Many anglers make up their own terminal rigs. Others get notions to change the hook arrangements on their favorite plugs. Singles also come in packages, already snelled for attachment to line or leader, and in complete ready-made rigs. And artificials, of course, already have their hooks, whether they be single, double or treble.

In the overall scene, single hooks predominate. Trebles probably are second, since so many lures carry them. Double hooks would be a poor third. They've been around a long time but usually do not rate with singles and trebles for effectiveness. Record-minded anglers check IGFA rules governing uses of single, double, and treble hooks.

Weedless Hooks

A headache shared by all fresh-water fishermen at one time or another is the snagging of hooks in aquatic vegetation and among stumps, rocks and logs. To minimize this problem as much as possible, manufacturers created weedless hooks. The chances are that no hook is snag-proof under all conditions, but the weedless type is a help. Since it is a hook's point that is going to snag on an

obstruction, the weedless feature consists of a thin-wire guard extending from the region of the hook's eye to its point. In effect it makes the point glide over an obstruction without snagging. The wire guard must be stiff enough to accomplish this yet be readily flexible so as not to interfere with a fish taking the hook. Weedless hooks are made unweighted or with a small sinker incorporated in the shank to aid in its "weedlessness." They also come with various types of bends—Aberdeen, etc.

Some anglers will not use a weedless hook for one reason or another, but the fact remains that this kind of hook can be fished in vegetation so thick that many other types would be ruled out.

Grading Hooks

The time-honored method of grading hooks for sizes uses a numerical system, and it has two ranges. One range is for smaller hooks. This range begins with the designation No. 1 and continues on to No. 20. On this rating scale, the *larger* the number, the *smaller* the hook. Therefore No. 1 is the largest in smaller hooks and No. 20 the smallest.

In the grading scale for big hooks, the designation is by a number, a slash (/) and zero. So the biggest hook after a No. 1 is a 1/0, and from there the scale climbs to 20/0. Thus the *larger* the figure, the *bigger* the hook. Here 20/0 is the largest. Note: Among certain patterns there are numerical size designations beyond No. 20 and 20/0. But that range, No. 20 to 20/0, suffices.

Hook size grading is based on a system established many decades ago in which the lengths of shanks were measured, with specifications that sizes 22 to 13 increase by ¹⁄₃₂ in. for each number, Nos. 12 through 3 by ¹⁄₁₆ in., and sizes No. 2 through 5/0 and on up by ⅛ in. Under these specifications, overall lengths of hooks (top of the shank to bottom of the bend) ranged from ⁵⁄₃₂ in. for a No. 20, through 1 in. for a No. 3, to 1½ in. for a 1/0, then increased by ⅛ in. for each larger size.

But this is an old size grading system with flaws. To begin with, it's based on shank lengths and doesn't take into consideration such important details as gauge of wire, style of bend, type of point, gap, etc. As a result, there has never been standardization of sizes among hook manufacturers. In other words, a 1/0, we'll say, in one brand can be larger overall than the same size marketed by another firm. And so it goes throughout the range, No. 20 to 20/0. Also noticeable are variations among different patterns of the same size designation.

Fortunately, these variations are not always critical, but it remains for a fisherman to decide on what hook patterns he likes, then get them in the appropriate sizes for the species sought. He can't always rely on being able to freely interchange two or three designs when they all have the same size designation. An angler can assume that hook strengths are approximately in proportion to their sizes. Thus a No. 1, for example, should be stronger than a No. 5, a 1/0 stronger than a No. 1, and so on. There are exceptions, of course, as among some fine-wire hooks used in live-bait fishing and certain artificials and, at the other extreme, hooks designated as double and triple strength. But in the main, that size:strength ratio serves as a rule of thumb.

In connection with some hooks, in addition to labeling for pattern (Mustad, O'Shaughnessy, Sproat or whatever) and size (No. 1, 2/0, etc.), you may encounter the letter "X" and the words "fine" and "stout." These designations refer to the diameter of wire used in the manufacture of those hooks, and this is what they mean: "1X Fine" = a wire diameter that is standard for *the next smaller size* of hook; "2X Fine" = wire that is standard in diameter for a hook *two sizes smaller;* and so on through "3X Fine," which is about the finest diameter in this particular grading system. Going in the other direction, a hook labeled "1X Stout" is made from wire that is standard in diameter for *the next larger size of hook;* "2X Stout" refers to wire whose diameter is standard for a hook *two sizes larger;* and so on through "4X Stout," which is about maximum at this end of the grading system.

You may never concern yourself with that Fine and Stout grading, but this is good to keep in your mental file: for certain species or under certain conditions it may be advantageous to go to a heavier (stronger) hook or a finer (lighter) one without appreciably changing the overall size. For example, for a particularly hard-fighting scrapper you might want to rig a stronger hook but hesitate to go to a larger one (for that added strength) because the fish has a small mouth. Here you can consider a

Stout. Or it might be advantageous when fishing with small live bait to use a finer diameter without going to a smaller hook. Here you can rig one in the Fine category.

Choice of Hook Sizes

Often there's latitude in hook sizes. For black bass, cod, striped bass and other largemouth species, a size or two either way isn't likely to make any difference so long as the hook strength is there. Among small and smallmouth species, however, sizes become more critical. Here a hook that is only one size too large can spell the difference between hooking a fish or losing a bait. Obviously if a fish can't swallow a bait it isn't going to get the hook in its mouth either. With such species it's important to learn precise hook sizes and how much latitude there is, if any. When in doubt with small or smallmouth species it's always better to go a size or two smaller rather than the other way. With such species hook strength usually isn't a key factor, and a difference in the next size smaller is therefore not critical.

And you can always drop in at a local tackle emporium, tell the nice man what kind of fish you're after, and ask him to outfit you with hooks. He will see that you get a suitable pattern in a proper size.

4. Trolling

Trolling can be defined as a sport-fishing technique in which a bait, some item of natural food, or a lure, an artificial attractor, is towed behind a moving boat. It's a very popular angling method, employed for many kinds of marine and fresh-water sport fishes all over the world.

Trolling offers two major advantages. First, it covers a lot of territory, thereby increasing chances of contacting fishes, especially those that are scattered, or travel solo or in small groups, or are constantly on the move. The second major advantage is that it imparts action to a bait or lure, thereby enhancing its attraction, particularly for those predatory game fishes that like to hunt their prey "on the hoof," so to speak. Drifting also imparts action to a bait or lure, but the towing speed cannot be varied and regulated as in trolling.

Trolling isn't without a drawback or two. For one, as you no doubt have gathered by now, it requires a boat. For another, the boat is in motion much of the time, which adds to fuel bills.

According to the kinds and feeding habits of the fishes sought, trolling may be at any depth, from the top surface on down to barely above bottom. In this respect it offers an added advantage of vertical coverage, increasing chances of finding the quarry at different levels. Similarly, trolling speeds, along with the distances of baits and lures astern, also are varied according to species (and locations too sometimes). All these details may become variables at certain seasons and/or in certain places, or at certain stages of the tide in salt water. They are predicated upon a number of items: (1) a species' diet; (2) any changes in feeding activity (many fresh-water and salt-water fishes are believed to fast at spawning time); and (3) where they are likely to be hunting prey at that time of year in a particular area. By increasing or inhibiting feeding activity, water temperatures can also play a role in trolling by influencing speeds and selection of attractors. They might even suggest trying some other technique for the time being.

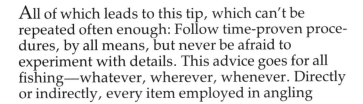

All of which leads to this tip, which can't be repeated often enough: Follow time-proven procedures, by all means, but never be afraid to experiment with details. This advice goes for all fishing—whatever, wherever, whenever. Directly or indirectly, every item employed in angling today (short of the angler, and I sometimes wonder about *him*) is a product of experimentation at some point.

Trolling is at its best with species that actively hunt and pursue their prey. Among them are some of the faster predators, including the tunas and bill-fishes (swordfish, marlins) in salt water and lake trout and walleyes in fresh water. There are the exceptions, of course. Outstanding among these—and this may surprise you—are sharks (of all people!). Although they actively hunt and will pursue prey if need be, sharks do not readily grab a trolled offering, at least not at speeds generally employed in trolling. I've fished for sharks innumerable times. Only once have I had a shark grab my bait or lure. It happened to be a mako, and the idiot seized a feather jig I was trolling for young bluefin tuna.

My theory is that sharks do not commonly take a trolled attractor because (1) they hunt primarily by scent (their sense of smell is probably the greatest of all fishes'), (2) their eyesight isn't too good (although this is still being argued), and (3) the bait or lure is moving too fast for them to really whet their curiosity. I've been meaning to experiment, trying a bait that has a strong natural scent (but it must be absolutely fresh) and trolling it at a very slow speed, barely making seaway (speed can always be increased a little), so that sharks can at least get a whiff of it if they can't see it too well.

Trolling may be only one of a few or several different methods used to catch many marine and sweetwater sport fishes. An example is bluefish. They are also caught by surf casting, chumming, jigging, etc.

Sometimes trolling is also employed as a probe to locate wandering schools of fish, whereupon the anglers switch to another, preferred method such as bait casting, jigging, bottom fishing or whatever.

Under Power

It's hard to believe nowadays, with kids of 12 to 14 galloping across lakes and bays in outboard boats, but in a long-gone era trolling was done with sail-powered craft. It has been done from paddled canoes and oared rowboats too, don't you think it hasn't. When my buddy Roger and I were youngsters, what kids of 12 to 14 could lay their hot, grimy little paws on an outboard motor! Old Rodge and I figured we were uncommonly lucky just to have something that floated and could be rowed, like his pa's old rowboat.

Today, with few exceptions, trolling is done under power, which can range from a single fly-weight outboard motor to a pair of muscular diesel inboard engines. Exceptions occur occasionally on some bodies of fresh water when anglers personally prefer the quieter operation of oars, and on small lakes where gasoline outboard motors are prohibited because of noise or some other reason. Even there, today's near-silent outboard motor—so popular among fresh-water bass fishermen—has largely replaced the human back and arms. One of the cleverest market names I've ever heard is that for a certain brand of electric outboard motor: Electric Sneakers.

Trolling is done with craft of many sizes and types, from little old rowboats with "kickers" up to dazzlingly luxurious 50-ft. sport-fishing cruisers such as the one on which I lived for a week on the Gulf of Mexico: hi-fi piped into the staterooms, each of which had its own head and hot-water shower, air conditioning throughout, lounge with bar and television, etc. And trolling tackle runs the gamut, light to heavy duty, according to the opponents sought and anglers' self-appraisals of their ability.

Mooching

There is another method of trolling that should be mentioned at this point. You might say that it is trolling with hiccups—and is called mooching.

The origin of this quaint term for a sport-fishing technique is lost in obscurity, but its name seems to have been born in the Pacific Northwest, where it very possibly was learned from the Indians. In any event, mooching has become a popular salmon-fishing procedure on the Pacific Coast, where it's employed on the ocean, bays, estuaries and tidewater areas. I understand that a variation of mooching also is used in bottom fishing in the Gulf of California.

Mooching depends for its effectiveness upon the attraction of a natural bait or an artificial suddenly taking off from the bottom, more or less on an upward course at an angle. The intended illusion is that of a small fish or other edible creature trying to get the hell out of there, which is a challenge to competitive-spirited predators.

Often a long rod, conventional or spinning, in lengths of up to 9, 10, even 12 ft., is a moocher's choice to aid in the casting part of the procedure. The reel needn't be proportionate to such rod lengths, but it should be able to accommodate, say, 100–150 yds. of 10- to 20- or 30-lb.-test monofilament or braided Dacron line. Actually, tackle is entirely up to its wielder's preference so long as it's sturdy enough. The reel's drag is set just enough to prevent line from peeling off without sufficient cause.

Some moochers use outboard power. Others favor rowing. There are three basic procedures: (1) The rig is allowed to sink to the desired depth. Then the boat moves ahead briskly for 10 to 20 ft., pauses to let the rig settle again, goes ahead some more, pauses, and so on—like trolling with the hiccups, as I mentioned. This not only keeps a bait or lure in motion; it also brings it upward at the desired angle. (2) The moocher makes a long cast (that's where the lengthier rods are helpful), lets his rig sink toward the bottom, then hand-retrieves the line in arm-length jerks. Retrieved line isn't cranked back on the reel but is allowed to coil neatly for the next cast. (3) The moocher anchors his boat or drifts and simply pays out line, letting the current work his bait.

Herring are a prime salmon-mooching bait. They're rigged whole when small. Somewhat larger herring are rigged as plugs. A plug in this instance is a herring with its head cut off at an angle behind the gills. Still larger herring are cut into strips called spinners, which flutter and spin in the water for eye-catching action. A sinker is involved, but only heavy enough to take the rig to the bottom. Hooks range anywhere from about a No. 1 to a 3/0 or 4/0, in proportion to the bait and the sizes of salmon running.

Mooching regulars will tell you that their method often produces salmon when trolling doesn't. I can't see why it shouldn't work for some other of the more aggressive sport fishes encountered near the bottom.

Tackle

Selection of trolling tackle comes down to individual preference. Many anglers wield spinning gear mainly because they figure that this equipment is all-purpose. That's a fallacy. Spinning tackle was designed primarily for casting. Expecting it to perform with equal efficiency in all methods is unfair to the equipment and its user too. Some extra-thrill seekers have even used fly-fishing tackle in trolling—up to a point—and have got away with it. But that's stunt fishing, so far as I'm concerned, and completely impractical.

Truth is, I don't even like spinning tackle for trolling. For casting you can't beat it. For trolling you can. Stay with conventional—revolving-spool reel—equipment. For details, see "Tackle & Accessories," Chapter 1.

Outriggers

Any boat that does appreciable trolling should be outfitted with outriggers. These are the long, skinny, polelike structures that ride vertically when not in use and are extended at about a 45° angle when in service. There are outriggers in numerous models and sizes, for boats as small as a 20-ft. outboard on up. There are even outrigger kits for do-it-yourself installers.

Outriggers are employed in surface trolling (as opposed to deep trolling, which we'll get to in due time). They perform four functions:

1. They let a boat troll more rigs than would be practical otherwise (notice I didn't say "possible").

2. They keep those rigs well clear of the boat, preventing them from tangling with other rigs being towed. The outriggers' reach also might lessen chances of scaring boat-shy quarry.

3. They impart a realistic action to baits and artificials, causing them to skip like frantic baitfish or

squid trying to elude enemies.

4. Outriggers provide an automatic "drop-back" —an interval of only a few seconds that can spell the difference between hooking or losing a fish. Each outrigger holds its fishing line in a clip attached to a halyard that operates like one used to raise and lower a flag on a jack staff. Between the clip and the angler's rod is a loop or length of slack line. When a fish strikes, the line pulls free of the outrigger clip, and its loop of slack allows the bait or lure to drop back with the fish, deluding him (one hopes) into thinking he has stunned or killed an item for lunch. The few seconds in a drop-back also give the fish a chance to mouth the bait so the angler can set his hook. The drop-back arrangement is designed for billfishes (marlins, etc.) and other species that may tap or nudge a bait before actually mouthing it. Without the automatic drop-back afforded by an outrigger, an excited angler might try to set the hook at once and so pull the bait or lure away from the fish before it has a chance to take the lure into its mouth. That could cause the fish to lose interest and swim away. The length of a drop-back can be varied by the length of slack line between outrigger clip and rod. The longest I've ever seen is that used in trolling for giant black marlin in the Coral Sea off Australia. There the loop of slack is so big it trails in the water. Depending largely on species hunted, outrigger baits and lures generally are trolled a bit farther astern than those on flatlines—the lines not in outriggers.

Ordinarily one line is trolled from each outrigger. But some boats outfit their 'riggers with two halyards so that two clips can be worked—two lines from each outrigger, in other words for a total of four, plus whatever flatlines the boat has out. This allows greater simultaneous experimentation with different baits and lures, as well as a comparison of them for actions and results. It may also lend an attractive illusion to some finned game of a little school of food fishes hurrying through the water. A drawback is that it increases the chances of rigs tangling with each other.

Kite Fishing

It has been speculated that the very first forerunners of outriggers may have been kites flown by ancient shore-bound fishermen to take their rigs out to surfaced fishes they couldn't otherwise reach. In time they may have tried the stunt in their boats too.

An old-timer once told me that in the early 1900s surf fishermen in New Jersey and on Long Island used kites to get their baits way out to where the fish—probably striped bass or bluefish—were. This stunt had a brief and limited revival on Long Island in the 1950s, but it didn't take. An obvious drawback is that wind direction must be just right.

Whatever kite fishing that persists today is done from boats. In this particular service I call a kite an aerial outrigger, and for it there are models referred to as "fishing kites," which are supposed to be more stable than other kinds. An aerial outrigger is used as a supplement to, not a substitute for, regular outriggers. The arrangement is similar. Attached to the kite's line is a clip whose grip is strong enough to suspend a rig yet release the line when a fish hits.

The late Tom Gifford, a now legendary Florida-Bahamas charter-fishing skipper and guide, used kites quite extensively in addition to the outriggers on his *Stormy Petrel,* and even developed his own kite-flying apparatus, secured to the boat's flying bridge. Tom could tell you how his aerial outrigger racked up sailfish, dolphin, big king mackerel, white marlin and other surface-cruising scrappers. With it he also caught striped bass off Long Island's Montauk Point, and he used to tell about famed angling author Harlan Major catching a 309-lb. swordfish on a kite rig offshore of Montauk in 1927.

Aerial outriggers can work in trolling or drifting by extending the boat's reach and so effect contact with fishes that might otherwise thumb their noses at you. Despite the success of Tom Gifford and other skippers I knew who occasionally used kites, I've wondered if kite fishing is worth the extra efforts it demands, except maybe as a unique and interesting change of pace. To begin with, you must get a kite designed just for this procedure. Then you need something with which to fly it. It has to be something that permits easy, rapid adjustment and readjustment of the kite's line. One skipper I knew used an old retired rod and reel. Also required is someone to stand by constantly to adjust and readjust the kite's height as the velocity of the breeze varies. Ideally the bait should be kept right on the surface to be most effective. Although Tom Gifford said he had seen sailfish, dolphin and king mackerel leap out of the water to grab a kite bait dangling a couple of feet in the air, an airborne bait has lost a lot of its appeal. "It just ain't natural," as an old bayman used to mutter about anything of which he didn't approve.

As I said, though, kite fishing is an interesting change. Try it sometime.

Most trolling is done right on the surface or just below it, at which levels it accounts for many kinds of marine and fresh-water finned game: marlins, striped bass, bluefish, muskellunge sometimes, salmons, still others. But there are also species and/ or times that demand deeper to very deep trolling, which may be anywhere from a few feet below the surface to 100 ft. or more down, as is done for big lake trout.

Trolling speeds, water friction, and upward thrusts of currents are major factors in how deep baits and lures will travel. And these rigs—even subsurface lures such as plugs designed to dive when activated—can go only so deep on their own. Beyond that they need assistance. For progressively deeper levels these aids include line with a metal core—to make it heavier—wire line, and such terminal tackle additions as trolling sinkers or drails and trolling planers (which function something like the diving planes of a submarine).

Downriggers

For the deepest trolling we have a device known as a downrigger, a kind of underwater outrigger. An old saying has it that necessity is the mama of invention. It's believed that the downrigger was spawned by a need to get rigs down to depths of 100 to 200 ft. to reach lunker-size lake trout. That was many years ago, and its inventor goes unrecorded and unsung.

The earliest downriggers were the crudest kinds of improvised, hand-operated devices. They've since been refined enormously, both functionally and aesthetically. Today's downriggers are much easier to use and adjust to varying conditions. And there are numerous models to meet different requirements and wallets.

This is your basic downrigger—think of it as a conveyance for a terminal rig but not actually part of the rig. Permanently mounted in the stern for cockpit use, a downrigger consists of a large, hand-cranked spool on which an adequate yardage of downrigger line can be stored and yet be ready for instant use. It's a kind of reel, actually. On the end of the line is the downrigger's sinker. Commonly this sinker is round, and its shape, along with its weight (roughly 5 to 10 lbs.), inspired the nickname "cannonball." (There are also streamlined sinkers.) Considerable weight is required to hold a depth against the boat's forward motion. A short arm, suggestive of a little fishing rod, extends out below the spool and helps keep the device's line clear of the boat. The final component of a downrigger is a special clip to hold the fishing line.

In operation, the angler's line is secured in the downrigger's clip, whereupon the device's line is payed out to lower the fishing line to the desired trolling depth. The downrigger will keep it there. When a fish hits, the angling line pulls out of the downrigger clip so that fish and fisherman are not hampered by the cannonball. Downrigger lines can be marked to indicate depths and facilitate returning to desired levels. I believe that some downriggers come equipped with a counter to indicate the amount of downrigger line out.

Once exclusively a fresh-water trolling accessory, the downrigger has entered the salt-water fishing arena, although its use is not as widespread yet. I've heard of a few instances in which downriggers have been used with success in deeper trolling for striped bass and big bluefish along the New York and New Jersey coasts. It would be interesting to try downriggers in extra-deep trolling well offshore.

General Trolling Advice

All other things being equal, proper trolling speed usually imparts enough action to a lure or bait. But there may occur times when just a little extra action increases a rig's attraction. A simple procedure I call jig-trolling can provide an extra touch. All you do as you troll is lift the rod tip a few inches to make the bait or lure spurt ahead, let it fall back, lift your rod again, let it fall back, and so on. I've had it produce better than straight trolling with striped bass and other game in salt water. I don't say it makes a difference every time, but it's worth a try.

Another maneuver worth a try when trolling blind—not knowing what fishes you might contact —is to swing the boat in a wide U-turn. This brings rigs up through different levels and may increase the chances of contact. Be careful where you execute this maneuver. In busy waters your contacts could be with other boats—know what I mean? *Crunch!*

Well-known angling author Frank Moss, formerly one of the East Coast's best charter skippers, reminds me of something I'm sure seldom occurs even to experienced rod-and-reelers: a boat's engine imparts sounds and vibrations to the water. Now the fish sought may tolerate that alien noise from a few, even several boats in the same general area but be scared away when the number of trollers exceeds a certain point. Similarly, fishes may tolerate boats' sounds and vibrations so long as they stay more or less at a steady level. Let there be a sudden upsurge—even by only one boat sometimes—and it can be enough to scatter the fish. That's why a change of trolling places may be indicated if too many craft are concentrated in a given area.

In 180° contrast are fishes that seem to be attracted by a boat's sounds and vibrations; or let's say that their curiosity is aroused, and it may be enough to incite them to hit the rigs being towed. Young bluefin tuna are an example. Something about a boat's white, bubbly wake intrigues them. I've had it happen dozens of times.

I've discussed this with a longtime friend of mine, veteran charter skipper Carm Marinaccio, for my money the best tuna-albacore-bonito skipper-guide on the whole East Coast. (I believe he's now retired and living in Florida.) "I don't know what it is about that bubbly water that attracts them," Carm said, "but it works. Maybe it's just curiosity, or they think the turbulence means food. Or maybe the boat's wake makes 'em mad because they think it's a foreign invasion of some kind, so they come up to see what it's all about. Who knows?" Carm knows it works. So do I, and I've never gone fishing for school tuna yet but what I haven't hung an old automobile tire or a fish basket right off the transom to generate an even more bubbly wash. School-size bluefin tuna will come up just a few feet behind the transom sometimes.

REMEMBER: Trolling is not only an angling technique in itself; it can also be employed to exploratory advantage to locate fish scattered over a wide area, whereupon some other method of hooking them may be desirable. Exploratory trolling can be suspenseful because you never really know for sure what you might scratch up.

As Captain Frank Moss has told me, there are times when trolling is the only practical method. Such occasions are when the fish are widely scattered, when fish are known to be present but other methods fail, and when the anglers lack the skill demanded by other procedures used in that area. (In passing, let me recommend Frank Moss's book *Successful Ocean Game Fishing;* International Marine Publishing Company; Camden, Maine.)

Trolling Tactics

Trolling tactics are open to all kinds of variations and adaptations according to fishes sought and characteristics of areas fished (water depths, presence or absence of currents, open or rocky bottom, presence and amount of aquatic vegetation, and the like). Accordingly, you might troll a drop-off or an underwater canyon by working your way along its edges or by crisscrossing it, or you might employ either or both of those tactics in working tide or current rips, where desirable game fishes are lured by the presence of little forage fishes tumbled about by the flow, and so on.

Surfaced schools of game fishes are approached with discretion. The boat maneuvers in such a way as to swing the trolled rigs along the edges or into the school without barging into it. The latter more often than not makes the fish sound, or submerge. Similar caution and procedures are involved when making passes at surfaced game fishes such as marlins and swordfish.

Not uncommonly, a surfaced school will sound in spite of all discretion. Even normally aggressive predators, not especially boat-shy by nature, exhibit unpredictable timidity occasionally and will disappear even before you can get to them. The next move is up to you, and you might as well try one before abandoning that area. For the time being you can assume that those fish are still in that general area.

One follow-up is to pause in the vicinity of where the school was last spotted and watch to see if it reappears. If it does, chances are it will be some distance off, in which case you can try again. The second attempt may produce the same results as the first, or the school might not reappear at all. In either case you might try one of the two following procedures:

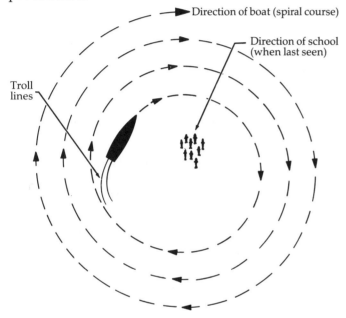

One method of relocating a sounded school

1. With rigs still out, the boat starts at about where the school was last seen and trolls in an ever-widening circle. By then the school might be miles away, or you might get to pass right over it.

How to troll a school
(Solid dots indicate boat's course. Little circles show swing of lure)

2. Another procedure (call it "direction trolling") is sometimes used successfully. It is the invention of the late Walter Drobecker, one of the best charter skippers ever to sail from Montauk, N.Y.

Judging the direction in which the school is headed when last seen, you try to guess their present traveling direction. Then you troll in that direction. You may be 359 ° out, but you might pass right over the school. Walt would have been the first to tell you that it doesn't work every time, but the fact that it works at all makes it worth trying. On at least one occasion Walt used this procedure to get me some shy young bluefin tuna. If you are that lucky and the fish are anything like young bluefin tuna, they might just rise to your rigs.

I said earlier that in trolling you should never hesitate to experiment. The fact is that some experimentation is the order of the day in trolling because of the variables involved. Here are three suggestions:

1. Start with assorted baits and lures. Here's where it's good to have more than one or two rigs out. You can try different kinds of naturals and artificials simultaneously, then change the other rigs accordingly when you find one that scores.

2. Also experiment with different rig depths, surface on down. The amount of line out is a variable affecting rig depths. Lengthening or shortening the yardage will make rigs ride higher or lower. You might arbitrarily start at a distance of somewhere between 60 to 100 ft. beyond the transom, then take in line or let it out to experiment. As mentioned, kinds of lines—regular, metal-core and wire—also influence the rig depths. Similarly, the choice of lures is a factor.

3. Do try different trolling speeds if necessary. A range of speeds may be recommended for a certain species. If that doesn't elicit a response, there's no law that says you can't go faster or slower. Remember, though, that trolling speeds also influence rig depths, especially with the so-called sinking-type lines. With those, the slower the trolling, the deeper the rigs will sink.

Last but far from least, some "commandments" for safe and sensible trolling:

1. Avoid busy waterways and other areas where there are numerous boats. Fishing is probably poor there anyway, and trolling might be hazardous.

2. Be sure of your boat and her engine and your ability as a skipper if you plan on doing any trolling just off an ocean-front beach, especially where there are rocks, and in inlets.

3. Approach and leave a trolling area at reduced speed to avoid any possibility of "spooking" fish.

4. While running free (not trolling, that is), give trollers plenty of clearance, especially when crossing astern of them. Remember their lines.

5. When trolling in close company with other craft, try to avoid excessively long lines, and keep your lines more or less uniform in length.

6. A boat battling a fish should be considered as having the right of way, since she's not readily maneuverable.

7. Avoid maneuvering too close astern of a trolling boat, as when observing, to avoid cutting her fishing lines. Similarly, even if a craft has Rules of the Road priority, so long as safety isn't involved she shouldn't cross abruptly and too close ahead of a trolling boat, forcing her to swerve sharply and possibly causing the fishing lines to be cut.

8. If another boat's lines are cut accidentally, common courtesy suggests that the offending craft stop, apologize, and offer to replace lost items. Only thing is, if the lost items include fish, the offending boat had better be ready for a lot of flack, and some of it could be pretty pungent.

9. When boats are working a small school of fish, it is suggested that they maneuver in a wide circle to give all hands a go at them.

10. Trollers try to seek plenty of open water as much as possible. But in areas where there's traffic it's their obligation to watch out for other boats and respect their rights.

11. When in the company of other boats, sensible trollers plan their patterns in advance, then maneuver in a pattern predictable by other skippers.

12. Remember that there are many dingdongs on our highways, and keep in mind that recreational boating—which includes fishing—draws a percentage of them too. Chances are you're far safer on the water than you'll ever be in an automobile—or even in your own home, if national safety statistics are an indicator. But you always must be alert for that one pineapple who shouldn't be allowed on a tricycle, much less operate a boat.

5. Bottom Fishing

The very first fish I ever caught—it was under the tutelage of my grandfather, Captain Thomas Raynor, when I was three or four years old—was a flounder hooked in a bay near my natal village of Freeport, L.I. That's another way of saying that the very first kind of angling I ever did was bottom fishing.

So it has been for uncountable tens of thousands of recreational fishermen down through uncountable decades. Bottom fishing, affectionately nicknamed "sinker bouncing," was their introduction too. I wouldn't be surprised if it's pretty close to a toss-up between casting and sinker bouncing as to which has initiated the greater number of beginners. In fresh water, I suppose, casting would get the nod, whereas bottom fishing would have the edge in salt water.

In any event, bottom fishing is one of the most widespread of all angling methods, globally used for a large assortment of marine and sweetwater species. Its variety of finned game is one of its attractions. Others, such as the simplicity of its tackle, will pop up as we go along.

If there's a keystone to all angling, it's the fact that fishes, like us humans, have to eat to live. (Also as in the case of us humans, opening their mouths gets them into trouble sometimes.) And another fact worth remembering by newcomers is that everything in fishing, from steps in procedures to selection and use of equipment, is based on sound reasons, time- and performance-proven.

A good angler is one who not only knows what to do and how to do it, but also *why* he does it, *which includes learning as much as he can about the habits of the species he seeks, most especially their feeding habits.* There's nothing difficult or complicated about this; and learning the *whys* will help you to remember the *whats* and *hows*. This holds for *all* kinds of fishing.

I compare the underwater world, salt and fresh, to a high-rise apartment house in which the tenants (fishes) occupy various floors (depths), from the ground floor (the bottom) up through intermediate levels to the top floor (the water's surface). The bottom is one of the busier levels, with a lot of different tenants. Some of these, like that flounder I mentioned earlier, literally hug the ground floor, seldom venturing more than a few inches above it. As a result, if you rig your hooks too far off the bottom you're not going to catch them. It's as simple as that. Many ground floor residents do not restrict themselves that much, but will wander around through some of the upstairs floors when seeking food or perhaps to escape hostile environmental conditions or elude enemies. When necessary, some of these will go all the way up to the top floor. Atlantic codfish are examples. Although catalogued as groundfish, or bottom dwellers, they may cruise 5 or 6 ft. or more off the bottom and even pursue baitfishes right to the surface, where they've been seen on occasion. Let me hastily add, though, that for all angling purposes cod are considered bottom fish.

For practical piscatorial purposes we can consider the bottom as a zone extending upward for 5 or 6 ft. above an ocean, a lake (a fairly deep one) or a bay floor. Bottom fishing is a simple way of bringing a rig down to a low zone.

Considering its hordes of participants in such heavily concentrated coastal sport fishing regions as southern New England, New York–New Jersey, Chesapeake Bay, southern Florida and the Keys—the Atlantic and Gulf of Mexico sides—and California, bottom fishing has to be the most popular salt-water method. It's a standard procedure aboard fleets of public fishing boats along the Atlantic, Gulf and Pacific seaboards, as well as on piers, docks and bridges and along channel banks and inlet shores. Surf anglers also fish the bottom for certain species. Just a sampling of the catches accounted for by bottom fishing includes several kinds of flatfishes—flounders, California halibut etc.—cod, pollock, black sea bass, assorted groupers, croakers, northern porgies, various snappers, sharks sometimes, eels, northern whiting and big bluefish.

Not uncommonly, bottom-fishing rigs nail intermediate- and upper-level species while being lowered or cranked in to check their bait. This is a mixed blessing, you might say. If those intermediate- and upper-level species are at least edible, O.K. But if they're disposable trash fishes or are pestiferous bait-stealers, they can be an infernal nuisance. What's worse, some of them—like the bergalls, dogfish (sand sharks), sea robins and northern puffers (blowfish) of Atlantic waters—can swarm around in such numbers that a bait can't get past them to more desirable bottom fishes at a lower level.

At Anchor or Drifting

Bottom fishing is done at anchor (still-fishing) or while drifting slowly. That done at anchor is the time-honored sinker bouncing, so called because at intervals, by lifting and lowering the rod tip, the angler allows the sinker to rise and fall. The angler can tell when his rig is on bottom when he senses a dull, muted thud. (Note: His hook may be anywhere from right above the sinker to a few feet above it, according to the species sought; but if his sinker bounces on the bottom the fisherman knows his hooks are at the level he wants them.) Checking may have to be fairly frequent when currents are brisk. Bottom fishing done while drifting is sometimes called bottom bouncing because the sinker is felt to bounce as it moves along a bottom's uneven surface.

Both versions, at anchor and drifting, have their advantages and a drawback or two. Drifting naturally covers more territory than still-fishing and therefore increases the chances of contacts with roving bands of fishes. By the same token, it also heightens the chances of a rig's getting snagged on something—a shellfish bed, a thick patch of vege- tation, etc. It also imparts motion to a rig, which does enhance a rig's attraction for some species. On the debit side again, bottom bouncing is impractical to impossible when bottoms are cluttered with stones or other obstructions such as thick aquatic vegetation or coral heads. It also can be impossible on artificial fishing reefs, of which there are increasing numbers along U.S. coasts. (Drifting may also pose safety problems in busy areas. As many as 400 boats, public and private, have been counted from the air on a summer's day in the New York–New Jersey region's famous "acid water" bluefishing grounds.)

Bottom fishing at anchor may be the only possible technique for certain species in certain locations. Fishing in the immediate vicinity of wrecks, over coral reefs, and on artificial reefs are among such locations. Even then, there's often a high mortality rate among rigs that can get hung up on various obstructions. Fishing at anchor can't match drifting's area coverage, but it can compensate for the difference with chumming (see "Chumming," Chapter 6). Drifting provides a continuous, attractive motion to a lure or bait that still-fishing can't match. But a still-fisherman can compensate to an extent by casting out and retrieving his rig at varying speeds along the bottom—

although risking hang-ups—or by jigging at intervals, that is, alternately raising and lowering his rig through a zone of a few feet just off the bottom.

Tackle

Notes on bottom-fishing weapons—or you can call 'em tools if you're a pacifist: Despite the method's enormous popularity and use, you'll seldom see rods and reels specifically labeled for bottom fishing in tackle catalogues, unlike trolling, fly-casting, bait casting equipment and the like. About the closest most catalogues come is the heading "Boat Rods"—a conventional type, generally viewed as a kind of all-purpose stick-aboard-boat, adaptable to bottom fishing, trolling and close-range casting. There's great latitude in the selection of bottom-fishing gear. Any outfit that satisfies angling requirements will do a job. By that, I mean sizes of fishes, their fighting habits, depths, etc. Most bottom-fishing regulars are not overly concerned about what tackle they wield, conventional or spinning, so long as it handles comfortably and catches fish. And that's all right. A prime requirement of tackle used in bottom fishing is that it have adequate sturdiness, or backbone. Ideally a bottom-fishing rod should possess adequate spine without an excessive stiffness, which could cost a lot of action with the smaller scrappers. An adequate amount of backbone is governed by the following factors:

1. Size of fish and behavior when hooked. It doesn't require an M.I.T. mentality to understand that first detail. Tackle wielded for opponents up to 40, 50 or 60 lbs. in deep water has to be much sturdier than that employed for 1- to 3-pounders in shallows. Similarly, fishes with a lot of fight will require proportionately heavier gear—depending upon the angler's ability—than that for species that quickly throw in the towel. By "behavior when hooked," I mean such maneuvers as exceptionally strong downward power surges that impose a sudden extra strain on rods, very long runs that necessitate trying to bring a fish under control before line becomes dangerously low on the reel, and the tendency of many species to dart to the nearest cover, which might be anything from a submerged log to a coral cave, from which the fish may have to be worked by the rod's power.

2. Weights of rigs, notably sinkers, and baits or lures. Sometimes overlooked by novices in salt-

water bottom fishing is the fact that deep sea action often necessitates heavy to extra-heavy sinkers to moor rigs on the bottom against the upward thrust of strong currents. These sinkers can run all the way from 8 to 16 oz. Fairly heavy baits may be involved as well. So far as I'm concerned, these details also impose certain limitations for the average angler on the spinning tackle that can be used satisfactorily in bottom fishing. I suggest that he ought to have a suitable conventional-type outfit as well.

3. Water depths. These contribute to the overall load on tackle because of water drag or friction on the line. The deeper the water, the more line out; and the more line out, the greater the water drag on it, which can be increased by currents.

Drifting or bottom bouncing can contribute to the effects of Nos. 2 and 3 above.

4. Fishing areas. A variety of rig-snagging obstructions faced by fresh-water anglers can put more pressure on a rod as well as the fish antics just mentioned.

Sinker bouncing and bottom bouncing with natural baits or artificials account for a long list of fishes from catfishes and hefty sturgeons in fresh water to porgies and giant groupers in salt. The caliber of tackle must be gauged accordingly, which means that if you haven't done so already, you might just as well decide now that there's no one outfit capable of handling all bottom-fishing assignments with equal efficiency.

Sure, you can swing spinning tackle in bottom fishing (up to a point). Many anglers do. But for greater versatility, considering those four factors described above, I'd suggest conventional-type equipment.

In that class, the closest to all-purpose rods for accommodating the majority of species caught by average bottom fishermen under average conditions would be as follows: For fresh water, 5- and 5½-footers handling lines up to 10- or 12-lb. test; for marine service, 6- and 6½-footers able to take lines up to 20-lb. test. Remember, I said for *average* everyday fishing conditions. If your targets are going to be in the league of giant sea basses topping 100 lbs., or if you'll be fishing in 300 to 400 ft. of water for the likes of tilefish, you'll need suitably stouter gear.

The tip sections of those all-purpose rods, or boat rods, have different degrees of flexibility, or "action," depending upon their length, kind of taper, caliber, and other manufacturer's and model specifications. There's no one special tip action for bottom fishing except that amount of backbone mentioned earlier. (For an explanation of tip actions, see "Tackle & Accessories," Chapter 1.)

Reels more or less match the rods on which they're mounted, but there's latitude. In bottom fishing, reel sizes are influenced largely by the strength and amount of line required. Bigger fishes naturally require heavier lines. Deeper water and longer-running battlers demand more of it. An average range of strengths is from 6-lb. test up through 20- or 30-lb. They handle the vast majority of fishes caught by the greatest number of bottom anglers. Lines of 40- or 50-lb. test would be used only for the heaviest bottom fishes. As for amounts of line, an angler fishing a shallow bay or lake can get away with about 50 yds. A hopeful angler working depths of 100 to 200 ft. may want at least 150 yds. And so it goes. The best bet is to keep the reel properly filled, which is to say within an eighth of an inch or so of its rim, because then it functions most efficiently. Chances are that yardage will be adequate under most conditions. If not, you'll have to buy yourself some heavier tackle.

Most bottom-fishing reel sizes go from 1/0 to 4/0 at the outside among the revolving-spool models, and from small to medium (spool capacity is the criterion) among spinning reels. For other features —some of which are desirable but not a must in bottom-fishing reels—see "Tackle & Accessories," Chapter 1.

Selection of lines is the angler's choice, and he develops preferences as he gains experience. In bottom fishing the choices are between braided and monofilament (single-strand) types and among such synthetics as nylon and Dacron, and among combinations of those types and materials. Many deepwater bottom fishermen like braided Dacron line because of its strength in relatively finer diameter, which decreases water drag and so permits rigging a somewhat lighter sinker than otherwise would be necessary. In another camp are sinker bouncers who favor nylon monofilament, arguing that monofilament lines generally are more wear- and abrasion-resistant than braided types. Abrasion resistance becomes an important quality on bottom-fishing grounds where lines come in contact with rocks, barnacles, coral and such growths as clusters of mussels.

See "Terminal Tackle," Chapter 2, for a discussion of terminal tackle for bottom fishing.

Much bottom angling, as already mentioned, is done in areas where many kinds of underwater objects await to snag rigs. It's a must, therefore, for sinker bouncers to always carry spares of all items they're likely to lose—hooks, sinkers and artificials. On some party or public fishing boats a limited variety of terminal tackle items can be purchased, but wise anglers do not depend on it. Same thing goes for public fishing piers and fishing concessions.

Sinkers

In bottom fishing, sinkers are a must in order to take the rig down and to keep it on bottom against the upward thrusts of currents or by the boat's forward progress in drifting. Since it's a heavy metal, lead is the standard material for sinkers. Another feature of lead is that it's readily melted and so can be cast into different forms. Some fishermen fashion their own sinkers using molds on the market. Sinkers are available in many shapes and sizes (see "Terminal Tackle," Chapter 2). Most commonly rigged among salt-water fishermen, especially for fishing at anchor, is the so-called bank type. In surf fishing a favored design is the pyramid. It holds well in sand. Two of the designs you'll see in fresh-water fishing are the ball type and the so-called dipsey. The former has a hole running through its center that allows the sinker to be loose on the line, an arrangement that allows more freedom to a live bait. The dipsey is a pear-shaped design with a built-in swivel. It is more suited than the bank type to drifting because its shape and tendency to roll along make it less apt to snag on something. For situations in which minimum sinker weight is required, there are the so-called split-shot type and the pinch-on. The split shot looks like an overgrown BB with a slot cut into it. The pinch-on is more elongated and has two tabs, one on each end, that are pressed closed to hold it on the line. Both of these fractional-ounce types can be attached either to the line or a leader by simply squeezing them fast. *Tip:* Pinch-on sinkers often tend to slide downward on the line or leader. They can be kept in position very easily. After folding the first tab closed, make one turn of the line or leader around the tiny sinker's body, then close the second tab on it.

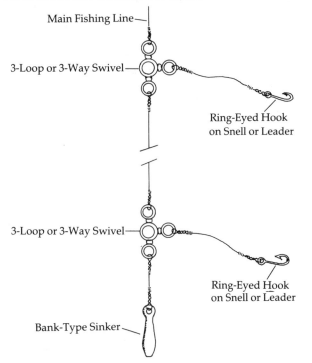

Main Fishing Line

3-Loop or 3-Way Swivel

Ring-Eyed Hook
on Snell or Leader

3-Loop or 3-Way Swivel

Ring-Eyed Hook
on Snell or Leader

Bank-Type Sinker

Basic One-Hook and Two-Hook Salt-Water Bottom Fishing Rigs

The most important no-no in the rigging of sinkers is overdoing the weight business. Don't use any more sinker weight than you need to keep your rig on bottom where it belongs. Any or all of the following are penalties for excessive sinker weight: It's hard to detect light nibbles at the bait; it can interfere with setting the hook, especially in the case of fishes with tough mouths or hard jaws; and it tires a fish—especially a small species—that much more quickly and so detracts from the action.

In salt-water bottom fishing, the weights of sinkers required vary from place to place and even in the same location, sometimes from one stage of the tide to another. The strength of the current is the factor. On a sheltered bay with weak tides—or on a lake—only a small sinker might be required, and the weight can stay the same throughout the day. In contrast, on ocean grounds 5 oz. might suf-

fice at one stage of the tide but have to be increased to 8 oz. at another stage because of changes in current strength. Or the converse could be true, a reduction from 8 oz. to 5 at different stages of the tide. The point is that you should carry a modest assortment of sinker weights. As an example, you might carry them in weights of 1 through 5 oz. This will enable you to put together combinations weighing more than 5 oz. should they be needed.

A rig should be checked at intervals to determine if it's holding bottom. Simply raising the rod tip a few inches, then quickly dropping it, will tell the story. If the rig is on bottom, the distant thud of the sinker hitting will be felt. If no thud is forthcoming, that rig is riding off the bottom and may be wasting your time. Add only enough weight to take it back to the bottom where it should be.

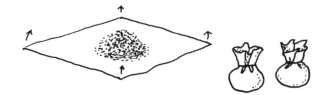

Homemade Substitute Sinkers

There is a simple substitute sinker—which is self-destructive—that you can make at home or put the kids to work on. It costs zilch and can save hooks, even entire rigs. You'll need any old kind of cloth—a discarded sheet is fine, and so is a retired dress or shirt. The only other items you need are some beach sand—a pailful should more than do—and a few feet of string. I specify string because it's weaker than twine, and you'll soon understand why this should be comparatively weak stuff. Light string such as is used in bakeries is fine. And you also need a little scale calibrated in ounces. Got a postal scale around the house?

All you do is fashion some bags from the cloth after cutting it into little squares. A measured amount of sand is put on each little square of cloth, whose corners can be lifted and tied together with the string to form a small bag of sand. In essence, this is the sinker. Fill the bags—whatever number of them you figure you need—with varying amounts of sand according to the range of weights of sinkers you most frequently use—for example, 1 oz. only or 1 to 3 oz. A refinement is to color-code the bags so that their weight is recognizable. Tying them with string of different colors is one way—white for 1 oz., green for 2 oz., etc. Another way is to vary the colors of the little squares used to fashion the bags. The sandbag is then substituted for a regular sinker. Here's where the weakness of the string comes in. It should be strong enough to secure the bag to the rig, yet weak enough to split after a tug or two, freeing the rest of the rig. The off-season is an excellent time in which to make up a supply of these rig savers.

When fishing in bays and inlet areas, look around for some clam diggers operating or a dredge. They disturb the bottom, releasing tiny shellfish and other miniature morsels that can attract sport fishes to that area. Try fishing in their vicinity. You also can do some profitable churning up of the bottom yourself. If the water is shallow enough, use an oar. Or do as some party boats do and take along a pole of suitable length to agitate the bottom alongside the boat, or scratch the bottom with an anchor at intervals.

Lures and Baits

Jigs are among the most versatile lures rigged in salt and fresh water, and they make up an enormous family. Lure manufacturers don't even know how many different models there are, and my bet is that one was invented even as I write this sentence. (That's exaggerated, but you get the idea.)

Most marine sport fishes will hit metal jigs, especially shiny metal jigs, at one time or another or at one level or another. One technique for bottom species is to let the lure hit bottom, then jig, or bounce, the rod tip, pausing briefly in between bounces. Imparting a little action to the jig enhances its eye-catching attraction. The pauses give slower-moving customers a chance to commit suicide.

There's a lengthy inventory of natural baits for bottom fishing. Overall the list takes in these items, among others too numerous to mention: small fresh-water fishes of a hundred or more different kinds and salt-water minnows, sand launce (sand eels), anchovies; assorted crabs—blueclaw, fiddler, lady, calico, hermit, whole or in pieces; clams—ocean (skimmer), hard-shell, razor, soft-shell, pismo; different species of shrimp; strips of squid; crayfish; conchs and snails; and worms—blood- and sand- . If you can lay your hands on an octopus, you can use that too, in pieces or strips. Also impaled on bottom-fishing hooks are pieces, chunks, strips and even fillets of other sport species. In sum, you have a lot of latitude in choices of baits for sinker bouncing. Try those recommended in a given area, but never hesitate to experiment.

I'm hampered by a lack of comparative statistics, but it seems safe to say that natural baits far outnumber artificials in bottom-fishing service. The variety of artificials in general use is relatively limited. As mentioned earlier, because of their weight metal jigs serve as their own sinkers. Among them are the so-called diamond jigs and mackerel jigs. There are also combinations of natural baits and parts of artificials. The latter consist of small, shiny spinner blades attached to line or leader ahead of the bait, so that their spinning motion and glitter will catch fishes' attention.

Crabs of various kinds can be pesky bait stealers, necessitating frequent replacements. In ocean bottom fishing, conchs or sea snails are bait thieves too. To thwart these larcenous critters when they become too much of a nuisance, try fastening a small piece of cork to the leader—just enough to keep the bait a few inches off bottom—out of the reach of the burglars. That's when you're fishing right on the bottom, of course.

As much as possible—which is to say, so long as they have attraction for the species involved—choose tough, durable baits for bottom fishing. It will cut down on the frequency with which you have to check your hooks to see if they're naked. Soft baits such as clams and worms can loosen or fall off a hook. They also tend to lose their attractive scent and take on a washed-out appearance in short order and should be checked and replaced accordingly. Tough baits include strips and pieces of squid, the rubbery "lips" of some clams, strips and chunks of fish that have the skin on (which they should anyway if it's silvery or white, because of its attraction).

After a while, especially when there has been a rather long period of inactivity at the other end of your line, you should check any bait. If not stolen, the bait may be mutilated or waterlogged beyond effectiveness. If at all in doubt about its condition, replace it.

Depth Sounders

The bottom is a survival region with food and a haven from predators. Certain bottom areas tend to be more productive of fishes than others. Because of increasing angling and commercial fishing pressures, it becomes ever more important to be able to locate such areas. That's why more and more sport fishermen are turning to electronic devices to help them in bottom fishing. Notable among these devices, widely used in marine and sweetwater fishing, is the depth sounder. Depth sounders are available in two basic versions: one that simply shows and another that shows and records. The former version offers the least expensive models; the latter provides a permanent record of depths and bottom characteristics.

There are many kinds of salt- and fresh-water bottoms, and practically all of them have some kind of angling promise, according to species: hard-packed sand, open and free of vegetation; mud; rock-strewn or stony; submerged boulders; weedy or (as in the case of impoundments) with submerged trees; shellfish beds or generously sprinkled with shells; the edges of drop-offs (where the bottom abruptly drops to a greater depth); and holes of various sizes. The only trouble is finding and pinpointing these places.

The problem is solved to a great extent by a depth sounder. The wise owner of this electronic aid learns to read it for more than depths. It will tell him much about the nature of a bottom, whether mud or sand, free of vegetation or weedy, as level as a billiard table or "corrugated," and so on. An angler who really knows how to read his depth sounder can even tell you when there are

fish under the boat—and maybe even what kind. I witnessed a particularly interesting demonstration of this during an outdoor-press gathering given by Johnson Outboard Motors in Waukegan, Ill. On the program was a coho fishing trip on Lake Michigan. At first, action was conspicuous by its absence. Then our skipper-guide said suddenly, "There are cohos under the boat," and he pointed to the blips on his depth sounder. His declaration was barely out of his mouth when the morning's first coho was in the boat. I had seen such fish identification before, charter skippers citing big tuna, probable blue sharks, etc. What made the Lake Michigan demonstration especially interesting was the fact that coho salmon were only recently introduced into the Great Lakes, and those we boated weighed only 2 or 3 lbs. (Incidentally, it's becoming increasingly infrequent to see a bass boat in the South and Southwest without a depth sounder.)

Depth sounders further assist marine anglers by helping them rediscover productive bottom areas and wrecks. In this respect they're used in conjunction with a U.S. Government navigation chart of the region that shows depths and kinds of bottom. Here fishermen must be able to read their depth sounders' information about bottom characteristics to match it with that on the chart. In this way they sometimes locate grounds unknown to others. Such information recorded by their sounders is zealously—and jealously—kept secret by charter and party boat skippers, especially the latter group, who are in bottom fishing exclusively. Any private grounds are trade secrets.

Approaches to Baits

A very helpful part of bottom fishing lore is learning to interpret and distinguish among fishes' different approaches to baits. The theory can be learned by reading angling literature and boning up on the species' feeding habits. But the practice can be learned only by experience.

Certain fishes, including a few of the larger ones, are distinguished by surprisingly light nibbles. They're the sneaks, and they can clean your hooks without your realizing it. In sharp contrast are the dynamic hitters. No nonsense. No preliminary fooling around. Often the force of their hit is enough to hook them automatically. And then there are those species whose approaches to baits

are variable and unpredictable, depending upon how hungry they are at the moment.

Experience—and only experience—can teach you how to differentiate among the species in the area fished. It isn't infallible. For example, a crab's bait thievery can be mistaken for a fish's light nibbles. (Check your hook for bait.) Or a forceful strike can come from a species not ordinarily encountered on the bottom. The point is, how you will strike your fish—that is, set the hook—is determined by how they approach and take the bait; and the more you can link certain approach characteristics with specific species, the better your chances of hooking them.

While there are sport fishes whose domain is exclusively on or close to the bottom, there are others who reside or spend much of their time at intermediate depths on up to the surface but also seek out the bottom on occasion, usually to feed. If those species are in the bottom zone in search of food, it means they're hungry; and if they're hungry they're obviously candidates for your baited hooks. Right? Right!

Sometimes this wandering leads to surprises, like one of the heftier rascals grabbing a rig intended for much smaller game. A late friend of mine, Carter Henderson, a lifelong bayman, used to tell an amusing story along those lines. Every year in late spring, several bottom anglers fishing Long Island's Fire Island Inlet would have something seize their rigs with a rod-bending jolt; that something then would streak off out of control. Invariably the encounter ended as abruptly as it began, with a popped line or a reel completely stripped of line. Occasionally there was a broken rod, and at least once, Carter said, a guy had his rod and reel yanked right out of his hands. All these fishermen would have tales about the giant fluke (the size of halibut, according to them), or sometimes the enormous striped bass, that got away. Those giant ''fluke'' and ''striped bass,'' Carter chuckled, were hungry brown sharks that cruised in and out of the inlet in search of food.

One of the common calculated risks in bottom fishing is that your finned opponent, as soon as he feels the restricting influence of the hook, will streak for any rocks, weed beds or other haven (he thinks) that may be handy, and get the line snagged on something. You may not be able to prevent this flight without a distinct risk of breaking your line. But you can try this (what do you have to lose if the line is fouled?): Slack off on your line and wait a couple of minutes. Your fish might just swim out and free the line for you.

Years ago Pacific Coast anglers conceived a technique to attract more bottom fishes. It's simple. All they do is create chum to attract the fishes by scraping off barnacles and mussels exposed by low tides on dock pilings, submerged parts of bridge abutments, rocks and other structures normally under water most of the time. The mussels' shells are cracked to let body juices escape into the water. Soon they draw the little fishes and other freeloaders, such as crabs, and in turn the freeloaders attract the desirable sport fishes.

There are always exceptions, but by and large, expanses of bottom with stones; gardens of vegetation such as eel grass, kelp or fresh-water aquatic plants; and rocks, reefs and wrecks are more likely to produce than large, open expanses of sand or mud that are barren of such things. But don't ignore plain, seemingly barren sand and mud bottoms completely. There might just be some finned game in transit.

6. <u>Chumming</u>

The origin of the term "chumming" is unknown. Even the mighty *Webster's New International Dictionary*, with its more than 600,000 entries, says that the word's origin, as applied to fishing, is "obscure." But the act of chumming is not obscure to fishermen.

Essentially, chumming consists of offering some item of natural food, in addition to bait, to attract fish to the angler's vicinity. It's a kind of telegraph line of communication, you might say. Its greatest application is in marine angling, where it is used for many different battlers, including striped bass, giant bluefin tuna, mackerel, bluefish, others. It's not as extensively involved in fresh-water fishing, although there is no reason why—barring strong currents that would dispel the chumming material too rapidly—it would not work as well as in fresh water.

The material used in chumming is called, to no one's surprise, chum. The list of chumming materials is as long as your arm, maybe longer. The reason is that any item on a given species' diet is theoretically a candidate for a chum line. One species alone may consume literally dozens of

different things. Wherever possible, the chum should be a favored food of the species sought. Certain kinds of chum, however, are versatile in that they attract more than one species. For instance, those herringlike fish called menhaden or, more popularly, mossbunkers, can be ground into a mushy pulp to lure sharks, mackerel, bluefish, bluefin tuna, bonitos, still other battlers. Another chum that will lure more than one species is chopped clams.

When practical, the chum is matched to the bait, or vice versa. The idea, of course, is that if the fish find the chum attractive they will go for the same food on a hook. Thus menhaden are used in chunks as bait in conjunction with mossbunker pulp; clams are minced for chum, impaled whole on hooks for bait; small shrimp are dropped overboard in clusters as a come-on and also stuck on hooks; and so forth. But it isn't necessarily mandatory to match chum and bait.

Chumming Materials—the Bait

The species involved influence a choice of chum. So does availability. Some kinds of chumming material are more effective than others but have a

big drawback in not being readily available locally, or are expensive when available. Current speeds and how fast a boat drifts on a given day also enter the picture. Some chum is dispersed before it can take effect if current or drift is too fast. This is not only a waste; it can be costly.

Effective chumming materials include, in addition to those already mentioned: (1) butterfish cut into pieces, clusters of which are dropped overboard at intervals, or pieces of butterfish and mackerel used to supplement a pulp chum; (2) the shells of freshly shucked ocean clams (confined largely to cod-fishing, in which these clams also are used as bait); (3) mussels, with their shells cracked to let attractive body juices escape; (4) many kinds of local fishes ground into a mush, including the trash species ordinarily discarded by commercial fishermen; (5) for sharks, the ground-up red meat of pilot whales, although the use of mammalian flesh, as either chum or bait, is forbidden by IGFA rules in world record contention; and (6) canned fish—jack mackerel and others—sold as pet food. The latter suggestion has an obvious economic limitation where large-scale chumming is involved.

Again according to species, incongruous items have found their way into chum lines: whole-kernel corn, boiled and uncooked rice, bread crumbs, uncooked oatmeal, even eggshells. Let it hastily be added, though, that such materials can constitute a form of cruelty, since the fish cannot digest them. If those fish are not caught, they can become ill, even die. It has been said, but contested, that whole-kernel corn, a popular chum for some of the flatfishes such as flounders, remains undigested in their intestinal tracts, enough of it causing a blockage that can prove fatal. As a conservation measure perhaps it would be better to avoid such items.

Chumming is of great value in attracting single fish or small groups that might otherwise pass too far from the boat to find the hooks, and to lure spe-cies that are normally scattered widely. It can also hold an ordinarily fast-moving school alongside a boat, at least long enough to extract some fish before the band moves on. On a broader basis, chumming in quantity by many boats, day after day, will keep one or more schools or many individual large game fish in an area.

Ground-up fish is an ideal chum because it extends outward from a boat at a considerable distance, dispersing downward and to the sides simultaneously, thus covering different levels in the process. Therefore it's also more economical than using pieces of fish or whole shrimp. Menhaden are sold as a mushy, oily pulp in large cans for this purpose. Anglers can buy frozen fish in packages or ask a local commercial fisherman for his trash fishes, then grind their own. But this is a messy and tedious process with a home meat grinder. Furthermore, any real quantity poses a refrigeration storage problem. Arrangements have to be made with a local fish market or bait station. In short, it's better left for times when the pulp is not available. By the way, there is no law against trying some kind of fish not ordinarily used for chum in a given area.

An important detail is that any ground-fish chum that has been under refrigeration for a while should be thawed before use. Well-frozen chum contains ice crystals that make it buoyant. Not only does it fail to sink properly; it may draw sea birds from miles around. As for quantity, there's no blanket rule because of the variables involved. Current speeds vary; so do drifting speeds. Similarly, more chum will be required in the vicinity of an inlet, with its tides, than on a quiet patch of ocean or bay. Only experience can provide a clue as to how much is required for a given species in a given area. In any case, it's always better to end up with a surplus than run short. If there's an appreciable quantity left over, inquire on the dock about a place to store it under refrigeration.

Rate of Chumming

There's no single blanket rule for the rate of chumming. Again, too many variables are involved. However, there is a rule of thumb that can be used as a basis, then adapted to almost any situation: When a ladleful of the pulp, or a cluster of shrimp or fish pieces, is dropped alongside, watch the material. Just before it disappears, repeat, and so on. *The cardinal rule in any chumming is that the chum line must not be interrupted.* If there's a kind of break in the line, any fish swimming toward the boat will come to the break, lose interest and swim away. The result is wasted chum and lost fish. A simple ladle is an old soup can securely nailed to a piece of wood about 18 inches long. It does fine.

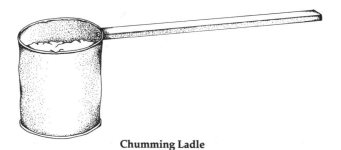

Chumming Ladle

Tips on ways to save chum and make it more effective: (1) Don't overdo it—that is, don't use more chum than you really need to get results. Over-chumming doesn't necessarily pay off proportionately. On the other hand, don't stint. That's false economy. (2) If you're using ground-fish pulp in quantity, ladle it over the side; don't sling it as though you were scattering grass seed. If there's any breeze, carelessly tossed chum can be blown back into the boat's cockpit or be splattered against the side of her hull—both messy. (3) If drifting, chum on the side away from the direction the boat is moving. If you chum on the opposite side, the boat will drift over the material and disperse it prematurely. (4) Ground-fish pulp, such as that from menhaden or mossbunkers, comes in big cans. It isn't necessary to use it in this concentrated form. Dilute it with sea water to the consistency of a stew as you go along. At the start you may have to take some of the mush out of the can to make room for a little water. (5) If necessary, a supply of pulp can be stretched by mixing it with sand (beach sand is good). The sand granules take on a coating of oil and scent from the chum. It will sink faster than the more buoyant pulp, however.

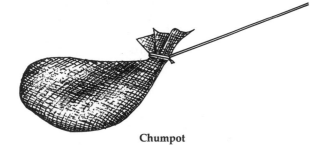

Chumpot

When smaller quantities of chum suffice, as when bottom fishing at anchor for, say, flounders and other flatfishes, a chumpot comes into its own. This is a very simple device. It can be a finely

meshed sack, such as oranges and onions come in, or a bag of similar size fashioned from finely meshed cloth. The mesh should be such that it allows juices and tiny bits of meat from the chum to escape into the water yet keeps the bulk of the material intact. Materials used in this form of chumming include mussels and clams, with their shells cracked just enough to let juices and tiny fragments of meat escape, and a coarse pulp made by grinding up fishes of various kinds. Tied on a suitable length of line, a chumpot is lowered to the bottom and bounced at intervals.

Also when fishing at anchor, mussels with cracked shells can be dropped overboard in clusters of two or three at a time, right alongside the boat, at intervals. You can chum with small shrimp (dead, so that they don't scatter) in this fashion too. The only trouble is, there should be little or no current running, otherwise the chum will be scattered before it can do any good. It's a more expensive way than the use of a chumpot.

Here's a simple chumpot: Get a can of fish food for cats, punch a few holes in the can so its contents can seep out, then tie a length of twine or old fishing line to it so that it can be bounced on the bottom.

For small, near-surface species the chum material can be placed in a floating bait car, called a killy car.

Lacking chum material, a chumming of sorts can be effected in very shallow water by stirring up the bottom at intervals with an oar or boat hook, or with a suitably long pole, as some public fishing boats use. Agitation of the bottom releases minute shellfish and other tidbits that fishes find attractive. Dragging an anchor along the bottom accomplishes the same thing. If you anchor in the vicinity of a dredge or clam diggers at work, they'll do the bottom-agitating for you without realizing it.

A unique variation of chumming—quite unintentional—used to occur offshore of Montauk Point, N.Y. Local big game fishermen discovered that giant bluefin tuna could be encountered in the wake of Russian trawlers' nets (this was before the 200-mile limit). The nets stirred up tidbits that attracted the tuna. Several boats took advantage of the discovery and docked with bluefins of 500 lbs. and more.

Another variation is called vertical chumming and can be employed to supplement a regular chum line when it is desirable to reach deeper levels closer to the boat or when the line is moving out rather rapidly. It is a simple stunt. Put quantities of chum pulp in ordinary paper bags and tie a suitable length of cord to each. Lower these bags over the side, one at a time. Start on or near the bottom with the first. When the bags have been in water a few minutes they weaken, and a sharp tug on the cord causes them to burst, releasing their contents. Try a different level with each bag.

Chumming can bring results when fishing is slow or dead and make it even better when it is good. When done properly it invariably gets results.

Drift-Chumming

To the writer's knowledge, "drift-chumming" is his own contribution to the argot of angling. But no matter. What counts is its meaning: to chum while drifting, as opposed to chumming at anchor.

Combining chumming with drifting heightens the advantages of both procedures: drifting, per se, naturally covers more territory than still-fishing, and therefore increases the chances of contacting fish. Chumming, in itself, reaches fish that might otherwise pass well beyond the boat; and drifting extends that reach.

In two ways chumming at anchor and while drifting are the same, for the material and frequency of release of chum overboard follow the same rule. But chumming methods can also differ. That difference is the amount of chum required on a given day. Understandably, drift-chumming can consume appreciably more. In both techniques the big factor is current velocity. The faster a tidal flow, the greater the chumming frequency, and therefore the more material used.

Drift-chumming is the most effective procedure in sport fishing for sharks. It can also be employed for other species that normally call for chumming. In the latter case, however, the baited rigs are moving with the boat, and they must not travel too fast for the fish involved.

Other Variations

A fairly fast drift also contributes to chumming frequency. There are times when a combination of swift current and brisk drift makes drift-chumming impractical. It can also be impractical in areas where there's too much boat traffic. In busy places drifting can be hazardous. Moreover, boats cutting across a chum line disrupt it and either impair or destroy its effectiveness.

At the other extreme are days when there's little or no current to carry the chum away from the boat effectively. In such circumstances there are two measures you can take. One is for the boat to move ahead very slowly under power, just far enough for a chum line to be established. This should be a few hundred yards at least. Then she pauses momentarily. By then, with luck, she has reached a place where there is some current. If not, she will have to continue under power until such a place is reached or the tide changes to create a flow. Usually such zero-current situations occur during periods of about a half-hour between changes in a tide. For economy's sake the boat can wait until change before chumming.

The other emergency remedy works only if there's at least a hint of a breeze. In this one a sail is jury-rigged forward. A tarpaulin, sheet or blanket —any piece of material large enough to catch wind —is attached to a mast stay and moored along its base. This crude "sail" will move the boat enough for chumming. If not, you'll have to use power.

7. Jigging

Over the years I've tried to track down the when and where of the application of the term jigging to an angling method (it's a commercial fishing technique too, by the way). I've learned several meanings of the word, but not one has anything to do with angling. Even *The Oxford Universal Dictionary*, a work which I esteem highly as an etymological source, is mute about the origin of "jigging" as an angling term.

Because of its spasmodic, bouncy, jouncy actions, I can only presume that the jigging in fishing was named for the jigging in dancing. What else?

I can tell you, though, that jigging is an ancient fishing procedure, dating so far back that we can't trace its beginning with any accuracy. Further, since man first fished to survive before he fished for fun, and so in a sense was a commercial fisherman centuries before he became what might be called an angler, it must follow that it was a l-o-n-g time before jigging became an established sport-fishing technique.

Vertical Jigging

Wherever performed, in recreational fishing or commercial operations, in salt water or fresh, jigging essentially consists of imparting an up-and-down or jerking type of motion to a rig. Jigging usually is thought of in connection with man-made baits or lures, but natural baits can be jigged too. There are two basic jigging procedures:

One consists of lowering the terminal rig (hereinafter understood to mean either a baited hook or an artificial, the latter without or with bait) to the bottom or to some desired intermediate depth, then reeling it in, lowering it again, reeling it in, and so on in a continuous process until the rig brings a response. This vertical jigging offers a certain advantage not found in such other standard methods as bottom fishing, trolling, and so on. Because of its nature, it covers several planes, along any one or more of which fish may be traveling. Vertical jigging is done at anchor and in slow drifting.

Jigging's prime objective is to impart some action to a bait or lure to make it more attractive to

70

quarry. Often this jigging action spells the difference between success and a skunking with an otherwise unproductive rig. ("Skunking," for the benefit of newcomers, means returning empty-handed from a fishing trip.) Even among lures that have their own built-in actions, jigging sometimes provides an extra touch that does the trick.

The other basic kind of jigging is a supplement to trolling, casting, bottom fishing and drifting. Once the rig is out where he wants it, the angler jigs it simply by short, spasmodic upward lifts of the rod tip. The rig need move only a few inches each time. If it's going to work, that's usually enough extra eye-catching action. According to the angler's own ideas, this can be a more or less continuous process or it can be punctuated with pauses of varying lengths.

That vertical jigging outlined above also is employed in ice fishing. You'll find details in this book's section devoted to that phase of hook-'n'-linin'.

In marine angling one jigging procedure or the other is used regularly on several species, including Boston mackerel, striped bass, bluefish, sea bass, others. It also can pay off in deepwater areas at sea, where it has accounted for groupers, assorted snappers, king mackerel, pollock, cero mackerel, fluke and others—even a tuna or two on occasion.

Fresh-water jigging nails assorted panfishes, black bass, walleyes, and several other scrappers.

Bait

Many kinds of natural bait see service in jigging. The list takes in just about every kind you'd rig for other angling procedures: whole small fish, alive or dead, or chunks or pieces of larger fishes; fish strips; worms; strips of squid; and so on. Ideally a jigging bait should be fairly tough so as to stay better on a hook. Soft baits, such as clams, might have to be secured with a few turns of thread.

Presumably, there being no historical information either way, the term jig was spawned by the jigging method to indicate a lure used specifically in that procedure. In any case, jigs have long since graduated to broader, more versatile use and are also rigged in trolling and casting. Jigs constitute an enormous family of artificials and are among the more widely employed fake attractors.

Artificials rigged in jigging include spoons, plastic worms (big in fresh water), plugs, bucktails and—but of course!—jigs.

Snagging or Snatching

There's a controversial form of jigging known variously as snagging or snatching. There's a fair amount of it in some parts of the country, but there's also a question of its being a sport. I'll tell you about it and you can judge for yourself.

Snatching or snagging begins by rigging one, two or more treble hooks with a small sinker to weight the rig and keep the line taut. The hooks are left unbaited because it's their bare points that do the job. The multi-hook rig is lowered or cast in among a school of fish, whereupon a rapid series of upward jerks of the rod tip (with luck) causes the treble hooks to snag one or more fish at a time, hooking them in various parts of their anatomy. Worked by an experienced snagger in a dense school of fish, it can do a job.

Except possibly in ice fishing, snagging/snatching is generally considered unsportsman-like. In some states—maybe many now—it's illegal.

Vertical jigging is an excellent exploratory operation, helping to determine what fishes may be available in a given area and at what level they may be feeding or cruising at the time.

For certain salt-water fishes—Boston mackerel are an example—a certain amount of jigging is essential at the very start of a fishing day because there's no way of knowing beforehand at what depth they may be. Here's where having more than one or two rigs in the water can be a time-saving advantage. The rigs are jigged at different levels until contact is made, whereupon the productive depth is noted and all rigs then are fished at that level. Jigging has a similar practical application in fresh water too.

Tackle

Both conventional and spinning types of tackle are wielded successfully in jigging. There are no set rules as to the caliber of tackle that should be used —I mean how light or how heavy. There can be no blanket rules because too many variables are involved: sizes and fighting characteristics of the fishes sought, weights of rigs (including sinkers) used, strength of current, and so on. Angling experience, as usual, plays a role too. Generally speaking, the more experienced a fisherman, the lighter he can go with his tackle. Thus a thor- oughly seasoned angler can win an argument with tackle as light as 6-lb. test, while another fisherman, given the same opponent, might require 30-lb.-test equipment.

If in doubt, and this is a rule of thumb that applies in all kinds of fishing, inexperienced participants might better go to tackle that's a bit heavier than needed than to the other extreme. That choice will cost them some of the fun of combat with certain species, but it will give them a better chance of landing all the fishes they hook.

Hang-Ups

This tip for the inexperienced and experienced alike: Much jigging, especially in salt water, is done around wrecks, reefs, rocks and other under- water obstructions. The reasons are that those obstructions attract lesser creatures (like tiny fishes, barnacles, crustaceans and mussels that serve as food for sport fishes, and also because jig- ging may not only be the best way to get at that finned game; it may be the *only* way under the cir- cumstances.

Point is, in any such fishing—jigging or even plain bottom fishing when rigs can and do drift— there are distinct chances of "hang-ups," or rigs getting caught in or on something down below. Sometimes careful tugging frees the rig. Many times it doesn't, and the line either pops or has to be cut. There's a mortality rate among hooks, sinkers, lures and other terminal tackle compo- nents. Wise anglers are ready with spares.

P.S. When other methods fail or produce poorly, try jigging. The results might surprise you.

8. Fresh-Water Fly-Fishing

No matter how much a man learns about fly-fishing or love, he can't live long enough to learn it all.

From start to finish, fly-fishing is an extraordinary test. The angler must not only make a phony insect bait look like some kind of real insect food to a fish, but he must also make the phony bait behave like its real life counterpart. This calls for real skill on the part of the angler, as fish see the real McCoy every day. Moreover, most fly-fishing lures are practically weightless, and it's up to the fisherman to present them properly in the face of obstacles that include breezes, overhanging tree limbs, precarious footing, interfering rocks, and sometimes little winged things that swarm around his head and dance in front of his eyes like spots seen during a bilious attack. And that isn't all. The fly fisherman must hook, fight and whip his opponent with weapons that to the uninitiated seem only slightly more substantial than an umbrella rib. But that's all part of the charm of fly-fishing, and it makes success that much sweeter.

Before discussing fresh-water fly-fishing further, let me sweep a couple of myths under the carpet. Fly-fishing is not overly complex. True, not all fly fishermen become crackerjacks and fewer become aces. What is important is that you don't have to be an expert to enjoy fly-fishing. In fact, much of the fun is in learning and improvement. What's more, with a little determination and patience you can become successful. And along the way you'll open

a succession of doors on newer, progressively more exciting vistas.

Among all the different angling procedures, fresh- and salt-water, fly-fishing is unique. It's the only one in which the line is the casting projectile, not a lure or a baited rig.

This is because of the extreme lightness of the artificials involved. They're so light they'd be impossible to cast any distance without additional weight for momentum. The line supplies it; it literally pushes the lure through the air, whereas in other kinds of casting the weight momentum of a rig pulls the line behind it. At this point, if you're not a fly-fisher, you might be asking: "Well, why not at least make the lures heavier, or maybe add a little sinker? Wouldn't that make casting easier?" Yes, it would. But it also would eliminate fly-casting as a technique. You will see why in due course.

With the extreme lightness of flies underlying it all, the casting of line becomes a pivot point around which fly-fishing tackle and its use revolve.

In fly-fishing it's particularly important that rod, reel and line be in balance with each other. Mismatching of just one of these three key items can lead to annoyance, frustration and discouragement.

Rods

A price we pay for the great diversification of tackle is the problem of selecting the right rod for our individual requirements. With a little thought the problem of selection can be whittled down to size.

Differences in materials won't be much help in fly rod selection. The greatest number of fly rods marketed today are of tubular, or hollow fiberglass. When a choice exists, it's usually between glass and split bamboo. Here price tags usually make up the buyer's mind quickly. Good bamboo models are much more expensive. The reason they're so expensive is the superb, highly specialized workmanship, which involves precision splitting of cane to meet critically fine tapers, then fitting those pieces together in tolerances so close that the finished rod looks like a single section of bamboo. There are still devotees who look upon fly-fishing with anything but bamboo as sacrilege.

But there are good to excellent tubular glass rods as well, and at prices that are more realistic for most of us.

As with other kinds of fishing, there can be no one fly rod to suit all assignments. If an angler intends to pursue his sport under a wide range of conditions and run the gamut of species, he might just as well make up his mind that he will require equipment in different calibers.

The factors entering into the selection of fly rods should include, first and foremost, lines to be used. To a novitiate it might seem like putting the cart before the horse, but a common procedure is to select lines first, then match the rods to them. Balancing of the two tackle components is that important, for it's the line that will (or won't, if mismatched) bring out the best performance in a rod. A line that's too heavy literally smothers a rod's action. One that's too light for its rod fails to

Overhand Fly-Casting for Beginners

The line hand is a kind of auxiliary reel in a sense. It works as a respository for line between casts and it maintains constant tension on the line to keep it free of slack. Coordination of the line hand is important as longer casts are developed.

1. The rod hand here grasps incoming line with the forefinger for the next cast, meanwhile preventing any slack. The line hand takes in a length, usually

the amount that can be pulled down in the distance between rod grip and when the arm straightens out. As each length is drawn down, it's stored in large, loose loops across the line hand. These loops must rest across the line hand neatly without tangles. They also should lie separately in the order in which the lengths were taken in: first length nearest the line hand's thumb, last length at the fingers' tips, ready to go again. After the last pull-down, the line hand should be free for the next cast.

2. Here the line is clear of the rod hand's forefinger as a cast is about to begin. The line hand, holding the loose loops in preparation for casting, maintains *light* tension between thumb and forefinger during the cast.

3. The cast, rod hand in motion. The rod swings upward to the limit of its back cast, then starts forward. Meanwhile, the left hand is stationary, holding the line securely.

4. Coordination between rod and line hands. Here the rod has completed its downward swing. At the precise instant the weight of the forward motion of the cast line is felt, the line hand opens so that the loops are free to follow each other in the shoot.

bring out the action. If an error is made, it's perhaps better to be a bit overweight than under, but that's roughly like saying a broken arm is better than a fractured skull. There's really no excuse for not matching lines and rods.

Other factors entering into the selection of rods are the lures involved, anticipated casting distances required for the most part, the user's skill and casting technique, and the species sought. All these are variables, and that's why there can be no pat formula for choosing one all-purpose fly rod. Last but not least is a personal factor: the rod must be comfortable to wield with a minimum of fatigue. That boils down to length and weight.

To repeat, there's no such animal as a fly rod that is all things to all fishermen at all times. However, we can wade through the vast canebrake of rods and come out with some useful generalities as starters. I've incorporated a number of helpful suggestions from nationally known fly-fisherman Leon Chandler in the following:

The logical start is for you to ask yourself, "Where and for what will I be doing most of my fishing?"

If your answer is small streams, you can rule out the longer, stronger, heavier fly rods. Recommendations would include rods in lengths from 7½ to 8½ ft., with 8 as an average. The rod would have medium-stiff action to handle level, double-taper or weight-forward lines (we'll come to those), as well as dry and wet flies, streamers, nymphs, and small popping bugs. Such a rod is about the closest you can get to an all-purpose model for panfishes, trout and bass.

If, on the other hand, your ambitions include lakes and big rivers, you will have to consider a longer, somewhat heavier model in the 8½- or 9-ft. class, with suitable muscle. There are even heavier rods in lengths to 9½ ft. and weights of 6½, 7 oz. And there are heavy-duty salmon rods that go even longer and heavier.

Within that range, aided by tackle shop personnel, you'll find the rod or rods that will suit your purposes admirably. If possible, take along an experienced fly-fisherman. When a choice has been narrowed down, try different models for feel; let your adviser try them too. Many tackle shops have indoor or outdoor areas where trial casts can be made.

You don't have to spend a small fortune for a good fly rod. On the other hand, don't stint. It's better to pay a little more than you expected and get a good rod than to economize and possibly wind up with junk. Points to check include the quality of its hardware—reel seat and guides—and ferrules. Check the number and alignment of its guides. Note how the ferrules mate. They should be snug, not loose nor overly tight. Pay some attention to how the handle feels. Handles are shaped in various ways to fit the hand comfortably. Grips are of cork, and it should be top quality.

You won't go wrong with equipment made by a well-known manufacturer. It's through consistent quality that a manufacturer builds and holds a reputation. Moreover, such a company stands behind its products.

Reels

Three types are in service in fly-fishing, and each has its own set of features, some of which may be more suitable to specific situations.

Single-Action

For years the most popular type has been the single-action. In this kind of fly reel each turn of the handle produces one revolution of the spool, a 1:1 ratio. Single-action fly reels enjoy enormous popularity because (1) they're versatile, readily adaptable to a full range of angling situations; (2) they're a simple mechanism; (3) they come in all sizes; and (4) very good ones can be had at realistic prices. There's no doubt that this is the best choice of the three for beginners.

That decision having been reached, the next step is to match the single-action reel to the rod on which it will be used. Here some consideration has to be given to its spool capacity. The size range runs from small, approximately 2¾ in. in diameter of frame to balance 6- and 6½-ft. rods, to large, measuring up to 4, 4½ in. in frame diameter, designed for sticks in the 9- to 9½-ft. lengths. For all-purpose fresh-water service, a 3¼- to 3½-in. size is suggested. It should go very well with that 8-, 8½-ft. rod.

The quality of the material and workmanship are details to look for. The way the spool turns and its clearance between flanges and frame can be indicators of quality—or lack of it.

Certain features add to a fly reel's price. One is a brake or drag mechanism. This is not as much of an all-round must as it is on spinning and conventional revolving-spool reels; still, it's good to have. A drag must be dependable, smoothly operating. It will take actual use to prove those details, but you can be sure of them in a quality reel turned out by a brand-name maker. The drag adjustment should be readily accessible. Another desirable feature is a quick-change spool. This is effected by activating a small release lever that allows a spool to be lifted out for replacement. With this feature you can change quickly from one type of line to another. It's easier than switching reels, and it saves carrying an extra one.

Multiplying

The multiplying type of fly reel offers the same retrieve advantage as conventional-type revolving-spool reels. That is, each turn of the handle produces more than one revolution of the spool. This is accomplished by gears and usually is in a ratio of 2½ or 3 to 1. The faster-retrieve feature is both a convenience and an aid. It saves time when taking in line to shift from location to location. Much more important, it quickly takes up any slack when fighting a fish. A common tactic among hooked sport fishes is to abruptly change direction, sometimes heading right toward the angler, in an effort to escape the line's restricting influence. This creates a belly of slack in the line, and if it isn't cranked in quickly a fish can throw the hook.

Multiplying reels come with adjustable drag and interchangeable spool features. They're available in a range of sizes to match different rods, with a judicious use of aluminum alloys to keep them light. For rod matching, the same general yardstick as for single-action reels can be used, always with line sizes in mind.

Automatic

The third kind of fly reel is the automatic. This is a pro-and-con affair, with anglers' opinions sharply divided as to its merit.

An automatic's biggest plus—and bone of contention—is its spring-driven mechanism that retrieves line when a button is activated. Line can be stripped from the reel by hand as needed, but the user doesn't have to crank it in. This is handy for taking up loose coils easily and quickly. However, the mechanism that effects this convenience adds appreciable weight to a fly reel, a detail some lightweight-rod wielders find objectionable. Criticisms that have been leveled at certain models are that they do not have sufficient spool capacity, and that line can bind if retrieved rapidly without proper tension for smooth winding on the spool. Another important criticism is that it can be difficult to feed or pay out yardage quickly when line is demanded by a running fish. That's bad news when harder-, longer-running game fishes, freshwater or marine, are involved. In connection with long-running species, it also must be mentioned that a spring mechanism limits the length of line in a single retrieve.

If extra weight doesn't bother him and small fishes are the objectives, an automatic can serve a beginner nicely. Sooner or later, however, he very likely will go to a single-action or multiplying reel. Most veterans probably would suggest starting with a single-action model.

Lines

A good part of a fly-fisher's affection for his equipment is lavished on his rod. Nevertheless, he will also admit that an equally important part of his gear is his lines.

To go back to something I said at the beginning of this section, fly-fishing is unique in that it's the line, not a lure or baited rig, that is cast.

In this respect a fly line becomes a kind of elongated sinker, but it's not quite as simple as that. A lead sinker used in surf casting, for example, is a compact weight. To achieve an equivalent weight in a fly line entails distributing weight throughout the line's length, and this poses a problem. Since a fly line's length is so much greater than a sinker's, there is a greater air-resistance effect, with the result that some of the propulsion effect of a cast is counteracted by that air resistance. Added to this is a certain amount of air resistance to the lure. Therefore, fly lines must be designed to offset this friction in order to maintain casting momentum as long as possible. This is especially important in fly-fishing because the line is in the air so much of the time.

The desired effect is achieved by altering the profiles of fly lines. Accordingly, they're produced in three basic types:

Level-Type Line

As its name hints, a level fly line has uniform diameter throughout, no taper. This type of line is understandably easier to produce than one with

The Double Line Haul

1. Line hand (left) reaches out as far as possible and begins pulling—just for an instant—before rod starts to lift.

2. A split second after step 1, both hands are teamed, the left pulling line, the right raising the rod.

3. Line hand continues to pull as the rod's upward lift accelerates to position shown.

4. The line hand stops pulling as the back cast straightens out. The line hand's pause is only for a fraction of a second and coordinates with the line's backward motion.

5. With straightening of the back loop, the line hand now moves upward for maximum reach for the next line pull.

6. Forward cast begins. Rod hand is pushing forward, line hand is pulling downward.

7. An instant after step 6, both hands are speeding up their respective actions.

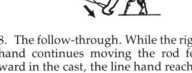

8. The follow-through. While the right hand continues moving the rod forward in the cast, the line hand reaches its maximum pulling distance.

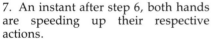

9. Casting hand stops as it reaches its maximum follow through, and the left hand releases the line for its "shoot."

taper, and this is reflected in its lower cost to the user. Because of its uniform diameter, which causes what we might call maximum air friction throughout, a level line will not perform as well as one appropriately tapered. Any taper, being of small diameter, naturally has less surface for air resistance. However, for beginners a level line can be suggested as a matter of economy at the start. It will serve in learning basic casting techniques, after which they can graduate to tapered lines for the finer points.

Double-Taper Line

In profile this kind of line has tip sections that taper downward to small diameters, while in between them is a heavier body section. It's this midsection that furnishes the weight. The tapered ends, being thinner, are more flexible, less bulky, set up less air resistance and, very important, allow a fly to land on the water's surface with minimum disturbance. A double-taper line also is easier to lift from the water than a level line, which means less strain on the rod. On an average, double-taper lines are 90 ft. long, of which each tapered section consumes about 8 to 12 ft., depending upon the manufacturer.

In addition to its advantages in use, a double-taper line offers an economy factor. Under average conditions, most casts are not much more than 50 ft., which leaves about 40 ft., including one tapered section, unused on the reel. At season's end this line can be turned around end for end, with the worn section on the spool, thus yielding that much more service.

A fine forward taper such as that provided by this kind of line is a must in proper presentation of dry, or floating flies. But a double-taper line is versatile and can also be used for shallow fishing with wet flies, nymphs and streamers.

Weight-Forward Type Line

Also known as the torpedo, Rocket (Cortland Line), or bug. A typical weight-forward line has a short, fine taper on its extreme end for the delicate presentation of a fly, then a heavier body section—the weight-forward portion—for casting momentum, followed by a long, comparatively slender section known as the shooting line or running line. In effect, the weight-forward portion is like a sinker, pulling the smaller-diameter running line after it; yet that slender front taper can present even a tiny trout fly as delicately as a double-taper line.

All lines in this category incorporate the weight-forward idea, but the proportions of their different sections vary somewhat from maker to maker. For example, there's a type that features a long forward taper and body sections, intended for use with small flies. Another type shortens its forward taper and belly portions to handle larger, more wind-resistant artificials. Cortland's Rocket line is an example of a well-designed weight-forward type. This line is 100+ ft. long. At its lure end is a very fine section 6 in. long, followed by an increasing diameter distributed throughout 12 ft., then 20 ft., of body—the weight-forward department—after which comes 4 ft. of decreasing diameter leading into 70½ ft. of slender running line. You can see why tapered lines cost more than the level type.

The principal advantage of this kind of line lies in its weight-forward arrangement. It aids in making longer casts with little extra effort. With its combination of heavier "head" and more slender running line, an experienced fisherman can extend his reach to 75 or 80 ft. without too much extra effort. It's therefore a prime tool when casting dis-tance is required, as well as when larger, bulkier flies and popping bugs are rigged. It's not restricted to those conditions, however. It must be remembered that there are weight-forward lines whose long, skinny front taper will present even small flies properly.

Shooting Head or Taper Line

Another refinement in fly lines is the development of the shooting head, or shooting taper, generally credited to Pacific Coast steelhead fishermen. A shooting head is a length—the average is about 30 ft.—of tapered line of proper weight for the rod involved, finest at its outermost end and becoming progressively heavier. This is interposed between the leader and a length of monofilament line (about 100 ft.). The monofilament, in turn, is attached to the backing line. The shooting head may have a loop at one or both ends for attachment to leader and mono line. The prime purpose of a shooting taper is the same as a weight-forward line, that is, greater casting distance with a minimum of extra effort. However, it's essentially a refinement for experienced casters and requires a more difficult handling technique, the double haul. Beginners and less experienced anglers might better ride with weight-forward lines (they handle better in a breeze anyway).

Floating Lines

There are two other divisions of fly lines: floating lines and sinking lines.

Originally there were only floating fly lines, so anglers were more or less limited to sport fishes that feed at or near the surface. Deep runners were out of reach. In time, as fishermen sought to deliver their come-ons to fishes lurking at lower levels, they accomplished their objective by attaching a sinking leader of suitable length to the floating main line. Varying the length of the leader regulated the depth at which the lure would go. Then came sinking lines, which I will get to in a moment.

Buoyancy in floating lines has been achieved by various means. Way back, fly lines were made from horsehair, then from a mixture of that and silk, and eventually all silk. Buoyancy was achieved by treating them with oil or some other repelling substance to prevent their becoming waterlogged.

Plastics technology brought the development of modern floating lines. One of the early inventions was a hollow line with an exterior made of a synthetic such as nylon. The only trouble was that water found its way inside the hollow core. Ultimately cores of braided nylon or Dacron fibers were developed, surrounded by a tough, water-repellent, buoyant outer coat. More recently, lines with even greater flotation have been created by surrounding the core with a layer of foamlike material containing millions of tiny air bubbles.

Sinking Lines

Sinking fly lines were developed to take wet flies, streamers and artificial nymphs down to deeper planes where game fishes often lurk, out of reach of standard floating lines. On big lakes and deep rivers fish often feed at these much deeper levels, and it's then that a sinking line comes into its own. (Seasoned fly-fishermen carry both floating and sinking lines to cover every possibility.)

Early sinking-type lines were manufactured with a fine-wire core for weight, but these developed handling problems, largely because of the inherent stiffness of the wire. Modern sinking lines take advantage of differences in specific gravity (weight) of different synthetics. Dacron, for example, is heavier than nylon. There are even degrees of "sinkability," with lines being classified as "medium-sinking," "fast-sinking," and "extra-fast-sinking."

Sinking lines have drawbacks that are important to novices. For one thing, they're harder to lift from the water than floating lines, and they exert a strain on a rod. For another, it can be more difficult to set a hook with a sunken line (a floating line is relatively unimpeded by water). A beginner might do well to accustom himself to handling floating lines first.

There's a kind of happy medium between floating and sinking types, and we have to mention a brand name to tell you about it. Cortland Line developed this "intermediate" in the 1960s under the name Sink-Tip. This line is designed to take a line reasonably deep yet be picked up like a floating line. The double effect is achieved by combining a main section that floats with a 10-ft. sinking tip section. Thus the main portion can be picked up easier than a fully sinking line; yet its tip will submerge a fly or nymph to depths of 4 to 5 ft. And since action is often only a foot or two down, Sink-Tip's coverage is ample for many situations.

Calibration of Fly Lines

For many years fly-line sizes—diameters—were indicated by letters. They began with A and ran through I to correspond to diameters ranging from 0.060 in. to 0.200 in. With this arrangement, a level line's diameter could be shown by a single letter, since it was consistent throughout. But combinations of letters—HCH, GAF, etc.—were required to show differences in diameters between the various sections of tapered lines.

The system worked fine while silk lines were still No. 1, since there was reasonable standardization among manufacturers. But the introduction of synthetics made the alphabet system impractical because diameters could no longer be used for calibration. In a given diameter, there are differences in weight among silk, nylon and Dacron. Further variations were caused by the different finishes on the newer lines. And since a fly line's weight is of cardinal importance in matching it to a rod, another system had to be devised.

It was established in 1961 by the American Fishing Tackle Manufacturers Association (AFTMA), a nationwide organization of equipment makers and firms importing tackle in the U.S., in a joint effort with the American Casting Association and International Casting Federation.

AFTMA selected a unit of weight as the basis of the new grading system. (A line's diameter, material, etc., are not the sole factors in this grading for size.) And because of the lightness of lines involved, AFTMA chose as its weight unit the grain. The term grain was derived from the weight of a grain of cereal. One grain is very light—7,000 constitute 1 lb.

In the AFTMA system the portion of line weighed to determine its designation is the first 30 ft. of its so-called working or front section, measured from the beginning of the taper but not counting any tip on a taper. Certain small plus and minus tolerances are allowed in meeting specifications. A number is then assigned to indicate each weight. In the new system the numbers run from 1 through 12 to indicate weights of 60 to 380 grains (with accepted tolerances), respectively.

So much for a line's weight. Now the system needed designations for level, double-taper and weight-forward lines, as well as an indication for anglers as to whether line was floating or sinking. These are simple: L for "level," DT for "double-taper," and WF for "weight-forward"; F for "Floating" and S for "sinking." To which AFTMA added ST to show a single taper and I for "intermediate," to indicate line that would float or sink.

Now you combine those letters with the numbers indicating weights. (Remember, it's the first 30 ft. of the working line involved in the weights.) Samples: L8F = level line, weight 210 grains, floating type. L5S = level line, weight 140 grains, sinking. DT9F = double taper, 240 grains, floating. WF11S = weight forward, 330 grains, sinking. And so on. Throughout the 1 to 12 weight range there are plus-minus tolerances ranging from 6 to 12 grains—pretty fine considering that there are approximately 437 grains in an ounce.

A Guide for Balancing Rods and Lines

Here's a guide for balancing fly rods and floating lines (courtesy of Cortland Line Company). It's intended only as a general guide. A tackle dealer can advise in precise matching.

Guide for Balancing Fly Rods & Floating Lines

Length/Weight of Rod (in feet)	Level	Double Taper	Weight Forward	Bug Taper
7, light action	L5F	DT5F	WF5F	—
7½-8, light	L5F	DT5F	WF5F	—
8, medium action	L6F	DT6F	WF6F	—
8½, light	L6F	DT6F	WF6F	—
8½, medium	L7F	DT7F	WF7F	WF8F
8½, heavy action	L9F	DT9F	WF9F	WF9F
9, light	L7F	DT7F	WF7F	WF8F
9, heavy action	L9F	DT9F	WF9F	WF9F
9½, medium	L9F	DT9F	WF9F	WF9F

Weights and their numerical designations in AFTMA standards:

AFTMA No.	Weight (in Grains)	Range, with Tolerances
1	60	54–66
2	80	74–86
3	100	94–106
4	120	114–126
5	140	134–146
6	160	152–168
7	185	177–193
8	210	202–218
9	240	230–250
10	280	270–290
11	330	318–342
12	380	368–392

Tapered Leaders

The prime function of this component of terminal tackle is to provide a gradual lessening of stiffness in the line-leader system so that it can continue the flow of casting momentum from the line and thus turn over the fly correctly. Difficulty in getting a fly to lie out straight for proper presentation can be caused by a poorly calibrated tapered leader. A recommendation is that the leader have a butt section that is at least ⅔ the diameter of the line's tip, and then gradually tapers downward to a finer diameter at the tippet end.

A level (uniform-diameter) leader is the easiest to make, naturally, but it has limited use in fly-fishing, where at best it's a makeshift substitute for a tapered leader.

A tapered leader has two sections: its butt, the heaviest portion, which connects to the line, and the tippet, which is the slender end accepting the fly. In presentation the tippet is the leader's business end, you might say, and its fineness is influenced by fly sizes and water conditions.

Many fly rodders fashion their own, starting with a section of monofilament in tests of, say, 25 to 30 lbs., then create a taper by joining short sections of material in 20-, 15-, 10-, 8-, 6-lb. tests, etc., until the desired tippet fineness is realized. All these sections can be joined by blood knots to produce a tapered leader of desired length. (An old do-it-yourself formula is 60-20-20—60 percent butt, 20 percent for tapering, 20 percent for the tippet, that last going about 20 to 30 in.) As you can see, a sizable number of combinations is possible with those sections' lengths and strengths. But a lot of time and effort can be expended in arriving at the right formula.

If an angler doesn't have a particular bent for experimentation, he can sidestep a lot of bother by buying knotless tapered leaders. These are packaged in various lengths, commonly 7½, 9 and 12 ft., with a designation to indicate the tippet end's size—1X, 2X, 3X, etc. Understandably, the smaller the fly, the finer the tippet must be if it's to be presented properly. Here is a general guide in selecting the proper leader tippet size (again, thanks to Leon Chandler and Cortland Line):

Guide to Proper Leader Tippet Size			
Tippet Size Designation	Diameter (in Inches)	Test (in Pounds)	Hook Size
1X	0.010	7	4 to 6
2X	0.009	6	6, 8, 10
3X	0.008	4.5	8, 10, 12
4X	0.007	3.5	12, 14, 16
5X	0.006	2	14, 16, 18
6X	0.005	1.5	16, 18, 20
7X	0.004	1	18, 20, 22

Fly-fishing often calls for frequent changes in flies in efforts to find the most appealing patterns. A fly is simply snipped off its tippet for replacement, but each time this amputation shortens the tippet that much more. It's a good idea, therefore, to carry level tippet material in several sizes for replacements. These spares also come in handy for lengthening a leader or changing a tippet section independently of the rest of the leader.

Leader and fly line should be united by a knot that won't snag in the rod guides. An answer is a nail knot. This makes a smooth, non-snagging connection. It can be made even smoother by coating with a rubber-based cement such as Pliobond.

A brand-new leader, or one stored on a reel for a length of time, often has springlike coils. These are removed by pulling the leader through a pinched rubber "cork." Lacking a cork, pull it under tension through two fingers pinched together.

Sometimes knots appear on the leader out of nowhere. Usually wind is the culprit. In any case, a knot should be taken out at once. It can weaken the leader by as much as 50 percent.

Tackle for Beginning Fly Anglers

Here's an outfit that has been suggested by casting instructors:

Rod

An 8- or 8½-ft. length (as a happy medium) weighing 4½ to 5 oz. (Rods with those specifications will handle 140- to 170-grain lines.) Until a newcomer finds out how serious he or she is about the sport, a good fiberglass rod is the ticket.

Reel

A lightweight single-action model, 3½ to 5½ oz., with a 3- to 3½-in. spool diameter and a clicker to minimize overruns. The reel's spool should be properly filled to within approximately ⅜ in. of the cross braces, with backing to fill it—even if the 30-yd. fly line is adequate in itself for the fishing involved. Fly line and reel will perform better if the reel spool is properly filled.

Line

The double-taper type is usually the easiest for beginners to manage. A more or less precise mating of line and rod is highly desirable in fly-fishing. And since lines come in different weights and rods have degrees of flexibility (or stiffness) that can vary, it's urged that beginners seek expert guidance in the matching. For backing to fill the reel spool properly, 15-lb.-test braided nylon or Dacron line will serve.

Lures or Flies

It never surprises anyone that the lures, or artificial baits, rigged in fly-fishing are called flies. As with any lures, artificials are designed and fashioned to simulate, in appearance and actions, items of fishes' natural food. In fly-fishing's case they include many, many kinds of flies and other insects, aquatic and terrestrial. Among lures are types created to imitate little fishes such as minnows and other creatures such as shrimp. Construction of all these clever fakes involves a myriad of materials, some of them quite exotic. Making them—fly-tying—also calls for an eye for details, imagination sometimes, an ability to improvise, and craftsmanship. Fly-tying is both an art and a hobby.

I've heard it estimated conservatively that there are at least 5,000 patterns of artificial flies, counting variations. Any census would have to be an estimate, because dozens, perhaps hundreds, of individual tyers' own original patterns and altered versions of standard patterns will never be known to the angling public. Additionally, fly-fishing's spread to salt water has spawned many more patterns and has opened a door on future increases without limit. (See ''Salt-Water Fly-Fishing,'' Chapter 9).

Artificial flies can be divided into three categories: wet flies, dry flies, and miscellaneous types.

Wet Flies

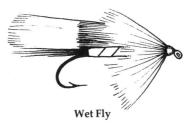

Wet Fly

In the modern concept, a wet fly is one designed to attract fish below the surface, as opposed to a dry fly (I'll get to this type later), constructed to ride on the water's surface and so draw fishes from below. Wet flies constitute an enormous family. Some are made in imitation of certain developmental stages (nymphs) of aquatic insects, or to suggest fresh-water shrimp, or tiny minnows, and so on. In each case, deception is accomplished by the lure's general appearance and size. Those details, in turn, are effected by the way it's dressed.

Among wet-fly dressings are four major styles:

(1) Feather wing: its dressing is a cluster of feather fibers from some bird, usually side or breast feathers. (2) Divided wing or double quill: the dressing consists of two pieces of feather, from feathers that are similar but from opposite sides of the bird (turkey, swan, duck, other). (3) Hairwing: here the dressing is hairs—animal hairs, such as those from a squirrel's tail. (4) Hackle: unlike the other three types, this one has no wings. Its dressing consists of hackles (feathers) wound around the lure's ''body'' (actually the shank of its hook) or attached as a collar.

With these variations, wet-fly patterns run into hundreds and hundreds. Each fly-caster develops her or his own very personal inventory of flies, with selections based upon the insects or whatever other local items of fish food they're trying to imitate, and also on the success they've had with them. There's no certainty that these will work for you, but a sampling of old faithfuls and favorites among veteran fly rodders includes these patterns: Royal Coachman, Quill Gordon, the Light and Dark Cahills, Gold-Ribbed Hare's Ear, Professor, Blue Dun, Black Gnat, March Brown and Silver Montreal. If I polled some other long-timers I'd probably get at least 50 more suggestions. Many wet flies were designed originally, or primarily, for members of the trout and salmon tribes, but can be rigged for a variety of fresh-water species.

An important detail in the selection of fly patterns is a determination of the months when the insects that they imitate are most likely to be around the water and so be food for trout and other fishes. Thus serious fly anglers must be entomologists of a sort. They must learn the species of natural flies common to their waters, their habits, and their peaks of abundance. For some fishermen, a study of the insects becomes a hobby within a hobby. Some really adept fly creators can take materials with them to streamside and match hatches, as the insects rise to the surface, fully developed.

Nymphs

Nymph Fly

Within the family of wet flies are a group of lures called nymphs, named for a developmental stage in the life cycle of many water-borne winged insects. Fake nymphs are a part of just about every fly rodder's lure kit, the patterns being tailored to the natural nymphs found in his favorite fishing waters.

To understand why artificial nymphs are effective fish-getters you must know the part played by their natural counterpart in aquatic ecology. Briefly, here's the way it goes, step by step: (1) The insect species, such as dragonflies, caddisflies, craneflies, deposit their eggs in streams, ponds and lakes, where they settle on the bottom. (2) Among stones, vegetation and debris the eggs hatch and develop into a larval form. Instinctively they make themselves as scarce as possible, hiding under stones and among vegetation. (3) With progressing development they acquire a "case," which encloses the developing wings. They then begin to approach their mature form. (4) Soon the nymphs must rise to the water's surface to earn their wings, so to speak. It's a journey fraught with peril, since there are numerous spectators, like hungry trout, bass and panfishes. Lucky is the traveler that manages to reach the surface uneaten. For many species of flies this emergence occurs in late spring or summer and is a detail of importance in matching artificial flies. (5) After nymphs arrive at the surface, the case enclosing their wings quickly splits, and the now winged insects are ready to test their flight equipment. First the wings must be allowed to expand, which is aided by a body fluid pumped into their tiny veins; then they dry. Drying is accomplished by crawling out on shore or on a branch. (6) The wings expand and dry quickly, and the nymphs take to the air.

Regular fly anglers should be equipped to capitalize as fully as possible on the various developmental stages of the different kinds of winged insects. Originally, fishing with man-made nymphs was confined largely to trout, but now it's also done for other species. Genuine nymphs, such as those of the dobsonfly, mayfly, caddisfly and stonefly, are used as live bait, anglers capturing them for that service.

It should come as no surprise to you to learn that the patterns of artificial nymphs are numerous. They parade through fly-fishing literature with such names as Green Damselfly (damselfly nymph), Alder Pattern (alderfly), Golden Stonefly, March Brown (another stonefly nymph), Caddis Nymph (caddisfly), Pink Lady, Iron Blue, Michigan Nymph, Greenwells Glory and Montana Nymph. All are in use in different regions at various times of the year.

Fishing with artificial nymphs is a specialty in its way. Many anglers consider it difficult. Much of the supposed difficulty involves insect lore that is foreign to the less experienced rod-'n'-reelers; but the best nymph anglers delve rather extensively into entomology or study of insects. Let me add that newcomers can easily acquire enough knowledge of the basics to have fun—and also catch trout.

Streamers and Bucktails

Streamer Fly

Another group under the banner Wet Flies are the streamer flies and bucktails. The main thing you need to know about construction differences between streamers and bucktails is a detail of their wings. Those of streamers are natural feathers

Bucktail Fly

from various birds, whereas those of a bucktail, also called a hairwing, are animal hairs. Contributing birds and beasts, according to patterns, include the swan, teal, turkey, stork, polar bear, fox, squirrel and deer. The term bucktail stems from the fact that hairs from the tails of buck deer have been used in lure creations.

Streamers and bucktails are created to imitate little baitfishes such as minnows on which trouts, salmons and other battlers dine. Both types are fished in similar fashion. Any choice between the two depends upon the appearance and lure actions desired, according to fishes sought. A streamer's eye-catching appeal, for example, may lie in the color and streaming movements of its wings. The bucktail's attraction, on the other hand, may lie in its lifelike markings and the pulsating movement of its wings. Durability also may be a factor in selection. Bucktails generally are better able than feathers to withstand assaults by sharp teeth. Streamer flies and bucktails sometimes are color-divided into two basic groups: imitators and attractors. Imitators are tied to simulate specific kinds of baitfishes in shape, color scheme, general appearance, and in any additional eye-catching features such as flash. Materials for this type of wet fly may be selected to achieve the appearance of a baitfish with a dark back and a light or silvery underside, without bars, stripes or other distinctive markings. That's a common pattern in nature. Or the intended effect may be a little fish with a pronounced lengthwise stripe, or perhaps one with vertical or oblique bars. Attractors are those streamers and bucktails which, in addition to their shape in the water, rely to a great extent on eye-catching color for their effectiveness. That's why their dressings usually are a bright yellow or white, or red and white, that time-proven combination used in so many fresh-water and marine lures. Tests have indicated that red, for some reason, is attractive to a number of different species of fishes. The lightness and visibility of white supplements it. Often the attractors' advantage over imitators is in murky water. Flash is another asset among streamers and bucktails. The bodies of little food fishes often catch light and reflect it in flashes, attracting the attention of predators. Flash can be achieved artificially by tinsel, wrapped completely around a lure's body or as a narrow, bandlike effect. A similar effect is created by "piping" the lure body with very narrow strips of the synthetic material called Mylar. Sometimes thin strips of Mylar are incorporated in the wings for additional flash. A few threads of a fluorescent color may also be tied into the wings. In sum, streamer flies and bucktails are designed, through form, color, action and additional attraction such as flash, to not only imitate baitfishes but also to function in varying water and light conditions, from bright, sunny days and clear water to overcast days, or other conditions of poor light and murky water. Wise fly anglers study the darting and erratic movements of baitfishes that their streamers and bucktails are designed to imitate, then reproduce these movements when working the lures. Streamers and bucktails may be cast from shore or from a boat, then retrieved to bring out their action; or they may be trolled. The largest artificial flies are among the streamer and bucktail patterns. I'll cite some of the names, not necessarily intending that any of them should be taken as recommendations: Nite Owl (streamer), Muddler Minnow (a famous pattern), Parson Tom (big streamer), Green Ghost (streamer), Alaska Mary Ann (bucktail), Dark Tiger (bucktail), Komish Sunrise Streamer, Jane Craig Streamer, Cain's River

Roaring Rapids Streamer, Black-Nosed Dace Streamer.

Dry Flies

As mentioned earlier, a dry fly is a surface lure intended to imitate some insect or little creature that has either fallen into the water or frequents its surface, or in the case of winged insects, hovers in the air above the surface and so could be captured by a fish making an extra effort. Its flotation is the No. 1 difference between a dry fly and a wet fly. Many fly patterns have both dry and wet versions. Thinking back to insects' nymph stage, you'll recall that they rise to the water's surface when they're ready for their debut as winged adults. This emergence, and the form of the completed insect, constitute the keystone of dry-fly angling, governing the way its lures are tied and presented or cast.

There are 12 or so basic dry-fly patterns, but they're the foundations for hundreds of standards and adaptations and personal creations. The 12 fundamental patterns are these: (1) variant, (2) bivisible, (3) spentwing, (4) hair body, (5) keel fly, (6) gauzewing, (7) divided wing, (8) downwing, (9) hackle, (10) fanwing, (11) parachute fly, (12) spider. Some of these basic designs, such as the divided wing, are intended to resemble insects in their natural forms. Other patterns, such as the variant, bivisible, fanwing and spider, are attractors rather than imitators and rely for their effectiveness more on such details as shapes and colors than on being faithful replicas of specific insects.

Mayflies, stoneflies, caddisflies and dragonflies are but a few of the insects imitated by dry flies. And this creativity has given rise to a terminology all its own. For instance, a mayfly, after its wings have emerged, is called a dun because of the drab gray-brown color of its wings. As a dun begins to mature, it becomes more brightly colored and acquires a long, taillike appendage. At this stage anglers nickname the dun a "spinner" because of its whirling flight patterns. After a mature female mayfly deposits her eggs, she collapses on the water's surface. At this stage an anglers' term for mayflies is "spentwings." Trout capitalize on the spentwing stage to the fullest, rising to the surface to cram their stomachs. At such times trout will also rise to greedily seize dry, or fake, mayflies.

Fly-tiers endeavor to style their artificials closely to the developmental stages of mayflies, as well as to those of the other species that hatch during the fishing months. This is known as "matching the hatch." The results are a large collection of dry flies. The parade appears almost endless. To list the available dry-fly patterns would be a project beyond the scope of this book. In passing I'd like to cite a few: Queen of Waters; Quill Gordon; Gold-Ribbed Hare's Ear; Iron Blue Dun; Rio Grande King; Rat-faced McDougal; Royal Coachman, fanwing and hairwing versions; Pink Lady; Mosquito; Light Cahill; Badger Spider; Dark Hendrickson; and the White Wulff and others in the Wulff series, creations of the famed U.S. angler and fly-casting teacher Lee Wulff.

Fly-rodding with dry flies is considered one of the most delicate, precise forms of angling. Because of this, plus a certain exactness required of its lures, and the challenges of landing scrappy fishes with light to very light tackle, fly-rodder purists say it is the ultimate of all sport-fishing techniques. But it isn't as difficult as impressions might lead you to believe. With basic knowledge and while practicing to become better, you can go for trout with dry flies and have a lot of fun, even if early mistakes get you hung up in underbrush or cost you fish.

Miscellaneous Types

Woolly Worms

The larval stages of many kinds of aquatic beetles stimulate fishes' appetites. Accordingly, there are artificials tied to simulate the worm- and caterpillar-like forms of aquatic beetles. They're often collectively called "woolly worms." They're fashioned from animal hairs or feathers—those of the peacock are one kind—and nylon. Some carry a dressing of tinsel or Mylar for added eye-catching.

The trouts and catfishes are particularly fond of beetle larvae. When the larvae are abundant, trouts will gorge themselves. And that's a cue to try a woolly worm pattern, matched as closely as possible to the larvae of the beetles known to be in that area.

Bass and Hair Bugs

Largemouth and smallmouth basses have voracious appetites. Their menus consist not only of insects and small fishes, including their own young, but also frogs and crayfish. And largemouth bass are not above gulping down mice and small birds that have fallen into the water. Angling for these two basses has sired a subfamily of small lures for use with fly tackle. Referred to as hair bugs and poppers, they're floating lures weighing only a fraction of an ounce—1/16 oz. or less.

Hair bugs are fashioned from animal hairs, fre-quently those of deer, secured around a hook in compact bunches, then trimmed to whatever imitative shape is desired. The underside is clipped rather close and flat so that it can't interfere with the hook's point. Variations include V-shaped tails and fanlike wings to conform with the simulation desired. They come in a multitude of designs and colors, and are intended to imitate, in form and action, assorted small creatures such as moths and frogs.

Popping bugs share part of their name and their sonic effects with plugs called poppers, mentioned in "Terminal Tackle," Chapter 2. Some bear a resemblance to those bigger lures, having a blunt or concave head end to generate a popping sound when worked in the water. Their bodies are rather bullet-shaped and made from cork, wood or plastic. Components in addition to animal hairs or feathers are tiny plastic or rubber skirts. Some models also sport winglike appendages made of bits of hair, feathers and even rubber bands. Popping bugs may imitate different kinds of critters such as insects, frogs and others. And some may not look like anything in nature. They all depend in part for their attraction on how they're worked in the water. Also in this group is a version designed to simulate a tiny minnow. The head end is usually of hair from a deer, and the tail is tied in such a way as to form a V, which pulsates and alternately opens and closes for added attraction.

General Lore About Lures

1. Whenever possible, purchase your flies in the area where you plan to fish. If that isn't possible, see if you can locate a professional fly-dresser and get his recommendations.

2. When building a fly inventory, be careful that you don't collect patterns without keeping a sharp eye on types. If you don't do this, you could find yourself with a whole bunch of patterns designed for the same service. That would be something like having 40 pairs of pants but no matching jackets.

3. One expert suggests a personal inventory of at least 24 dry flies for starters. He points out that there are about eight types of dry flies used along U.S. trout streams, so that you should have three flies of each type. The eight suggested are hairwing, divided wing, bivisible, spider, fanwing, midge, hair body, and downwing. Patterns suggested to represent the eight types are (hook sizes in parentheses) Grey Wulff (No. 12), Light Cahill (No. 12), Brown Bivisible (No. 12), (dry) Muddler Minnow (No. 10), Irresistible (No. 12), Fanwing

Royal Coachman (No. 12), Black Midge (No. 20), and Blue Dun Spider (No. 14).

4. For maximum versatility in sunken patterns, a basic fly collection should include four types: wet flies, nymphs, streamers and bucktails. The following are general suggestions as to type and pattern from experts:

Wet flies. (1) divided wing in patterns of Parmachene Belle, Leadwing Coachman and Black Gnat; (2) hairwing in patterns of Royal Coachman, Silver Doctor and Western Bee; (3) feather wing in patterns of Quill Gordon, Dark Cahill and Grizzly King; (4) hackle in patterns of Brown Hackle Peacock, Black Spider and Gray Hackle Yellow. Fly rodders in the East might have wet flies tied on No. 12 hooks, while Westerners can go to a somewhat larger No. 10.

Nymphs. Because nymph patterns are highly localized, it's virtually impossible to make a suggestion that will work all over. But expert Al McClane offers half a dozen patterns that could be worthwhile starters: Green Caddis, Breadcrust, Mossback, Hendrickson, Stonefly and Hardback. All are dressed on No. 12 hooks except the Green Caddis, tied on a No. 14. Al adds that it's important to increase the range of pattern sizes as time goes on, especially for Western trout fishing, where hook sizes go to No. 6 among simulations of large stonefly nymphs.

Streamers and bucktails. There are more than 12 artificials imitating minnows. Three are considered basic and should be included while building a fly inventory. The recommended streamers and pattern names are (1) the feather-wing streamer in Golden Darter and Chappie; (2) the marabou streamer in white and black; and (3) the bucktails in the Mickey Finn and Blacknosed Dace patterns. You should have at least two each of these three basic types. You might do well to get local recommendations on hook sizes beforehand. A No. 6, 3X long hook has been suggested as a starting size, with smaller and larger sizes being added according to needs as the collection builds.

Accessory Gear

There's a parade of items designed to heighten the enjoyment and success of fresh-water fly-fishing. Some could be classified as essential, others as helpful, and still others as good-to-have-if-you-can-spare-the-extra-bucks. The following are among major items:

Waders. Much fly-fishing is done in streams, shallow parts of lakes and other wadable areas. So a pursuer of the sport should own waders to be fully equipped. Hip boots are serviceable in small streams and shoaler places, but they obviously limit the wearer's range. A recommendation is to get chest-high waders. They should have soles of non-skid material. Slippery, mossy stones are treacherous. Another thing: Don't go by shoe sizes. Get waders large enough to accommodate heavy socks for warmth. Stream water can be mighty cool to feet and legs. Check your waders periodically for leaks. Take them into a dark place and shine a flashlight inside them. Patch any holes you find.

Fishing Vest. This garment has become an essential to fly-fishermen accustomed to wandering appreciable distances in search of action. A vest allows taking along a surprising assortment of items, from odds and ends to fly boxes, spare reels, and even lightweight rain gear. A well-designed vest has pockets of different sizes all over the place. It's literally a tackle cabinet you can wear. Fishing vests are made from durable, water-repellent material, and they provide a measure of warmth too. If you're a non-swimmer you might inquire about a type of vest that incorporates buoyant material to make it a kind of life preserver. It could be a vital refinement when stepping into a deep hole or being upended in a strong current of any depth.

Clipper. Clippers are indispensable to fresh-water anglers. Essentially a common fingernail trimmer, the clipper is designed for amputating flies for replacement, trimming line and leader ends, etc. One model also has an awl for clearing hook eyes and a small disgorger for removing hooks from fishes' mouths.

Hone. Here's a must. It's a small sharpening stone designed especially for keeping hook points needle-keen. Stows easily, even in a fishing vest pocket.

Fly Carriers. There's a variety. A small, compartmented box of strong plastic with a see-through, hinged lid is popular for small dry flies. There's also a lightweight plastic box with a slot arrangement to hold streamers, nymphs and wet flies and keep them from tangling with each other. Smaller wet flies and nymphs can be toted in a compact container that has a magnet to hold them. Also popular is the fly book. One kind resembles a long wallet; another is box shape and outfitted with a zipper. Both are lined with sheep's wool to protect flies.

Landing Net. This item is discussed in "Tackle & Accessories," Chapter 1. Suffice it to say that situations arise in which a net cinches capture of a fish that might otherwise be lost.

Thermometer. This item is also discussed in "Tackle & Accessories."

Rain Gear. There have been great developments; notable are the featherweight parkas and jackets that fold compactly for easy carrying.

Tape Measure. This device is a must for staying within laws governing minimum keeping lengths of sport fishes. There's one handy gadget on the market that combines a tape measure with a small hand scale.

And don't forget a good pair of sunglasses and spare tackle items.

Memo: A fresh-water fisherman isn't likely to overlook a license and special permits required in his state. It's when visiting another state that he can run afoul of the law if he hasn't checked requirements beforehand.

9. Salt-Water Fly-Fishing

It was inevitable that ultra-light-tackle regulars in the marine-angling fraternity should focus on the fly-fishing equipment of their fresh-water brethren and try fly tackle on salt-water game fishes. As a result, a new facet of sport fishing was born. That was decades back.

It's still a kind of specialty; yet it is recruiting more and more followers every year. Salt-water fly-fishing is in fact possibly the fastest-growing facet of recreational fishing.

Popular Fly Patterns

Today's marine fly rodders will tackle just about anything, ladyfish to sharks (some topping 100 lbs. have been landed). Name almost any of the popular marine game fishes—within reason, that is—and chances are that it has been caught on fly tackle. With the development of the sport it follows that there's an ever-widening selection of artificial flies, including streamers of both hackle and hair types, shrimp types, and fly rod popping bugs. Just listing them could turn out to be a chore, for more are being created every day. However, I'll offer some popular patterns, together with the hook sizes generally used and any species for which they have proved to be especially effective. (Mention of specific species doesn't rule out their use for others.) These represent a distillate of many patterns, some of which have been used with equal success on the Atlantic and Pacific coasts, as well as in the Gulf of Mexico and Florida waters.

First, nine patterns designated as classics by pioneer salt-water fly-rodder and fly-tier Kenneth E. Bay of New York City: (1) Bonbright Tarpon Fly, 5/0 hook; (2) Dean Bead Head, 1/0; ladyfish, bonefish, small tarpon; (3) Gibbs Striper Fly, 1/0; (4)

Bonbright Tarpon Fly

Dean Bead Head Fly

Horror Fly

Rhode Tarpon Streamer Fly

Sands Bonefish Fly

Horror, 1/0–3/0; bonefish and permit; (5) Loving Bass Fly, 1/0; striped bass; (6) Palmer Diller, 1/0; striped bass; (7) Pigtails, also 1/0 and for stripers; (8) Rhode Tarpon Streamer, 3/0–5/0 hooks; (9) Sands Bonefish Fly, 1/0.

A sampling of other popular models: (1) Ballyhoo, 1/0 hook; assorted Florida fishes; (2) Lyman's Terror, 2/0; striped bass; (3) McNally Smelt (he did?), 3/0; various gamesters; (4) Bluefish Streamer, 2/0, 4XL and other hook sizes; (5) No-Name Bucktail, No. 2 hook; bonito; (6) No-Name Streamer, 3/0; tuna and other battlers; (7) Silver Outcast, 4/0; various game fishes; (8) Pink Shrimp, hooks Nos. 6 to 2; bonefish and permit; (9) Skipping Bug, long-shank 3/0; striped bass and Florida species; (10) Bomber, 5/0–7/0; sailfish, amberjack.

Also these: (11) No-Name Tandem Streamer, two No. 2 hooks in tandem; albacore, barracuda, sharks, yellowtails; (12) Sea-Arrow Squid, 3/0, XL shank; albacore, groupers, sharks, striped bass; (13) Jetty Bug, Nos. 4 to 8 hooks, 3XL shank; bonito, spotted bass, perch; (14) Glass Minnow, 1/0; bluefish, bonito, mackerel, snappers; (15) Orange Blossom Marabou, 2/0; stripers, other species; (16) Spiro, 3/0, keel type; bluefish, snook, striped bass, tarpon, weakfish; (17) Argentine Blonde, 1/0–3/0 hooks; assorted game fishes.

To repeat, the foregoing are only a sampling. There are many more.

Whatever any lure's pattern, its hook *always* must have maximum sharpness. This is extra-important in fly-fishing because the rod's flexibility impedes driving the point home.

Tackle

Tackle for fresh-water fly-fishing can double in brass in marine use, up to a point. But unless it's designed for the heavier fresh-water action, it's usually too light for salt-water service. Larger, heavier, bulkier (more wind-resistant) artificials are involved. And often there are long casts in breezes sweeping across open water. Additionally, salt-water fly rods require suitable length and backbone, plus corrosion-resistant hardware.

Rods

Common rod lengths are 9, 9½ ft. when the largest lures are involved, casting distance is required, and opponents are bigger, like tarpon. But these sticks can be tiring to wield for any great length of time, and many regulars go to shorter, lighter rods in 8- to 8½-ft. lengths. They're not the peers of the longer sticks for meeting the requirements mentioned above, but they account for themselves handsomely with a wide range of gamesters from hefty bluefish and striped bass to small tarpon.

Because of the fly sizes and a need for at least some casting distance, a slower-action rod is favored in marine fly angling. Simply explained, "slow" here means that the rod's tip section is slower to return to its normal state after being bent. It's more flexible, in other words. A "fast" tip, in contrast, returns to normal more quickly after being flexed because it's stiffer. A fast tip can have too much stiffness for satisfactorily casting salt-water flies. At the other extreme, too much flexibility is not desirable either, because it will not respond quickly enough when fast placing of a lure is required, and it may not have enough spine for control of tougher opponents.

For a marine fly rod to be ideal it would have to amalgamate sufficient resiliency for casting bulky flies suitable distances with enough spine to set the hook and play the fish—all in consideration of the species the individual seeks. This happy marriage is not always possible. Consideration has to be given to required casting distances, if appreciable, and opponents' sizes. Certain situations demand longer casts than others. Working shallow water for easily "spooked" game such as bonefish is one such instance. Here's where the longer 9½-ft. rods come into their own. Further, their flexibility, or whip, affords maximum action with the smaller scrappers. But, by contrast, this same flexibility will work against an angler when arguing with larger and deeper-running species and those likely to streak for the nearest rock or coral mass. The longer rods may not have enough spine to raise and control such fishes. The shorter—8½-ft.— somewhat stiffer rods are more suited to these larger and deeper-running fish because they have more backbone. But more spine usually means less resiliency, and they won't cast as far. So if both varying casting distances and a wide range of species are involved, an angler may not be able to have it both ways in the same rod. He might better make up his mind that he will require two outfits. If one rod is to do, he could consider an 8½- to 9-ft. length and strike some sort of happy medium between slow and fast action. This could pose a calculated risk when long casts and bigger game are involved, but chances are the outfit will handle most of the battlers with whom he tangles.

Many salt-water fly-fishing veterans probably would advise not becoming overly concerned about rod weights. Weights can complicate the selection picture unnecessarily. The real criterion is how a rod feels in handling and whether or not it can be wielded over long periods without causing fatigue. Some tackle shops have an area inside or outside where customers can make practice casts to compare rods for feel.

Glass dominates the salt-water fly rod field. There are some regulars, like their fresh-water brethren, who stay with split bamboo; but the greater overall utility and durability of glass, not to mention its muscle, make it more desirable. And price differences make it more financially appealing.

Reels

Salt-water fly reels must have the construction, notably inside, to withstand the rigors of combat with hard-fighting and often long-running game fishes. Very important, they must also have line capacity and a dependable, smooth—accent that— adjustable brake system.

Capacity is major because 100 yds. or more of backing line must be accommodated in addition to fly line and leader. Open-water fishes are inclined to run and therefore demand line, and with fly rods there's no choice but to give it to them. For smaller or shorter-running species such as bluefish, striped bass, northern weakfish, sea trout and the like, 100 to 150 yds. or backing in tests to 12 or 15 lbs. should suffice. With distance runners or larger game—bonefish, tuna, tarpon, permit and so on—200 to 250 yds. of backing are not excessive, with strengths going to 20-lb. test on an average and to 30 lbs. for the larger species. Braided Dacron is highly recommended over nylon

or monofilament for backing. To determine whether or not the reel will accommodate the required amount of backing, spool the fly line on first, followed by the backing. When the spool has been filled, take backing and fly line off, and spool them back on in the right order.

A reliable, smoothly operating drag is especially important in a salt-water fly reel as a means of applying pressure on a fish. A drag that sticks or stutters is bad in any reel. If a brake gets sticky or freezes, if only for an instant, during a run, a broken line is the likely result. Corrosion resistance is important in salt-water reels too. Helpful are interchangeability of spools for changing of lines, and a quick-take-apart feature for cleaning.

The majority of salt-water fly reels are of the single-action type, that is, one turn of the hand = one revolution of the spool. But there are also multiplying reels, whose gear ratios effect more than one spool revolution with each turn of the handle. A choice between the two is personal. Many regulars favor the single-action type. However, a multiplying reel's obvious advantage is in its faster retrieve. Not only does this mean more line recovered per handle turn when cranking in a fish, it also means quicker elimination of any slack that may occur when a running opponent suddenly changes direction—a common maneuver, by the way.

Lines

Bulkier lures and wind are standard situations in salt-water fly casting. They are also the reasons weight-forward fly lines are favored in this sport. Weight-forward lines have been developed just for salt-water fly-fishing to facilitate casting under those conditions. And since much of the activity is with game fishes at or near the surface, floating-type lines are fine for most situations. Floating lines are particularly suited to beginners because they cast and pick up easily. Veterans carry both floating and sinking types, the latter for deeper-water fishing around reefs, or where there are fairly strong currents, or when it's necessary to get a fly down to a cruising prospect as quickly as possible.

You'll hear "shooting heads" mentioned as an aid in windy-weather casting. A typical salt-water shooting head utilizes the weighted portion of a fly line, about 25 to 30 ft., minus the thinner running line ordinarily attached. And this suggested arrangement comes from my friend Mark Sosin, outdoor writer and a topflight salt-water fisherman: To a loop at the shooting head's end, via a clinch knot, attach a length of monofilament running line, 30- to 50-lb. test. Mark suggests about 100 ft. Secure this to your braided Dacron backing by means of two nail knots, jammed together. One knot is tied into the mono around the backing; its mate is tied in the Dacron backing around the mono. They're tightened and pulled snugly so that they jam together.

As in fresh-water fly-fishing, matching of line and rod is important for a properly balanced outfit. Enough so, in fact, that marine regulars advocate deciding on line first—according to the flies that will be used most frequently and anticipated breeze conditions, then matching a rod to it, rather than the other way around. On an average, manufacturers market their fly lines in lengths of 25 to 35 yds. Generally a long line isn't necessary in salt water since distance casts usually aren't the order of the day, and it becomes increasingly more difficult to set a hook with longer lines. For these reasons regulars frequently lop off 10 ft. or more from lines coming in 30- to 35-yd. lengths. This also has the advantage of leaving a bit more room for backing line, which in salt-water action is more important than the fly line itself, since long runs may be involved.

Leaders

In the leader department, the salt-water fly rodder faces different requirements than his streamside counterpart. The fresh-water buff must use an appropriately tapered leader to lay his extremely light artificial delicately and lifelike on the water. In salt-water fly-fishing, presentation is not as critical, and the angler has to be more concerned with the fight to come. Similarly, in fresh-water fishing with dainty dry flies, water drag on the line becomes important. That isn't a factor in salt water. There, the fisherman is more concerned with being able to satisfactorily fling the larger flies, along with wor-

rying about possible abrasion from underwater structures and even from the gill covers and rough scales of his opponents. Therefore, whereas the streamside angler leans to favoring limper, softer-finish leaders, his marine brother favors somewhat stiffer, harder-finish monofilament, at least for the section—butt portion—that connects with the fly line.

There are all kinds of arrangements in fashioning leaders. Time-honored is one in which a series of short lengths of leader material, in progressively decreasing diameters toward the tippet end, are connected to form the desired taper. This arrangement has been in widespread use for years because many salt-water fly rodders prefer to fashion their own leaders in accordance with personal ideas and theories. It works, but a procession of knots passing through the guides could be a headache in fighting a fish of any size.

Mark Sosin suggests a superior setup: The leader begins with a 6-ft. butt section of hard mono, 30- to 40-lb. test. This longer butt, he notes, carries the fly and helps to turn it over, and there's only one nail knot, that between leader and fly line, to pass through the guides. Mark further suggests coating this knot with some rubber-based cement such as Pliobond to further reduce the chances of its snagging and abraiding in the guides. Next comes the tippet section, at least 18 in. of mono, secured to the butt section via a Bimini twist and an Albright knot. Mark also suggests a shock leader, 12 in. or so long, of light wire or fairly heavy monofilament, for fishes with toothy mouths or razor-sharp gill plates, like snook, for example. The same knot arrangement is used to incorporate the shock leader.

Still another leader arrangement is called "60–40–40": 60 percent of leader length for the butt portion, 40 percent for taper between butt and tippet, and 40 percent for the tippet.

Action Notes and Tips

Salt-water fly-fishing is like trolling in that it can be done blind (target unseen) or when a fish is sighted. The analogy can be extended by saying that in both kinds of blind fishing the idea is to cover as much likely water as possible. In fly rodding this is accomplished by a series of casts and retrieves in a pattern—it may be through a 360 ° arc, for instance—calculated to best cover places with promise. (This is the best argument for tackle that is comfortable and non-tiring to handle.)

Weight-forward lines help, but long casts usually are not necessary. The fisherman shoots his line in comfortable casting distances. All things being equal, the odds for or against his chances of success are theoretically the same as in blind trolling, although the latter does cover more ground. Having worked one patch of water to his satisfaction but without contact, the caster moves on to another site.

Sight-casting is something else again. It's more

encouraging than blind-casting because a target is seen. But it also calls for accuracy in placing the fly so that it will intrigue the fish into striking, and for speed, since the target is probably cruising. Misjudging in either department could mean kissing that fish goodbye. It's a good test of reflexes, not to mention skill. The angler has to be alert and at the ready when a target is sighted. One procedure goes as follows: Enough line has been stripped from the reel beforehand and is ready to go. The angler holds his lure—carefully, by its hook shank or dressing—and a loop of line, with 15 or 20 ft. of slack from the rod tip. A roll cast is made, taking the loop from the rod tip as the fly is released. A back cast shoots another 10 to 15 ft. of line, and then the caster aims right for his target. All this is done in less time than it takes to describe it. Needless to add, it takes a lot of practice.

Speaking of practice, regulars will tell you that if you can cast 50 ft. it's enough for most salt-water situations. But there's one qualification: if 50 ft. is your maximum, you're likely to have problems making that distance every time. If you have a greater maximum, 50-ft. casts should be comfortable.

A detail to remember in sight-casting is that the target is probably cruising. Marine fishes are a restless lot and are frequently on the move. You will find that speed and direction will change according to species, water conditions, and an individual fish's hunger at the moment. The more active types move right along while scouting; others prowl slowly. There are fish that hang in a current, barely maintaining seaway, so to speak, while they wait for the tide to sweep food to them. One of the things that make sight-casting difficult is judging how close to a fish to place a fly. There's no set rule. The distance ahead might be only a yard or two with a slow-mover, but might be increased to several feet if the fish is moving at a pretty good pace. With any luck the target will maintain the same direction and not be distracted by a passing tidbit. Consideration also has to be given to the species' spookiness. Some are always jittery, and dropping a lure too close sends them hightailing elsewhere. It should also be remembered that in shallows and in clear or dead-calm water fishes are more apt to be jittery anyway.

Many marine fly rodders favor the strip-retrieve technique for imparting motion to the fly, rather than by using the reel. On completion of a cast the line is momentarily pressed against the butt by a finger of the rod hand. Then, with the rod's tip-top aimed directly at the lure, the free hand pulls on the line to manipulate the fly. Accented advantages of this method are that the position of the rod helps in setting the hook while being ready to pick up line if another cast is necessary.

Setting the hook depends upon how enthusiastically the fish hits and the toughness of its mouth. Sometimes the force of a strike sets the hook automatically. Planting it in a leathery mouth with a fly rod can be tough, and many a fish is missed in the process. The usual short, upward lifts of the rod tip can be aided by hand tugs on the line. Once the hook bites in, the fish is going to take off, and with the likes of bonefish and permit that rush can be a scorcher. Any loose line had better be free to follow. From there on in the fish is played with both rod and reel, and always the angler has to be ready to crank in any slack that might develop when his fish suddenly changes direction. Any belly in the line provides an opportunity to throw the hook.

Drag adjustment is also a factor in setting the hook (and sometimes in broken lines). In salt-water fishing there are two degrees of drag: one for setting the hook, the other for playing the fish. The striking or setting drag often is greater, particularly with tough-mouth species. Once the hook is planted, brake pressure can be eased off if necessary to let the fish run, then tightened a bit later to bring pressure. Needless to add, at no time should the drag approach the breaking strength of the weakest component of the line system, which includes a leader.

Setting a drag properly is a nebulous detail. Through experience, most seasoned fishermen develop a certain feel for it, aided by thorough familiarity with their reels. It becomes instinctive. Others use a small hand scale. Except, maybe, in cases of small or lightly fighting species, the drag should be set beforehand. If a drag is too light, the hook can't be set properly and line will peel off too fast when the fish runs; and with revolving reels that spells backlashes. At the other extreme, a drag that is set too tightly can cause the hook to pull out of a soft-mouth fish or can pop the line or leader.

A lot of fishermen use a small hand scale. The procedure is to tie the line to the scale, held by a companion. Then the angler lifts steadily on his rod until it's at an angle of about 45 °. The fellow holding the scale notes its readings throughout. Suggested for a salt-water fly rod outfit is 15 percent of the leader tippet's breaking strength.

The adjustment of a drag, either way, during a battle is a tricky thing at best, especially since the adjuster is occupied with other things. There's absolutely no guide except experience. It can be remembered, though, that a drag effect can be momentarily increased or decreased by raising or lowering the rod tip. Added pressure can also be exerted temporarily with fly tackle by letting the line run through the fingers between the reel and the first guide, but this has to be done carefully. And with long-running opponents it must always be remembered that there's an automatic increase in drag as more and more line leaves the reel.

In any case, if a fish demands line, let it take yardage. Don't try to stop, or "horse," a fish when it runs. Feel for signs of turning and slowing, and then capitalize on the opportunitites to regain line. When necessary, exert as much pressure as you think your outfit will tolerate, but don't be over-eager. Many times you'll reach an impasse,

otherwise known as a "Mexican standoff," when neither side budges. This is a test of patience, and you'll have to be prepared to give or take line, as the case may be.

Last but not least, be ready for almost any kind of antics when the fish is brought close to capture. At this stage a fish can summon a reserve of energy and be off like a shot again, or can jump or sound. You may have to fight that rascal for another round or two. Aboard boat, a landing net or gaff will clinch victory. Someone else should be handling this assignment. It has to be done carefully. Fish have been lost right at the boat, literally knocked off hooks by overzealous net and gaff handlers. On a beach or sand flat a fish can be landed by carefully leading him onto an exposed bar or in through shallow water to the beach. It goes without saying that a fellow trying to lead his fish with one hand and gaff or net with the other has to be especially careful.

10. Surf Casting

In traditional imagery a classic surf fisherman stands knee-deep in an apron of foam on a lonely, wind-swept strand extending to the horizon. Just beyond him waves rear upward, curl shoreward and thunder upon the beach. The only sound is the age-old song of the breakers, punctuated by raucous cries of sea birds wheeling low. In the classic surf fisherman's hands is a rod of Calcutta cane—bent under strain, of course—long and husky enough to pass for a small flagstaff. From its tip a line vanishes into white water out yonder. What he is battling is of no consequence here. The scene alone summarizes the exciting challenge of this form of angling: personalized, toe-to-toe combat with both participants strictly on their own.

There are details this traditional picture doesn't show. The many times when a rod isn't bent under the rush of a finned opponent . . . the penetrating chill of pre-dawn hours . . . the fierce tangles accompanying backlashes . . . the frustration when fish are feeding just out of casting range, when a strong breeze from the wrong quarter makes it impossible to reach them . . . the fish that are lost when a fatigued line parts or is abraded through by a rock. But all these things are part of surf fishing's magnetism too. More than any of his

brethren, possibly with the exception of blue marlin and swordfish hunters, your surf angler is an incurable optimist. And success is all the sweeter thereby.

The classic surf fisherman of yore was a "squidder," so called because of his fondness for a heavy solid-lead artificial known as a squid, molded in the shape of a sand eel (sand launce) or some other small forage fish on which his quarry fed. On occasions he also flung heavy bottom rigs or whole eels. The bulkiness of his rigs, coupled with his frequenting of ocean-front beaches where considerable casting distance was involved, necessitated stout rods with long tip sections and butts, the latter for casting and playing husky surf game such as big striped bass and channel bass. The reels were appropriately large and gutsy too, able to accommodate a couple of hundred yards of linen line. It was heavy gear, awkward and tiring to use. It separated the men from the boys, as the saying goes.

But those were the years before the advent of spinning tackle, an innovation that altered the surf-fishing picture. It was a vast improvement.

For one thing, spinning tackle is easier to use than the conventional-type surf gear once in exclusive service. With a little practice, even a novice can attain respectable casting distance with a spinning rod. For another thing, there is the absence of backlashes, or line tangles on the reel, which are enough in themselves to discourage a lot of new-comers. Furthermore, spinning tackle's inherent casting quality has made it possible to use shorter rods. No longer does a surf caster have to feel as though he or she is wielding a small flagpole. Additional lightness is achieved by the use of hollow fiberglass rods and metal alloys in reel manufacture.

But don't misunderstand. There is heavy-duty surf spinning equipment too, and conventional (revolving-spool reel) tackle is still much in service. Beach conditions still vary from place to place, and fishermen still differ in their preferences.

Today's surf-fishing equipment, collectively, is far more versatile than its predecessors. That is, there's a far greater selection of weapons. This is because surf fishing itself has broadened in concept. It remains a salt-water casting technique, but no longer is it confined to ocean-front strands. Surf fishing today includes angling on jetties and sea-walls, along the shores of inlets, channels, bays and sounds, and from boats maneuvered just beyond the breakers.

Another factor contributing to this broadening is a certain de-emphasizing of great casting distance as a prerequisite to success. In the old days it was a common belief that a successful surf fisherman had to be practically of Olympics casting caliber. While it's true that casting distance is important when schools of fish are feeding well away from shore, it's also a fact that many catches are made within 100 ft. or so of where casters are standing. It all depends upon such local conditions as the contours of a beach, breeze direction, velocity, etc.

Surf tackle is primarily casting equipment. Before it can catch any fish it has to be able to reach them with whatever natural bait or artificial is currently in use. An ideal outfit is one that blends flexibility for casting with enough backbone to argue with a hefty, stubborn opponent. It also must be comfortable to wield over long periods. In this regard, incidentally, newcomers are apt to overlook the detail of rod butt length. A surf rod's butt must be sufficiently long to provide the required leverage, yet should not be so excessively long that it repeatedly jabs its wielder in the ribs. As you might suspect, an individual's height and arm length are factors in the selection of a proper butt length.

For several reasons, some of which are outlined above, there can be no blanket recommendations for a single all-purpose surf fishing outfit. Too many variables involved. What I can do, however, is catalogue the equipment in use and perhaps make some suggestions along the way. As major guides in selection you might consider these points: (1) species involved and their general size ranges; (2) local conditions under which you will be doing most of your surf fishing: open, often breezy ocean front, rocky shores, relatively calm waters, jetties, or from a boat; (3) rigs involved—primarily artificials or natural baits, or both? This is important when rigs are heavy, especially with spinning tackle. The equipment has to be able to cast them satisfactorily. (4) With Nos. 1 through 3 in mind, comfort in use.

Conventional Surf Tackle

For our purposes let's divide conventional surf tackle into light, medium and heavy categories:

Light

Overall rod length runs 8 to 9, 9½ ft., making it possible to cast artificials up to about 2½ oz. and sinkers to 3 or 4 oz. The rod should be rated to handle lines to 20-, 30-lb. test. In the light category are the so-called popping rods, which are really shorter, lighter versions of the time-honored squidding rods. Also in this group are jetty rods. Most of these have shorter butts, to about 24 in., to facilitate handling on the more precarious sections of jetties. On these structures casting distance is less of a factor than on a beach, since the "jetty jockey" is already some distance from shore or

working an inlet channel beside the structure.

Tackle in the light class can be used for the following conditions, singly or in combination: calm or light surf; smaller bottom rigs or lures; fishes up to 20, 25, even 30 lbs. (which covers much of the game ordinarily sought). Light surf tackle also serves nicely in casting from a boat toward shore.

Medium

This surf tackle is perhaps the closest to a happy medium. Rods go 8½ or 9 to 10 ft. overall. They're resilient enough to fling artificials up to 4 oz., sinkers to about 5 or 6 oz., and should be rated to handle lines up into the 30- to 40-lb. tests. As with tackle in the other two categories, it will handle lighter and even a bit heavier rigs than those just mentioned, but usually with some sacrifice of performance.

Medium-caliber weapons will accommodate the vast majority of fish encountered in surf situations, including lunker-size striped bass. It must be remembered, though, that the heavier any equipment is, the less the sport with smaller fishes.

Heavy

Surf gear in the weight class ranges up into heavy-duty two-handed rods that can cast artificials of up to 5 and 6 oz., whole eels, and baited rigs with sinkers weighing 6 to 8 oz. Rods go to 10, 10½ ft. long; some are up to 11, 12 ft. A lot of leverage is needed, and their butt sections consequently are long, to 30-plus in. These rods are used with lines in 40-, 45-lb.-test strength. These are more or less specialized weapons, designed for beach use when it's necessary to cast heavy rigs long distances or fight bigger battlers in rough water and strong current or undertow, and when arguing a stubborn opponent away from a rock or other submerged structure. This equipment is not the easiest in the world to wield, and it's fatiguing. It's not recommended for beginners.

Reels

Surf reels are matched to these rods. Matching is not a matter of precision, but it should take into consideration the same factors governing the selection of its rod. Most important, it should have a smoothly operating, dependable drag or break system (a sticky drag spells popped lines and lost fish). Many surf species can tear away on long runs, and considerable line is already out after casting, so the spool must hold ample yardage. A length of 150 yds. is not too little; 200 to 250 is a better figure.

For casting efficiency it should also have a free-spool feature for casting. All conventional reels come with that anyway. Recommended as well are reels with wide spools. Many surf models incorporate this feature. A wide spool not only facilitates casting; it also allows for wider distribution of the line thereon, which minimizes an automatic braking effect as more line leaves the reel.

Backlashes are caused by a reel spool spinning out of control and overrunning the line. Some reels incorporate anti-backlash devices of one kind or another. None will eliminate backlashes completely, and veterans usually dispense with them because they can cut down on casting distance. Instead, they rely on thumb pressure—judiciously applied—on the reel spool as line zips out in casts. Lightweight metal spools are favored over the older, heavier types because they do not gain as much momentum, the culprit in causing backlashes.

Surf reels usually have a higher retrieve ratio than models used for other kinds of fishing. This gives greater flexibility in retrieve speeds in working lures and also allows any slack line—which can be caused by wave action and the fishes themselves—to be taken in quickly. The retrieve ratio should be at least 3:1. Even greater flexibility is provided by models with two retrieve speeds, 3 or 3½ to 1 and a faster rate, interchangeably by flipping a lever. The advantage is that the faster rate can be used when it's desirable to retrieve a lure rapidly; and then, when the fish is hooked, the reel can be shifted to the lower rate for paying out.

Spinning Tackle

Here we have light, medium and heavy grades too. As in the case of conventional tackle, the grading is arbitrary, flexible, and subject to individual variations.

Light

Rods run 7–7½ ft. to 9–9½ ft. overall, butt end to tip-top guide. A matching reel is in the small to small-medium size, holding about 150–200 yds. of 10- to 20-lb. line. Tackle in this caliber is fine for the smaller surf-run gamesters such as bluefish,

northern weakfish, the smaller "schoolie" striped bass, etc., and for the lightest rigs—little artificials to 1, 1½, maybe 2 oz., sinkers to 2 or 3 oz., light line, the smallest fishes, and when appreciable casting distance isn't required. Lines to 10-lb. test are popular strengths.

Medium

Like its conventional counterpart, this is a good middle-of-the-road caliber. Overall rod lengths go to 9 ft., 9½ or so in some models. They have fairly

Overhead Casting, Open-Face Reel

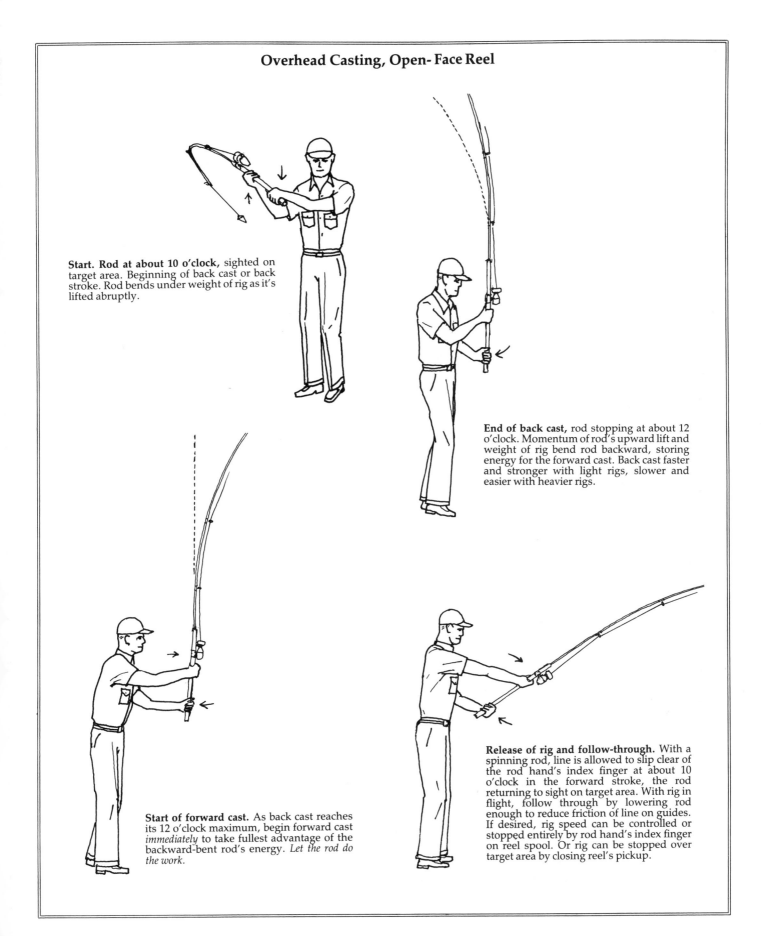

Start. Rod at about 10 o'clock, sighted on target area. Beginning of back cast or back stroke. Rod bends under weight of rig as it's lifted abruptly.

End of back cast, rod stopping at about 12 o'clock. Momentum of rod's upward lift and weight of rig bend rod backward, storing energy for the forward cast. Back cast faster and stronger with light rigs, slower and easier with heavier rigs.

Start of forward cast. As back cast reaches its 12 o'clock maximum, begin forward cast *immediately* to take fullest advantage of the backward-bent rod's energy. *Let the rod do the work.*

Release of rig and follow-through. With a spinning rod, line is allowed to slip clear of the rod hand's index finger at about 10 o'clock in the forward stroke, the rod returning to sight on target area. With rig in flight, follow through by lowering rod enough to reduce friction of line on guides. If desired, rig speed can be controlled or stopped entirely by rod hand's index finger on reel spool. Or rig can be stopped over target area by closing reel's pickup.

long butt sections, to 24, 25 in., for two-handed casting and plenty of leverage. They handle lines to 20-lb. test, a good strength for this outfit. Artificials go to 3 oz., which is representative of the majority most frequently used in surf fishing. Baited rigs with sinkers to 3 or 4 oz. The reel is one of the medium-size spinning "mills" able to accommodate at least 200 yds. of line used. It's a versatile outfit that can handle opponents up to big bluefish and the huskier striped bass and channel bass.

Heavy

Rod lengths run up to about 10 ft. (some have gone even longer) overall and combine a "whippy" tip section with a long butt for hurling lures weighing up to 4 and 5 oz. A balancing reel is one of the larger, huskier surf spinning models able to take a minimum of 200 yds. of the line used. Line strengths go up to 20- and 30-lb. test. As a margin against abrasion in rocky areas, some anglers go to 40-lb. test, or at least incorporate a monofilament leader in that strength. When the heaviest species are anticipated, 40-lb. line is used. These outfits are what you might call the big guns of surf spinning, suited to the bigger artificial, heavier bait rigs, rough water, and the largest surf-run species. But they're heavy, somewhat cumbersome outfits and tiring to cast for any length of time.

General Notes

An angler might best go with medium-caliber tackle, at least as a starter. And here the ideal rod is one with fast-taper construction. Its topmost tip section is flexible enough to cast the lighter lures and rigs, yet there is power and backbone in its middle section and butt. It allows for considerable latitude in assignments.

The larger surf rods are long indeed, and may pose a problem in transportation and storage. Many anglers favor one-piece sticks, feeling that ferrules, or joints, cut down on casting action and are also potential weak spots. It's a point well taken, but of doubtful importance to the average once- or twice-a-week fisherman. Transporting these long rods requires a rack on the outside of the car, and storing them properly can be a headache. Rods that disassemble by means of ferrules are easier to tote and put away. You'll have to decide on any inferiority in strength and casting action.

As for lines, both monofilament and braided types are in service, all of synthetic materials such as nylon and Dacron. Many anglers stay with monofilament for spinning gear and braided line for conventional tackle, although mono is used with the latter too. Monofilament is somewhat more resistant to abrasion than braided line, an advantage in places where there are rocks and other

underwater obstructions. On the other hand, mono has more stretch, which can make it tougher to set a hook in a running fish, and is not as easy to handle in its heavier strengths. If abrasion is a threat, a compromise is a monofilament leader in a strength somewhat heavier than the line's.

Leaders commonly are incorporated in terminal tackle for various reasons, and usually are fairly short. Wire is a must if the fish have toothy mouths or sharp edges on their gill covers. Otherwise, monofilament does nicely, is easier to handle than wire, and may be included either because of that abrasion factor or because the user feels it has decreased visibility in water. In any case, terminal tackle hardware is kept at a minimum. For artificials a snap swivel at the end of the line will facilitate quick lure changing.

There's an army of lures employed in surf fishing —plugs, jigs, etc., as well as a variety of baits. You'll be wise to check locally as to which are currently the most productive in the areas you intend to fish.

Jetty & Pier Casting

In a way, "surf casting" has become a misnomer. Or let's say that this phase of piscatorial activity has outgrown its name. Today the term has broadened to include casting also from jetties, ocean-

front piers, and other shoreside locations. A couple of generations ago, "surf casting" told exactly where the method was practiced. Not any more.

Ocean-front jetty fishing has many adherents wherever it's allowed. (In some places jetties may be off limits to anglers for their own safety.) This method has both advantages and disadvantages.

These are jetty fishing's biggest advantages over fishing from the adjacent beach: (1) Since you're already "out to sea," so to speak, considerably less casting distance may be needed to reach fish. (2) Fact is, the extension of a jetty out beyond the breakers often makes it possible to contact fish which otherwise would remain beyond reach from shore. (3) By providing places in which to hide from predators and so attracting little fishes and other food items, and by accumulating barnacles and mussels, which also serve as food for some species, jetties are in themselves a kind of artificial fishing reef. (4) Jetties flanking inlets can be especially productive, since sport fishes move in and out of those gateways in search of food. Often tidal currents erode a channel right alongside a jetty, which channel becomes a thoroughfare for prowling game fishes. Note this: Timing in inlet fishing is very important, whether from shore or a jetty. Many species—bluefish, for example—make hit-and-run excursions in and out of the gateways. If you happen to be there when they do, you'll get fish. At least some of that luck can be created by being familiar with the habits of the fish sought.

Ocean-front jetty fishing's biggest drawbacks are matters of safety. Specifically, it's a matter of safe footing. Jetties and seawalls with a reasonably flat, level surface are one thing. Those composed of great piles of rocks are something else again. Footing is tricky enough when they're dry; and when they're wet or covered with mosslike vegetation they're treacherous and can be especially dangerous. It goes without saying that anyone venturing out on a jetty at night without some means of illumination ought to have his or her head examined. And always, day or night, jetty fishermen should be outfitted with so-called creepers or some other suitable kind of non-skid footwear.

Another problem on jetties may arise when attempting to land a fish. The angler may not be able to get close enough without having to scramble over dangerously slippery rocks. There are long-handled gaffs for such situations, but sometimes they're not long enough, in which case the angler might better gamble on successfully working his catch in over the slippery rocks rather than climb over them himself. He has to exercise common sense and judgment, but a broken line (even with a lost fish) is better than a broken leg— much better.

Another potential danger on jetties, particularly on old crumbling ones, sounds more like a gag than an actuality. Be assured that it isn't. It's the possibility of being cut off from shore or trapped out on the end of a jetty by a rising tide and waves. Some jetties may become completely submerged during extra-high tides or when the sea goes into one of its surly moods. Even though they rarely if ever become completely covered by water, many other jetties may be unfishable at high tide.

At the other extreme—not dangerous, but not productive either—are jetties that are left practically high and dry, or at least with very shallow water around them, at low tide.

It pays to scout a jetty beforehand, studying the water conditions around it at different stages of the tides, getting an idea of the extent and velocities of currents swirling around it, looking for any sand bars—lighter-colored water—that have built up and for darker water indicating channels and deeper sloughs, and for tide rips—white water— and eddies that tumble small fishes, crabs and other tidbits about for easy capture by game fishes (one of the reasons why surf fishing for striped bass and a number of species is usually better in and around white water than in dead calm). Ask other anglers about that jetty's productivity at various stages of the tide and different times of day and where the productive areas are. They may lie or say they don't know, but ask 'em anyway—you might get lucky.

There's a systematic way to fish a jetty. You begin on one side arbitrarily, choosing a location you think might have promise. You make a series of casts, back toward the beach, then out straight in front of you, then out toward the seaward end of the jetty. If that station produces, fine, otherwise you take a casting position farther out on the jetty and repeat the series of casts through approximately 180 °. Giving each station a fair chance to produce before moving on, you work your way out along one side of the jetty, do a lot of casting in different directions out at its seaward end, and then, if you still haven't made contact, work your way back toward the beach on the jetty's other side. Note: In the case of some inlet jetties there may be only one side and the seaward end to fish. Ocean currents may have built up a little beach on the other side.

Chances are fairly good that many of the contacts you make will be less than 50 ft. from the jetty's edge, maybe within 25 or 20 ft., or even right alongside the rocks. From a local tackle shop or other fishermen get a line on what artificials and natural baits seem to produce best (and for what species). Keep in mind that game fishes frequently cruise close to rocks, knowing instinctively that they'll find little food fishes, shrimp, crabs and other food items in among the rocks. Try artificials made to simulate such creatures, casting them as closely parallel to the jetty as you can. In whichever directions you cast, try varying the speeds of your retrieves. On inlet jetties let tidal currents carry your rig out a way, then retrieve it, varying the retrieve speed. And try working lures at different levels—near-surface on down. You may have to use some weight, like split-shot or pinch-on sinkers, to take your rig to the desired depth, but don't overdo it.

Ocean-front pier fishing, of which there is much on both the Pacific and Atlantic coasts, is an equivalent of jetty fishing in that it extends the anglers' reach. But there are outstanding differences. One is that the pier has safe footing and has rails. Another is that a pier requires less casting than a jetty and in fact is more like bottom fishing than surf casting.

There are public fishing piers that charge a fee, usually modest; and there are some, municipally or state-operated, that are free. Fishing piers are very popular and are a solution to the problems of people who fish only occasionally, and then for a couple of hours each time, for anglers who do not like to fish from boats for one reason or another, and for fishing parents with children (they believe) still too young to take along in a boat. Many fishing piers are starkly simple—just a big platform out over the water. Others incorporate refinements that include lights for night fishing (which also attract little bait fishes that draw more desirable finned game), snack bars, a bait station, rental of rod-and-reel outfits, and sales of tackle items, toilets, and a chumming machine that spews ground-up fish pulp into the water to attract sport fishes.

Tackle wielded in jetty and pier fishing is varied, to put it mildly. Sooner or later you'll see just about every kind, conventional, spinning and spin casting, short of fly rods and big-game equipment. Mostly it's what could be generalized as light to medium tackle. With casting distance not a prime requisite, the rods in pier and jetty fishing tend to be somewhat shorter than those used primarily in casting. And they should have a pretty good backbone. On some piers at certain stages of the tide fish have to be cranked upward from a height. On jetties it is often necessary to control a fish to prevent his running in among rocks that could abrade the line or prevent landing that fish. Quite commonly anglers bring their boat-fishing tackle, spinning and conventional, to piers and jetties.

Carrying tackle items such as lures, extra line, spare reel, hooks and leader material, along with such essential items as fisherman's pliers, flashlight and knife, can be a pain. That's why many jetty jockeys travel as light as possible, taking only the items deemed necessary and forgoing the standard tackle box in favor of a knapsack type of carrier, or maybe a shoulder-suspended canvas bag, to leave both hands free when climbing over rocks.

Accessory Gear

These are accessories with varying degrees of use and helpfulness, according to circumstances, and not necessarily in order of importance here:

1. Sand spike. For beach anglers. It's a rod holder with a pointed leg that is thrust into the sand to moor it. This is not an absolute essential, but it does hold a rod and reel when not in use and keeps the reel out of the sand. Some surf casters also use it to hold their outfit between strikes, but I advise against that because it means a delay in trying to set the hook when a fish hits. Besides, it's lazy man's fishing.

2. Creepers. Some form of non-slip footwear (such as ice-creepers) is a must in jetty fishing. Slippery rocks are treacherous. Safety footwear is cheap insurance against a broken leg—or worse.

3. Gaffs. There are short-handled models for carrying on the belt in beach fishing. There are also long-handled gaffs for jetty service, and they should be painted white so as to be seen better at night. With a lively surf or a tough opponent, even a short-handled gaff can be tricky to wield, and many a fish has been knocked off the hook as a result. That's why many veteran surf anglers dispense with a gaff and depend upon wave action and experience to help land their fish. When large surf-run fishes are involved, some regulars substitute a persuader—a short, heavy club—for a gaff. On jetties it's a different proposition. Often a gaff, perhaps one with a long handle, is essential

because you just can't get close enough to your fish otherwise.

4. Tackle carriers. The choice is between a standard tackle box and a compartmented bag, usually an over-the-shoulder type, to carry the essentials. Jetty jockeys prefer a shoulder bag or similar carrier because it's easy to tote. Same goes for beach fishermen who have to walk any distance.

5. A light. This is a must in night fishing, for changing lures, rigging hooks, untangling backlashes, etc. A flashlight becomes more important on jetties at night, when footing can be especially dangerous. Even better is an angling adaptation of a miner's head lamp, which leaves the hands free.

6. Clothing. This isn't a problem for warm-weather fishermen. All they have to worry about is sunburn and foot cuts from shells and other bottom objects. Simple prevention takes care of those. Northern surf anglers need proper clothing for comfort in chilly weather and cold water. Non-leaking, hip-length boots with warm socks inside are a must, or, better yet, chest-high waders with warm inner clothing. Also essential are outer garments that keep wind and water out. (As you probably know, wind contributes to the chill factor.) Some surf casters and jetty fishermen wear foul-weather gear—jacket and pants—over warm inner clothing. Waterproof insulated parkas are good, and a hood not only lessens loss of body heat through the head (this loss can be considerable without any covering) but also protects the neck and ears against chilling wind.

7. Sunglasses. These are an important item and should be of quality. Cheap sunglasses are almost as bad as none at all. The Polaroid type is recommended. Not only does it protect against harmful glare on water and sand; it enables the wearer to see through glare to detect sloughs, cuts alongside sand bars, and other areas with promise.

"Reading the Water"

No surf angler worth his or her salt goes into action without surveying an area beforehand. In addition to obvious indicators such as sea birds circling and swooping low over a patch of water (to seize small fishes chased to the top by predators) and surface commotions created by game fish clobbering a panicked school of bait, there are subtle signs that can be put to good use if a fisherman knows what to look for. They apply generally.

Studying a beach area is best done at low tide, from atop a dune if possible. (Here's where the sunglasses help.) The angler seeks out holes and sloughs alongside sand bars or near the beach, detectable by their somewhat darker water. These are places where surf-run game fishes prowl in search of food. Also worth scouting are channels and bars in and around inlets and around jetties, along with places where currents collide in white water that can tumble bait about to attract finned game.

You should also take note of any holes, cuts and bars just off the beach but beyond casting range. Maybe you can have a go at those with a boat.

So long as local ordinances do not prohibit them and private property doesn't make accessibility too difficult, a beach buggy (for the uninitiated, a vehicle adapted for travel in loose sand) is great for scouting beaches and surf fishing in general. It can cover a lot of territory.

An old surf fishermen's recommendation is to fish two hours before and two hours after a high tide. This is often valid advice, but it can't apply to all areas at all times. Bait fishes and their pursuers do not read fishing books. Another old rule is that at least some chop on the water is always preferable to a slick calm. This also is valid counsel. Dead water, such as that between changes of tides, is seldom productive. A third "rule" is that the hours from dusk until dawn are often more productive than daylight when the sun is high in the sky. This is true for several species, including striped bass and bluefish, but doesn't rule out daylight hours even for them. Some fishes simply go into deeper water by day to avoid either the brighter light or the warmer water of the uppermost levels. Some fishes provide better action at night because they prey upon creatures—eels, for example—that are nocturnal prowlers. All things considered, you shouldn't go wrong by fishing two hours before and two hours after a high tide at dusk, after dark, or just before dawn.

You should try various stages of the tides and different hours of the day. It's also important to experiment with artificials and natural baits. Use the standard lures and baits for a given area but don't hesitate to try something different. Fishes can be moodily selective in their responses, and there's no predicting what they might hit. Sometimes a change of bait or artificial can make an immediate difference. A smart procedure is to inquire locally to get ideas for a basic selection, and also experiment with your own artificials.

Artificials should be worked according to manufacturers' suggestions, but this doesn't exclude experimentation. Varying the speed and nature of retrieves is often helpful. Theoretically a strike can come at any time from the instant a lure plops on the surface, and you should be ready to engage your reel accordingly. A retrieve should cover all water, right on through the breakers. Game fishes often pursue prey surprisingly close to a beach. With any lure the retrieve is usually begun the instant it hits the water, and an effort is made to work it hard just behind an oncoming breaker

because the water is apt to be clearer—and the attractor more visible—than in a wave proper. Along the same lines, retrieves may have to be slower at night and in sand-clouded water to give fish a chance to spot your offering.

And don't overlook surf casting from a boat. Not only will it give you contact with fish otherwise beyond casting range; it sometimes is more productive than when fishing the same artificials or natural baits from shore. Only thing is, you want a competent skipper and a completely dependable engine. This can be a dangerous sport.

There's more to successful surf fishing. Some of it is lore acquired by talking with and watching other anglers. Even better is know-how acquired through personal experience, and the only way to get that is to fish.

11. Big-Game Fishing

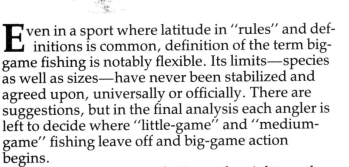

Even in a sport where latitude in "rules" and definitions is common, definition of the term big-game fishing is notably flexible. Its limits—species as well as sizes—have never been stabilized and agreed upon, universally or officially. There are suggestions, but in the final analysis each angler is left to decide where "little-game" and "medium-game" fishing leave off and big-game action begins.

So far as I'm concerned, size and weight are the criteria for big-game status. The kind of fish, if it figures at all, is secondary. For me, contrary to some suggestions that persist, big-game status doesn't begin with fishes in the 100- to 200-lb. bracket, whatever their fighting qualities and whatever the number and assortment of sportsters included. There are excellent battlers in the 100- to 200-lb. class, but I don't think they should be classified as big game when it's considered that sizes among the largest sport fishes already caught top half a ton, and in a couple of instances—both white sharks—top 2,000 lbs.

I'm inclined to side with my distinguished colleague, Frank Woolner, angler-scribe and *Salt Water Sportsman* magazine editor, when he arbitrarily sets the minimum weight at 500 lbs. for fishes to qualify as big game. That narrows down membership in the elite group, confining it to the likes of giant bluefin tuna, black marlin, blue marlin, and giant sea bass, broadbill swordfish, possibly striped marlin yet to be caught (the ceiling at this writing is 400-450 lbs.), and the larger sharks, notably makos, whites, or man-eaters, great hammerheads, tigers, duskies and threshers, along with possible additional heavyweights revealed as time goes on.

All of the aforementioned big-game-class bruisers except one are recognized by the International Game Fish Association as species worthy of world-record recognition. That present exception is the dusky shark, a tough customer (larger than the blue shark and porbeagle, both on the IGFA list), which may one day get deserved recognition as an opponent of world-record caliber (if so requested by enough fishermen).

I suggest 500 lbs. as the minimum weight for fishes to qualify as big game. Since that's an unofficial arbitrary, flexible figure let me also suggest that it can be revised downward, say to the vicinity of 250 to 300 lbs., perhaps in a special light-heavyweight division, to admit a greater variety of species and a greater span of ages among anglers. That would be more economically feasible for more anglers too. Be advised that hunting such elephants of the sea as black marlin, swordfish and blue marlin can be expensive, especially if you have to travel to such faraway places as Australia, Peru and Mauritius.

As an old saw has it, records are made to be broken; and understandably there could be changes even as I write this, with new kings enthroned. However, existing IGFA all-tackle world-record weights (the very heaviest recognized by that association), even if fractured within the next five minutes, will do nicely to give you an idea of how high you'll have to set your sights.

Latest Big-Game Records	
Bluefin tuna	1,496 lbs.
Black marlin	1,560 lbs.
Blue marlin, Atlantic	1,282 lbs.
Blue marlin, Pacific	1,100 lbs.
Giant sea bass	563½ lbs.
Broadbill swordfish	1,182 lbs.
Mako shark	1,080 lbs.
White shark	2,664 lbs.
Great hammerhead	717 lbs.
Tiger shark	1,780 lbs.
Thresher shark	802 lbs.

The maximum size potential of dusky sharks has yet to be determined. Lengths to 11 ft. are on record (no weights given for those), but I personally know of a 640-pounder brought in by a charter boat. So far the blue sharks and porbeagles honored by IGFA record recognition have been in the 400–450-lb. bracket and 450–475-lb. class, respectively.

I mentioned that records are made to be broken. Some seem imperishable. Witness these, with dates and places that were still in effect at time of writing:

Longtime Records
Black marlin, 1953, Cabo Blanco, Peru
Pacific blue marlin, 1966, Mauritius (in the Indian Ocean)
Giant sea bass, 1968, Anacapa Island, Calif.
Swordfish, 1953, Iquique, Chile
Mako shark, 1970, Mayor Island, New Zealand
White Shark, 1959, Ceduna, South Australia
Tiger shark, 1964, Cherry Grove, S.C.

Trolling

Big-game angling procedures are fundamentally the same as some of those used for far smaller fishes. There is trolling, probably the most popular big-game method because it's used for swordfish and all the marlins. And there's fishing at anchor —rigs at various depths—with chum, a procedure that racks up giant bluefin tuna. It also racks up sharks, but a superior sharking method is to drift and chum.

Trolling's widespread popularity throughout marine and fresh-water angling can be credited to three cardinal advantages: 1) It covers a lot of territory, thereby enchancing the chances of contacting fish, especially those that are loners or travel in very small groups or pods. 2) It's excitingly suspenseful because you never really know what your rig might dredge up. 3) Its production record, overall, is good, although it may not always get you exactly what species you want, but what method does? (See "Trolling," Chapter 4.)

Most big-game trolling is done blind—the quarry unseen. At best you might know or hear that some of your intended prey are in that general area, or you might radio-talk with a boat that has spotted fish in the area, or, if you're real lucky, you might even get to see a few yourself. But the

chances are that you'll be trolling blind, hoping for contacts. This is the case, usually, with all the marlins, from the lithe "little" white marlin on up to that deep-chested elephant of the sea, the black marlin, and with some other heavyweights such as swordfish, in certain areas.

Sighted trolling is in order when a target is seen on or near the surface and there's an opportunity to present a bait or lure right then and there. This is the favored technique in that catch-blessed arena from southern Massachusetts to the southeastern offing of Long Island. In that arena it's also the procedure for white marlin. Both species loaf on the surface at times, where exposure of their tail's upper lobe (and the dorsal fin in the case of the swordfish) betrays them. The boat then maneuvers to bring the bait (whole squid in the aforementioned region) or lure practically under the fish's snout.

Speaking of white marlin, here's a story about a trolling experience that no one talked about for quite some time.

With her owner and a professional skipper and mate, there were about eight of us aboard the 50-ft. sportfisherman *Jo-El* one early July day offshore of Shinnecock Inlet, L.I. Five of us were fishing writers. Our prime target was swordfish, with white marlin as a secondary quarry. The truth was that we were prepared to be content with the latter, knowing how high the odds were against even sighting a broadbill. But rod-and-reelers out after swordfish are among the world's greatest optimists, and eight pairs of eyes, most of them on the flying bridge, where height provided better distance vision than in the cockpit, scanned the sea throughout every point of the compass. Mile after mile slid under our keel as we sailed farther off-shore . . . then back inshore a way . . . then east'ard . . . then back west'ard . . . and offshore again. Zilch. Finally, about midafternoon, we decided to hang it up. It seemed as though we'd covered half the Atlantic Ocean. All we'd had was a boat ride with sunburn and eye strain to show for it. I don't remember who made the discovery, but suddenly there was a yell, "Hey, there's a white marlin!" We looked, and there sure enough was. Are you ready for this? There was a marlin right alongside the boat, less than 20, 25 ft. from the cockpit, on a course parallel to ours! We could've smacked him with an oar. We had no way of knowing how long he'd been there, but he wasn't sticking around. He began to ease off on his throttle and drop back, and by the time we got a couple of baits over and put about he was gone. It was a long time before any of us mentioned that incident.

I've been privileged to have fished for assorted big game in such widely scattered regions as the Indian Ocean's Mozambique Current off South Africa, on the seaward side of Australia's Great Barrier Reef in the Coral Sea, in the Pacific off Ecuador, in Nova Scotia and in the Caribbean. With the exception of swordfish off my native Long Island, it has been my experience—or poor luck—that seldom are real heavyweights of big-game angling seen right at the surface with any semblance of regularity. There are occasions when they do show for a specific reason. For instance, they may leap out of the sea and go into aerial acrobatics in desperate attempts to rid themselves of parasites, some of which may annoy the fish in a way that fierce flies drive land animals crazy.

Conceivably a feeding frenzy can also bring big-game fishes to the top. I'm sure that was the cause of one of the most spectacular sights I've ever witnessed in sport fishing. It was in the Strait of Yucatán off Isla de Cozumel, and I saw acres—and I mean acres—of migrating giant bluefin tuna esti-mated at 500 to 800 lbs. churning the sea white and leaping clear of the water. I was told that such migrations can occur during a span of about three weeks in May. Our host landed one, about 500 lbs.

Other sporadic appearances at the surface are thought to be a kind of mating or pre-spawning ritual. I saw a number of black marlin while fishing off Cairns, Australia. Incidentally, the females are monsters ranging from 800 to more than 1,200 lbs. The disparity in size between females and males is startling. The males can attain 500 lbs., but a more common maximum is 300 to 350.

Big-game trolling speeds vary according to the species sought, whether natural baits or artificials are used, and such variables as location, current, local recommendations and personal ideas of skippers and veteran fishermen. One veteran I knew used to follow this blanket rule: With fresh natural or live baits, troll slowly, up to about 4 knots; and with artificials, troll faster, up to about 9 knots, even 10 on occasion. Slower trolling with natural baits provides an opportunity for the quarry to smell as well as see the offering.

But that veteran troller would be among the first to concede that there can be no hard and fast rule for proper trolling speeds, and that those speeds are invariably open to experimentation. All fishes have certain set feeding patterns; but their appetites, like humans', are subject to moods, and who can predict them? Some species are more aggressive or faster than others.

The same thing goes for trolling distance astern. One set of suggestions advocates letting out 60 to 120 ft. of line as a starter. Here's where putting out three or four rigs at different distances can be a timesaver. You note which rig gets response, then adjust the others accordingly. Here again you'll have to experiment. As with trolling speeds, getting results may be largely a matter of trial and error. Each situation can be different. Just keep in mind that you may have to let out a bit more yardage in shallower water and, conversely, take in some line in deeper water. An exception to that latter rule is in extra-deep trolling, in which case more line may have to be let out to get down to where the fish are at the time.

Teasers

Generations of ocean big-game anglers have included "teasers" in their kits of tricks. These teasers are strictly a trolling device, towed astern with the rigs as an extra attraction-getter. They carry no hooks. Their function is to attract game fishes' attention through their motion in the water, with the aim of teasing the quarry into seizing the rigs. In other words, trolling teasers are only a come-on. By themselves they catch nothing.

Salt-Water Teaser

The simplest teaser is a block of wood, maybe 9 to 12 in., about 2½ or 3 in. square, which is shaped to a crude point on one end to make it a little streamlined. It is painted a bright color—yellow, red, white or in combinations. A hole is drilled through the pointed front end, and a length of nylon rope is attached for towing. There are also store-bought teasers made from tough plastic or wood. Some of these are dressed with bright-colored skirts of synthetic materials or natural feathers, with flashy strips of metal foil for still more attraction. By varying teasers' sizes, shapes and degrees of streamlining, it's possible to create different kinds of teasing actions in the water—zig-zag motion, bouncing, a bubbly wake, and so on.

In the overall ocean-fishing scene many kinds of teasers, some of them outlandish, are devised and improvised. For young bluefin tuna and their cousins the bonitos and albacores, trollers often tow a bucket, a fish basket, or even a discarded automobile tire right at the transom to generate the bubbly, foamy water that those gamesters find so intriguing. I've never seen it, but I hear tell that chromed car-wheel covers have been towed as teasers, and even garbage-can covers. In Nova Scotia, teasers for bluefin tuna consist of what they call daisy chains of small fishes such as herring and mackerel. Theoretically, anyway, many objects could serve as eye-catching teasers. One improvisation that comes to mind is a bunch of shiny teaspoons or tablespoons tied together in a procession and towed. Or how about shiny tin cans?

Teasers' greatest service in big-game angling is notably in marlin fishing. One or two teasers may be used, depending upon the boat's size and the number of rigs out. A teaser can be towed on a line secured to a bitt in the boat's stern. Another arrangement is to rig a second halyard on an outrigger and tow it from that. A teaser rides in the general vicinity of the rigs, and its line should be readily accessible for lengthening or shortening as needed. A big objection to teasers is that they can tangle with fishing lines. Some fishermen won't use them.

Outriggers

It seems safe to state that the vast majority of ocean fishing boats—and not just those out after big game—are equipped with outriggers, their big advantage being that they allow trolling of up to four rigs simultaneously. Four rigs are maximum so far as I'm concerned. But I've known boats that trolled five or six—two from outriggers, the others right from rods. Multiple-rig trolling is good because it provides opportunities to experiment with such vital details as baits, lures and trolling distances astern. Its drawback is that there are chances of lines tangling—depending, of course, on how well separated they can be kept. Apart from an appearance of greed, trolling five or six lines increases anglers' chances appreciably. But pandemonium can break loose when two or three rigs are hit at the same time, as often happens when a school of hungry fish is contacted. I don't even want to think what it could be like if four or five are hit simultaneously, the fish taking off in different directions.

Cockpit Deportment

Speaking of pandemonium, which has been facetiously called a "Chinese fire drill" (I've never been able to find out what a Chinese fire drill is, but it sounds like confusion) brings up a couple of important details of cockpit deportment in big-game fishing.

To begin with, members of the fishing party should decide beforehand the order in which they will occupy the boat's fighting chair and how long each one's turn in the chair will last. It further should be mutually agreed that whoever is in the fighting chair when a fish hits gets to play that fish. It's his or hers for better or for worse until, or if, a popped line do them part. It also should be understood that when a fish is on—hooked—all other lines will be brought out of the water as quickly as possible. This is so that they won't interfere as the hooked fish is fought and brought to boat. It also prevents something that could be very awkward indeed: the hooking of another big fish at the same time. It has happened.

One more thing: If you're fishing with a charter skipper, have an understanding beforehand about the disposal or keeping of the catch. If any misunderstanding can occur, it will probably do so if the catch is marketable (like swordfish, striped bass, and other table species). The odds are high against a squabble, but here and there one does occur.

Drop-Back

In trolling for marine game fishes, especially bill-fishes—marlins and others with long, narrow snouts—an important part of the procedure is a drop-back. This is what its name implies: a dropping back of the rig when a fish shows active interest. It's an important step because it gives the fish a chance to seize your bait or lure. For the whys and hows of drop-backs, see "Trolling," Chapter 4.

When a line is being trolled from an outrigger, the drop-back is automatic. Sometimes—swordfish are a case in point—a drop-back by hand is favored. In this technique someone who must know what he's doing assists the angler in the fighting chair. The assistant stands at the transom, a few neat coils of the angler's line ready to pay out. As the boat starts her pass at the fish, the aide holds the trolled line in his hand. If and when the fish shows an encouraging response to the offering, the assistant lets some line pay out through his fingers, a drop-back that leaves the bait or lure with the fish, with the hope that he'll grab it. Sometimes the rig sinks without further response, and the fish seems to follow it down. There may be action shortly, or nothing. Both the angler and his helper have to be alert, and the suspense can be really exciting.

Leaders and Lines

Leaders are a standard component of terminal tackle (all parts of the outfit beyond the line's far end: hooks, hardware such as swivels, lures, etc.) in big-game angling. Some regulars still rig wire-cable leaders after the heaviest big game because they're tremendously strong. In my opinion, they're unnecessarily strong, since any combination of line and leader is only as strong as its weaker component, which is usually the line. Over the years cable leaders have been replaced by wire, since cable is bulky and hard to handle. Wire leaders, in turn, have been replaced to a degree in recent years by heavy monofilament in instances where metal leaders are not a necessity. Monofilament is easier to handle than wire, which has an inherent stiffness and can also kink.

Conditions that suggest or demand wire leaders include 1) fishes with rough scales or skin, such as sharks, 2) possible abrasions caused by contact with the filelike roughness of 'billFish's jaw' elongated upper jaw (these fishes can get a leader wrapped around their bill, called bill-wrapping), 3) possible fatal abrasion of ordinary leader material against the boat's bottom when the fish is brought alongside for gaffing, and 4) sharp teeth and knifelike gill covers.

Record-minded fishermen must keep in mind that the IGFA limits leader lengths. See IGFA note at end of chapter.

Another common procedure in big-game fishing is to double the line (a swivel or snap swivel already on it) for so many feet, tying it every 18 to 24 in. or so with dental floss or light fishing line to facilitate its passage through rod guides. Doubling the line does provide extra strength, but only when there are at least a few turns on the reel; otherwise the line has only single-line strength. A double line can be helpful when an obstreperous fish is brought right alongside the boat and some added line strength may be needed.

NOTE: IGFA rules also limit the length of a double line. See the IFGA note at end of chapter.

Fishing at Anchor

Big-game fishing at anchor can be productive, but chumming is a must. Big-game fishes generally are loners and widely scattered (which is why they have lived long enough to become big game); and without chum to draw them to a boat's vicinity the chances of contacts are very slim. Even with chum, still-fishing isn't one of the more productive methods. It does save fuel, though.

A potential danger in big-game fishing at anchor is that a large, very muscular opponent will become uncontrollable and rush away on a series of long runs that threaten to strip the reel of line. It happens. There are only two alternatives: be prepared to lose the fish or, if you can get the boat's anchor up in time, take off after the fish, cranking madly, to get line back on your reel. Atlantic Coast giant bluefin tuna boats have an answer to this problem. At the upper end of their anchor line is a buoy, to which the boat ties up until a giant tuna is hooked, whereupon the boat is easily released from the buoy to give her mobility in fighting the big fish. She can pick up the buoy afterward.

A good compromise between still-fishing and trolling is drifting, with chum. It covers territory as trolling does, but without consuming fuel, and there's already mobility as needed when and if a fish hits.

Tackle

A digest of big-game tackle, with notes on baits and lures:

Rods

As among most salt-water rods today, the great number of big-game sticks are of fiberglass—strong, tough durable. In general, rods designed expressly for big-game fishing are characterized by a somewhat shorter but noticeably stouter tip section, with more spine, or backbone, than other rods wielded in boat fishing. Further, they're outfitted throughout with roller guides instead of the common ring type, to assure a smooth flowing of line out and back, with minimum wear on line and guides, in long-winded battles. Two grips, one on each side of the reel, are also a characteristic. Also, and very important, there is a double-locking reel seat to assure that the reel won't work loose in combat.

The caliber of rods wielded in big-game fishing —we're talking about quarry weighing at least 500 lbs., remember—ranges from about the 50-lb. class, considered light for the real heavyweights, through 80-lb. gear to the extra-heavy 130-lb.-line equipment. A choice is up to the angler, based on his or her search for angling thrills and appraisal of their ability.

Reels

They're of the revolving-spool or conventional type, matched to the caliber of the rods on which they're mounted, which means they must have suitably sturdy gears, a good drag system, and a proper spool capacity. (See "Tackle & Acessories," Chapter 1 for details of spool capacities and other reel features.) Strong all-metal spools are an important feature. Synthetic line wound back tightly on a reel is capable of exerting a pressure great enough to fracture a plastic spool. And these reels should be corrosion-proof inside and out.

Gauged to rods and line strengths and lengths needed, conventional big-game reels range from a 10/0 to a 12/0 for 80- and 130-lb.-test lines. For 50-lb. lines you might see a 9/0. For a lot of 130-lb. line you will see a 12/0 from time to time, but it seems to me that they're gradually fading from the scene, or at least are less numerous than they once were.

Another feature of big-game reels is a means of attachment, incorporated in the reels' end plates, to a harness that fits across the angler's back to enable him to put his back into a fight and take some of the strain off his arms. This harness is snapped onto the reel.

Lines

They're variously of the braided and monofilament types, according to individuals' choices. Nowadays they're virtually all synthetics, nylon and Dacron. In big-game action their range of strength is from 50-lb. test through 130-lb. test, the maximum allowed by the IGFA in record contention. Monofilament is available in greater strengths than 130-lb. test, and as such may be used as leaders with the heaviest lines when wire leaders are not required. IGFA allows monofilament stronger than 130-lb. test to be used as leaders only.

NOTE: IGFA requires that a sample of the line on which the fish was caught accompany an application for a world record, and tests that sample. It's very important, therefore, that a line test out at the strength stated on its spool and not over that. Better that it test under than over if it must go one way or the other.

Hooks

Big-game regulars develop personal preferences in hook patterns. Their two greatest criteria for good big-game hooks are those for fishhooks in general: good penetration and dependable holding ability once it penetrates. Mustad patterns are widely rigged in big-game theaters. Design names often noted include O'Shaughnessy, Martu, Sobey and Pfleuger-Sobey. Sizes range from about 9/0 up to 16/0 and sometimes to 20/0, according to the species and expected sizes of the finned game sought.

Rigs, Baits, and Lures

There's really only one basic big-game rig: a snap swivel on the end of the line, which may or may

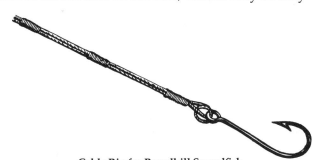

Cable Rig for Broadbill Swordfish

not be doubled, to facilitate changes of rigs; a leader; and the rig, which may be a hook for a natural bait or for some kind of artificial. Dozens of variations—different leader lengths, a fixed or swinging hook, the number of hooks, choice of a lure, etc.—are possible to suit different situations.

Considering the species and methods involved, there's probably more fishing for the real heavyweights with natural baits than with artificials. Dozens of kinds of fishes are used, alive and dead, whole or in chunks, or as flapping fillets or waving strips. This is only a sampling: mackerels, flying fish, mullet, herring, butterfish, balao (ballyhoo), bonitos, northern whiting and eels. Whole squids are a good bait, alone with tentacles fluttering astern or in combination with a piece of fish.

Natural baits are rigged in big-game trolling, fishing at anchor, and drifting. Artificials are primarily for trolling. Those rigged for marlins include realistic plastic squids, fake eels, and large versions of the so-called Hawaiian lures and the pluglike Kona Head lures used so successfully in the Pacific.

Have you ever wondered how it's possible to conquer one of those giant fishes going 800, 1,000 lbs. or more on line rated at 130-lb. test? It's possible because at no time during the contest does the fisherman let the *force* being exerted on the line by the tug-o'-war between him and his opponent exceed 130 lbs. To prevent it he relies on a sense of feel that he develops with experience. He lets his fish run when he knows that he can't stop the rush anyway, carefully feeling for certain signs—a slowing of the fish's run, a pause here and there—that tell him that his opponent is tiring and that make him alert to chances of cranking line back on the reel safely without exerting enough stress to risk breaking the line. This seesaw action, this give-and-take of line, adds up to what constitutes skill in playing or fighting a fish.

A big-game fish's weight in itself could break the line if the fish simply lets himself sink. Fortunately, the heavyweights don't realize this, and much of their bulk is supported by buoyancy, so the angler doesn't get its full effect. Knowing when to yield line as an opponent demands it becomes extremely important—vital—in successfully fighting that fish. Be assured, the heavyweights are so powerful as to make a strong man and heavy-duty tackle look weak by comparison, and there would be no holding the fish. Dynamometer tests of the pulls of certain sharks dramatically show the potential power of big-game fishes. A 10-ft. hammerhead, from a standing start, registered an initial pull of 1,500 lbs. Given a running start of 50 to 60 ft., an adult silky shark weighing no more than about 350 lbs. broke a new 12-thread manila rope testing at about 1,350 lbs. Large white sharks reportedly have broken chain with a breaking strength of 3,800 lbs. And giant bluefin tuna may be even stronger, pound for pound.

Shark Fishing

There have always been some anglers who seek sharks for the sport of tangling with them. But not until the 1950s did the activity really begin to find a place for itself as a part of sport fishing. Shark fishing now is an established part of the big-game angling scene. In testimony to this are the IGFA's recognition of several species as suitable candidates for world record honors, and the increasing numbers of shark-fishing tournaments.

Sharks provide a good taste of big-game fishing, with considerably greater chances of success than in searches for blue-chip species such as marlins,

sailfish and swordfish. Because of that, because of a widespread profusion of opportunities, and because a professional skipper-guide is not required (although helpful), it's considerably less expensive.

Sharks can be sport-caught by four hook-and-line methods. First I'll mention three of them. The fourth is the best technique. I'll save it until last because I'm going to concentrate on it.

Techniques

1. Surf casting. This is uncommon, but it's done in some parts of the world. It requires certain ideal conditions. For any chances of real shark fishing, a beach should slope very steeply—or form a drop-off—into fairly deep water. Even in these locales, conditions must be such as to attract food that will draw sharks in the first place. A jetty extending into fairly deep ocean water or alongside a deep channel would be more likely to produce than a surfside beach. In Durban, South Africa, I met members of a club devoted exclusively to surf casting for sharks where they catch white sharks and other species up to 1,200 lbs. It's a sport only for the rugged and nimble-footed. Hospitalization insurance is a worthwhile accessory. As you would surmise, surf fishing for sharks of any size, whether from a beach or a jetty, calls for stout tackle and stamina.

2. Still-fishing. Coupled with chumming—a must—this will produce; but unless you happen on an area that is well populated with sharks at the time, chances of success are appreciably less than in technique No. 4. The same chum and baits can be employed in both methods.

3. Casting from boats. This is reserved for experienced light-tackle addicts and is practical only when targets are sighted at or near the surface. Blue sharks are one species commonly seen in the uppermost levels; makos are spotted occasionally. Most sharks travel deeper and would require chum to draw them within casting range. The limitations necessarily imposed by lighter gear make it a specialized activity. Sharks up into the 200-lb. class have been nailed on medium spinning tackle. Salt-water fly-fishermen have made conquests too. Two catches, 117½ lbs. (10-lb. tippet class) and 272 lbs. (12-lb. tippet category), both Florida products, were recorded years ago. The odds against an angler bringing a shark to gaff on such lighter-caliber equipment are high.

At this point it should be mentioned that trolling is not a standard sharking procedure. By and large, it's not too effective. Paradoxically, sharks are active predators and can swim like the dickens; yet they seldom respond to trolled bait. I can recall only two instances when sharks smacked trolled lures. Both were makos, and the artificials were red and white Jap feathers set out for tuna. A few other species—the Pacific Coast's salmon shark is one—have been reported as accepting slowly trolled artificials from time to time. The point is, though, that blind trolling isn't dependable.

Sharks hunt primarily by scent. As for natural baits, perhaps they're moving too fast under average trolling conditions for sharks to catch the scent. Further, sharks' eyesight is considered poor in distance vision. Perhaps very slow trolling, with some dribbling of chum astern, would get results. Good opportunity for experimentation there.

4. Drift-chumming. Now we come to technique No. 4, most effective of all: drifting and chumming. It can be used for any species of shark anywhere. Many of the species sought are essentially loners, traveling in small groups, and may be widely scattered. Any ocean is a big place, and how is a fisherman going to be apprised of where the sharks are? The angler has to find out for himself, and drift-chumming is the best way. This method covers more territory than fishing at anchor, imparts attractive motion to bait, yet does it more slowly than trolling; and most important, it appeals to sharks' extraordinarily keen olfactory sense. Further, in the technique I'll detail for you there's also vertical coverage of different planes, near-bottom to near-surface, at which sharks are likely to be cruising.

At this point a couple of tips should be injected. Locate one of the steep drop-off shelves, where sharks often prowl, with a chart and depth sounder, then drift-chum on a zigzag course along its edge. Also—*mark this*—sharks are night feeders. Theoretically, almost any patch of open ocean, inshore—except in real shallows—and offshore, constitutes territory with potential. A chum line will tell you how well you guessed. You can try an area on speculation, but give it a chance to produce, then move on to another if it fails. Once in a while, en route offshore, you may sight a shark loafing at the top. If the fish meets with your approval, start chumming and get a baited rig over. You have a fair chance of a hookup. Later, if necessary, you can slice fillets off that fish for bait for other sharks.

Your all-important line of communication is the chum. With it you can reach a wanderer way off yonder, maybe the only one in that particular area. Without chum you won't have a prayer in most instances. A very good shark chum is the mushy, oily, bloody pulp of ground-up menhaden or mossbunkers. (See "Chumming," Chapter 6.) Sharks find this smelly stuff mouth-watering. Lacking ground 'bunkers, you can substitute almost any species, even trash fishes discarded by commercial netters. It must be ground into a pulp for distribution. Ground-up animal flesh—whale meat, for instance—and blood are also attractors, but don't use either for chum if you're record-minded. IGFA rules forbid it.

The purpose of a chum line is to lure customers to waiting hooks. For this reason it's imperative that any chum line not be interrupted. Just a small gap will defeat its objective. A chum line should be started as soon as a prospective area is reached, the boat with her engine off and drifting. If you're lucky, response will come within minutes. What's more likely, it will take a while before the handout tickles the nostrils of a possible customer. It may not come at all in that particular area. If there are no sharks in the vicinity, nothing in the world is going to work. A chum line should be given at least an hour in which to produce before being abandoned. If it fails, move on. Often it pays to move farther offshore rather than inshore.

Three rigs are fished simultaneously in drift-chumming. But before we get into those we need to clarify the tackle situation. A lion's share of credit for development of shark fishing as a sport goes to a Montauk, N.Y., charter skipper named Frank Mundus.* The finer points of drift-chumming are the results of his astute observations and continuous experimentation. The effectiveness of his ideas are attested to by the fact that more than a dozen IGFA world records have been set on his boat *Cricket II*. Additionally, efforts by Frank and his charter clients probably contributed to IGFA recognition of certain species of sharks as worthy of world record honors. Part of Frank's refinement of shark fishing was a different grading of tackle. This was essential because medium or heavy gear for other gamesters is too light for sharks. He set up this general calibration: (1) Light: lines and rods in classes over 20-lb. test to 40- and 45-lb. test; (2) medium: over 45-lb. test through 60-lb.; (3) heavy: over 60- to 80-lb. test; and (4) extra-heavy: over 80- to 130-lb. test or stronger. Frank has an ultra-light classification too. This takes in light to medium conventional spinning tackle, as well as salt-water fly-fishing equipment. Weapons this light are not practical in shark angling. They're only for crackerjacks, seekers of extra thrills, and anglers willing to risk lost fish.

* In case you are interested, Captain Mundus and I collaborated on a book devoted to shark fishing. The title is *Sportfishing for Sharks;* Macmillan, New York.

Standard Shark Rig

The standard shark rig consists of a single hook on a wire leader. The connection between leader and line can be made through a two-loop barrel swivel of suitable strength, but even better is a snap swivel on the line to facilitate the fast changing of

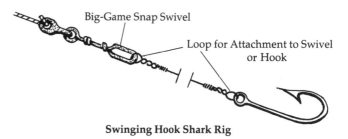

Swinging Hook Shark Rig

baited rigs and for shifting a rig to a heavier or lighter outfit if required. All the well-known hook patterns serve. Captain Mundus favors a Martu because of its good penetrating power. Hook sizes are gauged more to sizes of the baits than to those of the fish: 10/0 to 14/0 is an average range. They can be had in double and triple strengths. A wire leader is a must, not only because of sharks' cutting fangs but also because of their sandpaper hides, which fray ordinary line on contact. Cable leaders are still rigged in some quarters, notably for the largest sharks, but leaders this heavy are not needed. Besides, sharks can get a cable between the cutting teeth on the sides of their jaws and cut it strand by strand, either severing it or weakening it so that it breaks later. It isn't necessary to go to extra-heavy wire. After all, the strength of a line-leader combination is that of its weaker component; and the heavier a wire leader, the harder it is to handle. Extra-heavy wire doesn't provide that much more protection against teeth and skin. However, shark leaders take some of their worst beatings when the monsters are brought alongside for gaffing. Here is where some extra strength is beneficial. A safe range is from No. 9 (104-lb. test in stainless, 114 in piano wire) to No. 12 (174-lb. in stainless, 198 in piano). For the largest battlers some fishermen rig No. 15, which tests out at 240 lbs. in stainless, 288 in piano wire. Lighter wire than No. 9 also is rigged—with lighter tackle—but it can be a calculated risk. IGFA regulations limit lengths of leaders, but not their materials or strengths. (Similar restrictions apply to the doubling of line at the leader.) A practical range in shark angling is 15 to 18 ft. It isn't wise to go less than 15 because some sharks roll up in the leader. If their girth is big enough, a few turns will bring the line in contact with their skin. A 15-ft.

leader is a good all-round length; an 18-footer adds a measure of protection in case of rolling. It would be even safer to go longer than that, but it's a dubious advantage. All wire tends to kink; the more you rig, the greater the chances of kinks that weaken, even break, leaders under strain. Longer wire also becomes increasingly more awkward to handle when sharks are brought to boat.

Hooks are rigged in two main ways:
1. Fixed hook. A needle-eye type is used. In this rig the end of the wire leader is fed through the eye, then wound around the shank in two tight turns—to make it fixed or stiff—before being brought through the eye again for the twist to secure it. About 3 to 4 in. of wire should be left after the final twist. This is thrust through the bait, then twisted on the leader to secure it. A fixed- or stiff-hook rig is used for dead baits.
2. Swinging hook. A ring-eye type is used. This is primarily for live baits to give them more freedom, but it can be used for dead baits as well. The important difference between this and a stiff-hook rig is that the two turns around the hook shank are omitted, along with the extra couple of inches of wire to pin the bait.

In both Nos. 1 and 2, the attachment of hook to leader is accomplished by 8 or 10 loose twists, crossing each other evenly in an X—the so-called bailing wire twists—next to the hook, followed by six to eight tight twists. The tight turns are made farther away from the hook because under great tension they tighten like a hangman's noose, possibly cutting themselves.

Baits

There's a rather wide choice of live baits. Among them are mackerel, eels, squid and northern whiting. Northern whiting have been found to be particularly good. These baits also can be used dead. The fact is, that any small fishes occurring in abundance in a region are potential shark bait, alive or dead.

Another shark come-on is a fillet bait. Fillets can be cut from the sides of tuna and other species too large to use whole or the sides of sharks already caught. If the fishes have bright white or silvery sides, cut the fillets from there. If shark meat is used, skin each fillet so that the white meat is fully exposed as an eye-catcher. An effective fillet bait is roughly triangular. The hook is embedded in the broad end, leaving the triangle's pointed end to trail. Slicing that point up the middle for about two inches will create two fluttering tails for added action.

As mentioned earlier, three rigs, at least one with a live bait, provide the best coverage: (1) Topmost rig: This is kept at an upper level by a block of cork—3 in. long by 2 wide and 2 thick or thereabouts—on the line about 25 or 30 ft. above the connection of line and leader. (2) Middle rig: This also carries a float, adjusted so that the rig will ride approximately midway between rig No. 1 and the bottom. Adjustment will be according to water depth, but the float will be attached farther up the line than No. 1's. (3) Bottom rig: No float for this one, because the boat's drift and the current will bring it up off the sea floor.

Having three rigs out offers the advantage of being able to experiment with different baits and tackle of different calibers. Generally speaking, the largest bait should go on the bottom rig, which also should have the heaviest tackle. Often the biggest sharks are down deep. Brakes on all three reels are set for striking drag—only enough to set the hook, then tightened later when necessary. And all three reels are left in free spool, with their clickers on. The clicker prevents line from peeling off as the boat drifts and also provides audible warning of activity at the bait. An observer topside on the bridge can help by watching for sharks moving in along the chum line.

Approaches to Baits

I can't repeat too often that sharks' approaches to baits differ among species and individuals. Their hunger—or lack of it—is a big factor. Some are sneaky. Others are aggressive and with some there is toying with the bait. There's this broad rule: The slower the pickup of the bait, the slower the striking of the shark. Conversly, on a fast pickup, strike fast. ("Striking" means setting the hook.)

Often a shark can be seen moving in along a chum line toward the topmost rig. This calls for close watching. He may be more interested in the float than the bait, in which case the float should be jettisoned before the shark makes a pass at it. Hits on the middle and bottom rigs are not seen, so their lines should be monitored constantly.

Once a shark is on, the other rigs should be reeled in at once lest one of them be seized too. Battling two sharks simultaneously could be fatal to one or both catches.

Their battle plans differ. Some streak away on long power surges, then settle down to dogged resistance and shorter runs. Few punctuate their runs with any leaps. Some bore deep. Others run wide of the boat in an arc, which necessitates maneuvering the craft to keep the fisherman pointed at his opponent. Many sharks stay out of sight throughout the battle. Some appear at the surface at intervals, and these often are the tricksters that complicate matters by rolling up in the leader. Others go into a rolling act when brought alongside the boat. Another tactic is to change direction and torpedo underneath the boat to the other side. If the boat can't be maneuvered quickly enough, the angler may have to walk his line around her transom, holding his outfit so that its line clears abrading surfaces.

Reel drags are tightened and loosened as needed. Don't try to let up on the brake during long runs or a power surge. So long as it isn't obviously too loose, leave it alone until the fish slows. During long-winded power drives you may have to loosen the drag a little, if anything. And remember this: A brake effect increases as more line leaves a reel. This may also necessitate easing off on a drag during very long runs.

Plenty of line is needed. Properly fill each reel to its capacity.

Final Capture

Final capture consists of these steps:
1. "Wiring-up." Someone seizes the wire leader *with gloves* when it breaks surface. If the shark gets wild, let go until he quiets down. *Caution: Don't let leader get wound around finger on hand!*
2. Gaffing. A flying gaff, its line already secured to a cleat or bitt, is sunk into the back close to the dorsal fin. Don't plant it too far forward or you may find the shark in the boat with you. The tail is then lifted with a straight gaff and a tail rope—a noose on about 10 to 15 ft. of ¼- or ⅜-in. rope—slipped over it. Keeping the tail out of water helps to slow down a shark.
3. Moving to the gin pole. With the shark quieted down, the beast is walked with the gaff and tail ropes to the gin pole and hoisted tail first out of water. A few turns of a belly rope keep the fish

secure and prevent it from threshing about and maybe knocking out a cabin window or biting someone.

Gin poles have their load limits. There must be sufficient clearance for the captured fish to be suspended clear of the water. Leaving a shark partly submerged and bleeding invites other sharks to a free lunch. If a shark cannot be hoisted on a gin pole, the alternative is to secure it by a tail rope as a tow. The boat should then head for port and call it a day because that fish is going to be in the way. In any event, no shark of any species or any size should be brought into a boat's cockpit while still alive; it could mean havoc, injury to someone, and possibly damaged equipment. Sharks can really throw their weight around. The only safe shark is a dead one. Hanging them on a gin pole will do it, although there are some that will still be alive two or three hours later. Towing them backward, which literally drowns them, works sometimes but isn't reliable. Besides, who wants to lose maybe an hour or more towing a shark around?

Be particularly careful about keeping spectators, especially children, away from any sharks that show a trace of life, Unless the jaws are securely propped open, keep all hands, including your own, out of a shark's mouth on the dock. There can be post-mortem nerve reactions causing the jaws to close. If a hook is that important, it can be retrieved in due time.

Makos are the most desirable species because they're among the fastest, most active, hardest-fighting sharks, and about three out of five add thrills by aerial acrobatics. Further, makos attain respectable bulk, all of it muscle. Weights go to 300–400 lbs. on the Atlantic Coast, up to 800 and more on the Pacific. But many other species await. Here's a sampling: (1) duskies, 250 to 500-plus; (2) blues, to about 150 average, known up to 300 lbs.; (3) tigers, up to 1,000 lbs. and more; (4) porbeagles to 300 lbs. Added to those are many others you could want to handle in packages from under 100 lbs. to over half a ton.

IGFA

Those who aspire to records must become familiar with the rules and regulations of the International Game Fish Association (IGFA), the official arbiter and keeper of salt- and fresh-world records. In addition to rules already mentioned, IGFA also has rules for rigging of hooks, and it has been prohibiting *wire lines*. Best way to keep up is to join. Dues are modest and will bring you helpful literature. Write to IGFA, 3000 East Las Olas Blvd., Fort Lauderdale, Fla., 33316.

12. <u>Ice Fishing</u>

Dunking rigs through holes in the ice has its own brand of magnetism, compounded of several things. It's good sport—gets fish for the table too—and a healthful activity that draws its followers out into the sun and air at a time of year when they otherwise would be cooped up. For many anglers it bridges a long gap between regular seasons, giving restless rod-'n'-reelers some action and helping to lessen winter's tedium. A less obvious attraction, but a strong one nonetheless, is its peculiar challenge. It's more of a battle with nature than open-water fishing, with the ice adding suspense and an aura of mystery. And don't overlook this: It's a chance to walk on water, a feat not possible for mere mortals at other times and therefore strangely appealing.

There are details on the debit side too.

Weather, for openers. Midwinter temperatures drop real low on ice-fishing lakes, and with a wind's chill factor they become downright polar. There can be accessibility problems posed by snow, especially in more remote areas. And there's a little work in preparation for action, like clearing snow from the surface and making a hole through which to fish. Sweeping away snow is minor. The work comes in chopping or boring a hole.

But these aren't big obstacles, with the exception of drift-blocked accessibility. Ice anglers learn how to dress to keep from freezing to death. Chopping or boring through the ice is accepted as an inescapable part of the game. Besides, there's equipment to facilitate the chore. We'll get to it later. What's more, you can add comfort—even a note of roughing-it luxury. Many veterans do their ice fishing in style in small portable huts that shelter them from bitter winds.

Ice fishing continues to gain in popularity throughout the northern U.S. It has been a major winter sport in the Midwest for decades, and it draws a large quota of followers in New England. Common on large Midwestern lakes are regular little villages of ice fishing shanties housing the faithful. Some are even laid out with "streets"— *named* streets, no less. In recent years the sport has fanned out to include more and more Western lakes, with increasing numbers of participants in the higher-country regions of Nevada, California and the Pacific Northwest.

Did you ask about the species caught? Ice angling accounts for many of the fishes hooked in open water: largemouth bass, northern pike, lake trout, yellow perch, walleyes, kokanee salmon, pickerel, crappies, rainbow trout, saugers, landlocked salmon, brook trout, smelt, bluegills and other panfishes, still others—all dependent upon regions, of course. *Note this:* It's important to check locally on any regulations governing species that can be legally taken by ice fishing in any given state, as well as on places and acceptable equipment. This also is an opportunity to inquire about areas with the most promise.

Ice fishing has two basic divisions. One involves the use of a gadget known as a tipup or tilt. The other is a form of jigging. Each has its variation from region to region or even within the same region. As in other kinds of angling, participants develop their own ideas and refinements. But the sport is built upon those two basic forms, with selection predicated upon species sought and personal preference. Equipment for both methods is simple and inexpensive.

Jigging

This technique is ordinarily employed for species an angler can expect to encounter in reasonable numbers, like bluegills, yellow perch, smelt and other panfishes. Accordingly, it is a common procedure to probe different places until a school, or at least a group, of fish is found. It means work, since a hole must be cut at each spot tried, but it can be rewarded by good catches. True to its name, the method consists of jigging a rig up and down through a span of inches, or perhaps a couple of feet, to impart attractive action to a bait or lure. As in jigging in general, some experimentation as regards depths may be required. For measuring depths, regulars carry a sinker-weighted length of twine marked at intervals.

Conventional-type outfits are wielded in ice fishing, but the rods are short so that the angler can be close to the hole. More traditionally the badge of a jigging regular is a very inexpensive device known as a jigstick. This is tackle reduced to its simplest form outside of a hand line. A jigstick is a short, glorified piece of wood. It has a handle for comfortable gripping, and the line passes through a simple guide at its outermost end. Line is stored by winding it between two pegs—the "reel." Knowing how much line is in each loop, the user can lower his rig to a desired depth simply by counting the turns as line leaves. Some jigsticks have a compartment in the handle for extra hooks and sinkers.

Since they do not absorb water like linen and are therefore less likely to freeze, modern snythetic lines are a blessing to ice anglers. (At least one manufacturer, Gudebrod Brothers, Philadelphia,

produces lines expressly for ice fishing.) On an average, strengths do not go above 10- or 12-lb. test so long as the diameters aren't too fine to handle in cold weather. Required yardage naturally depends upon depths fished. Hooks are gauged to the baits and sizes of the finned game sought. Those—and baits—rigged for the likes of panfishes must be small. A sinker of suitable weight to take the rig down—fast in deeper-water locations—completes the terminal tackle. Scraping and sandpapering the lead to bring out its brightness adds attraction. Natural baits for panfishes and other little fellows include worms, grubs and small minnows. Pieces, strips and slices of fish also see service. In shallow-water angling for the smaller fishes some regulars tie in a float, or bobber, to signal bites. Flashy artificials and lures known as ice flies are also rigged, but usually in conjunction with some natural bait.

In shallow-water jigging for panfishes such as crappies and bluegills, the ice angler feels for nibbles before trying to set his hook. In deeper-water fishing he doesn't wait for bites but employs the so-called jig-and-snatch technique. This consists of jigging the bait or lure repeatedly, making it dance for eye-catching motion, then suddenly jerking it upward, the objective being to snatch, or hook, a passing fish. Experienced jiggers work fast enough to extract numbers of fish from a school with this procedure. Some speed is necessary because the rig must be lowered again quickly after a fish is unhooked, before the others lose interest and move off. *Tip:* Also to save time and effort, bait in this deeper-water jigging should be tough as well as appealing so that it doesn't have to be replaced frequently. A piece or strip cut from a local species often meets this requirement.

Because of the simplicity and greater portability of their gear, jiggers are more mobile than their tipup brethren. The nature of their method more or less demands it. So they're less able to use a little

shanty for protection against the elements. They usually settle for warm clothing and a portable windbreak.

Tipup or Tilt Fishing

Although he seeks larger game too, a jig angler often looks primarily for quantity, since many of his quarries are small. A tipup fisherman, by contrast, usually is out after larger species such as walleyes, northerns, chain pickerel and, where permitted by law, trout and salmon. He generally sets out a number of tipups or tilts—also in compliance with any state regulations governing their use —in what he thinks are likely locations. Then he sits by, alert to responses, unlike the jig angler, who wanders over the ice to try different spots.

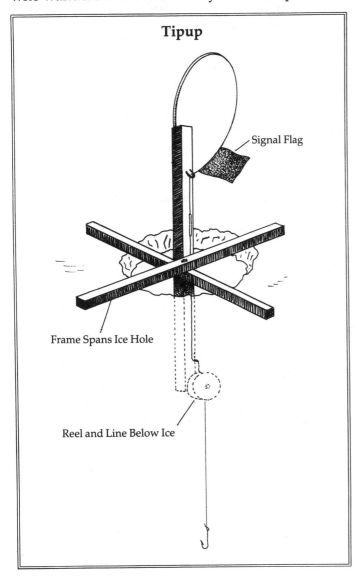

Tipup

Signal Flag

Frame Spans Ice Hole

Reel and Line Below Ice

The tilt fisherman waits for customers to come to him. The jig angler tries to go to the fish. In this respect tipup angling calls for more patience than the other method. It also demands good protection against cold and wind.

Tipups or tilts can be store-bought or homemade. Either way they all share the same basic components and function in the same way: support the line, as would otherwise be accomplished by a rod, store line in reserve for depths and fishes' runs, and signal when a fish hits. A tipup's essential components are a simple base for mooring, a spool to store line, and an arm—carrying a little flag on some models—that is triggered into jerking upward to signal bites.

There are two basic designs. One is the above-ice model. On this the line emerges from the ice hole and goes to the arm-triggering mechanism. The other design has its line spool below the surface, where a hit causes it to turn and activate the signal arm. Both types have their advantages and debits. The above-ice model is more convenient to manage when a fish is hooked. It usually can also be more sensitively adjusted to light bites. A drawback is that in very cold weather there must be frequent checking to see that the hole hasn't frozen and closed around the line. Scooping out slush and thin ice from a hole is a chore with the underwater type too, but since its line doesn't come out through the opening it can't become locked in ice. But this also gives rise to its drawback. The underwater spool has to be lifted from the hole before the line can be grasped, a hand-chilling job. Both kinds of tilts have their advocates.

Every angler has his preference in line—monofilament or whatever. Tipup lines usually are a bit heavier than those in jigging, not so much because of larger or tougher fishes encountered, although that's part of it, but because they're easier to handle with cold-numbed fingers. As in jigging, the yardage on a tilt's spool is according to depths customarily fished. An important thing to remember is to allow enough for a reserve after the rig is set, to handle any runs.

Again the rig is simple. A sinker of suitable weight —only enough to take the rig down, hold it in position, and keep the line taut—is tied to the end of the line. Tipup fishermen carry sinkers in assorted weights to meet varying conditions. Hooks are more or less gauged in size to the baits and the weights of anticipated opponents, and are tied in at various distances above the sinker, according to personal ideas. Using a small snap swivel to make the connection is a good stunt. It facilitates changing hooks and baits when hands are cold. When toothy opponents such as northerns and pickerel are involved, a short wire leader should be interposed just ahead of the hook. It can be fine wire.

Dead-fish baits can be rigged for tipup fishing, but live offerings are superior. Minnows are among the standards. These are gauged approximately to the sizes of the species sought: to about 2 in. long for panfishes and the like, 3 or 4 in. for larger game such as trout and walleyes, and up to 6 in. or so for aggressive predators like pickerel and northerns. Some care must be exercised in selecting hook sizes for live bait so as not to injure or kill it, thereby subtracting a lot of its appeal.

Experimentation with depths is often the order of the day in tilt fishing. A simple lead line—a length of twine, marked every so many feet, and a sinker —first determines the depth in that spot, after which the tipup's line is adjusted so that the rig dangles at the desired level above bottom. It's common practice to arbitrarily start just above bottom, then if no action is forthcoming, try successively higher planes.

Tilt fishermen set up as many outfits as local regulations allow in a pattern they deem effective. Because it takes time to set up and adjust gear, tipup anglers are less mobile than their jigging brethren, and this more stationary procedure can be colder. Wise followers at least have a windbreak of sorts, and a Thermos or two of hot soup. Fancier is one of those little shacks, maybe with a catalytic heater to make things even snugger.

Accessories & Gear

Some means of cutting through ice is an obvious essential. Hatchets, crowbars and axes will do the job. So will a device called a spud, a long-handled implement with a sharp metal end designed for ice chopping. For years a spud was the tool for the job. Like axes, it's effective but spells unnecessary work. Superior is an ice auger, created expressly for drilling a neat hole quickly and with less effort than with a spud. Ice augers are marketed with bits, or cutting ends, in different diameters interchangeable on some models. Often they're collapsible for easier carrying and storing. Most models in use are hand-operated and reasonably priced. There are also power-driven augers—even less work, but considerably more expensive. Another standard item of equipment is a skimmer, which is like a strainer with a long handle, for scooping out slush and any ice forming in a hole. A skimmer is cheap.

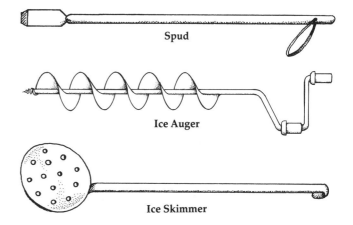

Spud

Ice Auger

Ice Skimmer

An ice angler also requires a bait bucket. A gaff is helpful, and safer than depending upon the line when bringing larger fish out of water. An old piece of cloth, a brush or a sawed-off broom is a refinement for clearing away any snow at the hole site.

This sport often lures its followers some distance from shore, especially on huge lakes, so it becomes important that they have everything they need with them for the day's activity. A priority item is an ample supply of bait, along with a carrier designed to keep minnows alive and lively. In addition to required gear, the check list includes spare hooks and sinkers in different sizes, extra line, plus any terminal tackle items they may use. It can be a cold, time-consuming hike back to get replacements.

Coming in for increased use in ice fishing, where it's a relatively recent arrival, is a self-contained—battery-powered—completely portable flasher-type sounder. It can function on ice just as it can in open water to give depth readings and indicate channels, drop-offs, patches of vegetation, presence of fish, etc. No depth sounder can operate without its transducer, which is the part that transmits and receives the ultrasonic signals by which the instrument functions. Completely portable units take their transducer right along with them.

If the ice is clear—not filled with bubbles or debris—a depth sounder can be used on its surface. Only thing is, to function, its transducer's surface must always be kept wet. This is accomplished by clearing snow for a clean area, then creating a little puddle of a mixture of water and antifreeze at the spot of transducer contact with the ice.

Reading a depth sounder through ice is a little confusing at first, and complicated by small flashes or blips at the zero mark, which are caused by echoes from the rough undersurface of the ice. When ice is filled with bubbles or debris, a hole must be cut through it for the transducer. Some fishermen fashion a simple bracket for holding the transducer at an angle of about 45 ° for fish scanning, but this eliminates bottom signals. And it should be remembered that cold weather affects battery life adversely, so a sounder should be protected against cold as much as possible when not in service.

Transporting gear out on the ice is no great problem. Enthusiasts improvise with assorted little vehicles. Simplest is a sturdy wooden box, with or without crude runners, that has a short length of rope for pulling. There are kids' sleds, along with some homemade sleighs. The going is tricky, but on big lakes with thick enough ice it isn't startling to see automobiles.

Proper clothing is about the most important item on an ice angler's inventory. It must provide protection against wind as well as a plummeting thermometer. Unless they have the haven of a shanty, ice fishermen are often at the mercy of a frigid wind sweeping across a lake; and in tipup fishing there's relatively little moving around.

Thermal underwear is an excellent foundation, on top of which can be a woolen shirt and insulated garments that provide warmth and windproofing without bulk or excessive weight. Protection against wind is particularly important because breezes contribute greatly to the chill factor. Protection of the head, neck and face is also an important consideration. Practical is a parka with a warm, insulated hood; and it's even better if the hood has a drawstring to tighten it around the face. A ski mask is practical for protection of the face. A hat with earflaps is minimum head protection, which drops to zero if the wind sends it skating across the ice at about 20 miles an hour.

Very important: Get the proper footwear. It should be insulated and completely waterproof. Accent the latter. Shoes that are not fully waterproof get wet on the ice from snow, slush or water; and soggy shoes mean the worst kind of cold feet. Best is all-rubber footwear. Suggested are hunters' boots, completely waterproof because of their rubber exterior, warmly lined, and reaching above the ankles. Keeping ankles warm is a comfort detail too. Ideally, shoes should also have skid-minimizing soles.

Also very important: Don't forget eye protection. Get good sunglasses. Glare from ice and snow can be fatiguing, even harmful, to eyes.

Additional protection can be devised. Many veteran ice fishermen build portable windbreaks that can be set up and moved when the wind shifts. More elaborate and comfortable, also much more expensive, is one of those one-room shanties we mentioned earlier. Inside, a fisherman drills his hole and fishes in comfort, snug against wind and foul moods of weather. A portable stove makes it even more comfortable, and a radio adds a touch of luxury. On many lakes where ice fishing is a regular winter event, these shanties can be rented.

Granted, ice fishing isn't for every angler. But the sport has a lot going for it. If you're still skeptical, take a winter swing through the Midwest.

Vital Postcript: It should go without adding that safety must be practiced at all times, with observation, common sense and the advice of experienced local fishermen as guides to what constitutes a safe ice thickness in a given area. And a smart procedure in any case is to *never go ice fishing alone in deserted places.*

13. <u>Popular Fresh-Water Fishes</u>

Some North American species profiled here are caught both in fresh and salt-water in varying degrees.

American Shad

SCIENTIFIC NAME: *Alosa sapidissima.* COMMON NAMES: Atlantic shad, white shad, shad. COLOR: Silvery, with bluish-green back, silver-white underside, with a dusky spot close behind the upper edge of each gill cover. SIZE: They are said to reach lengths up to 30 in., weights up to 12 lbs., among exceptional specimens. Average range, males, is 1½ to 6 lbs.; for females, 3 lbs. to 8. FAMILY: It belongs to the herring tribe, among whose other members are the hickory shad, menhaden and mighty tarpon. DISTRIBUTION: Range is southern Newfoundland (strays) and St. Lawrence River estuary (in numbers) on down to Florida's St. Johns River. A closely related species lives in the Gulf of Mexico. Transplanted in Pacific coast waters many years ago, they range from southern California to Alaska. HABITS: (1) They're anadromous, which is to say they spend most of their lives in salt water but move into fresh-water rivers to spawn. (2) Water temperatures of 50–55 ° F. can trigger spawning runs into rivers in spring and early summer. Fishermen capitalize on these runs, which occur progressively later toward the northern part of their distribution. (3) Shad travel in large schools, a break for rod-'n'-reelers. WHERE CAUGHT: Coastal rivers, from estuaries on inland. HOW CAUGHT: Trolling and casting from boats and shores are the methods. BAITS & LURES: Artificials are small and include fractional-ounce but shiny spoons, bucktails, spinning lures, bright white or yellow jibs, and those created especially for shad fishing. On the Pacific coast, buffs also use

American Shad

pieces of sea worm and small strips of fish. TACKLE: Tackle should be light (6-lb.-test line or lighter), spinning or conventional. Increasing numbers of anglers fly-cast, using wet and dry flies in white, orange and yellow patterns

---

Arctic Char

SCIENTIFIC NAME: *Salvelinus alpinus.* COMMON NAMES: Some of these regional tags are Canadian; others are used by Eskimos: Arctic trout, hardhead, salmon trout, Alpine trout, sea trout. COLOR: Char are chiefly a silver hue during that phase of their life spent at sea. When they enter rivers to breed, their color scheme runs like this: the back becomes bluish, olive-greenish or a brown; sides are pale to fairly gaudy shades of red, red-orange or orange, extending to the belly. Unlike trout relatives, the Arctic char lacks profuse spotting; but some specimens bear vague, blotchlike markings in pink, reddish-orange or cream color. SIZE: The average runs 2 to 8 lbs. Landlocked chars often are dwarfs. In contrast, a giant one upwards of 25 lbs. is occasionally hooked at sea. FAMILY: Ichthyologists group the Arctic char with trouts. This fish is also catalogued as a salmonid, a general label that covers trouts, salmons and their allies. The Arctic char resembles the well-known Dolly Varden trout. DISTRIBUTION: Regions are the circumpolar northern waters of the Northern Hemisphere and include Alaska and northern Canada, Northwest Territories to Newfoundland, Labrador and New Brunswick. HABITS: (1) Arctic chars are anadromous, spending part of their lives at sea and returning to rivers to spawn. Usually in late spring or early summer, adults run downriver to the sea; in summer, many linger in the vicinity of estuaries and river mouths, where they eat ravenously to store nourishment for the cold weather ahead. Some may linger in brackish water. In late summer and autumn the spawning migrations occur—from the sea into estuaries and then upriver. (2) Arctic chars travel in large schools. (3) While at sea and downriver, the natural food of chars consists of little forage fishes such as capelins, sand eels and the like, plus crustaceans. As the fish progress upriver, insects such as caddisflies, etc., become increasingly a more important part of their diet. WHERE CAUGHT: Best fishing is right after they return to the rivers—in mouths, estuaries, lowermost sections. HOW CAUGHT: Casting from shores and boats. BAITS & LURES: Although items of natural food—shrimp, sand eel, etc.—should draw response, most angling is with artificials—small versions of spinners and spoons, along with dry and wet flies. TACKLE: Accent is on light gear, because these are small fish. Spinning tackle of 4- to 6-lb.-test is fine. Fly rods provide even more action.

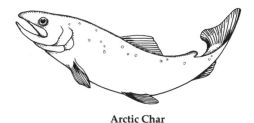

Arctic Char

Atlantic Salmon

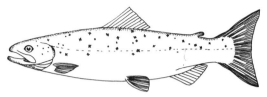

Atlantic Salmon

SCIENTIFIC NAME: *Salmo salar*. COMMON NAMES: Regionally, in eastern Canada and Maine, landlocked salmon, Sebago salmon. Also sea salmon, silver salmon. COLOR: While at sea, the salmon's body displays a dark steel-blue color along the back, brilliant silver below, with numerous black dots and tiny X-like markings on the upper half of the body and head. After a period in fresh water, a nondescript brownish-red, often with large blackish spots, appears on the body. In fresh water the males—ever gaudier of the two sexes among wild creatures—take on splashes of orange or red. SIZE: An overall average is about 10 to 20 lbs. Any above that, say, 40–50 lbs., are increasingly exceptional. They used to be much bigger. Traditionally, Canada's province of Quebec has produced the heftiest on this continent, up into the 70-lb. class. A modern U.S. record, set in Maine, was 28 lbs. 1 oz. Years ago Europe produced some giants: 79 lbs. 2 oz. (Norway), 83 lbs. (England), and what still is the gran'pappy of 'em all, 103 lbs. 2 oz. (Scotland). FAMILY: Salmonidae is the family's scientific name. Under its banner parades a large and distinguished group embracing Pacific salmons (king, coho, etc.) and the trouts (rainbow, brook, etc.). DISTRIBUTION: Range covers the North Atlantic seaboard, including coastal rivers, western Greenland to southern Massachusetts. Atlantic salmon once inhabited every large river to the sea from Canada's Maritime Provinces to Cape Cod. But industrialization—notably dams that blocked spawning runs—plus pollution, along with over-exploitation by commercial fishermen, have brought the fish to the status of an endangered species. Curtailing of commercial operations and cooperative action by conservationist groups, aquatic biologists and government agencies in the U.S. and Canada appear to have saved the Atlantic salmon from extinction. But it will be a long time before they are as numerous as they once were. HABITS: (1) While still young, Atlantics leave their natal rivers to spend about one to three years at sea, gluttonizing (I think I coined a word) and growing rapidly. (2) They're voracious predators and gorge themselves with herring, smelts, capelins, small mackerel, young haddock, sand launce, flatfishes (soles, etc.), little sculpins and shrimp. (3) For anglers, Atlantic salmon are at their best—plump, sassy and at peak vigor—when they enter rivers on spawning runs, fresh from the sea. These runs' starting times vary, from just before early spring to as late as October. Anglers should check locally beforehand. (4) Their spawning journeys are legendary, taking them upriver 100 miles or more when no dams interfere. At sea they wander varying distances from their home river. Many stay within a radius of up to 50 miles, but tagging experiments have revealed that stragglers may wander more than 500 miles. All return to their natal rivers to spawn. WHERE CAUGHT: Estuaries and coastal rivers. HOW CAUGHT: Walking the riverside, wading streams, looking for salmon pools, and from canoes and other little craft. Traditionally there's only one way to fish for Atlantic salmon: with fly tackle. BAITS & LURES: Prime attractors, because of fly-fishing's popularity, are dry and wet flies in a wide range of patterns and sizes. Whenever possible, anglers should inquire locally beforehand. Atlantic salmon are also caught on live baits, as well as on plugs, spoons and other artificials, but there may be regulations against some of these in certain areas. TACKLE: Fly tackle is urged for supreme sport, but anglers are advised that the caliber can vary between U.S. and Canadian areas.

Black Bullhead

SCIENTIFIC NAME: *Ictalurus melas.* COMMON NAMES: Yellow-belly bullhead, stinger, bullhead, and horned pout. COLOR: The body color, probably influenced by environment, is variously black or a darkish olive or yellowish-green along the back, with off-white or yellowish sides and a white or yellow ventral surface. The dorsal fin is black. Usually there's no mottling. SIZE: One of the smallest members of the catfish family, with lengths in inches and weights under a pound. A 2-pounder is a big one. Despite their size, though, black bullheads are popular panfish, especially among small-fry rod-'n'-reelers. FAMILY: As I've just noted, the catfish clan, Ictaluridae. Among numerous relatives: brown bullhead, white catfish, yellow bullhead, flathead catfish, channel cat. DISTRIBUTION: From New York throughout the Midwest to North Dakota, Colorado and Wyoming, southward to Texas and including Kansas, Louisiana and Alabama. WHERE CAUGHT & HABITS: (1) Black bullheads are familiar residents of ponds, reservoirs, small lakes and slow-flowing streams, where they favor muddy bottoms. (2) They generally prefer shallow, moderately warm, muddy or silty water to clear, cooler, deeper places. (3) Like other catfishes, they have chin barbels, called whiskers, which are feelers to help them locate food on the bottom. (4) They're omnivorous eaters, consuming insects and their larvae, small fishes, young crayfish, other fishes' eggs, worms, small crustaceans and mollusks. That menu offers a wide choice of baits. (5) They feed most actively at night—a cue to fishermen. HOW CAUGHT: Simple one-hook bottom fishing. BAITS & LURES: Almost any item of their natural food should do; and if it has a strong scent for murky and dark water, so much the better. TACKLE: Lightest possible gear.

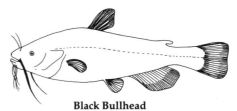

Black Bullhead

Blue Catfish

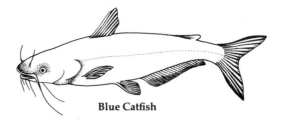

Blue Catfish

SCIENTIFIC NAME: *Ictalurus furcatus*. COMMON NAMES: Blue cat, great blue cat, chucklehead cat, forktail cat. COLOR: Grayish blue or pale blue is the body color above, with silvery reflections. Lower down on the sides this color gets even lighter, fading to a white or silver-white on the belly. The blue cat closely resembles his cousin the channel catfish, a similarity heightened by a bluish color phase among some specimens of the latter. The black spots on the channel cat's body, absent on the blue cat's, are a means of separating them. SIZE: Weights to 30 lbs. are quite common. An angling record stood at 97 lbs., a 4-ft. 9-in. rod-bender from the Missouri River in South Dakota. Blue catfish are known to reach 100 lbs. FAMILY: The catfishes, Ictaluridae, a family that also includes the bullheads. DISTRIBUTION: Ohio, through Minnesota to South Dakota, then southward to Texas, the Rio Grande River, and northern Mexico. The species' principal habitat is the far-flung Mississippi River system, including its mightiest tributary, the Missouri. Blue cats also have been introduced into coastal rivers on the U.S. eastern seaboard. HABITS & WHERE CAUGHT: (1) Blue cats are most at home in large rivers and spacious impoundments or reservoirs, where they scout for food over sandy, pebble or gravel, and rocky bottoms. (2) Unlike other catfishes that thrive in sluggish and muddy waters, blue cats prefer clearer, moving rivers. (3) Like other catfishes, they're omnivorous feeders, with a lusty appetite. Small fishes of many kinds, laced with crayfish and other tidbits, make up their diet. Also like other cats, they have sensory appendages, or barbels, on their chin to help locate food on the bottom. HOW CAUGHT: Fishing from shore in deeper water and from boats. Then there's that unique method called "jugging," long practiced in the South and Southwest to catch the larger members of the catfish family. Simplified, it consists of suspending a baited rig at the desired depth by means of a jug of some sort, perhaps one of those plastic containers that household bleach comes in. That outfit is set adrift and the fisherman follows in a boat until a catfish grabs the hook, whereupon the angler hauls his fish in as on a hand line. A refinement is to attach the jug in such a way that it can be replaced quickly by a rod and reel right after the cat is hooked, giving the fisherman the greater sport of battling the fish with tackle. TACKLE: Type and caliber can be its wielder's choice—short of fly rods and other ultra-light equipment. What must be kept in mind is that blue catfish are strong fighters and attain respectable sizes. Too, there may be river currents to put further strain on the tackle.

Bluegill

SCIENTIFIC NAME: *Lepomis macrochirus*. COMMON NAMES: Sun perch, bream (often pronounced "brim"), blue sunfish, copper-belly, copperhead. COLOR: Basically body color is a blue, an olive, or a greenish-blue on the back, fading to a lighter shade below. There are variations. Some individuals have orange or a yellow color on their sides, with splashes of orange or reddish orange on the underside's forward section. Some bluegills are marked on the sides with dark vertical bars of the same color as the back. SIZE: Many are under a foot in length. Any over 12 in. are a good size. Maximum is about 14–16. Weights go up to 4 and a fraction lbs. in exceptional fish. FAMILY: Bluegills belong to the fresh-water sunfish tribe, Centrarchidae. DISTRIBUTION: Their natural range is from southern Canada—Ontario and Quebec—and Lake Champlain westward through the Great Lakes region to Minnesota, southward through a stretch from Arkansas to Georgia, and on to the Gulf states and northern Mexico. The species was implanted in California and Washington State waters in the late 1800s. Since then, their adaptability and desirability as a pond fish have led to their introduction into thousands of ponds and small lakes throughout many other states. Bluegills are considered their family's most widely distributed representatives in the U.S. They are also among the best known and most widely sought fresh-water panfishes. HABITS: (1) They have great adaptability, which means they can be stocked readily. (2) They consume aquatic insects, small crustaceans, and a certain amount of plant life. Their growth rate varies with areas and availability of food. Generally speaking, growth is faster in the South than in the North. WHERE CAUGHT: Waters highly favored by bluegills are quiet, with vegetation in which they can find food and haven from foes (Bluegills are heavily preyed upon by larger fishes). During the day the bigger bluegills usually hang out in deeper water, shifting to shallower areas in the evening and early morning to feed. The smaller individuals generally linger in shallower places closer to shore. HOW CAUGHT: Simple casting of baits and little artificials from shores and boats; also by fly casting, which offers about the best sport with these small fish. BAITS & LURES: Bluegills accept a variety of natural baits— worms, grubs, etc. They're also taken on an assortment of little lures—jigs, spinners, flies, etc. All hooks must be very small. TACKLE: Tackle can be simple and inexpensive, which, coupled with the fact that bluegills are often available in quantity, makes the fish especially popular with youngsters. But it should be as light as possible. Fresh-water spinning and fly casting outfits are recommended.

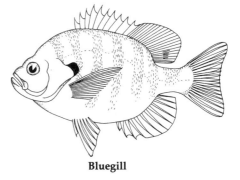

Bluegill

Brook Trout

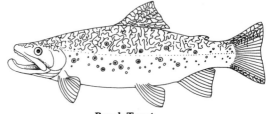

Brook Trout

SCIENTIFIC NAME: *Salvelinus fontinalis.* COMMON NAMES:
Over the years, speckled trout, squaretail, eastern trout, native
trout, char, silver trout, mountain trout, still others. But
"brook trout," often shortened to an affectionate "brookie,"
has weathered the passage of time best of any. COLOR: It's
intricate and has many variations among males and females
and from place to place. Here's a general description: olive or
greenish-brown, with yellow, on the back and upper sides.
This fades gradually on the sides, yielding to an off-white on
the belly. Wiggly markings, termed vermiculations, adorn the
body's upper half and dorsal fin and serve as a field mark to
separate the brookie from other trouts. At spawning time
males acquire a splash of red or orange on their lower sides.
Other markings are pale yellow spots peppering the sides,
along with tiny red spots, each rimmed in pale blue. They are
colorful. Another clue to brookie identification is the white
leading edges of the lower fins and bottom edge of the tail, set
off by a slender margin of black. SIZE: Overall, depending
upon regions, weights go to approximately 2 or 3 lbs. Any up
to 5 lbs are considered exceptional, although Far West states—
Idaho, Wyoming and Montana—occasionally report 4- and
5-pounders. (My friend ichthyologist-angler Ed Migdalski of
Yale University landed a 5¼-pounder and a 7½-pounder the
same afternoon at Encampment, Wyo.) Environmental
conditions are believed to be a strong factor influencing sizes,
even to stunting brook trout. Labrador and Canada's Hudson's
Bay region have yielded sizable numbers of the larger brookies.
FAMILY: The tendency is to group the trouts—brook, rainbow,
brown, etc.—and salmons together under one family name,
Salmonidae. DISTRIBUTION: Originally brook trout were
indigenous to eastern North America, Labrador to Georgia,
where they long were a prime fresh-water game fish. In the old
days eastern Canada and Maine produced the largest brook
trout, one of which was a 31½-in., 14½-lb. rod-bender caught
in the Nipigon River, Ontario, in 1916. Thanks to hatchery and
fish-planting procedures, distribution of brook trout
subsequently fanned out through the Midwest to the Far West
and in the South in areas that do not become too hot, since
brookies can't take excessive heat. HABITS: (1) Brook trout like
cold, pure water, in lakes and freely running streams. (2) They
seem happiest when water temperatures are well below 65 ° F.
(3) Overly warm waters (70 ° F.), pollution, dams and run-offs
from farmlands (insecticides, other pollutants) impose
restrictions on their distribution; but when their environmental
demands are met, they thrive. (4) Brook trout feed on many
kinds of insects and little fishes. They also forage along the
bottom for small crustaceans and mollusks. (5) Brookies are
essentially non-migratory, but coastal rivers of eastern Canada
and the U.S. Atlantic seaboard have harbored populations of
sea-run fish nicknamed "salters." They shift back and forth
between fresh water and salt water, generally fattening up
while at sea to reach somewhat larger size (to about 4 lbs.) than

those keeping to fresh water exclusively. Salters have a different color pattern: dark greenish-blue above, silvery lower down, white on the belly, with only a few pinkish dots. WHERE CAUGHT: Streams, ranging in size from brooks to rivers; large ponds and lakes (often stocked in those bodies of water). HOW CAUGHT: Primarily by fly-fishing, but also by bait casting and some trolling and plug casting. BAITS & LURES: Live baits include small minnows, local insects. Artificials include dry and wet flies, streamers, nymphs, small plugs, little spoons and spinners. Often those last two take the largest brookies. TACKLE: Go ultra-light—fresh-water spinning or fly casting.

Brown Bullhead

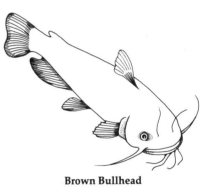

Brown Bullhead

SCIENTIFIC NAME: *Ictalurus nebulosus.* COMMON NAMES: Horned pout, speckled bullhead, mud pout, common bullhead, squaretail catfish. COLOR: Body hue is a nondescript brown or olive-brown, usually with darker mottling on the sides and a white or yellowish color below. SIZE: An average is about 8 to 10 in., with weights under 1 lb. Maximum is about 18–19 in., 4 lbs. FAMILY: A member of the catfish clan, Ictaluridae. Numerous cousins include the black bullhead, channel catfish, yellow bullhead, blue catfish. DISTRIBUTION: Across southern Canada, Nova Scotia and New Brunswick to Manitoba; throughout the St. Lawrence River region and the Great Lakes country; in the East from Maine to Florida. The species has been introduced extensively in North American waters, notably those of western regions. HABITS & WHERE CAUGHT: (1) Brown bullheads are very hardy, and because their oxygen requirements are low they adapt to sluggish streams and small ponds. (2) They're bottom feeders. The "whiskers" around the mouth are called barbels. They're sensory appendages to help locate food, and like most members of the catfish family, they have a lusty appetite. They consume smaller fishes, insect larvae, small crustaceans (including crayfish), and other items they find on the bottom. (3) Their habitat preferences run to quiet waters, often in sluggish segments of creeks and streams and deeper parts of ponds and lakes, favoring weedy areas. (4) They feed most actively at night. (5) Summer is the season. HOW CAUGHT: Simple bait fishing on the bottom. BAITS & LURES: Brown bullheads accept a variety of baits—pieces of fish, or even meat, pieces of worm, other items from their natural diet. TACKLE: It should be as light as possible.

Brown Trout

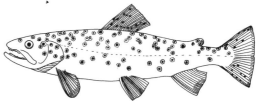

Brown Trout

SCIENTIFIC NAME: *Salmo trutta.* COMMON NAMES: "Browns" and "brownies" are about the only others, and those are used only when it's known that the subject is trout. Faded into disuse are "Loch Leven trout" (a Scottish name), "German trout," "German brown trout" and "Von Behr trout," those last three based on the fact that the species was imported into the U.S. from Germany. COLOR: The back and upper sides are a shade of brown, sometimes mentioned as having olive, greenish or golden tints. Farther down, this color becomes a lighter shade, a yellowish-brown or cream. Dark brown or near-black spots pepper the head, back, upper sides and part of the dorsal fin. These spots may have a halo of lighter hue. Lesser numbers of orange-red spots, also with pale halos, are scattered along the sides. The tail is brownish, sometimes tinged yellow. A variation among sea-run brown trout, as well as among some of those residing in large, deep lakes, is a silvery body color with scattered black spots. Spots help to separate brownies from brook trout and lake trout. Only a few spots, or a complete absence of them, on the brown trout's tail help to separate this fish from the rainbow trout, whose tail carries many spots. SIZE: The range, depending upon age and nourishment, goes up to 8 or 10 lbs. Although an Arkansas champ of 31½ lbs. and a Scottish giant of 39½ lbs. are on record, any brownies over 10 lbs. become increasingly more exceptional. Generally speaking, those confined to streams are the smallest. Those that can run to sea, called salters; and those inhabiting lakes, impoundments and large ponds where food is abundant reach greater size. FAMILY: Scientific family name, Salmonidae, trouts and salmons. DISTRIBUTION & WHERE CAUGHT: Thanks to hatchery procedures and the species' adaptability, brown trout are found in brooks, rivers, ponds and lakes throughout much of Canada and most of the United States. HABITS: (1) The types of lures that can be rigged for brownies are influenced by a lengthy menu, among whose items are small fishes—minnows and others, worms, crayfish, mollusks, and the larval and adult forms of many kinds of aquatic and terrestrial insects. Frogs, even birds, mice and other little land animals have been found in the stomachs of big brown trout. (2) They're very active night feeders, a detail turned to good advantage by after-sundown anglers in the summer. (3) Brown trout are also active surface feeders, especially during hatches of caddisflies, mayflies and the like. That's a detail of value to fly-fishermen. (4) Perhaps it's because they're more wary, but brownies are harder to catch than other species of trout. That greater challenge undoubtedly contributes to their enormous popularity. HOW CAUGHT: Although casting artificials or natural baits from shore or boat accounts for browns, and so does trolling (natural baits or lures), fly-fishing traditionally is the method (it's followers say it's the *only* method, but they're prejudiced). Much credit is given to brown trout for development of fly-fishing in the United States. BAITS & LURES: On the list are minnows, adult insects, spoons, spinners, small plugs, bucktails, streamers, dry and wet flies; patterns are matched to the kinds and current stages of development of insects in the area. TACKLE: The choice is up to you—conventional, spinning or fly casting, but keep it very light.

Carp

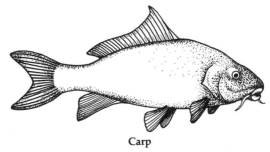

Carp

SCIENTIFIC NAME: *Cyprinus carpio.* COMMON NAMES: German carp and, according to variations in number and location of their scales, scaled carp (most of body covered with scales), mirror carp (scales only in patches on back), and leather carp (without scales or nearly so). COLOR: Olive, greenish or bronze-green on back and upper sides, fading to a lighter shade lower down, then white or yellowish underneath. The fins are an opaque gray-green or brownish, occasionally with reddish tinges. Dark outer rims on the scales lend an effect of fine lines on the body. SIZE: Up to 10 lbs. or so on an average, occasionally to 25. Old records mention much heftier carp: 55 lbs. 5 oz. (Minnesota); 58 lbs. (Lake Erie). FAMILY: Carp are classified with the Cyprinidae, the minnows, largest group of fresh-water fishes in North America. Our friend *C. carpio* is in fact a big bully boy of a minnow. Goldfish are cousins. DISTRIBUTION: Carp were introduced into Europe from China and Japan centuries ago. From Europe they were brought into the U.S. in the 1800s. Here, as in Europe, they thrived (an understatement), aided by their hardiness, adaptability, pond cultivation and transplanting. Carp have been reported for just about every state. HABITS: (1) Carp consume a variety of items. On the lengthy list are insect larvae, small mollusks and crustaceans, little fishes of various kinds, eggs of other fishes, and bits of aquatic plants. (2) They prefer comparatively warm, shallow water if it has an abundance of food. But they adapt readily to an assortment of environmental conditions, including all kinds of bottoms—mud, sand, etc.—clear or silty water, and a fairly wide range of temperatures.
(3) Carp are a controversial species, liked and sought by many anglers, detested and scorned by others. Carp are liked by their fan club because they provide inexpensive fishing for rod-'n'-reelers of all ages and are a table fish. In many instances carp also provide sport for city dwellers in outlying areas when other kinds of angling are not accessible. Carp opponents charge that the fish multiply to the point that they ruin an environment for more desirable sport species. Granted, carp are very prolific, can take over a body of water, and are difficult to control when they get established; but in fairness it must be added that in some instances the deterioration of a fishery blamed on carp might very well have been due to man-created causes. WHERE CAUGHT: Brooks, streams, ponds lakes. HOW

CAUGHT: Casting. BAITS & LURES: Standard is a so-called doughball type of bait, which can be fashioned with the fingers from a slice of water-dunked bread and molded to a hook. Veteran carp hunters have their own recipes for this dough bait, some of which recommend adding a little sugar, or perhaps a dash of cheese, as an added attraction. At times, notably in the spring when aquatic insects are hatching, carp will respond to flies, such as nymphs, fished near the bottom. TACKLE: Light spinning and spin-casting equipment are good. Hooks should be small—about a No. 2. Molded to the hook, a dough bait covers its point and barb.

Chain Pickerel

SCIENTIFIC NAME: *Esox niger*. COMMON NAMES: River pike, jackfish, pike or pickerel, chainsides. COLOR: Greenish or bronze, or a mixture of those two, overlaid with the darker reticulations, or chainlike markings, that inspired the species' most popular common name. SIZE: These are influenced by food supplies and water temperatures, but chain pickerel are small fish. Average range is 1 to 3 lbs., with a potential to 5 or 6 lbs. (In the past some states have imposed a minimum keeping-size length.) FAMILY: Chain pickerel are members of the pike family, Esocidae, along with the celebrated muskellunge. Northern pike, redfin pickerel and grass pickerel are also relatives. DISTRIBUTION: Eastern Canada, southward through the U.S. East, to Florida, and westward to include parts of Alabama, the Mississippi River system, northern Texas and southern Missouri. Greatest centers of abundance are in the Northeast, but Georgia and Florida match Yankee states when it comes to sizes. HABITS: (1) The preferred habitat of chain pickerel is quiet, relatively shallow water with plenty of weed cover and lily gardens. To a certain extent they're also found in slow-moving streams, even brackish coastal creeks. (2) They're noted for an omnivorous, savage appetite, with a mouthful of formidable teeth to satisfy it. When young they eat little fishes, insects, small crustaceans and other lesser aquatic citizens. As adults they're primarily fisheaters, but when a banquet mood is on them they'll tackle just about anything that moves—frogs, newts, mice, smaller chain pickerel, even snakes at times. (3) They feed all year, indifferently day or night, but are often erratic. WHERE CAUGHT: From shore or boats, in ponds and lakes with weed cover, in depths to 10 ft or so. *Note:* Falling water levels in summer may force the fish to move farther out from shore to find suitable cover. Chain pickerel are also caught through the ice. See "Ice Fishing," Chapter 12. HOW CAUGHT: Casting baits or small artificials and ice fishing. BAITS & LURES: Minnows are standard, both in open water and through ice. Chain pickerel also respond to fractional-ounce artificials—little spoons, plugs, spinners, etc.

Chain Pickerel

Note: It's better to have single hooks than doubles and trebles on artificials rigged for chain pickerel. They smack a lure so enthusiastically that they engulf it. A treble or a double hook makes it that much tougher to remove. TACKLE: Any kind, ultra-light to light, so long as it can cast the required artificials satisfactorily. In ice angling, tipups or jigsticks or light rods. Fly tackle also is wielded in open-water fishing. Here lures include minnow-pattern flies, streamers (alone or in combo with eye-catching spinners), frog and mouse imitations (P.S.: If you're wondering how fish get to eat mice, the little Mickeys and Minnies fall into the water every so often.)

Channel Catfish

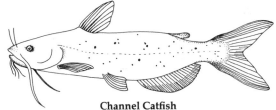

Channel Catfish

SCIENTIFIC NAME: *Ictalurus punctatus.* COMMON NAMES: Channel cat, spotted catfish, Great Lakes catfish. COLOR: It varies, from grayish or silver-gray to blue to a mixture of yellowish brown and silver above and on the sides, becoming silvery or white below. There's casual peppering with blackish dots (hence the "spotted catfish"). Channel cats closely resemble their cousins the blue catfish. SIZE: Sport-caught channel cats go to about 2, 2½ ft. long and weigh up to 12–15 lbs. maximum. Their size potential, as proved by commercial catches and an occasional rod-'n'-reel whopper, extends upward into the 50- and 60-lb. classes. Channel cats usually run third to flathead catfish and blue cats for size. FAMILY: The catfishes, Ictaluridae—what else? DISTRIBUTION: Southward from Canada, through the U.S. Great Lakes region and Midwest, to the Mississippi River and tributaries, then on to Texas and Mexico. Propagation and stocking have extended the species distribution to the eastern U.S. and as far west as California. HABITS: (1) They're more inclined than most of their kin to frequent moving water, and they favor open, clean floors of sand, gravel or rocks rather than mud bottoms and weedy places. (2) They're very adaptable to a variety of environments and are compatible with other fishes, which makes them good candidates for fish farming—pond propagation—for both sport and market. (3) Like other catfishes, they're primarily bottom feeders—note the barbels on the chin. Their diet consists of larval and adult insects, small fishes, parts of water plants, and sometimes seeds that fall into the water from shoreside plants. WHERE CAUGHT: Lakes and large rivers. HOW CAUGHT: Drifting a bait in a current in fairly fast water, where channel cats often feed. Among productive areas are current races below dams. BAITS & LURES: Fishing is with natural baits. Pieces and strips of fishes are effective. Strip baits are best cut from the silvery or lighter-colored undersides of the fishes because it adds to their visibility. TACKLE: Whichever type is wielded, conventional or spinning, it has to be sturdy enough to handle fish of the channel cats' size, keeping in mind that there can be appreciable added strain imposed by currents.

Chinook Salmon or King Salmon

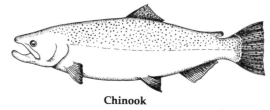

Chinook

SCIENTIFIC NAME: *Oncorhynchus tshawytscha*. COMMON NAMES: In addition to the short labels "kings" and "chinooks" when talking about this species, talking specifically about salmon, there are some regional names like tyee, quinnat, and spring salmon. "King salmon" is a favorite in Alaska and California, while you might hear "tyee" quite often in British Columbia and Washington. In Oregon and Washington you're likely to hear the nickname "blackmouth" (from the color of the inside of the species' mouth) applied to young, maturing king salmon, popular targets in Puget Sound and the Strait of San Juan de Fuca. Incidentally, the chinook also has black gums, a detail which helps separate him from his cousin the coho, or silver salmon (see page 134), whose gums are white. COLOR: While spending part of their lives at sea, wolfing all the food they can hold and growing, chinooks are silvery for the most part, with some greenish-blue along the back. Numerous small, irregularly shaped back spots speckle the back and upper sides, as well as the dorsal fin and tail. In fresh water, especially as spawning time approaches, the males take on a dark, dull orange-red color, with black on the head, while the females' color becomes brassy. SIZE: Chinooks are kings of the Pacific salmons for size. A broad general range, so far as anglers are concerned, might be 8–10 to 35–40 lbs. On record in Alaska are 50- to 80-pounders, real muscle-testers. Oregon's famed Umpqua River has produced chinooks in the 80-lb. class. Heavyweights up to 92 lbs. have been extracted from British Columbia's Skeena River. And that these salmon occasionally reach, even top, 100 lbs. was proved by a 126½-pounder captured in an Alaskan fish trap. FAMILY: Salmonidae or salmons (a tribe which also includes the trouts), is the family's scientific name. Within this family chinooks are grouped with the coho, pink, chum and sockeye salmons under the subheading Pacific salmons. Five Pacific salmons occur in North America. A sixth, cherry salmon (*Oncorhynchus masou*), is found in Asia. DISTRIBUTION: From Alaska to (probably the southernmost extreme) about San Diego, Calif., according to California's Department of Fish and Game. This range includes Pacific Ocean waters and the many estuaries and rivers tributary to them, such as California's Sacramento, the Columbia, and Canada's mighty Yukon. Overall distribution has been seriously curtailed by dams, pollution and commercial exploitation. HABITS: (1) After time at sea—up to 6–8 years—in which to gorge themselves on herring, anchovies and other small fishes to grow, king salmon return to coastal rivers to spawn. Mostly these returns occur in spring and autumn, but anglers also can capitalize on summer. Since times vary from region to region, fishermen will do well to check in advance the areas they plan to fish. (2) Their travels upriver are legendary, even for salmon. Longest are their spawning migrations in Canada's Yukon River system, more than 1,000 miles inland. (3) Chinooks feed at different levels, surface on down. At the surface they may betray their presence by commotions as they assault small fish. (4) Commonly chinooks and cohos are found in the same area, the kings usually at a deeper level than the silvers. Since cohos also feed at the surface, any commotions at the top might be caused by them alone or by a mixture of kings and cohos. WHERE CAUGHT: Inshore ocean belts, straits (like San Juan de Fuca), sounds (like Puget), estuaries and rivers. HOW CAUGHT: Trolling at different levels (upper for cohos, lower for chinooks) and different speeds (1 to 2 m.p.h. for chinooks, 4 to 7 to 8 m.p.h. for cohos). Also caught by a Pacific Northwest technique called mooching, a kind of stop-and-go trolling, and by casting from boats. BAITS & LURES: Herring is a good bait for Pacific salmons—rigged whole, or cut in the shape of a fishing plug, or as a small fillet that spins. Other baits are anchovies, Pacific sardines and candlefish. A large, shiny metal flasher is often rigged ahead of the bait as an eye-catcher. Casting spoons of various designs and sizes also account for chinooks. TACKLE: Conventional gear is suggested, considering the species' fighting quality and size potential and the methods involved. Deep trolling may necessitate a trolling sinker or other device to get the rig deep enough. Mooching can also put a strain on tackle. Suggested is a so-called boat outfit whose rod is able to handle lines up to about 40-lb. test.

Ciscoes

"Ciscoes" is the familiar collective name for eight North American species or subspecies in a group catalogued with the Salmonidae (salmons and trouts). For our purposes here we can consider them all as one species. SCIENTIFIC NAMES: All begin with *Coregonus*, followed by *alpenae*, *artedii*, *hoyi*, *johannae*, *kiyi*, *nigripinnis*, *reighardi* and *zenthicus*. (There, aren't you glad you asked for them?) COMMON NAMES, often used interchangeably: Lake herring (for a resemblance to the marine herring, but not related), blueback, fresh-water herring, common cisco, grayback, shoal-water herring, tullibee and shallow-water cisco. COLOR: The scheme is mostly silvery, with some very dark blue or grayish green along the back and white on the underside. SIZE: Collectively, ciscoes go from about 6 to 20 in. in length, with weights ranging from about ½ lb. or less to 2 lbs. Some reach 3–5 lbs., and exceptional specimens of 6, 7 and 8 lbs. have been reported. Sizes depend upon species, and on food supplies and growth rates in

Cisco

different areas. FAMILY: As already mentioned, the Salmonidae. DISTRIBUTION: Collectively, ciscoes are cold-water fishes widely distributed from eastern Canada and the U.S. East to the Midwest and Great Lakes, north to central Canada, and on to British Columbia and Alaska. HABITS: (1) Ciscoes travel in schools. (2) They favor cold, clear, well-oxygenated water. In summer they go deep to escape warm water, but return to shoaler areas when those waters cool sufficiently. They're fatally vulnerable to oxygen deficiencies when trapped in shallow areas that warm quickly. (3) They feed on aquatic and terrestrial insects and their larvae, small crustaceans and little fishes. WHERE CAUGHT: Lakes. HOW CAUGHT: Casting or jigging live or dead baits or artificials. Best action is in fly casting. They're caught from boats, docks and, in winter, through the ice. Best fishing times, any season, are usually from just before sunup into early morning, then in the evening and at night. BAITS & LURES: Live minnows, salted minnows, shiny spoons and spinners, brightly colored beads in combination with a bait, and dry flies. Ice fishermen rig natural baits, such as minnows, and the small artificials designed for ice angling. *Note:* Hooks must be small. TACKLE: Any kind of tackle, so long as it's very light. Ciscoes are good sport on extra- and ultra-light gear. Try fly casting.

Coho Salmon

SCIENTIFIC NAME: *Oncorhynchus kisutch.* COMMON NAMES: Silver salmon. COLOR: In common with other Pacific salmons, the coho's body coloration while at sea is a steely blue on the dorsal surface and upper sides, turning to silver lower down and white below that. Small dark dots pepper the back and upper section of the tail. Also as among other Pacific species, this color pattern changes after the fish enter rivers to spawn. There's a general darkening effect in both sexes, the males often developing a dull red shade on the sides and the females assuming a nondescript brassy-greenish color. Typically among salmons at breeding time, there's also that strange alteration of the jaws to produce a hook (kype), or knob effect, which gives the fish a grotesque look. Their white gum color is a detail separating cohos from chinooks or king salmon, which have black gums. SIZE: Cohos are born in rivers but grow up at sea. In the ocean, while still juveniles, they feed chiefly on shrimp, then concentrate on herring (mainly) and other small fishes as they grow, varying their diet with squid and small crustaceans. Development is rapid. After a year at sea they weigh 2 to 3 lbs., and growth continues at a good clip until a silent signal summons them to rivers to reproduce. This usually occurs during their third year, although a certain percentage of individuals may remain in the ocean somewhat longer. After maturity their weights range from 6 to 10 to 12

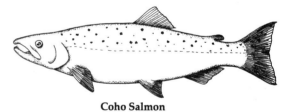

Coho Salmon

lbs., which is also the approximate span in sport-fishing
catches, give or take a couple of pounds, to less than 5 and up
to 14, 15. About the largest ever authenticated for angling was
an exceptional British Columbian hefty weighing 31 lbs.
FAMILY: A member of the Pacific salmons group within the
Salmonidae family. DISTRIBUTION: Originally coho salmon
were natives of the Pacific Coast and its rivers, from California
to Alaska, with an accent on Washington, British Columbia
and southeastern Alaska. They have also been caught in the
Pacific as far south as Los Coronados Islands, Baja California.
Throughout that segment of seaboard they earned a legion of
followers because of their combat tactics. Subsequently their
reputation spread eastward, and attempts were begun to
transplant the species to suitable environments in the
Midwest, notably in Lake Michigan. The transplantings were
outstandingly successful. And although that inland sport
fishery is still relatively young, it attracts thousands of anglers
and promises to become one of the Great Lakes' prime
piscatorial attractions. More recently than the Lake Michigan
stocking, experimental plantings were made in Lake Erie and
Lake Ontario. At this writing it's still early for a long-range
prediction, but earlier indications have hinted at success.
HABITS: (1) Throughout their Pacific seaboard distribution, the
time they enter rivers, and consequently their spawning
period, can be anywhere from July to February or March.
(2) Generally coho salmon do not journey as far upriver for
spawning as do chinooks. (3) Most young cohos start their
migration to sea when about a year old and only about 6-in.
long. They move downstream in groups of 10, a dozen, 40 or
50, doing much of their traveling at night because the voyage is
fraught with perils from swimming and flying assassins. While
still in the rivers they nourish themselves with insect larvae
and tiny crustaceans. It's believed that once they leave their
natal rivers they linger for a short time close to shore—gaining
confidence, no doubt—then disperse to seaward, possibly
fanning out for appreciable distances. (4) The Great Lakes have
become a sea for those transplanted fish mentioned earlier, and
they follow the same general pattern as their Pacific Coast
counterparts, instinctively moving out of tributaries to mature
in the lakes, then returning to their home streams to breed. In
Lake Ontario it was discovered that precocious young males,
nicknamed "jacks," return after only a year or 18 months.
Presumably this occurs in Pacific Coast regions too. (5) Anglers'
opinions differ, but the majority would probably rate cohos
second only to chinooks among Pacific salmons for action
quality; and at that the kings' greater sizes are probably a
factor. Cohos hit and fight enthusiastically. Even small ones
are scrappy, as I can testify after spinning-tackle arguments
with 3- and 4-pounders on Lake Michigan. At any size they're
magnificent light-tackle fish, and what particularly endears
them to coho aficionados is their maneuver of fighting close to
the surface and jumping. WHERE CAUGHT, HOW CAUGHT,
BAITS, LURES & TACKLE: (1) Trolling is No. 1 for ocean-run
silvers, with herring—whole, plugcut, or fillet—as the leading
bait. Other fish baits are also rigged, along with such artificials

as spoons. Cohos travel at a higher plane than chinooks, usually within 30 ft. or so of the top, so trolling isn't as deep. Even so, wire line and/or a trolling sinker of suitable weight may be necessary to reach them. If a fairly heavy sinker is required, it should be of the breakaway type that is detachable from the rig to let the salmon fight unhampered. Suggested trolling speed is 2 knots, approximately 2¼ m.p.h. (2) Ocean-run cohos are also caught by live-bait fishing, the boat at anchor or drifting. Preliminary experimentation often required to learn at what depth they're traveling. (3) Shoreside casting around bays, estuaries and river entrances accounts for cohos as they come in from the sea. However, there should be a fairly deep channel within casting distance because salmon prowl these waterways to capitalize on food fishes moving in and out with tides. The method is to repeatedly cast and retrieve until contact is made. Spin fishermen can have a ball working spoons and other small artificials. Fish strips, especially herring, are good attractors in shoreside casting. Ghost shrimp and a piece of crayfish tail also are effective. Some anglers add a "flasher," or spinner blade, 3 or 4 ft. above the hook. Hook sizes are 1/0 or 2/0 to 4/0, on a short leader for easier casting. (4) Cohos are taken on spinning lures and artificial flies in both salt and fresh water. Trolling a streamer fly, or combination of a fly and a spinner, is another ocean fishing procedure. It should work on bays and estuaries too when silvers are feeding. Hooks go from No. 1 to 3/0. When used in tandem with artificials, spinners are 1/0 to No. 4, and silver is a good finish. (5) At sea, trollers watch for signs of surface activity, either the fish pursuing prey, or sea birds concentrating on a patch of ocean. When silvers are so engaged in active feeding, trolling a streamer fly, or fly-and-spinner combo, at fair speed will bring hookups. So will casting a fly to a surface-feeding school. (6) Along rivers a good team is spinning tackle and small artificials. Shiny, erratically wobbly spoons are a suggestion. It must be remembered, though, that cohos or any other Pacific salmons are not at their best in rivers. It often happens that the farther upstream you go, the poorer the fighting quality of the fish—understandably, what with the rigors of their travel. That's why it's important to learn when a river run begins so as to catch them while still fresh from the sea. On their spawning runs they do not feed.

Crappies, Black and White

The popular name of these fish, crappie, should be changed. It has a derogatory connotation, "crappy" being a U.S. slang expression for anything of poor quality or otherwise inferior. Fortunately, it hasn't hampered these little fellows' popularity one iota. They're among the most commonly sought of American panfishes, respected for both their tackle action and edibility. Along with their relatives the bluegill, pumpkinseed

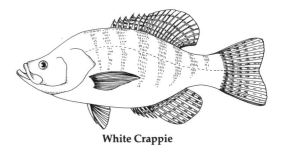

White Crappie

and other sunfishes, they're catalogued under the scientific family name Centrarchidae, sunfishes. Among crappies' regional names are speckled perch, silver crappie, strawberry bass and calico bass. Forget "perch" and "bass." They're misnomers.

Crappies are distinguished by deep bodies, flattened from side to side—as opposed to rounded—and rather large mouths. Other specifications are the prominent dorsal and anal fins, deep caudal peduncle (tail base), and well-developed tail with a somewhat convex trailing edge. They're small fishes. Lengths of 10- to 12-in. are considered fair sizes.

Black Crappie *(Pomoxis nigromaculatus)*

This species' range now is wide. Overall, it extends from southern Canada's western sections eastward to Quebec, through the Great Lakes region to portions of Nebraska and Pennsylvania, then fanning out to include the vast Mississippi River system, to northern Texas on the west and northern Florida on the east, from there it goes to at least eastern North Carolina. Extensive plantings in Midwestern and Far Western waters have broadened distribution even more.

Black crappies like clear, quiet water, favoring areas with gardens of vegetation. They seem to be less tolerant of silt-filled water than their cousins the white crappies. Too, they're more of a schooling species. Their food consists of aquatic insects, worms, small fishes of different kinds, and little crayfish. Their basic color is silvery, with a green or yellow cast, becoming darkest on the back. From gill covers to the base of the tail the body carries darker, irregular spots and mottling. Some are also evident on the fins.

They're light-tackle game, of course, and they respond to baits that include small minnows, worms, pieces of crayfish. They will accept artificials too, and are caught on little spinning lures and dry and wet flies.

White Crappie *(Pomoxis annularis)*

The white resembles the black, from which it is distinguishable by body mottling and the number of spines in their respective dorsal fins. Whereas the darker markings on the black crappie are distributed haphazardly, those on the white crappie are barlike. The anterior portion of the black's dorsal fin carries seven or eight spines. Its counterpart of the white has six.

Orginally, the distribution of white crappies stretched from Nebraska to Lake Ontario, through the Ohio River and Mississippi River systems, on to Alabama and up into North Carolina. As in the case of black crappies, their distribution has been enhanced by introduction into additional states. In their distribution, white crappies are more numerous in the Southern sections, possibly because of their greater tolerance—than black crappies'—of silty waters.

Their food and feeding habits are similar to the black crappies', and they will respond to the same natural baits and artificials. Again, the lightest kind of tackle is indicated.

Cutthroat Trout

SCIENTIFIC NAME: *Salmo clarki.* COMMON NAMES: For some reason this fish is one of those species that amass an extraordinarily large collection of nicknames. One researcher tracked down no less than 70. Here's a sampling to give you an idea and show regional influences: Columbia River trout, Yellowstone cutthroat, Piute trout and cutthroat, Montana black spotted trout, coastal cutthroat (California), Colorado cutthroat, Tahoe cutthroat, southern Rocky Mountain trout, Snake River cutthroat, Utah Lake cutthroat and intermountain trout. COLOR: Perhaps the best clue to identification is the bright orange or red streaks on either side of the lower jaw, the marks giving the fish its name. Because of the wide range of color variations, few authorities would want to venture what might be called a "typical" color scheme for cutthroats, if indeed there is such a thing. Variations occur from region to region, presumably influenced by type of water and environment, race, etc. As a result some inland forms may be, we'll say, yellowish or yellow-green with splashes of red on the head's sides, or greenish-brown above with greenish-yellow sides and pink tinges below; while coastal residents are dark green or greenish blue on the back, a lighter shade of same on the upper sides, and silvery below. Spotting of body and fins, usually dorsal and tail, is common among cutthroats, but this too is very variable. The spots are roundish and black, but vary in size and profusion from race to race. SIZE: Sea-run cutthroats usually do better than landlocked forms in sizes. Their potential is from about a pound or a little over to 3 or 4, and up to 15, 16 and 17 lbs. for exceptional catches. Tops for inland cutthroats is about 5 lbs., but larger specimens are reported from time to time. None of the present-day fish seem to come up to those caught during the first two decades of this century. There's mention of 10- to 20-pounders extracted from Western lakes. FAMILY: Salmonidae family—salmons and trouts. DISTRIBUTION: This much-respected gamester is a resident of western North America, with an overall scope extending from Southern Alaska to northern California, thence inland to include western Canada and the Rocky Mountain states. HABITS: (1) Further complicating the color-pattern picture is that they hybridize with other species to create still more combinations. In areas they share, cutthroats cross with rainbows and golden trout, the offspring retaining some of the physical traits of each parent but with its own color scheme. Still further, as among Pacific salmons, there are color

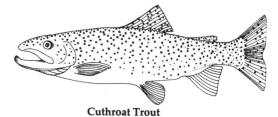

Cuthroat Trout

differences between sea-run cutthroats and their inland
counterparts. (2) Another field mark is teeth in the rear of the
mouth at the base of the tongue (hyoid teeth). These teeth help
to separate cutthroats from rainbows and steelheads.
(3) Among cutthroats with access to the sea, youngsters may
accompany their elders downstream in the spring to salt water.
Or they may remain in their natal streams for as long as two or
three years before migrating to ocean or lake. Some coastal
individuals may spawn without going to sea. Adult fish can
spawn two or three times. (4) Anadromous cutthroats that go
to sea usually remain there one or two years before returning to
their rivers, and do not wander too far. Characteristically, they
fatten up while enjoying the sea's bounty. The food of these
sea-run trout consists of small fishes and crustaceans. River
forms dine on insect larvae when small, advance to adult insect
forms, little fishes and crayfish as they grow larger. WHERE
CAUGHT: In habitat cutthroats are also variable. As their
nicknames hint, they occur inland and also are coastal,
migrating to the sea. Waters in which they are found include
mountain lakes, large ponds, streams and coastal rivers. HOW
CAUGHT, BAITS, LURES & TACKLE: Cutthroats rate as good
sport fish, although a notch below browns and rainbows for
combat activity. In salt and brackish water they provide good
sport on light conventional tackle and medium spinning
equipment. Trolling is one method, usually slow, and the fish
will respond to several kinds of small artificials, towed slowly.
They also are caught on strip bait, shrimp and crayfish tails.
Usually they're found in relatively shallow water. Estuaries,
river mouths and rocky areas are among places with promise.
Inland cutthroats also rise to an assortment of artificials that
include small dry flies, wet flies, nymphs, small spoons,
spinners and bucktails, along with minnows, worms and
crayfish. They're especially good fly-rod opponents. A SAD
EPILOGUE: Cutthroats are dying out in some areas and are
already gone from others they once inhabited. Several factors
contribute to this ''genocide.'' Cutthroats cannot compete
successfully with other fishes for food. Pollution and dams
have exacted tolls. And finally, they do not stand up well
under increasing angling pressures.

Dolly Varden

SCIENTIFIC NAME: *Salvelinus malma*. COMMON NAMES:
Regionally, salmon trout and bull trout. COLOR: Dolly Vardens
can be very variable in color, according to habitat, so it's
impossible to offer a standardized pattern. Those confining
themselves to inland waters are generally a nondescript
darkish shade, olive or greenish-brown on the back, somewhat
lighter or silvery farther down. Typically, though, the sides are

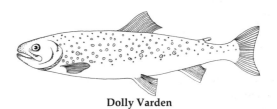

Dolly Varden

speckled with small, round spots that can be orange, red or
yellow, and the belly is a shade of white. Sea-run individuals
tend to be silver. The fins are without spots, bars or other
markings, but the underside fins—pectoral, ventral and anal—
are usually edged with white in front. SIZE: Stream specimens
tend to be the smallest, while those inhabiting lakes and large
rivers, along with some of the sea-run fish, go up to 8 lbs. and
heavier. Maximum size is generally given as approximately
20 lbs., but there are heavier ones on the books. Years ago Lake
Pend Orielle, Idaho, surrendered a 32-pounder. FAMILY: A
member of a famous family, Salmonidae, and kin to trout, the
Dolly Varden is a species of char. It closely resembles the Arctic
char *(Salvelinus alpinus),* and authorities still argue as to
whether or not they are the same species, or the Dolly Varden a
subspecies of Arctic char. DISTRIBUTION: In the U.S., Dolly
Vardens have northern and western distribution, including
Alaska, Oregon, northern California, Idaho and Montana.
HABITS: (1) Young Dolly Vardens feed chiefly on insects, later
extending the menu to take in assorted smaller fishes and the
eggs of other species. (2) In waters they share with Pacific
salmon they stand indicted for being very destructive of the
eggs and fry of chinook and kokanee or sockeye salmon, as
well as eating quantities of trout eggs. They have in fact been a
serious predatory menace to the commercial salmon fishery.
WHERE CAUGHT: Inland they inhabit lakes, rivers and
mountain streams. Along the coast there are sea-run
populations, the fish returning to their native rivers to spawn.
HOW CAUGHT: Trolling and casting from boat or shore. BAITS
& LURES: The fish respond to wet flies (occasionally to dry flies)
and other small artificials, such as shiny spoons. They also will
accept strip baits, herring, anchovies and shrimp. TACKLE:
Opinions of the Dolly Varden's fighting qualities are highly
personal, ranging from only fair to excellent. Much depends
upon the angler's opinion of what constitutes a good game
fish, the caliber of his tackle, the situation, and the size and
performance of individual fish. This western char is not alone
in that varied response. Same thing holds for many marine and
fresh-water fishes.

Flathead Catfish

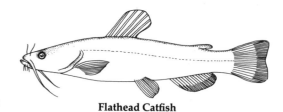

Flathead Catfish

SCIENTIFIC NAME: *Pylodictis olivaris.* COMMON NAMES:
Regionally, shovelhead catfish, mud cat, yellow catfish.
COLOR: Brown or olive-brown, blotched or mottled with a
darker tone of the main hue. The basic color's shade differs a
bit according to the nature of the bottom in the fish's area—
darker for a muddy floor, lighter over sand. SIZE: If there's an
average range in sport catches, it's probably a modest 2 to 4
lbs.; but an incentive is a potential that climbs up into the
20-, 30- and 40-lb. classes, even heavier in exceptional

instances. On the basis of commercial takes, these cats reach at least 80 to 100 lbs. FAMILY: The flathead catfish is one of the larger ictalurids, a fancy term for catfishes, from their family's scientific label, Ictaluridae. Note the fleshy barbels around the mouth, trademark of catfishes. DISTRIBUTION: In all, their range is from Iowa and South Dakota eastward to Pennsylvania in large rivers, southward via the Mississippi Valley to Gulf Coast states, then via the Rio Grande into Mexico. HABITS: (1) They're rather lazy by nature yet are omnivorous eaters. Smaller fishes are their menu's chief item, but they also consume crayfish and aquatic insects, the latter in both larval and adult forms. (2) Productive angling areas include the deeper parts of sluggish pools. In some locales they're also caught in the tail water at large dams. Here the cats probably lurk in wait for baitfishes swept to them by currents. WHERE CAUGHT: Flathead catfish inhabit large rivers, where they seek out quiet places away from the flow. HOW CAUGHT, BAITS, LURES & TACKLE: Catfishing methods are diversified. Rods and reels are standard, of course, but sometimes hand lines are used for larger cats. Trot lines are employed too, but these are more a commercial or quantity procedure than a sport-fishing technique. A unique method for hefty catfishes is jugging. See page 124. Whatever the method, rigs are set for the bottom for flatheads. Among natural baits are cut pieces of local fishes, crayfish, and whole small live fishes. Flatheads also take artificials such as spoons and leadhead jigs, bumped or trolled along bottom. They give a good account of themselves on a line. Tackle must be suitably sturdy if the larger ones are expected.

Fresh-Water or Black Basses—Largemouth, Smallmouth, Spotted—

These fishes are listed scientifically with the sunfish family, Centrarchidae, and "black bass" is their common grouping label. There are 10 U.S. members of the group, catalogued as species and subspecies. The classification varies among ichthyologists, but generally the black bass group consists of six species and four subspecies. In any case, they are the largest members of the sunfish tribe, and in their ranks are the enormously popular largemouth and smallmouth basses.

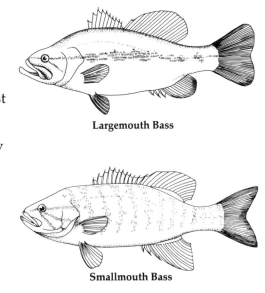

Largemouth Bass

Smallmouth Bass

All these basses share certain physical traits and habits. They are stout-bodied, solid-looking fishes. All have a dorsal fin composed of a fairly stiff spinous portion and a higher, softer, rounded rayed section. The tail is well developed, with a thick base and somewhat convex trailing edge. Their mouths are of good size, even on the so-called smallmouth bass. Their scales have comblike edges. They all favor warm water. Their varied diet consists of small fishes—sometimes their own juniors, frogs and tadpoles, insects and their larvae, worms and crayfish, and other crustaceans. They have been known to eat mice, even birds, on occasion.

Because of their varied diet, all black basses respond to a variety of natural baits, including crayfish, earthworms, frogs, insects, lampreys and several others. Bait selection varies from area to area and is governed by availability and, to a greater extent, anglers' personal ideas. Probably the most widely used bait is minnows. Bass love them, so when in doubt, use minnows. Be sure to hook them carefully in the flesh of the back near the dorsal fin. According to the fisherman's ideas, and the sizes of the bass, the minnows may be anywhere from 2 to 6 in. long, even longer. Similarly, they may be allowed to swim free for maximum action or, if desired, kept a desired depth by suspension from a bobber or float. Black basses also respond to an assortment of plastic and metal artificials—an enormous assortment. There's a host of lures designed to simulate small fishes, insects and other items on bass menus. Popular on big impoundments in the South and Southwest, such as Texas' Toledo Bend and Lake Sam Rayburn, is a plastic red- or purple-colored worm. Then there are the so-called bass bugs in a myriad of forms. To those are added literally hundreds of plugs, spoons, flies, spinners, etc. It has been said that more artificials are designed and produced for largemouth bass alone than any other kind of sport fish, fresh-water or marine.

Black bass angling is so far-flung that at any given time of year there are bass fishermen in action somewhere. Utilizing the huge assortment of natural baits and artificials available, bass anglers fish every conceivable type of water, from streams and small ponds to big lakes and reservoirs. Accordingly, methods and tackle vary from region to region to embrace spinning, fly casting, live-bait fishing, plugging, bugging, trolling, and bait casting from boats and shores.

Largemouth Bass (*Micropterus salmoides*)

Here is a battler on a pedestal all its own. From the double standpoint of numbers of anglers fishing for them and their devotion to the species, largemouth bass rate among the nation's topmost fresh-water game fishes, rivaled in esteem only by trout and salmon.

Most classifications list largemouths as one species under the Latin handle given above. Other cataloguings divide them into a species and subspecies: northern largemouth, *Micropterus salmoides salmoides*, and a subspecies larger than the northern variety, Florida largemouth, *Micropterus salmoides floridanus*. This is of no consequence to anglers, but it gives taxonomists something to argue about. The fish, of course, couldn't care less. For our purposes here it will suffice to consider them as a single species, and let the taxonomists fall where they may.

Originally, largemouth bass were native to waters in southern Canada's eastern reaches, the Great Lakes and Mississippi River regions, and on down to Florida and Mexico, with a further extension in the southeastern U.S. from Florida northward through the Carolinas to Maryland. In time the species was introduced in the Northwest, California, New England and elsewhere, until now virtually all states offer largemouth fishing.

Like other black basses, largemouths are warm-water fish. Their preference runs to shallow, quiet—even sluggish— waters, usually with mud bottoms. They also favor waters well supplied with aquatic vegetation—those well-dotted with lily pads are classic. Plants harbor small fishes and other creatures on which largemouths feed, and also provide them a haven and often a spawning site. Because basses favor weedy places, they are seldom encountered beyond them. Waters around submerged stumps and trees have potential for the same reason. When the foregoing conditions are satisfied, their habitats include farm ponds, slow-moving streams and even standing bodies of water, impoundments and reservoirs, lakes of all sizes, and bayous and other backwaters.

While still young they subsist chiefly on assorted aquatic insects and their larvae, with small crustaceans for a change of diet. En route to adulthood the menu becomes broader and more ambitious. Smaller fishes, frogs in various stages of development, worms, crayfish, and even their own young join the list. In some regions, notably those in the northerly parts of their range, feeding lessens during the colder months, picking up again in the warmer days of spring.

Growth rates and adult sizes vary according to availability of food and extent of feeding. Thus there's considerable difference in those specifications between northern and southern largemouths. The latter have a distinct advantage in their longer feeding season (northern largemouths eat less during the colder months, remember), coupled with a normally abundant food supply. As for size, the state of Florida generally yields the largest of this species—some go up to 15 lbs., and there have been a few reported in the 20-lb. class. The northern breed, on the other hand, has a ceiling of about 11 lbs., and those are whoppers. In either region, north or south, most bass fishermen are happy to boat 2- to 4-pounders.

The basic body color of the largemouth bass is a green or brownish-green, darkest atop the head and along the back, fading to a lighter shade on the sides. A dark, somewhat irregular but readily distinguishable band runs along each side from gill cover to tail. Largemouth and smallmouth basses bear a resemblance to each other, but certain details separate them. They will be pointed out when we come to smallmouths.

All kinds of light tackle—fly-fishing, spinning, bait casting, etc.—are pressed into service for largemouth bass, with techniques suitable to the areas involved. Greater variety exists among anglers' opinions as to which baits and artificials are most effective. Each group of attractors—bass bugs, plugs, flies, live minnows, streamers, and so on—has its fan club, with choice influenced by personal success. The sonic popping designs are particularly popular because they attract by both sight and sound. Another group of buffs will argue for flies, specifying combinations of brown or white and another color, or all-yellow. A third faction argues for live minnows; a fourth for plugs—surface types, poppers, etc., in various colors such as red and white. Still another group swears by plastic worms. So it goes.

A largemouth hunter fishing unfamiliar waters will do well to check locally as to the most effective baits and artificials, and about the best fishing hours as well. Largemouths can smack a lure at any hour of day or night, but often the most productive hours come during early morning and in late afternoon, or in the evening.

Smallmouth Bass (*Micropterus dolomieui*)

Now is a good time to point out the differences between smallmouth and largemouth basses. In examining the color pattern, one sees that the smallmouth's has a passing resemblance to the largemouth's but is darker atop the head and along the back. The greenish color is somewhat lighter, with a noticeably brownish or bronze hue (the latter leading to a regional nickname, "bronzeback"). Too, the smallmouth's underside is white. The darker body markings differ also. On the largemouth, there's a broad band running longitudinally along each side. On a smallmouth the darker overlay takes the form of several vertical bars. Their intensity and distinctness usually vary with the darkness or lightness of habitat background. As for mouth size, there's not as much difference as the name smallmouth might indicate. A classic field mark in separating the two basses lies in their upper jaws. The smallmouth's does not reach backward beyond the rear rim of the eye, whereas that of the largemouth does. Another identification aid is the notch between the spiny and rayed sections of the dorsal fin. On the largemouth this is much deeper, almost separating the two sections.

At one time the range of smallmouth bass was more confined than now. Originally they were indigenous to the St. Lawrence River and its tributaries in the East, the Great Lakes region in the Midwest, and sections of the Ohio, Mississippi and Tennessee rivers. Then came a duplication of the largemouth story. With sport fishes as fine as these, nature should be given a hand. From the last half of the 1800s on, transplanting and stocking introduced smallmouths to New England, the Middle Atlantic States, and eventually on across the U.S. to Idaho, California and Oregon.

Throughout their range, smallmouths' habitat preferences are diametrically opposite those of largemouths. Whereas the latter favor warm, undisturbed waters, smallmouths like cool, clear water with a lively flow. Lakes and streams with gravel floors, or studded with large stones or boulders, are smallmouth hangouts. So are streams whose currents swirl past large stones and boulders, with riffle areas alternating with cool, deep pools. Again unlike largemouths, whose fondness for aquatic vegetation is legendary, smallmouths avoid such areas and carry on a lifelong love affair with rocks instead. Too, they're not as tolerant of silty waters as largemouths.

Increasingly larger items of food are eaten as the youngsters grow. As adults they subsist on smaller fishes, many kinds of insects—beetles, dragonflies, grasshoppers, etc.—and crayfish. Typically, their growth rate is determined by abundance of food and whether they reside in northern or southern waters. With abundant food they grow rapidly. Conversely, if they live in an overpopulated area where there is brisk competition for food, growth is slow and may even be stunted. Again like largemouths, those in northern waters gradually cut down on their feeding activity in autumn. With colder weather they seek the insulation provided by deeper water, then apparently fast throughout the winter. Not until early spring do they resume feeding.

These bass run smaller than largemouths, but they have their own legion of devotees, the more loyal of whom may even prefer smallmouths. They're excellent game fish. From seizing a bait or artificial to landing, they battle energetically, often punctuating their argument by leaps clear of the water. As in the case of largemouth bass, anglers can take their cue from the fact that smallmouths are inclined to feed more actively during early morning and evening hours. They can also be caught at night.

Much of the challenge in successful smallmouth angling lies in selection and presentation of a bait or artificial. No blanket rules are possible, since baits, lures and procedures change from region to region according to locales and time of year. Broadly speaking, natural baits include minnows, hellgrammites, worms (night crawlers) and crayfish. Artificials run the gamut from bass bugs in insect and frog patterns, through dry flies and streamers, to surface plugs and darters. Many smallmouth regulars insist that the best action comes with a fly rod and surface-riding artificial. However, bait fishing and spinning have their followers too, and on large lakes anglers often go deep with spoons and plugs. Again, it is wise to check locally. Considerable precious fishing time and effort can be saved in this way. Meanwhile, it does no harm to carry at least a modest inventory of bass bugs. These are generally smaller for smallmouths than for largemouths. Floating types, including poppers, in frog and insect patterns, usually are effective. Rubber models, with legs for added action, are good. So are deer-hair floaters. Add flies and streamers.

Areas where smallmouth may lurk include the vicinity of (1) shelving rocks, (2) stony points extending out into a lake, (3) clear water around boulders, (4) rock-strewn streams with a good flow, (5) deep pools with riffles, (6) bars, (7) gravel bottoms between patches of aquatic vegetation, and (8) rocky reefs of large lakes.

Spotted Bass *(Micropterus punctulatus)*

Related to both the smallmouth and largemouth basses, the spotted shares some characteristics with those species and suggests, in fact, a cross between the two. There are also differences. As far as the color scheme goes, the spotted's back is olivaceous, punctuated with numerous darker mottlings of varying size, some of which may be roughly diamond-shaped. Like a largemouth, it has a dark band, interrupted, running lengthwise along each side, but below that are the black spots that give the fish its common name. In that dotting it also differs from the smallmouth and carries vertical bars on its sides. As for the mouth, the upper jaw does not extend backward beyond the posterior rim of the eye, as does the largemouth's, and the notch between spinous and rayed sections of the dorsal fin isn't as pronounced. Still further, the black spot on the gill cover's trailing edge is usually better defined on the spotted bass than on the smallmouth and largemouth. More apparent is the difference in size. *Micropterus punctulatus* is the smallest of the trio. A length of 18 in. and a weight of 4 lbs. constitute a big one.

Among common names for this fish you may hear Kentucky bass or Kentucky spotted bass. As commonly occurs, there is discussion as to whether all spotted bass are of a single species or should be subdivided into species and subspecies. This needn't concern fishermen, but it has led to such aliases as northern spotted bass, Alabama bass and Wichita spotted bass.

Distribution of spotted bass extends from Ohio and West Virginia to Kansas, Texas and Oklahoma, then sprawls southward to Gulf of Mexico states and eastward to western Florida. They favor the types of habitats of those cousins, bearing out the suggestion that spotted bass are a cross between smallmouths and largemouths. Like largemouths, in northern expanses of their distribution, the spotted like the deeper sections of slow-moving streams with mud bottoms. In southern parts of their range they are more like smallmouths—preferring cool and clear deeper-water lakes or streams with gravel bottoms, riffles and pools.

As youngsters they nourish themselves with insects and their larvae and tiny crayfish, later broadening their diet to include small fishes, crustaceans and the like. Spotted bass residing in rivers seem to participate in downstream migrations, leaving the headwaters for the deeper pools or lower-river sections. Presumably this is to escape autumn and winter cold in the shallows. With spring, the travelers return upriver to their summer environment.

Angling methods, artificials and natural baits are substantially the same as for smallmouths.

Grass Pickerel and Redfin Pickerel
Esox americanus vermiculatus and *Esox americanus americanus*

As their scientific tags indicate, one is considered a subspecies of the other. Together they commonly are referred to as "the little pickerels" because they are the smallest representatives of the five-member pike family (Esocidae) in North America. Also because of their diminutiveness, they're far overshadowed in

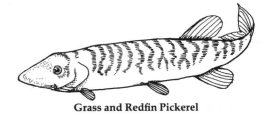

Grass and Redfin Pickerel

the angling theater by their larger kin, the famed muskellunge, northern pike and chain pickerel (see pages 155, 157 and 130).

Grass Pickerel

This western subspecies of the redfin is sometimes called mud pickerel. Distribution range covers St. Lawrence River, New York's Lake Champlain, and tributary streams of Lake Ontario, Lake Erie and Lake Michigan; through the Midwest to western Pennsylvania, thence southward, west of the Appalachian Mountains, to include sections of Missouri, Arkansas, Oklahoma, eastern Texas, Louisiana and Alabama. In the main, though, their distribution is concentrated in the drainage systems of the Great Lakes and the Mississippi River.

Redfin Pickerel

The redfin pickerel is regionally nicknamed barred pickerel, banded pickerel, grass pickerel, trout pickerel, and, like its close relative, little pickerel. Distribution range is chiefly through the Atlantic Coast drainage zone, from the St. Lawrence River southward to Georgia, northern Florida, and Alabama.

The Two Pickerels

The "little" in "little pickerels" is appropriate. Average maximum dimensions for both species are lengths of 10 in. and weights under a pound. Fifteen-inch specimens are reported occasionally but are exceptional.

The two are scaled-down versions of the larger pikes, sharing such characteristics as elongated, shallow body; single dorsal and anal fins, similar in size and shape and positioned one above the other far back on the body; well-developed, V-forked tail; a long head with protruding lower jaw and numerous teeth. The basic color is greenish or brownish, or a mixture of the two, with darker vertical bars on the sides. These separate them from adult chain pickerel, whose markings are chainlike. The bars are usually more distinct on the redfin, and grass pickerel lacks the reddish tinges on the fins that give its cousin its name.

Grass and redfin pickerels sometimes are confused with the young of the larger pikes. These details aid in differentiation: unlike muskellunge and northern pike (but in common with chain pickerel), their "cheeks" and gill covers are fully scaled; and they have proportionately shorter, broader snouts.

Habitats of the two species include shallow, weedy areas of streams and lakes, with preferences running to places with little current and a soft floor. The denser the aquatic vegetation, the more they like it, and for this reason they are often encountered in swamps and quiet backwater creeks. Similarly, they may hang around the mouths of tributaries, but do not seem to like spacious open water. It has been noted that they favor clear water that is free of pollution of any kind and excessive silt.

As youngsters they devour small aquatic insects and little crustacean forms, gradually expanding their diet as they develop to engulf tadpoles, larger insects, and assorted little fishes such as minnows, darters, young perch, etc. Also included at times are worms, algae, and bits of aquatic plants.

Neither species is big on anglers' programs. Of the two, redfins come in for more attention, and they can be surprisingly scrappy for their size on the lightest kind of rod. Tiny spoons and spinners, even mini-plugs, will draw response. Since little pickerels favor areas with vegetation, the cue is to seek out weed patches, sunken logs and the like, and cast to such places. Retrieves are usually at a lively clip.

Green Sunfish

SCIENTIFIC NAME: *Lepomis cyanellus*. COMMON NAMES (regionally): Green perch, rubber tail, blue-spotted sunfish, sand bass. Those are mentioned only in the interest of details. Forget 'em. COLOR: Color is an aid to identification. The body is an olive-green, with brassy glints on the lower and under sides. The fins are dusky, the dorsal and anal fins and tail often edged in an off-white or pale shade of yellow or orange. SIZE: 8 or 9 in. are about maximum. FAMILY: Relatives include the bluegill and pumpkinseed (see pages 125 and 159), along with other sunfishes labeled redear, spotted, longear, redbreasted, orange-spotted and others. DISTRIBUTION: Through introduction, green sunfish now have a wide distribution that includes the expanse between Colorado and South Dakota in the West through the Great Lakes region, to western New York in the East, plus California, plus the Mississippi Valley, Alabama, Georgia and New Mexico. They are also reported for drainage streams along the Atlantic Coast. HABITS: In running streams they prefer areas with slower-flowing water. Their diet consists of small fishes, insects and little crustaceans. WHERE CAUGHT: In various areas they're found in brooks, streams, rivers, ponds, reservoirs and lakes. They can live on silt or mud bottoms and seem to be more resistant to siltation than some other species. HOW CAUGHT, BAITS, LURES & TACKLE: Green sunfish are small, but they're lively little fellows on appropriately light tackle. Worms are good bait. They also take crickets and grasshoppers. The larger fish can be caught on small spinning artificials and flies.

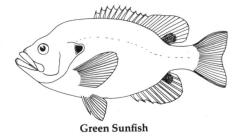

Green Sunfish

Hickory Shad

SCIENTIFIC NAME: *Alosa mediocris*. COMMON NAMES: Shad herring, fall herring. COLOR: American shad (see page 120) and hickory shad can be confused with each other because of strong profile similarities. They both have a deep, rather plump body—somewhat more so in the hickory's case—and a single small dorsal fin about halfway back, plus a deeply forked tail. Their color patterns are similar, too—silvery with bluish-green back—although there are subtle differences on the hickory shad. The tip of the hickory's snout is sooty or dusky, and there are faint dusky stripes running longitudinally on the sides. These are best seen when the fish are alive or immediately after catching. SIZE: Maximum size is about 2 ft. and a weight of 2 to 3 lbs. A 15-incher weighs about 1½ lbs.; an 18-incher, 2 lbs. The largest U.S. river-running herring is the American shad. FAMILY: Like the American shad, this fish is an affiliate of the herring family, Clupeidae. Also like the American shad, it is related to the mighty tarpon. DISTRIBUTION: Overall, the species' distribution is from the Bay of Fundy, Newfoundland, southward to Florida, but the hickory is more of a southern resident than the American shad. HABITS: (1) Whereas American shad and menhaden are plankton eaters, the hickory shad is more piscivorous, or fish-consuming. It devours small fishes of various kinds, including young herring, launce or "sand eels," anchovies, silversides, young porgies and cunners (bergalls), varying the menu with squid, fish eggs and little crabs. (2) Hickory shad are like American shad and their cousins the alewives in being anadromous—spending their lives at sea but running into estuaries and rivers to spawn. After reproduction, the adults probably return to the sea, followed at a later date by the young of that year. WHERE CAUGHT: Close inshore in salt water, also in estuaries and rivers. HOW CAUGHT: Casting of baits and artificials, some trolling of those attractors. BAITS & LURES: Hickories are good sport on light tackle. Like American shad, they put up gallant resistance when hooked. Being fisheaters, they respond to such natural baits as silversides, launce, etc., as well as to squid. But these come-ons must be in small portions on appropriately small hooks. Small live baits are also used. Hickory shad will accept artificials, but they too must be little. Shiny spoons are good. Flies and bright-colored spinning lures, such as jigs dressed in white or yellow, also attract them. TACKLE: Light gear, of course, spinning or conventional.

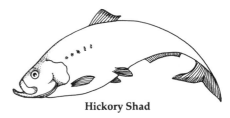

Hickory Shad

Kokanee

SCIENTIFIC NAME: *Oncorynchus nerka*. COMMON NAMES: Kokanee salmon, landlocked sockeye, kickaninny, Kennerly's salmon, redfish, blueback, silver trout, walla, landlocked

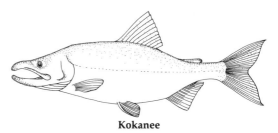

Kokanee

salmon, *Koko* (Indian) yank, and little redfish are regional aliases of a dwarfed, landlocked version of the anadromous sockeye salmon. Some ichthyologists differentiate between the kokanee and sockeye by adding *kennerlyi* to the former's scientific label. COLOR: Before they spawn, their predominant color is silver on the sides and belly. During the breeding period males take on a reddish body color—hence the "red" in regional names—while the head becomes greenish. The females become less colorful, a darkish gray on the sides and greenish along the back. There are variations in colors among both sexes, as well as in the degree of spotting among males. *Note:* Also at spawning time, male kokanees develop a noticeable hump on the back, plus hooked jaws. Hooked jaws, common among Pacific salmons at breeding time, are curving, grotesque-looking extensions consisting of cartilage. They're called kypes. SIZE: In body form the kokanees and their progenitors the sockeye salmon are identical. The major difference is in size. Runts among salmons, kokanees' average maximum is about a pound. Many in anglers' creels run less than that. FAMILY: The family name is Salmonidae. DISTRIBUTION: Originally Alaska, British Columbia, Washington, Oregon and Idaho. Over the years they have been introduced into numerous other states, including California, Nevada, Utah, Montana, Wyoming, Colorado and North Dakota, and eastward with varying degrees of success in Maine, Vermont, Connecticut and New York. They're primarily a Western sport fish, however, inhabiting lakes and reservoirs. Plantings have increased the species' distribution in its native states. HABITS: (1) Kokanees feed chiefly on plankton. (2) Kokanees are the only kind of Pacific salmon that matures in fresh water. Others run to sea to grow up. (3) When spawning time comes, the kokanees shift to tributary streams or to shallower areas of their lakes and there turn out carbon copies of themselves. WHERE CAUGHT, HOW CAUGHT, BAITS, LURES & TACKLE: Kokanees reside in the deeper waters of lakes and reservoirs. Angling methods are trolling artificials, bait fishing at anchor, and, to a lesser extent, fly casting. Trolling is usually at a slow rate, with small spoons and wobblers. Sometimes shiny spinners or flashers are rigged ahead of the lures for extra attraction. Natural baits include worms, salmon eggs, maggots and kernel corn. When the fish are at the surface, small flies produce. Although kokanees are little fellows, they're exceptionally scrappy on very light tackle.

Lake Trout

SCIENTIFIC NAME: *Salvelinus namaycush*. COMMON NAMES: Familiarly called lakers. In Alaska and Western states you will hear the name is mackinaw. In Maine and other northeastern states it becomes togue. Additional regional labels are gray trout, salmon trout and Great Lakes trout. COLOR: Because of lakers' wide distribution, their colors vary appreciably from

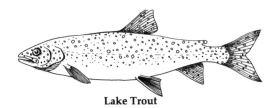

Lake Trout

POPULAR FRESH-WATER FISHES   151

region to region. The range is from a greenish or greenish-gray to shades of brown, often dark. Color of the belly is more or less standard—white or cream. Among some specimens is a yellow or orange tinge on the lower sides, and hints of orange, yellow-orange or pink on the lower fins. Standard is a profusion of whitish or light-colored spots, varying in sizes and shapes. These pepper the head, most of the body, dorsal fin, adipose fin and tail. The profusion of spots and the noticeably forked tail are good field marks for identification. SIZE: It is the largest of the trout group and is topped for size in its family only by chinook salmon. It depends upon areas, but lakers up to 30 lbs. in sport catches are not unusual. Forty-pounders are about maximum for anglers. But these fish are known to attain considerable size. Specimens up into the 60-lb. class have been documented for recreational fishery. Commercial netters in the past have captured brutes weighing up into the 80's and, in a few instances, heavyweights in the 100-lb. bracket. FAMILY: The lake trout is scientifically classified as a char in the family Salmonidae. DISTRIBUTION: Lake trout are native to North America. Their natural distribution extends from Alaska and Yukon Territory across Canada to Labrador, thence southward in sufficiently cool waters from Western states (by introduction) eastward through the Great Lakes to New England and New York State's Finger Lakes. Water temperatures limit southward distribution. Other restrictions are imposed by their need for large expanses, considerable depths, and well-oxygenated water. HABITS: Young lakers fan out in fairly deep water, nourishing themselves with insects and small crustaceans. Later they become almost exclusively fisheaters, devouring such species as whitefish, perch, alewives, kokanees, and whatever others are available in reasonable quantity. Food supply naturally influences their growth rates and ultimate size. When their normal larder is low, lake trout will turn in desperation to aquatic insects and even planktonic forms. The result is readily seen in slower growth and stunted individuals. WHERE CAUGHT: A principal habitat is deep, clear, cool lakes. In some regions they also reside in rivers tributary to such bodies of water, provided conditions of depth, clarity, water temperatures, food, etc., are satisfied. HOW CAUGHT, BAITS, LURES & TACKLE: Deep trolling is the most common method of catching lakers. Natural baits and artificials such as large spinners and spoons are rigged. Wire line may supply enough weight to take a rig deep enough, but these fish can go quite deep, and it may be necessary to add a trolling sinker. Coming into greater use for real deep trolling is a kind of underwater outrigger called a downrigger. (See ''Trolling'' Chapter 4.) In shoaler areas lakers are caught on spinning, fly, and bait-casting equipment, with plugs, spoons, spinners, streamer flies and spinning lures getting results.

Lake Whitefish

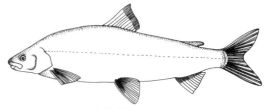

Lake Whitefish

SCIENTIFIC NAME: *Coregonus clupeaformis*. Because of some minor physical differences, lake whitefish in certain areas are more precisely catalogued as a subspecies, with a third Latin word added to their scientific name to so designate them. But this is a technicality that need not bother anglers. COMMON NAMES: Common whitefish is another name, and you can add Great Lakes whitefish and inland whitefish. Also, it's frequently a regional practice to prefix ''whitefish'' with the name of a particular lake, e.g., Lake Huron whitefish. COLOR: This whitefish is a pale green or olive green, sometimes with faint brown tinges, along the back and uppermost sides. Below that, it's silvery and white on the belly. Darker shades of the topside color are noted for some specimens. The fins are whitish or grayish-white, except the tail, which is dusky or darker. SIZE: Lake whitefish are quite long-lived, known to reach the age of 25. A general average for Great Lakes whitefish is 2 to 4 lbs. In other inland bodies of water it's 1 to 3. Fish over 4 lbs. and up to 10 and 15 become progressively more rare. Many years ago, 20-pounders were not uncommon. FAMILY: This species is classified with a group under the head Whitefishes, included with Salmonidae, a distinguished family embracing salmons and trouts. DISTRIBUTION: Lake whitefish are indigenous to northern North American regions. Their distribution extends from Alaska, the Northwest Territories and British Columbia in the west, across Canada to Ontario and the Maritime Provinces, Newfoundland and Labrador, then southward into northern New England, New York and the Great Lakes. HABITS: (1) Lake whitefish consume aquatic insects and their larvae, small crustaceans and mollusks, nymphs, and land insects, according to whatever items are in best supply in their waters. Fly-fishermen might want to note that they're fond of caddisfly and mayfly larvae. (2) They're a schooling species, and under normal conditions are usually quite abundant. The trick, however, is to locate a school. Here's where knowing an area, or getting some fisherman who does, can save a lot of time. (3) Whitefish generally nibble a few times before actually mouthing bait and hook, so a certain amount of patience is required. An important thing to remember is that the hook must be set carefully, by a gradual tightening of line rather than by a smart upward lift of the rod tip, because of their soft mouth parts. WHERE CAUGHT: These whitefish are cold-water residents. Their prime habitat is deep, clear lakes, but they also occur in rivers. Alaska's Yukon and Kuskokwim are cases in point. For a while in spring in large lakes, they may move into shallower areas, water temperatures being low enough there; but as soon as those places begin to warm under an advancing spring's sun, they shift back to deeper water. Another mass movement into shoaler areas, this time to spawn, takes place in autumn, when those waters have cooled sufficiently. BAITS, LURES & TACKLE: Pieces of cut fish —local species such as suckers—are the bait. They, like the hooks, must be small (maybe No. 8 or 6). The rig is fished on bottom, gently jigged continuously to impart extra attraction. Because of their soft mouth they should be reeled in carefully. Another technique involves chumming. But here local regulations must be checked, for chumming and/or the method may be illegal in that area. Where allowed, the procedure consists of lowering the chum, finely chopped minnows or other fish, in a pail to the bottom, where it is spilled. With any luck this will attract a group of whitefish, whereupon they can be foul-hooked—also known as snagging or snatching—by upwards lifts of the rod tip. The hooks may be tied to the line in a series or attached directly to a sinker. Canned kernel corn and boiled rice are also employed. Ice angling for lake whitefish is becoming increasingly more popular. Again bottom fishing is the method, with chumming when allowed. Live or salted minnows are the bait. Salted minnows are also used as chum. Snagging is combined with chumming for ice fishing if it is permitted by law—and, it's suspected, when it isn't. We mentioned earlier that lake whitefish consume the larvae of caddisflies and mayflies. When there are hatches of these insects, fly-fishermen get in their licks.

Landlocked Salmon

Landlocked Salmon

SCIENTIFIC NAME: *Salmo salar.* The scientific tag for this fish is a ditto of that for the Atlantic salmon. Why? Because the landlocked salmon is essentially an Atlantic salmon. The most important difference to fishermen is that the former resides only in fresh water, whereas anadromous Atlantics spend part of their lives at sea. COMMON NAMES: Ouananiche, lake Atlantic salmon, Sebago salmon. COLOR: The two forms are identical anatomically. Size difference is the most obvious way to separate them. Landlocked salmon are smaller. About the only other aid in separation is the characteristic silvery color of sea-run Atlantics. Among the landlocked there are the variations in color patterns typical of salmonid fishes. SIZE: Occasional specimens up to 7 to 10 lbs. are reported in sport catches, but a creel average is more in the neighborhood of 2, 2½ lbs. *Note:* Visiting fishermen should check state regulations governing minimum keeping sizes and catch limits. FAMILY: One of the Salmonidae, or salmons. DISTRIBUTION: Deep, cold, well-oxygenated lakes are a prime habitat requirement of landlocked salmon. This has always contributed to the limitation of their distribution. Orginally they occurred in Canada's Maritimes and the province of Quebec and in suitable lakes in New England, plus a few in New York, including Champlain and Ontario. Maine has long been a leading U.S. landlocked salmon region. Over many years it has also produced some of the largest fish. A record 22½-pounder came from Maine's Sebago Lake, way back in 1907. HABITS: (1) Like Atlantics, they can spawn more than once. (2) When very young they eat aquatic insects and tiny invertebrate creatures. Later their diet expands to include many kinds of forage species such as yellow perch, suckers, minnows, etc. WHERE CAUGHT: Deep, cold, clear lakes with plenty of oxygen. HOW CAUGHT, BAITS, LURES & TACKLE: The better landlocked salmon angling begins in spring when the ice moves out, and continues into June. Some of the fish move upstream after spawning; others move downriver. During this period they're still in fairly shallow water and can be reached by fly casting, spin casting of small artificials, or by near-surface trolling of streamers, small bucktails and live smelt. Smelt are a logical choice as a natural bait, since they are a forage species for landlocked salmon. They also inspired a smelt-pattern streamer. For maximum sport, veterans recommend small dry flies on No. 18 or 16 hooks. With the warming effects of late spring and early summer, the salmon range outward into deeper water. Now a change of techniques to deeper trolling or still-fishing is indicated. Again live smelt become a logical choice for both methods. Trollers also rig small spoons.

Mountain Whitefish

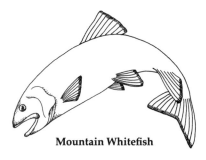

Mountain Whitefish

SCIENTIFIC NAME: *Prosopium williamsoni.* COMMON NAMES: Rocky Mountain whitefish, and, regionally, mountain herring and pea nose ! COLOR: Typical of whitefishes, the mountain species possesses a rather slender body similar to that of a trout. In body shape and color mountain whitefish resembles lake whitefish, although the body is more cylindrical. Its color is brownish, gray-brown or gray-blue topside, giving way to silvery below and white on the ventral surface. SIZE: They're not large fish. Specimens weighing 3 and 4 lbs. are on record, but the average is less than 2 lbs. and more like 1. FAMILY: This species belongs to a fresh-water tribe whose family name, appropriately, is whitefishes. They're considered relatives of trouts and salmons, Salmonidae. Generally classified under the group title with mountain whitefish are species of ciscoes and lake whitefish. DISTRIBUTION & WHERE CAUGHT: Mountain whitefishes inhabit the colder streams and lakes of the U.S. West. They're encountered throughout the Rocky Mountain region and on out to the Pacific Northwest and British Columbia. HABITS: (1) Mountain whitefish can adapt themselves to a fairly wide diet, depending upon what their local larder holds in quantity—going from tiny planktonic forms to aquatic insects and their larvae. (2) Also depending upon the food situation, they may dine at various levels, bottom to near surface. Accordingly, they will rise to the top for artificial flies when hungry, a behavior that hasn't gone unnoticed by anglers. HOW CAUGHT, BAITS, LURES & TACKLE: They're a controversial species in the angling arena. Many trout fishermen consider them undesirable, since they favor the more desirable salmonids for food and thus cheat fishermen of potentially larger trout. Many fishermen, however, enjoy the lively light-tackle sport they afford. Mountain whitefish can be real sporty on fly tackle. Even some purist trout hunters are glad to tie into them during the colder weather between seasons. Since mountain whitefish feed on insect larvae and even their own eggs, natural stonefly nymphs and salmon eggs are effective baits. Generally they're most apt to rise to artificial flies in the warmer months, and will also accept small spinners. Casting or drifting an artificial or natural bait near the bottom, depending upon time of year, is a technique. They are good action on either fly gear or light spinning tackle.

Muskellunge

SCIENTIFIC NAME: *Esox masquinongy.* Three subspecies have been described: Great Lakes muskellunge *(Esox masquinongy masquinongy),* Ohio or Lake Chautauqua, N.Y. muskellunge *(Esox masquinongy ohiensis),* and Wisconsin or tiger (or northern) muskellunge *(Esox masquinongy immaculatus).* Their common names provide clues to their general distribution. Separating them can be complex and serves no practical purpose here. COMMON NAMES: "Musky" is the popular common name in the U.S. According to one source, the name originally came from two Indian words, *mas* ("ugly") and *kinonge* ("fish"). Because of the freedom taken with pronunciation and spelling, there are said to be more than 50 regional names and variations of "muskellunge." Here's a sampling: muskalong, masquenonge, 'lunge or 'longe, masqualonge, and masqueallonge. Other area names are great pike, barred muskellunge, blue pike, and great muskellunge. COLOR: The musky's profile is typically a pike's. Muskies' colors are subject to some differences and have been described variously as brownish and olive-brown along the upper surfaces, becoming lighter below. There are darker side markings that take the forms of irregular bars or large spots. SIZE: By any name muskies are up near the top on the long list of inland sport fishes in the U.S. Prime reasons are size and fighting power. Fifteen- to 25- and 30-pounders raise no eyebrows among musky regulars. Forty-pounders are on the books, as are hefties up into the 50- and 60-lb. classes. *Note:* Visiting anglers should check on minimum legal keeping sizes in the states fished. They vary. FAMILY: Muskellunge are in the pike family, Esocidae, along with northern pike, chain pickerel, grass pickerel and redfin pickerel. All are of the genus Esox. DISTRIBUTION: Broadly speaking, from Canada's province of Ontario, the St. Lawrence River and western New York, out through the central Great Lakes states and northward to Minnesota, including the Ohio River and

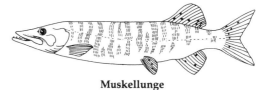

Muskellunge

Tennessee River systems. Pennsylvania, West Virginia, Kentucky, Michigan and Wisconsin are among the states offering musky fishing. Successful artificial propagation and stocking have done much to expand the species' distribution. HABITS: (1) Like northern pike, they have a reputation for being voracious, omnivorous feeders. They're chiefly fisheaters, devouring minnows, yellow perch, walleyes, suckers, bluegills, or whatever other species are in good supply in that area at the time. The stomachs of large muskies also have yielded young ducks and geese, frogs, crayfish, salamanders, assorted shore birds, snakes, and small animals such as mice, rats, squirrels, chipmunks and muskrats. (2) It has been noted by biologists that muskies feed most actively in water temperature of about 68 ° F., slowing down as the thermometer moves to either side of that mark, and stopping altogether when temperatures climb high. (3) Several factors influence muskies' mode of life. Food supply and its distribution are among the most important. Water temperatures, naturally, are another. So are changes in water levels, understandably. (4) They do not seem to be extensive travelers. In summer, populations are more or less stationary, occasionally shifting into deeper water if food needs dictate. In rivers such movements, if they occur, are likely to be upstream in summer, downriver in autumn. WHERE CAUGHT: Throughout their range muskies occur in lakes of different sizes—from the Great Lakes on down, along with rivers and streams. Their favored habitat is quiet, clear water with gardens of weeds and other cover. Commonly they frequent shallow areas, but scouting for food takes them into deeper water. Except in large rivers such as the St. Lawrence, those residing in streams are likely to be smaller—to 5 lbs. or less—than muskies inhabiting lakes. Like northern pike, muskies often lie in wait for food. Except in summer, when they shift to deeper lake water, they're likely to be found in depths up to 12 or 15 ft., and areas with beds of weeds are likely territory. In rivers muskellunge often seek out the quieter backwaters away from the main flow. Here too they favor areas with cover. Other places with potential include the edges of drop-offs in channels. HOW CAUGHT, BAITS, LURES & TACKLE: During summer's heat muskies will retreat to deeper areas with up to 50 or 75 ft. of water. Deep trolling of plugs, spinners and other artificials on wire line, according to regions, is the way to contact them. Here again, *state and local regulations should be checked*. The use of wire lines may be illegal. Some general tips offered by musky regulars: (1) Usually afternoon is the best time of day. (2) Prime months are September and October (this does not necessarily hold for all regions, however). (3) Muskies are completely unpredictable. One day any of several artificials or baits will draw a response. The very next day they will ignore everything. (4) Repeated casting in the same area often is the ticket. Muskies are loners, and it may require several casts to get one interested in your offering. Short or medium casts are favored over long ones, and lively, uninterrupted retrieves are usually more effective than slow cranking with pauses. (5) Sometimes a musky will pursue a lure without grabbing it. It may be necessary to repeat casting and retrieving. (6) In feeding, muskies tend to grab a smaller fish in the middle, then work it around in the mouth for swallowing head first. They can seize a plug in similar fashion, which makes it difficult to set the hook until the jaws relax. Veteran musky fishermen recommend striking the fish several times in rapid succession. (7) Local weather and water conditions may (or may not) play a part in success. Inquiries are worthwhile. (8) There are artificials designated as prime for muskellunge, designed to be worked in different ways. Follow the directions accompanying them.

Boating a lively, toothy rascal such as a musky can be tricky. Not recommended for the inexperienced is a method used for the smaller muskies and other species with a mouthful of biters: seizing the fish by pressing thumb and forefinger into the eye sockets. Safer is a landing net, but it must have a deep bag, because these fish are long-bodied. The larger muskies are best gaffed. Care must be used in removing the hook. Muskies are slippery. Tools are a pair of long-nosed pliers and a piece of cloth with which to grasp the fish. If a musky is to be released, the fisherman is going to have his work cut out for him if he wants to retrieve his lure without fatally injuring the fish.

Northern Pike

SCIENTIFIC NAME: *Esox lucius*. COMMON NAMES: Northern, great northern pike, jackfish, pickerel, snake, jackpike. COLOR: Aiding in the identification of northern pike is a color scheme that goes to shades of green, darkest on the dorsal surface, lighter below, with a white underside. Also characteristic are numerous whitish or pale yellow-white, oblong spots, extending like dotted lines along the upper sides from head to base of tail. On the fins are dark spots. SIZE: There are so many variations among growth rates in different regions that it's impossible to state maximum potential size in sport catches. However, a potential does go to 15 and 20 lbs., although most of the fish caught are smaller. Among the largest sport-caught northerns on record are a 46-pound 2-ouncer (New York) and a 53-pounder (Ireland). FAMILY: In addition to this fish, the pike family, Esocidae, in North America includes the famed muskellunge, chain pickerel, redfin pickerel and grass pickerel. In common with these relatives, the northern pike possesses a distinctively long, slender body and long jaws (the lower protrudes somewhat on northern pike) well armed with sharp teeth. DISTRIBUTION: An ancient breed whose progenitors are believed to have evolved in Europe during the Cretaceous Age, 60 million years or more ago, northern pike are widely holarctic in distribution, which is to say their range is in northern regions of North America. In the U.S. they occur in a northern belt that stretches

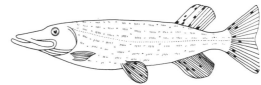
Northern Pike

from New England, New York and Pennsylvania through the Great Lakes states, Iowa and part of Missouri, to Nebraska. The species doesn't occur naturally west of the Mississippi River, but plantings have extended its range to include some more southerly waters and regions as far west as Colorado and Montana. U.S. distribution also includes Alaska. The species' Canadian range, broadly speaking, is from Labrador, New Brunswick, and part of the province of Ontario to the Northwest Territories and British Columbia. HABITS: (1) Like other pikes, northerns favor waters with plenty of weed and brush cover, and they are aggressive predators, preying primarily upon other fishes. (2) Although they wander in open water in scouting for food, northerns' chief movements are at breeding time, when they seek shoal areas. If these shallow places are nearby, fine. If not, the breeders will journey reasonable distances to find them. Trips of nearly 50 miles have been recorded. (3) Northern pike have always had a reputation for being voracious. Mature northerns are chiefly piscivorous —fisheaters. In their stomachs are found just about every species of smaller fishes available in their areas, not excluding young pike. In the manner of many other predators, northerns prey upon whatever finned neighbors happen to be in best supply at the time—which is perfectly sensible when you stop to think about it. When forage fishes are in temporarily short supply, they turn to other items, and here they can be equally non-selective. There is no exaggerating their consumption of frogs—tadpoles, adults, snails, mice, crayfish, crustaceans and insect forms. Young waterfowl and snakes have also been reported in their digestive tracts. WHERE CAUGHT: Because of the regional variables involved, chiefly water temperatures and the kinds, habits, quantities and distribution of forage fishes, there can be no blanket rule as to the best depths in which to hook northern pike. Many are caught in less than 15 ft. of water. In summer, for example, they often frequent weedy areas in such shallow water. But I must repeat that water temperatures and availability of food are key influences. Accordingly, when water temperatures rise too high or if the forage fishes they fancy at the moment are in deeper areas, northerns will shift. Also, as summer progresses and temperatures climb, northern pike often show a reluctance to bite. This could be due to a kind of heat-induced lethargy or to a summertime abundance of food. Much of the better angling is in cool or cold weather. There's also good action for a while right after a spawning run, when northerns are especially hungry. Broadly speaking, early morning is probably the best time of day. HOW CAUGHT, BAITS, LURES & TACKLE: Casting and trolling are standard methods. Northern pike will smack almost any kind of attractor, natural or man-created. Live baits, such as large minnows, are successful. So are many kinds of plugs, shallow- and deeper-running models, along with spinners in combination with natural bait, streamer flies and shiny spoons. There's so much variation that visiting anglers should check locally (and while they're at it, ask about the most productive fishing hours). Northern pike also offer an excellent opportunity to experiment with natural and artificial baits.

Light tackle is the ticket to best action. Northern pike are tough
fighters when hooked, a Class A sport fish.

Pumpkinseed

SCIENTIFIC NAME: *Lepomis gibbosus.* COMMON NAMES:
Pumpkinseed, also called common sunfish, yellow sunfish.
COLOR: Olivaceous body with bluish spots; half a dozen wavy
blue lines radiating outward from the mouth area past the eyes
to the gill covers. When the fish is young, the forward portion
of the belly is orange or yellow. Characteristic are the hard
black gill covers tipped in orange or red. SIZE: Their maximum
size is appreciably less than bluegills. Eight or 9 in. and a
weight in ounces are maximum. FAMILY: One of the true fresh-
water sunfishes, Centrarchidae. DISTRIBUTION: Over the years
this sunfish has been distributed widely around the U.S. and in
eastern Canada. Now the species' scope is from there
southward through the Northeastern states to Georgia,
westward through Pennsylvania and Ohio to the Mississippi
River system, and beyond to Iowa and the Dakotas. The
species was introduced to West Coast fresh waters in the late
1800s. HABITS: (1) Pumpkinseeds commonly are found in the
same areas as their relatives the bluegills. See page 125.
(2) Their food consists of insects, worms, small crustaceans and
mollusks, and to a lesser extent, little fishes. Their growth rate
is governed by available food, and is stunted if supplies are
inadequate. WHERE CAUGHT: The pumpkinseed's habitat is
ponds and other quiet waters, preferably those with soft floors
and plenty of cover such as aquatic vegetation, sunken logs,
etc., usually in relatively shallow areas close to shore. HOW
CAUGHT, BAITS, LURES & TACKLE: Pumpkinseeds and
bluegills frequently are caught in the same waters. This
contributes to their angling popularity, along with the facts
that they're usually plentiful, are easily caught from shore on
the simplest, lightest kind of tackle, and readily take a variety
of baits that include garden worms. Worms also are a bait for
catching them through ice. For a little more sport, try fly tackle
with wet flies. Yellow is reported effective. Pattern is
secondary.

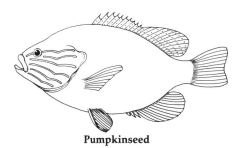
Pumpkinseed

Rainbow Trout

SCIENTIFIC NAME: Ichthyologists want to be precise. It's part
of their job. But in this rascal they met a challenge. The species'
seemingly interminable variations in color patterns alone are
enough to drive scientists right up a wall. At one time no fewer
than 17 different groupings were recognized, and each

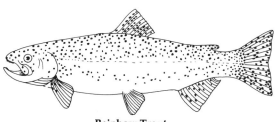
Rainbow Trout

assigned a Latin name. Not only are there color variations from population to population but within populations as well. To delve into those complexities serves no practical purpose. Therefore we'll consider all rainbow trout as one species— *Salmo gairdneri*—recognizing only two major subdivisions, steelhead trout, which are sea-run rainbows, and Kamloops trout, which are inland rainbows. COMMON NAME: Rainbow. COLOR: To say that there are numerous variations in color patterns among non-migratory rainbows is an understatement. A few random samplings will give you an idea. Back and upper sides can be brownish or greenish, or blue or blue-green on young individuals, with a paler shade of the same color on the flanks, followed by a silvery underside. There's usually a band of color running along the sides. It might be red or reddish pink or reddish violet, or an iridescent mixture of several colors. Commonly, non-migratory rainbows are profusely spotted in black atop the head and along the back and upper sides, including dorsal and adipose fins and the entire tail and its base. Immature inland individuals may have spots or lack them and, when small, carry dusky markings. And so on. Whatever color variations, rainbows possess the standard trout body configuration and complement of fins. The mouth's interior is white, a detail separating the steelhead or sea-run rainbow from chinook and silver coho salmons. Superficially the rainbow resembles the cutthroat but differs in lacking the latter's splashes of red on the lower jaw and teeth on the rear of the tongue. SIZE: Top weights for rainbows have been given as 48, 50 and 52 lbs. but are challenged by some authorities. All conditions being optimum, the steelhead and lake-grown Kamloops forms are usually the biggest. It's difficult to state averages. But one consensus of steelhead catches reveals a mean of 8 to 10 lbs., with individual fish as high as 12. Less common are specimens from 16 to 20 lbs., with fish to 25 lbs. or better. Steelheads up to 36 lbs. are mentioned for California and British Columbia. On record are lake-dwelling Kamloops trout up to 37 lbs. FAMILY: Grouped with the Salmonidae, with other trouts. DISTRIBUTION: At one time, in the continent's western and Pacific coastal reaches, from Alaska and the Aleutians to northern Mexico. Since then the species has been hatchery-propagated and widely distributed throughout North America. The western Rockies and Sierra Nevadas are part of its range. HABITS: (1) Infant rainbows may remain in their natal streams for different lengths of time. For some it's a few months, after which they shift to lakes. Others may linger in streams and tributary rivers for a year or two, or more, before making a move into lakes or down to the sea. Still others never leave the streams. (2) Young rainbows subsist chiefly on aquatic insect forms and small crustaceans. As they grow, they add terrestrial insects and small forage fishes. SPECIAL NOTES ON STEELHEADS: They're the migratory rainbows, the fish heeding a call to run downriver to the sea to spend a few years of their life in salt water. There they dine well on smaller fishes and squid, along with forms of crustaceans known as amphipods. When the time comes to return to their native rivers, steelheads are robust and sleek, with the silvery color

and steely blue back characteristic of sea-run salmonid fishes. Also typical of salmonids, there is a change in color as they proceed upriver and spawning time approaches. In general the color darkens and spotting becomes more profuse. A reddish band appears on each side, more pronounced among the males. It has been said that there are spawning-bound migrations of steelheads somewhere on the Pacific Coast at just about every season of the year. These movements too are variable from region to region. Times can be checked locally because it is then that anglers go to work. The youngsters' stay in their natal streams can last a year or two or more before they run to sea. In the ocean they linger anywhere from a few months to four years. Rainbows have been called the most migratory of trouts, especially in the steelhead form. It's known that steelheads wander considerable distances at sea. To further complicate the picture, there are rainbows that migrate downriver toward the sea but do not go beyond tidal waters, then return upriver for spawning. These treks also can involve considerable distances. It is because of their river journeys that dams have threatened their very existence in several areas.
WHERE CAUGHT, HOW CAUGHT, BAITS, LURES & TACKLE: Rainbows are truly great game fish, especially the steelheads. A rather wide choice of techniques is open to steelhead hunters, with differences and variations all over the place. In California, for instance, many are caught by trolling small artificials in brackish water. They also are caught by fly casting. Surf casters using shrimp or strip baits take some from sandy beaches near river mouths during spawning runs. Marine worms, ghost shrimp, salmon egg clusters and crayfish tails also figure in methods. Fact is, rainbows in their various forms are caught on a wide variety of natural baits and artificials. The real rainbow purists stay with flies. But there are many places in which anglers must be prepared to adapt when conditions demand it. There's that old and proven maxim that anglers should try to match their lures or baits as closely as possible to the diets of the species involved; and in the case of rainbows it involves consideration of their regions. For example, fly-fishing is likely to be most productive where the trout feed chiefly on insects and perhaps small crustaceans. In contrast, with Kamloops trout that fatten on forage species such as ciscoes and young kokanee salmon, spin fishing and trolling of spoons and plugs are likely to be more effective. Dry flies are used with deadly effectiveness on rivers and lakes. But stream fishing is the sport that readily appraises an angler's ability. For example, river rainbows favor fast-moving water. To place a floating pattern properly and argue with a tough opponent in a current requires a better than average skill. Generally speaking, rainbows tend to move around more toward dusk, and on lakes and streams they can be seen rising, especially during periods of insect hatches. From California's Russian River northward to the coastal streams of Oregon, (the Umpqua, tributaries of the Columbia, others), and Washington's Kalama, Skyomish, Wind rivers, etc. and northward to British Columbia, steelhead fly-fishermen gather at times of the fall and winter runs and, in some areas, for

summer showings too. There's fishing from shore and from boats. Both fly tackle and spinning gear figure largely in the rainbow trout fishery, but for steelheads the equipment runs heavier. These fish run to respectable size, remember, and every inch is muscle. Steelhead rods go from about 8 to 9, 9½ ft. long. Their prime requisite is power, well distributed throughout. Single-action reels with an adjustable brake are more popular than automatic fly reels, although they are used too. Reading the water is a vital part of steelhead fishing success. These trout prefer moving water. Therefore, riffles are likely places, as are narrow, fairly fast runs at the heads of pools or alongside them, or between boulders. Channels with a steady, consistent flow also offer promise, along with slicks at the tail ends of pools, where the water is shallow and begins to pick up speed before the next riffle or series of little rapids. Bottom and near-bottom fishing with conventional and spinning tackle has its advocates too, with natural baits and artificials being rigged. Sinker weights must be gauged to current strengths in the areas. Spare sinkers, hooks and lures, or an ample supply of bait, are indicated, because hang-ups and loss of terminal tackle in this method can be high, due to rocks, sunken logs and other obstructions. Still another technique is to drift a natural bait—shrimp, worm or whatever —and let it pause at the end of each drift, then retrieve slowly. Steelheads have been known to follow a drifting bait before grabbing it. *Note:* Check on state and local regulations governing steelhead fishing.

Redbreast Sunfish

SCIENTIFIC NAME: *Lepomis auritus.* COMMON NAMES: Among several area nicknames: Redbelly, red brim or bream, longear sunfish, robin, redbreast bream. COLOR: Generally yellowish on the sides. The "redbreast" in their common name stems from the fact that their underside turns a vivid red or red-orange during the breeding season. The identification clincher is a long black tab, without white, yellow or red trim, on each gill cover. SIZE: Maximum size is about 10 to 12 in. and a pound. FAMILY: True sunfishes, Centrarchidae. DISTRIBUTION: Chiefly an eastern U.S. species, redbreast sunfish range from New Brunswick, Maine, and Lake Ontario southward, east of the Appalachians, to the Carolinas, Georgia, Florida and Alabama. Introduction has brought them to Oklahoma, coastal rivers in Gulf states and eastern Texas. HABITS: Even as adults, their mouth is rather small, so their diet consists of insects and whatever small fishes and crustaceans they can accommodate. WHERE CAUGHT: Although some are caught in ponds and lakes, they're most abundant in rivers and streams. HOW CAUGHT: Casting of baits and lures. BAITS & LURES: For anglers they can be very

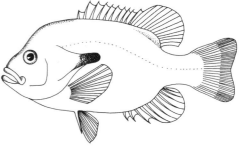

Redbreast Sunfish

cooperative, accepting a variety of natural baits and artificials—
so long as they are small. Little spoons and spinners are
effective, along with mini-plugs, popping bugs and flies.
TACKLE: They're little guys, but scrappy on very light tackle.

Redear Sunfish

SCIENTIFIC NAME: *Lepomis microlophus*. COMMON NAMES:
Regionally, shellcracker and stumpknocker.COLOR: Redears
most closely resemble the pumpkinseed (see page 159),
another sunfish. Differences are a lack of dorsal fin spotting
and no bluish bands on the sides of the head. The redear's
body color is olive, overlaid with spots in a darker tone of the
same color and dusky bars on the sides. SIZE: Fastest and best
growth has been noted for clear-water areas. Maximum sizes
are about 10 to 12 in. and weights of 1, 1¼lbs. Occasional
heavier specimens are reported. FAMILY: Sunfishes,
Centrarchidae. DISTRIBUTION: The range has been broadened
considerably by stocking. Originally the species was native to
central and eastern portions of the South—the lower
Mississippi River sector, Alabama, Georgia, Florida. Hatchery
and farm pond propagation and plantings have broadened the
range to extend northward to the Midwest and westward to
Oklahoma, Texas and New Mexico. HABITS: (1) Throughout
their range, redears serve as both a forage and sport species,
and because of their diet are not heavy competition for other
fishes subsisting on insects. (2) Although they can exist in
turbid water, redears thrive better in clear water. Their
preference is for quiet areas, and they get the nickname
"stumpknocker" from a habit of lingering in the vicinity of
submerged stumps and logs. The alias, "shellcracker," stems
from their fondness for snails and mollusks, whose shells they
crush with grinding teeth located in the throat. WHERE
CAUGHT: Redear sunfish occur in lakes, ponds and rivers.
HOW CAUGHT: Simple casting from boats and shores. BAITS &
LURES: Natural baits are favored over artificials for these fish,
and they include worms, grubs and pieces of shrimp. TACKLE:
Hooks must be small, Nos. 8 to 6, because redears have little
mouths. It goes without saying that tackle should be extra
light. Fresh-water spinning equipment is good.

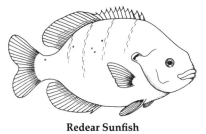

Redear Sunfish

Sauger

SCIENTIFIC NAME: *Stizostedion canadense.* COMMON NAMES: Sauger is the most widely used common name nowadays. But aliases such as sand pike, river pike, jack salmon, and jackfish persist regionally. COLOR: An olive or greenish-gray, darkest on the dorsal surface and upper sides. The underside is white. Extending downward from the back are irregular darkish-brown or olive bars. Points of difference between the sauger and the walleye are two or three rows of distinct black dots on the first dorsal of the sauger (the walleye's is vaguely blotched) and a white tip on the lower lobe of the walleye's tail (absent in the sauger). SIZE: Differing from region to region, sport-caught size ranges can be from less than a pound to 1½, and 1 to 3 lbs. Some of the heavier saugers are recorded for the Missouri River system, up to 3–5 and 4–6. Maximum size seems to be in the vicinity of 8 lbs. Approximate length-weight relationships: 14–15 in., just under 1 lb. to a pound; 18 in., near or at 2 lbs.; 20 in., 3 lbs.; and roughly a pound for each 1½–2 in. thereafter. FAMILY: This fish is in the perch family, Percidae, with the walleye (see below), and looks very much like that species. DISTRIBUTION & WHERE CAUGHT: Overall distribution of saugers fans out from Canada—Hudson Bay drainage system eastward to New Brunswick—southward through the Great Lakes, then eastward and westward to West Virginia, Iowa, Montana, Oklahoma and Alabama, and in the Mississippi, Missouri, Ohio and Tennessee rivers. Throughout their range they are native to the largest rivers and lakes, and for some reason do not thrive in smaller bodies of water. They need much more living room than walleyes. As a result some of the better sauger fishing is in big impoundments and in the waters below dams. HABITS: (1) When young they feed on insect larvae. As they get older they turn to a fish diet varied with insects and crayfish and other crustaceans. (2) For reasons not yet known, they travel considerable distances and seem better able to live in silt-filled waters than walleyes. In their journeys they exhibit seasonal runs, some of which are pronounced in autumn and early winter. HOW CAUGHT, BAITS & LURES: Angling procedures are trolling and casting artificials, and still-fishing with live bait. TACKLE: Spinning gear is suggested for casting, light conventional tackle for trolling.

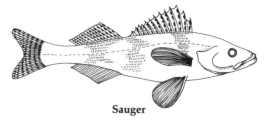

Sauger

Walleye

SCIENTIFIC NAME: *Stizostedion vitreum vitreum.* COMMON NAMES: One is walleye pike. Others, perhaps better forgotten, are yellow walleye, pike, pike-perch, pickerel, jackfish and yellow pike-perch, plus still more regional tags. Any reference to pike is misleading, because they do not belong to the pike

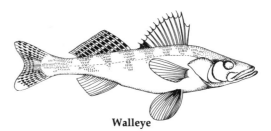

Walleye

tribe. COLOR: The walleye's color pattern is subject to some variation. In the main, the body is a shade of brown with olive or yellowish tones, darkest on the back and upper half, somewhat lighter below, becoming white or yellowish-white on the underside. There are indistinct darker markings in brown or near-black along the dorsal surface and sides. The rounded pelvic fins are an off-white or yellowish, and the tail's lower lobe is dipped in white. SIZE: An approximate length-weight yardstick is 13–14 in., 1 lb.; 18 in., 2 lbs.; 20 in., 3–4 lbs.; and a minimum of about a pound for every 2 in. thereafter. On stringers, walleyes go to about 3 lbs. A 5-pounder is considered good; anything over that to about 7 or 8 lbs. is braggin' size; and any fish larger than that are potential contest contenders. Among the largest on record are a Canadian 22¼-pounder and a Tennessee catch weighing just short of 25. FAMILY: Some 99 members of the perch family, Percidae, are described for the United States and Canada. DISTRIBUTION: Originally native to Canada and the northern regions of the U.S., walleyes have been nursery-propagated, introduced and planted so extensively that their distribution now can be said to cover most of the United States and much of Canada. They're a major fresh-water game fish in both countries. HABITS: (1) Walleyes are voracious hunters, devouring quantities of minnows, perch, panfishes, and what-have-you. Their voraciousness can be either a blessing or a curse. In large bodies of water their consumption of forage species contributes to a balance of life. In smaller lakes it can pose serious food competition for other game fishes. (2) Walleyes like lots of living room. Tagging experiments reveal that in breeding travels and other wanderings they journey as much as 100 miles and more. (3) Walleyes are a schooling species. Therefore when there's one, there are likely to be others. But these schools move around, and may require some hunting. Usually all the members of a given school are about the same size. (4) They tend to congregate over gravelly, sandy or rocky bottoms, and on the edges of currents and eddies. They also prowl deeper pools along undercut banks. (5) As a rule, walleyes are near the bottom, which is a cue to rigging. (6) By day, especially in warmer weather or bright sunshine, they seek out deeper, cooler or shadier places. On overcast days they may visit shallower areas in search of food. Important: they feed a lot at night, from dusk on into the predawn hours. Also at night, they leave deeper water to prowl shoaler areas. WHERE CAUGHT: For the most part, walleyes inhabit the larger lakes, rivers and streams. They require cool, clear water with reasonable depths in which to escape summer heat. HOW CAUGHT, BAITS, LURES & TACKLE: More walleyes probably are caught by trolling and casting, but slow drifting with a spinner and minnow combination near the bottom can pay off too. They will also respond to deep-running plugs and spoons, and to sinking or deep-running plugs (red is an effective color) that are cast and then worked near the bottom. Metal-cored lines and small trolling sinkers will take a trolled rig deep. Jigs can also be used if worked deep. An old stunt is to locate the fish by trolling a deep-running artificial, then pause to jig just off the bottom. Walleyes are caught in so many places that several techniques and variations have been developed over the years. Trolling a spinner and night-crawler combination is still another. Plastic worms and small eels are also rigged, and hooks of artificials can be garnished with strips of pork rind. Such attractors often draw "short-strikers"—fish that hit short of the hook. Adding a second or tail hook usually takes care of them. Live-fish bait is about as dependable as any, since walleyes are primarily fisheaters. They are not targets for fly-fishermen, since they invariably are deep and won't rise to a dry or wet fly. However, anglers have reported success at dusk and at night in shallows, using streamers on sinking fly lines and working them close to the bottom.

White Bass

SCIENTIFIC NAME: *Roccus chrysops*. COMMON NAMES: Barfish and silver bass. COLOR: The basic color of white bass is silver. As on its relative the yellow bass, the back and sides carry narrow, dark or dusky stripes running horizontally from behind the head to the base of the tail. On the white bass these are unbroken. On the yellow bass those below the lateral line are interrupted. This striping and the general coloration have prompted the regional nickname "striped bass," an understandable but confusing misnomer, becoming even less desirable as the real striped bass are introduced in more and more inland waters. SIZE: As in the case of yellow bass, after their first autumn, growth is approximately 1 to 2 in. per year greater for southern fish than for northern, averaging 17 in. and 15, respectively, at age 5. At 10–10½ in., white bass weigh roughly half a pound. This doubles at 13 in., doubles again by 16 in., and reaches 3 lbs. at 17–18 in. Their maximum weight appears to be about 5 lbs. FAMILY: As pointed out, white bass are a close relative of the yellow bass in the Serranidae family. They share the distinction of being the only two representatives of that tribe living exclusively in fresh water. DISTRIBUTION: Left to nature, the distribution of white bass was once limited to the Great Lakes region, portions of the Mississippi River drainage system, and a couple of the more southwesterly central states. But that has been changed radically as white bass, unlike yellow bass, have proved to be a good species for stocking. The creation of impoundments such as Lake Sam Rayburn and Toledo Bend in Texas, and Clark Hill Reservoir on the Savannah River between Georgia and South Carolina, has also contributed to the wider distribution of these fish. Today distribution fans out beyond Missouri, Arkansas and Kansas to include lakes in the South, Oklahoma and Texas. HABITS: (1) When very small, white bass subsist on plankton, later taking on insects and their larvae as they are able to accommodate them. Eventually their menu swings to smaller

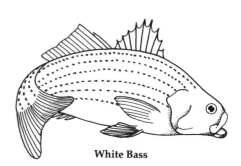

White Bass

fishes. Gizzard shad are popular. They also accept perch, bluegills, crappies and the like, adding insects and crayfish along the way. (2) During daylight hours white bass generally are in deeper water, shifting to the shoals at dusk to feed. Angling is usually best at this time, and again during the early morning hours before the sun is high. (3) On the basis of their performance in big impoundments, they seem to require lots of living room and ample gravel, stony or rocky floors on which to reproduce. WHERE CAUGHT: White bass occur in lakes, rivers and large streams and favor reasonably clear water. HOW CAUGHT, BAITS, LURES & TACKLE: In deeper water the technique is to slowly troll a spinner and minnow combination near the bottom. Live minnows are also effective in deeper fishing, as well as in the shallows. At dusk, when they come into shallower water to forage, they often come near the surface. Here spinners, little plugs, flies and small spinning lures get results. White bass travel in schools, and if one or two are extracted, the promise is for more. In any case, they call for the lightest kind of tackle. On that they will provide a lot of lively action.

White Catfish

SCIENTIFIC NAME: *Ictalurus catus*. COMMON NAMES: White cat, cat. COLOR: The white cat is typical of its breed in form. A shade of blue or gray-blue on the dorsal surface and sides, changing—sometimes abruptly—to a white belly. And there are those standard catfish sensory appendages, the whiskers, or fleshy barbels, about the mouth and snout, which aid in locating food items along the bottom. SIZE: Fully grown, they run smaller than channel cats. A sport-fishery range is from about 10 to 18 in., with weights to 3 lbs. But heavier fish are hooked. The maximum size is in the vicinity of 10 to 12 lbs. FAMILY: The white cat's clan is the Ictaluridae, or fresh-water catfishes. North American relatives include the blue, channel, and flathead catfishes and the bullhead. DISTRIBUTION: Originally meted out by Dame Nature in coastal rivers and streams from New York State's mighty Hudson down through the Chesapeake Bay region, and in tributaries of the Gulf of Mexico to Texas, this popular cat has had its range extended considerably by wide plantings in the Northeast, southward, and westward as far as California and Oregon. HABITS: (1) White cats favor places where there's a sluggish flow with a muddy floor. If need be, they can adapt to clear, flowing water. (2) Further, like their kin, they seem to be better able to withstand pollution than your average fresh-water residents. All this makes them fine fish for stocking. (3) Not uncommonly, white cats share the same neighborhood with channel cats, or maybe it's vice versa. In any case, the former can be distinguished by their tail, which isn't as deeply forked

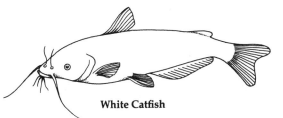

White Catfish

and has lobes that are slightly rounded on their ends, rather than pointy as on channel catfish. (4) White catfish reproduce along about June or July, the parents fashioning shallow nests and providing protection of eggs and newly hatched infants. These fry hang around in schools throughout their first summer, eating whatever they can wrap their little mouths around. By the time autumn nears, they're 2 in. or so long. (5) As they grow they become omnivorous feeders, devouring smaller fishes, crustaceans and aquatic insects. WHERE CAUGHT: Streams, bayous, ponds, quiet backwaters. HOW CAUGHT, BAITS, LURES & TACKLE: As I've said, white catfish bite readily. Assorted natural baits will attract them, but small live minnows are as good as any. Rigging is for near the bottom, which is where they're likely to be cruising for food. Bottom bumping with jigs will take them too. Whatever the tackle wielded, it should be very light.

Yellow Bass

SCIENTIFIC NAME: *Roccus mississippiensis*. COMMON NAMES: In various locales, yellow perch (a bad label, since it's the legitimate name of a perch, and this fish doesn't belong to that family), stripe, barfish and streaker. COLOR: The yellow bass's color is a dark greenish topside, becoming yellowish and silver on the sides, white underneath. Both this fish and the white bass are marked by longitudinal stripes, suggesting those of the striped bass; these extend along the back and sides. The difference is that those on the lower sides of the yellow bass are broken, whereas those on its cousin are uninterrupted. SIZE: The profiles of this fish and the white bass are strikingly similar. But there are differences separating the two. Most obvious is size. Yellow bass in sport catches are usually no longer than about 10 or 11 in. and weigh less than a pound. Any over a pound could be called jumbos. Maximum size isn't known, but probably is in the vicinity of 2–3 lbs. FAMILY: It is a true bass, a fresh-water representative of the huge Serranidae family. To the north this species is replaced, in a manner of speaking, by its close relative, the white bass (see page 166), which it resembles in appearance, habits and life pattern. DISTRIBUTION: A resident of the southern U.S. midlands, from the lower sections of Minnesota, Wisconsin, Michigan and Indiana down to the Tennessee River drainage system in Alabama, and Oklahoma, Louisiana and Texas. HABITS: (1) As they grow, their items of diet gradually increase in size to include insect larvae and minute crustaceans. (2) Usually they have to be reached deep. Only once in a while do they come up near the top. (3) Yellow bass are schoolers, which means that if a group is contacted it's good for more than one or two fish. WHERE CAUGHT: Lakes and streams. HOW CAUGHT: Casting baits and artificials from shores and boats. BAITS & LURES: Live

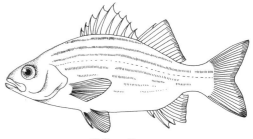

Yellow Bass

minnows and worms are standard naturals. Little artificials—spinners, flies, spoons and miniature plugs—also rack them up. TACKLE: They're lively on a hook, but it requires the lightest kind of tackle to bring them out.

Yellow Perch

SCIENTIFIC NAME: *Perca flavescens.* COMMON NAMES: Regional nicknames include lake perch, ringed perch, striped perch. COLOR: Basic color is a yellow or greenish-yellow overlaid with dusky or dark bars extending downward on the sides from the back. The underside is a light shade of the ground color or a whitish. The dorsals and tail are more or less the same color as the back. Pectoral, pelvic and anal fins run to a shade of orange. SIZE: Most catches weigh less than 1 lb., but some waters produce 1- to 2-pounders on occasion. Recorded is a New Jersey jumbo weighing just a hair under 4¼ lbs. A 13- to 14- in. yellow perch weighs about a pound; 12-, 10- and 8-inchers go about 12, 8 and 4 oz. FAMILY: Yellow perch join walleyes, saugers, blue pike, and many other species in a family, Percidae, or perches, with approximately 99 members in Canada and the United States. DISTRIBUTION: Yellow perch are far-flung in distribution, perhaps the most widely allotted representatives of the family. Overall, their range stretches from central and eastern Canada on down through the Midwestern U.S. to Kansas and Missouri, thence eastward, where it runs from Nova Scotia to South Carolina. Over the years, extensive plantings have supplemented the natural occurrence considerably by bringing yellow perch to lakes as far west as California and Washington, as well as other regions. HABITS: (1) As they grow, their menu expands to small fishes, insects, snails and young crayfish. (2) Yellow perch travel in schools wandering indifferently in shallow and fairly deep areas. (3) Since they travel in schools and bite readily, catching one is almost surefire promise that others—perhaps many—can be taken from that same area. Even the greenest fisherman has a good chance. Fact is, yellow perch provide an unexcelled opportunity to indoctrinate a youngster —or wife—in the delights of angling. (4) Yellow perch eat insects, snails, small fishes, crayfish. By day they feed in deeper water, then move shoreward at dusk. They're an important forage fish for larger game such as muskellunge, lake trout, walleyes, northern pike. WHERE CAUGHT: They can be caught from shores, docks and boats—the last sometimes necessary when the fish seek deeper, cooler waters in summer. They're available all year, and have become a staple in ice fishing. HOW CAUGHT, BAITS, LURES & TACKLE: Small minnows are a good all-round bait for yellow perch because they can be rigged in any season, including wintertime ice

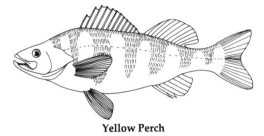

Yellow Perch

fishing. Worms also are effective. Generally the bait is fished on or a foot or so just off bottom. They also respond to small artificials such as spinners, flies and spinner-and-fly combinations if those lures are worked slowly. Slow, near-bottom trolling with small minnows has produced too. Tackle —spinning or conventional—is very light for open water. For ice-fishing gear, see Chapter 12.

14. Popular Salt-Water Fishes

Some North American species profiled here are caught both in salt and fresh-water in varying degrees.

Amberjack

SCIENTIFIC NAME: *Seriola lalandi.* COMMON NAMES: Regionally, great amberjack and greater amberjack. COLOR: Back a shade of blue; lavender or purple undertones and hints of yellow or gold on sides; underside silvery or white. While the fish is still alive, a dark yellowish band runs from head to tail. This fades rapidly when it is boated. On each side of the head is a dusky band; these two bands meet atop the head to form a V. SIZE: Sport range, 5 or 6 lbs. to 30, with a potential up to 80 lbs. On record are specimens topping 100 lbs. FAMILY: The Carangidae, or jacks, of which there are many representatives. DISTRIBUTION: Overall, from southern Massachusetts (as summer strays coming north with the Gulf Stream) to Florida and on down to Brazil, including Bermuda, the Bahamas, West Indies. HABITS: (1) Larger amberjacks tend to travel in small groups, pairs and alone, whereas those to 15 or 20 lbs. move in schools. (2) Mostly they feed on small schooling fishes and squid. (3) The largest of the Atlantic Ocean jacks are pelagic (open-sea) wanderers. WHERE CAUGHT: They frequent reefs, deep holes and drop-offs. HOW CAUGHT: Deep trolling, deep jigging, fishing deep at anchor, and occasionally by boat-casting artificials in the vicinity of a wreck. BAITS & LURES: Both live and dead baits are used— mullet, pinfish, squid, small grunts, pilchards and large shrimp. Artificials include assorted plugs, such as deep-riders; large spoons, bucktails, and feather lures in different color combinations. TACKLE: Conventional tackle suggested, its huskiness commensurate with the wielder's ability. Amberjacks are enthusiastic battlers—and remember their size potential.

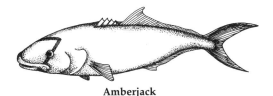

Amberjack

American Eel

SCIENTIFIC NAME: *Anguilla rostrata*. COMMON NAMES: Eel, silver eel, fresh-water eel. COLOR: Dark muddy-brown or olive-brown on back and upper sides; a lighter shade of that color, tinged with yellow, lower down on sides; belly a dirty yellowish-white. Darker shades are found over a mud bottom, lighter shades over a sandy bottom. SIZE: Average range is 15 to 24 in. Maximum is 3–3½ ft., although 4-ft. specimens and weights up to 16½ lbs. have been reported. Females are larger than males. FAMILY: The family, Anguillidae, also includes such lovelies as the slime eel, conger and long-nosed eel. Closest relative is the nearly identical European eel. DISTRIBUTION: Range includes coastal waters and streams from eastern Newfoundland to the Gulf of Mexico, and also West Indies and Bermuda. HABITS: (1) They're found in salt, brackish and fresh water. (2) Eels are greedy feeders, eating anything, alive or dead, they can wrap a mouth around: small fishes of many kinds, shrimp and other little crustaceans, etc. (3) They're chiefly nocturnal, which means they attract game fishes—striped bass are one species—which feed on them at night. (4) Locally they spend the winter buried in mud, where they're speared for food. WHERE CAUGHT: Bays, salt-water and brackish creeks, tidal and fresh-water rivers, channels. HOW CAUGHT: Bottom fishing with small baited hooks, also on a contraption known as an eel bob, and in baited traps called pots. BAITS & LURES: Almost any kind of fish in small pieces, worms, clams, mussels. Artificials not used. TACKLE: A simple hand line will do, but eels can be lively sport on extra-light tackle. SPECIAL NOTE: Alive and dead, in pieces or whole, eels are bait for game fishes that include marlins, sharks, striped bass and bluefish.

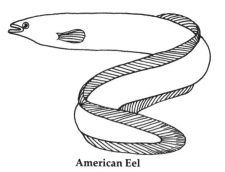

American Eel

Atlantic Cod

SCIENTIFIC NAME: *Gadus callarias*. COMMON NAMES: Cod, codfish. COLOR: There are two main color phases, gray or greenish-gray and reddish-brown. Numerous variations exist, include shades of olive-gray, brownish-gray, sepia brown, dark gray. Belly is white. SIZE: Commonly 10–15 lbs. to 30–40 lbs., with a potential to 60 lbs., even heavier. FAMILY: Cod is also the name of this fish's family, a group that includes the American pollack, tomcod, haddock. DISTRIBUTION: Range is Labrador to North Carolina. HABITS: (1) Cod live on or near the sea floor. (2) They favor cold water and tend to migrate seasonally to find it. Where there's satisfactorily colder water all year, there may be stationary populations. (3) They're gluttons, insatiable predators. On their long list of natural foods are small fishes, crustaceans, mollusks, squid, etc., even

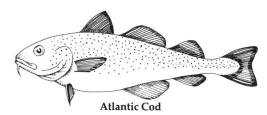

Atlantic Cod

their own young. WHERE CAUGHT: Ocean, inshore and offshore. Favored is a hard bottom—packed sand, gravel and rocky areas—with broken shells. Wrecks are also a haunt. HOW CAUGHT: Bottom fishing. Two hooks may be rigged, one near the bottom, its mate a few feet above it, to cover different levels. BAITS & LURES: Surf or skimmer clam is good cod bait, and the empty shells can be dropped overboard as chum. Cod also take pieces of squid, herring and other fishes. Lures are not used, although hungry cod have been known to grab a shiny spoon or a bright jig. TACKLE: Conventional type is suggested. It should be sturdy. Cod rigs are heavy because of their sinkers—currents can be strong; fishing may be in more than 100 ft. of water.

Atlantic Croaker

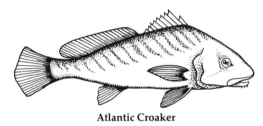

Atlantic Croaker

SCIENTIFIC NAME: *Micropogon undulatus*. COMMON NAMES: Just plain croaker or golden croaker. COLOR: Body is a light silver-gray, with an iridescent sheen on back and upper sides. Lower sides and ventral surface are white. Oblique, irregular rows of brownish spots lend a bar effect. At times a yellowish tinge infuses the tail and anal fin. SIZE: One- to 2-pounders are angling averages, although 3- to 5-pounders are caught. About tops is 6 to 8 lbs. FAMILY: One of the Scienidae, a large tribe catalogued under the heading Drums and Croakers, so called because of their—surprise!—drumming and croaking sounds. They're quite vocal. Relatives include channel bass and black drum. DISTRIBUTION: Massachusetts and Rhode Island on down to North Carolina, but uncommon north of New Jersey. Also found off northern Florida on both Atlantic Ocean and Gulf of Mexico sides. HABITS: (1) They're bottom feeders, foraging over hard-packed sea floors and areas strewn with shells. (2) They move inshore and into bays when waters warm in the spring, then go back out to deeper offshore ocean waters in autumn to escape winter cold. They're not true migrators. (3) Mostly they consume small crustaceans, such as shrimp and crabs, along with some mollusks, marine worms and other invertebrates. WHERE CAUGHT: Inshore waters, inlets, bays, channels. HOW CAUGHT: Bottom fishing. Because of their underslung mouth, adapted to feeding right on the bottom, the hook must be rigged accordingly. Bait should hug bottom. BAITS & LURES: Baits include small pieces of sandworm or bloodworm, clam, squid, or what have you. Artificials generally aren't used. TACKLE: Any tackle, conventional or spinning, must be very light. Atlantic croakers are small fish.

Atlantic Mackerel

Atlantic Mackerel

SCIENTIFIC NAME: *Scomber scombrus*. COMMON NAMES: The regional names are Boston mackerel, often shortened to "Bostons," and tinker mackerel, when about 10, 11 in. long. COLOR: Back and upper sides of body are dark steel-blue or greenish-blue, almost black on the head. Upper sides are overlaid with 23–33 dark, vertical or oblique wiggly bands, technically called vermiculations. Jaws, gill covers and lower sides of body are silver, without markings. Lengthwise on each side of the body is a dark narrow stripe, often indistinct. SIZE: Angling averages are 12–18 in. and weights to 2½ lbs., but they go to 22 in. and weights of 3 to 4 lbs. on the high side. FAMILY: The Scombridae, or mackerels, comprise a huge tribe with representatives all over the world—Pacific mackerel, king mackerel, ceros, frigate mackerel, Spanish mackerel, many others. Close relatives are the tunas and bonitos. All share certain family resemblances, such as a superbly streamlined body, prominent and indented tail, and finlets (small triangular-shaped processes along the midlines of the body's rear section, top and bottom). DISTRIBUTION: Gulf of St. Lawrence, Canada, to North Carolina, is the range, with centers of abundance that include New England, New York, New Jersey. HABITS: (1) They travel in enormous schools, some of which are strung out over miles. (2) Despite their huge numbers, they're among the more erratic of marine fishes, sometimes vacillating between great quantity and great scarcity. (3) They're migratory, approaching the U.S. East Coast in spring and moving northward toward Canadian waters, lingering in coastal belts for a few weeks, even into summer, then disappearing offshore in autumn. They're believed to winter offshore along the rim of the continental shelf. (4) They eat just about anything their mouths can accommodate, such as eggs and infants of other fishes, sea worms, crustaceans, little fishes of various kinds. (5) They're fast-moving. Chumming will hold a school around a boat, but it takes a bit of doing. (6) These mackerel have no air bladder (standard equipment for many fishes). As a result, they must keep in motion or sink. This means they won't dawdle at a bait or lure but must accept or reject it almost at once. WHERE CAUGHT: Chiefly open ocean, inshore and offshore. But they also invade large sounds and bays. HOW CAUGHT: A favored technique is chumming and jigging, the boat at anchor or on a slow drift. Trolling small artificials also produces, but not in such quantity. Boat casting when the fish are at the surface. BAITS & LURES: A shiny mackerel jig, hook unbaited or baited, for chumming and jigging; small, shiny spoons, chromed wobblers and little bucktails in trolling; those artificials, plus red, white and silver-bodied flies for boat casting. TACKLE: Choice is yours—conventional, spinning or fly casting, but it must be light. Bostons are good sport on very light tackle. SPECIAL NOTE: Since these are quantity fish and easy to catch, they're a good starting point for youngsters and others you're trying to get interested in fishing.

Atlantic Permit

SCIENTIFIC NAME: *Trachinotus falcatus*, formerly *Trachinotus goddei*. COMMON NAME: Great pompano, so called because it is the largest of the pompanos. COLOR: It's variable, according to age and where found. Youngsters are a silvery hue and black, or sometimes nearly all black. Older permits in shallow water are blue or silver and blue on the back and upper sides, with silver lower down and yellow on the underside. Over all is an iridescence. Deeper-water permits tend to lose their blue and yellow hues, retaining only some blue on the back, and becoming largely iridescent silver. SIZE: Atlantic permits reach respectable sizes. An average range in the sport theater is from approximately 10 or 12 lbs. up to 25 or 30. The species is believed to attain weights in excess of 50 lbs. You would have to top 50 lbs. to be an International Game Fish Association world record challenger. FAMILY: Carangidae family. The Atlantic version has a close relative in the Pacific permit, ranging from Ecuador to Baja California. DISTRIBUTION: North Carolina to the Florida Keys and around into the Gulf of Mexico in southern Florida. Stragglers wander as far north as Massachusetts and as far south as Brazil. A prime U.S. permit-fishing arena awaits in southern Florida, from about Cape Florida through the Keys to the Dry Tortugas beyond the Keys. Here Atlantic permits are among the largest and most numerous. Let it be added hastily, though, that nowhere do they seem to be especially abundant. HABITS: (1) Permits are schooling fish when young, then travel in small groups or even become solitary as they grow older. This is probably due to differences in feeding habits at various ages. (2) They are bottom feeders. (3) When young they consume many different kinds of small invertebrates. Later they eat small fishes, crabs, mollusks, shrimp and, if they can get them, crayfish. (4) Permits seem to feed most actively on flats during the last phase of a flood tide and the early phase of the ensuing ebb tide. In such shallow water, groups of them generate little surface swirls that betray their presence to permit-wise fishermen. Sometimes the backs and tails are partially exposed as they feed nose-downward. WHERE CAUGHT: Their daily life takes them through channels and cuts into deep holes and around wrecks. They also come into shallow water over sand and mud flats, much in the manner of bonefish, where they root for tidbits with their snout. In searching for them at such times, anglers should keep in mind that permits, being larger and deeper-bodied than bonefish, require more water on the flats. Their appearance in such areas, therefore, is a bit later than that of bonefish during a rising tide. *Note:* For permit hunters the name of the game is patience and careful searching —with Polaroid sunglasses. Without sunglasses that cut surface glare, chances of sighting permits are poor. Even with such lenses it can be difficult to spot them. HOW CAUGHT & TACKLE: Light tackle—spinning and conventional types— usually is recommended for these battlers. But a fact of life is that unless fishermen know how to cope with tough fighters

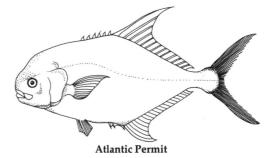

Atlantic Permit

on light tackle they will lose a fish. Permits are tough customers. Even small ones put up a knock-down-drag-out fight. Fact is, the contest can resolve itself into a test to see which has the more stamina, fish or fisherman. A permit hooked in shoal water will always streak for deeper water. En route it uncorks a bottle of tricks that include all kinds of gyrations and other stunts in efforts to throw the hook. Adding complications, the battle route may be strewn with coral heads, clumps of marine flora and other obstructions on which a line can snag—and break. So a permit that is fought successfully is a triumph indeed. The greatest sport lies with light or light-medium tackle. Conventional and spinning kinds are wielded, but the latter is favored in most instances. Commonly in service is a medium-action, 6½- or 7-ft. spinning ''stick'' with matching salt-water reel. Hooks go to about a 2/0. Points and barbs must be needle-sharp to penetrate a permit's leather-tough mouth. Permits have been landed with fly rods too. It should be added quickly that fly-fishing for these roughnecks demands not only a high degree of skill but also heaping measures of optimism and luck. Some permits are nailed in deeper water, but the favored procedure is the same as in bonefishing. That is, they're stalked on the flats and cast to. BAITS & LURES: Most permit fishing calls for live crab or shrimp bait. Permits are sight feeders, as opposed to those species attracted to a bait by scent. Therefore they will also respond to artificials. It's much more difficult to fool them with man-made lures than with natural baits, however. It's even more difficult to tempt a lone-feeding permit, concentrating on a small patch of bottom—head down, as usual—than it is a member of a feeding school. Unless an angler is bound and determined to try a small bucktail jig, spoon or the like, he might better stick with natural attractors in the favored procedure.

Atlantic Sailfish

SCIENTIFIC NAMES: Given variously as *Istiophorus americanus, Istiophorus albicans, Istiophorus platyperus*—ichthyologists can't seem to agree. COMMON NAME: Sailfish, usually shortened to ''sail.'' COLOR: Handsome. The functionally streamlined body is a vivid cobalt or steely blue, topside. This shades away to gleaming silver on the sides and belly. The sides of some individuals carry vertical rows of pale spots that look like bars at first glance. The fish's distinctive trademark, the detail inspiring sailfish as a common name, is the exaggerated dorsal fin, which towers above its owner. This ''sail'' is a bright, rich blue, liberally sprinkled with black oval or round spots. SIZE: Because of their body slenderness, Atlantic sailfish are deceptively light for their length. An average length, overall, including the pointed ''bill,'' is about 7 ft. Weights average in the 40- to 50-lb. bracket. Overall lengths have been recorded up

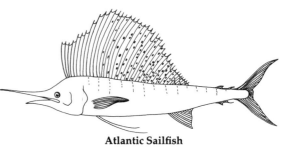

Atlantic Sailfish

to 8½ ft., and weights top 100 lbs. among exceptional specimens, with a potential that has gone as high as 141 lbs. FAMILY: The tribe, known scientifically as Istiophoridae, includes the Pacific sailfish (see page 222), the marlins, and the much lesser known spearfishes. All these are also called billfishes. DISTRIBUTION: From about the Virginia capes to and including Florida—especially Florida—where boating a sail was once as common among tourists as writing postcards. They have been found as Gulf Stream stragglers as far north as Massachusetts in summer. Range also takes in the Gulf of Mexico and the Caribbean. HABITS: (1) Atlantic sails are anything but fussy feeders. Foraging at various levels from the surface to the sea floor, they devour squid and smaller fishes such as mackerels, young tunas, jacks, balaos ("ballyhoos"), herring, southern porgies, other available species. (2) Their approaches to baits and artificials are individualistic and variable and range from smacking a bait with their bill to seizing it quickly, to "studying" or toying with it; then, after frustrating the angler, they may lose interest and leave. (3) They're oceanic wanderers. WHERE CAUGHT: Open ocean. In Florida, among the greatest Atlantic sailfishing regions, they're boated inshore and offshore, on out to and including the Gulf Stream, and are practically all-year game. An area with great sailfishing potential is Isla de Cozumel, Mexico. HOW CAUGHT: Trolling baits or lures; drifting with live or dead baits. Trolling is standard. *A special technique:* Essentially it's a combination of trolling and fly casting. But—get this—hookless artificials are used. They can resemble small fishes in shape, or better yet, strips of fish cut in the shape of a small fish. These lures are trolled to attract sailfish to the surface, whereupon—precise timing is needed here—the boat is stopped dead in the water and the fly caster goes quickly to work. This technique has also accounted for Pacific sailfish and striped marlin. BAITS & LURES: (1) Whole small fishes such as pinfish, blue runner, mullet and ballyhoo, alive and dead. The first two are popular live ones. (2) Strips of fish. (3) Shiny spoons and feather jigs in various color combinations (red and white, green and yellow, etc.). Lures not considered as productive as natural bait. (4) For that trolling/fly-casting special, popping bugs and streamer flies—white an effective color for both. TACKLE: Conventional or spinning tackle. The lighter the tackle, the greater the sport—and the greater the challenge to the wielder. Needless to add, fly casting offers the greatest challenge.

Barracudas (Family: *Sphyraenidae*)

Several species are described for North American waters. Each has certain individual differences, but all share family characteristics that unmistakably stamp them as barracudas:

Great Barracuda

(1) elongated, very slender body; (2) long head with rather large eyes; (3) big mouth, its lower jaw projecting beyond the upper, and both jaws armed with numerous sharp, wicked-looking teeth; (4) two dorsal fins, positioned well aft of the head; and (5) a well-developed, deeply forked tail. All are active, vicious predators. Here are some members of the family.

Pacific Barracuda (*Sphyraena argentea*)

Overall distribution of Pacific barracuda is from Alaska down to the Gulf of California; however, the species is rare north of California's Point Conception. It's believed to be the only representative of the Sphyraenidae family in California waters, and so has acquired an alternate common name, California barracuda. There are regional aliases too, such as scoots, barry, snake, log, scooter and, like all barracudas, simply 'cuda.

This fish's color pattern has a metallic gray, sometimes almost black or a nondescript brown, on the dorsal surface. That fades to silver-white on the sides and belly. Lacking are the darkish bars seen on its relative the Mexican barracuda and the black side mottling of the great barracuda, another cousin. The tail has a yellowish tinge.

Pacific barracuda can be caught off Mexico all year, but in California waters the best seasons are spring and summer. Apparently there are northward migrations from Mexican waters in the spring, for schools of them appear offshore of San Diego in March, after which they build to that season's peak and extend northward to areas off Los Angeles (San Pedro) and Santa Barbara. Some can be hooked north of Point Conception, their apparent northern limit in California, in late summer. Comes cooler weather in the fall, they disappear, probably to move well offshore, then return southward until the next year.

Among barracudas in general, this Pacific species is medium size. Lengths go up to about 36, 40, 44 in., with weights to 10 lbs. or so. They're active hunters, preying upon smaller schooling fishes of several kinds, along with squid.

If "popularity" is the word for an attraction that gets them killed, barracuda have a measure of it in southern California, where they're caught mainly from boats. Shoreside anglers on rocks and piers also go at them. In seasons when tunas and other more frequently sought targets are in diminished supply, barracuda become an important item on boats fishing south of Point Conception. Boat methods are casting and trolling. From rocks and piers it's casting, of course. Usually these scrappers are fished at or near the surface, but they also are contacted at lower levels. They respond to live and dead baits such as anchovies, queenfish and sardines; strip bait about 5 in. long; and artificials, notably colored feathers, ¼ to 1 oz. In night fishing, boat lights shone into the water will attract little baitfishes, which in turn draw barracuda.

Hooks go from No. 2 to 1/0, usually with short shanks, on wire leaders to guard against the barracuda's dental armament. When in a feeding mood, these fish throw caution to the winds and strike readily. During the early phase of their run, however, they can be wary, chopping a bait in half or mangling it and eluding the hook. A cure for these larcenous "short-strikers" is to rig two hooks. These can be spaced 3 or 4 in. apart, both with their points and barbs in the bait, the trailing hook near the bait's free end. The two hooks are linked by a short length of wire. Another method, employed for short-strikers with smaller mouths, is to bridle a trailing hook, ring-eye type, on the bend of the orginal hook and impale the bait on both.

Mexican Barracuda *(Sphyraena ensis)*

Generally Mexican barracuda run smaller than the Pacific barracuda, an average being about 3 lbs. They're typically 'cudas in appearance and habits and can be separated from the Pacific breed by noticeable dark bars on the body's sides.

Relatively little is known about this species other than that its general distribution is from Baja California and the fish-fertile Gulf of California southward to at least Panama.

Bait casting from boats will catch them, but anglers are divided as to their sporting qualities. Obviously, very light tackle is a must.

Guaguanche *(Sphyraena guaguancho)*

Guaguanches are a tropical Atlantic species ranging from Florida and its Keys—possibly a bit farther north in summer—and the Gulf of Mexico on down to Brazil. They're among the smaller 'cudas, reaching lengths of 18 to 24 in. The body form is typically barracuda, and these fish are among the clan's slimmest members, which makes the tail appear disproportionately larger. Along the back their color is a gray, often with a greenish cast. The sides and belly are silver, without any darker spots or mottling.

Schools of guaguanches prowl shallow bays, where they're caught by casting small lures and by fishing at anchor with pieces of bait or small live bait. Very light tackle—salt- or fresh-water spinning, bait casting, or fly casting—is required for best action, due to their small size.

Great Barracuda *(Sphyraena barracuda)*

This fish is king of the barracuda family in size, hence the "great" in the name. Specimens up to 40 and 50 lbs. are on the books. There's mention of 5- to 6-footers in the 100-lb. class in angling literature; but these are to be considered oversized brutes of record caliber. In sport catches their weights are more likely to go up to 15, perhaps 20 lbs.

Warm-water citizens, great barracuda have their greatest North American concentration in Florida, notably along the Keys, and also are encountered in lesser numbers in the Gulf of Mexico. Their distribution also embraces Bermuda, the Bahamas archipelago, the West Indies, and the warm seas on down to Brazil.

The typical 'cuda body and large mouth armed with sizable,

fearsome-looking teeth, mark this savage predator. The back can be a shade of blue, medium to dark, or a greenish. On the upper sides above the lateral line this darker color has a series of curved edges that resemble scalloping. The lower sides are silver, becoming white on the ventral surface. Dark spots and blotches of irregular shape are scattered along the sides below the lateral line. The fins are dusky or sooty. Generally great 'cudas of the open sea are darker on the back than those of shallower waters and around reefs.

Throughout their distribution the younger fish will come into shallow water only a few feet deep. In clear water they sometimes can be seen suspended motionless as though waiting for something. This seems to be a habit shared by various kinds of barracudas.

Great barracuda also frequent reefs because of the abundance and variety of food. As trollers after marlin and tuna have discovered, they also are encountered in the open sea at varying distances from shore. The larger 'cudas usually are taken offshore, although big ones are spotted occasionally on flats and in other shallow-water areas at high tide.

Great barracuda are fisheaters, grabbing any smaller species that may be available. If they can capture prey with minimum effort, fine. But if need be they can turn on the speed, as evidenced by their assaults on lures trolled fairly fast. Their speed capability is even more impressive during the first run or two after being hooked.

Areas with potential include reefs, inshore flats on a flooding or high tide, rims of channels, underwater shelves, mangrove shores and open sea, both inshore and off. Great barracuda do not seem to be a schooling species, although the youngsters may be encountered in groups of some size. Like bluefin tuna, they tend to become loners or travel in pods (small groups) as they grow older—changing hunting habits are probably a factor.

Various techniques will account for these 'cudas. In Florida's Keys, small and medium specimens are caught from bridges, causeways and docks, and stalked on the endless sand flats. Casting is the method in all these instances, so spinning tackle is ideal. Several different kinds of artificials are effective, including spoons, top-riding plugs, spinner and bait combinations, and bucktails. Many 'cudas, whatever their species, are attracted by artificials that shine and glitter. Bright spoons, therefore, are a natural.

Barracudas are insatiably inquisitive. Paradoxically, though, despite this curiosity and an inborn aggressiveness, great barracuda can be very wary toward artificials. A plug plopping into the water close by is more than likely to spook the fish, and it will take off like a silver arrow. Therefore the attractor should be cast so that it lands several feet—perhaps 10 or 15— ahead of the target, then should be retrieved within the fish's field of vision. This can pose problems in areas where their color and water glare combine to make them difficult to pinpoint.

Casts and retrieves must be repeated. Some individuals will stalk a lure before striking—or losing interest. Much lies with the speed of retrieve and how an artificial is worked. As a rule of thumb, the lure should always be made to perform erratically. This gives an impression of an injured creature, attractive to most fish. Smaller 'cudas will respond to medium-speed retrieves, but fast cranking is best with larger, older and wiser specimens so that it minimizes the opportunity to see that an artificial is a fake.

Spinning tackle is favored. Also used are plugging and bait-casting rods and light, all-purpose sticks such as those commonly wielded on boats. The lightest conventional-type surf tackle can be used if casting distance is a requisite, as from a dock or shore.

Fly tackle wielders will have a test of casting skill and patience with these fish. Streamers, small bucktails and the so-called popping bugs get results if placed properly and rapidly retrieved.

For barracudas the hook must always be preceded by a wire leader. It need not be long. Light wire of 8 to 10 or 12 in. should suffice.

Shiny spoons can be effective in ocean trolling. Strip and chunk fish baits also get results, along with surface plugs of various designs. Still-fishing, or drifting, with live bait around reefs should also account for 'cudas. In any case, there should be a fair supply of bait on hand. Barracudas can tear bait off a hook or render it useless by shredding. Their teeth can do a job on plugs and other non-metal artificials too.

Black Drum

SCIENTIFIC NAME: *Pogonias cromis*. COMMON NAMES: I've heard "drum" and "drumfish." COLOR: Body is silvery, with iridescent tints; dusky, often brassy, on the dorsal surface, while the belly is gray-white. All the fins are blackish or sooty. After death the fish turns a dark gray, like badly tarnished silver. SIZE: In sport fishing, from about 3–5 lbs. through 10–20 to 30–40, and occasionally to 50–60 lbs. Catches belie the fact that black drums can and do top 100 lbs. An IGFA world record stood at 111, a champ caught off Cape Charles, Va. The largest one I ever heard about was a 148-pounder, commercially caught in Florida years ago. FAMILY: Family Sciaenidae, among whose other members are the channel bass or red drum—the popular redfish of the Gulf of Mexico, several species of croakers, and the U.S. East Coast's famous weakfish. It's a family noted for its sonic talents—drumming, croaking, thumping and purring, sounds believed to variously attract mates, express belligerence, and show alarm or annoyance. DISTRIBUTION: Overall this goes from about Massachusetts to northern Florida on the Atlantic seaboard, then down to Argentina. It also extends into the Gulf of Mexico. Favoring warm waters, black drums are uncommon north of New

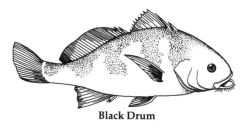

Black Drum

Jersey. HABITS: (1) They favor inshore waters and come fairly close to beaches. (2) They're bottom feeders (note the mouth low in the head and the chin barbels, features of bottom-dining species). (3) Crabs are a major item of diet (and so are good bait). Also consumed are clams, shrimp and mussels. The black drum's jaws are outfitted with flat crushing teeth to take care of shells. WHERE CAUGHT: In the surf along sandy beaches; from ocean-front piers; from boats and shore in inlets, sounds and large bays; occasionally in lower tidewaters. Generally speaking, they move inshore when weather warms in spring, remain through the summer, then shift back offshore with cooler weather. HOW CAUGHT: By rigging for the bottom, whether surf casting or boat fishing. BAITS & LURES: Natural baits are better than artificials here. For black drums they include pieces of crab, clams, mussels, strips of squid, chunks of mullet, shrimp. TACKLE: Black drums are not spectacular fighters, but they're stubborn and have enough bulk to lend authority to their arguments. Conventional tackle is suggested, and it can be gauged roughly (say, 20- to 30- lb. test gear) to the sizes of the drums currently running.

Black Marlin

SCIENTIFIC NAMES: *Makaira indicus* (or *indica*). You may also see this beast listed as *Makaira marlina*, *Makaira nigricans*, or *Makaira mazara*. There's confusion; and to add to it, those last two labels are also applied to the blue marlin at times. COMMON NAMES: I've come across only one, "black," and that used only when it was understood that the subject was marlins. In Hawaii, I understand, they sometimes use the name "silver marlin." COLOR: Body color is dark blue, almost black sometimes, on the back and uppermost sides, fading to dark silver below. Some specimens show tinges of bronze or brownish on the upper surfaces. Vague stripes, in lighter blue, may appear on the massive shoulders and upper half of the body while the fish is still alive, but fade quickly. This marlin also "lights up"—takes on an eerie pale green glow, like phosphorescence—when brought to gaff. SIZE: At this writing black marlin takes second place only to white sharks for the IGFA title of The World's Largest Game Fish. The known angling potential, based on an IGFA world record set years ago by the great Texas big-game angler Alfred C. Glassell Jr., goes up to 1,560 lbs. I know from personal experience that the Coral Sea off Australia has black marlin to 1,300 lbs. or better. One afternoon fellow Long Islander Virgil Price and I docked in Cairns with two fish 994 and 1,002 lbs. FAMILY: One of the Istiophoridae, or billfishes, along with blue, white and striped marlins, Atlantic and Pacific sailfishes, and spearfishes. DISTRIBUTION: Black marlin are not known in the Atlantic.

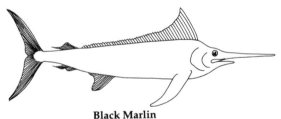

Black Marlin

Pacific range runs from southern California to Mexico and the Gulf of California, and in waters surrounding Hawaii. HABITS: (1) Little is known about this magnificent billfish's feeding habits and diet, other than that he seems to hunt food at various levels, near the top on down, and eats a variety of other fishes—various mackerels, young tunas, bonitos, dolphins, flying fish, mullet, many others, plus squid. (2) Those that I saw may have been extra hungry, but they didn't mess with the trolled bait. They came right up behind it and literally inhaled it, and some of our baits were whole 15- to 25-lb. bonitos. (3) Black marlin have been known to dive so deep during a fight that it became impossible to raise them with rod and reel. WHERE CAUGHT: Offshore in the open ocean. HOW CAUGHT: Trolling with fresh-dead or live baits or artificials. Trolling is slow, to about 4 knots with baits; faster, up to 9 or 10 knots, with artificials. Also, drifting or fishing at anchor with live or dead baits. BAITS & LURES: Among the naturals, many kinds of whole fishes from the species' diet; also whole squid; also strips of fish. Among the artificials, large, shiny spoons, big feather lures, so-called Kona Head and Knucklehead types; also plastic or vinyl fish and squid. TACKLE: Conventional tackle only. Some experienced anglers who know what they're doing use 80-lb.-test weapons; a few daring souls have tried 50-lb. tackle. Mostly, though, it's 130-lb.-test equipment. And there are times when you wonder if *that's* heavy enough!

Black Perch or Black Surfperch

SCIENTIFIC NAME: *Embiotoca jacksoni.* COMMON NAME: Black surfperch. COLOR: One of the more colorful members of his family: olive green or reddish-brown on the body, with eight or nine dark vertical bars on the sides, and thick yellow to orange-brown lips. Ocassionally the pelvic and anal fins are reddish or yellow. In the San Francisco sector, some specimens in the fall and winter are jet black with blue crescents in the middle of their scales. The color pattern helps to identify the black surfperch. SIZE: Maximum is about 14 in. and 1½ to 1¾ lbs. FAMILY: This is one of 20 surfperches, family Embiotocidae, found in California waters (19 are marine species, the 20th is fresh-water). DISTRIBUTION: Black surfperch range is from California's Bodega Bay to Baja California. HABITS: They subsist on a variety of foods, including small crustaceans, mollusks, marine worms and moss animals. WHERE CAUGHT: They're generally found over seaweed-covered rocky bottoms and in the vicinity of ocean-front piers. In bays they linger around beds of eelgrass. HOW CAUGHT: Bait casting. BAITS & LURES: Among the baits for them are shrimp, little sand crabs, and pieces of mussel or sandworm. TACKLE: Spinning and conventional tackle is used, with light lines—6-lb. is ample—

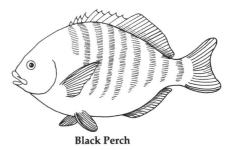

Black Perch

and small hooks, about a No. 5. In rocky areas, with braided lines, a leader of monofilament somewhat heavier than the main line offers a measure of protection against abrasion.

Black Sea Bass

SCIENTIFIC NAME: *Centropristes striatus.* COMMON NAMES: "Sea bass" is the one most widely used. Being a popular species, this bass has acquired a number of regional aliases. I'll mention a few that are strange: Hannabill, black Harry, talywag, and black Will. COLOR: There's variation, but commonly the body coloring is a dark blue-black, or a dark grayish-brown, which fades to a paler shade or becomes an off-white on the belly. Whitish markings on the scales give an effect of lengthwise rows of dots, almost like narrow bars. Some specimens have whitish markings on their dorsal fin. The other fins usually are a darker shade of the body color and mottled. SIZE: The smallest ones caught by anglers go from a few ounces to ½ or ¾ lb. These are taken in bays and harbors and are sometimes spoken of as "pin bass." Bays yield fish up to about 1½ lbs. The largest sea bass are ocean-caught and have a size potential to 5½ lbs. At around 8 lbs. you start getting into a world-record class. Adult males develop a pronounced hump behind the head, leading to the nickname "humpback." The biggest sea bass are usually these humpbacks. FAMILY: Black sea bass are a marine bass, members of that large worldwide family labeled Serranidae. The fresh-water basses, Centrarchidae, are relatives. DISTRIBUTION: The range covers the Atlantic seaboard from Maine to northern Florida. Historically the most productive grounds have been in that stretch from Long Island, N.Y., to North Carolina. HABITS: (1) They're bottom dwellers but range a few feet above the bottom in searches for food. (2) They favor clean, clear water and frequent areas that contain rocks, stones or beds of mollusks. (3) Like tautogs (see page 241), sea bass often hang around wrecks, the underpinnings of piers, bridge abutments, breakwaters, large rocks and other long-submerged structures that attract lesser creatures that in turn are attractive to sea bass as food. (4) Their diet includes assorted little fishes, among them the young of other species, along with sea worms, mussels, barnacles, and crustaceans such as small crabs and lobsters and shrimp. WHERE CAUGHT: Ocean, inshore and offshore; in and around inlets and adjacent channels, bays and sounds. HOW CAUGHT: Bottom fishing at anchor is the principal method. Some anglers use two hooks, one right on the bottom, its mate a couple of feet above it, for better coverage. Two-hook rigs also produce mixed bottom catches of porgies and sea bass. Two hooks, however, increase the chances of snagging on something. Jigging with a shiny, 3- or 4-oz. diamond jig (3/0–4/0 hook) also produces sea bass. BAITS

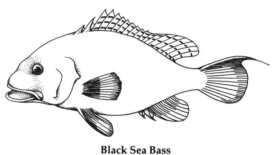

Black Sea Bass

& LURES: Sea bass will accept many kinds of bait: sandworms, bloodworms, strips of squid, pieces of clam, pieces of shedder crab, and live killies. A diamond jig is about the only artificial I've ever heard being used for them. TACKLE: Conventional and spinning equipment is used, and it should be light for maximum sport. The only thing is, it also should be able to handle the sinkers rigged in ocean bottom fishing.

Bluefin Tuna

SCIENTIFIC NAME: *Thunnus thynnus.* COMMON NAMES: On the U.S. East Coast young bluefins to 100 lbs. or so are referred to as school tuna because of their habit of traveling in large groups, while the older fish, 300, 400 lbs. and up, are called giants. An old nickname, no longer used, is "horse mackerel." "Tunny" has been a name in Europe since the days of ancient Rome. COLOR: The massive but functionally streamlined body is a dark midnight blue, almost black, sometimes with greenish reflections, on the back. Sides and belly are silver or silver-gray, with pink iridescence and occasionally with bands or large spots or blotches of silver. The powerful tail is dusky silver; the ventral and pelvic fins are black above, silver-gray below. SIZE: Based on IGFA world records, which have been inching upward in recent years, bluefin tuna are known to attain weights of at least 1,300 lbs. Maybe those 2,000-pounders the ancient Romans wrote about are possible after all. A general range in the sport fishery is from about 12 or 15 lbs. for small "schoolies" up to 500–700 lbs. for the giants. Bluefin tuna are among the world's largest recorded sport fishes, trailing only the white shark, tiger shark and black marlin. FAMILY: Bluefin tuna are catalogued with the mackerels, Scombridae, a worldwide family whose members include the tunas, bonitos, albacores, and many species of mackerel. Profile comparisons of scombrids (taken from Scombridae) reveal several shared family resemblances: beautifully streamlined body (in the case of the bluefin tuna this streamlining includes a slot into which the dorsal fin folds to lessen water resistance); a prominent, more or less crescent-shaped tail; large mouth; and finlets (those small triangular processes along the midlines of the back and belly just ahead of the tail), which are yellow on the bluefin tuna. DISTRIBUTION: Off the Atlantic Coast from Labrador and Canada's Maritime Provinces to Mexico and the Caribbean, including Bermuda, the Bahama islands, and the Gulf of Mexico. I've seen schools of giants, estimated to 800 lbs., on the move northward off Quintana Roo, Mexico, in May. On the Atlantic Coast they're seasonal migrators, moving northward and closer inshore in late spring and summer, back down and offshore in autumn. The greatest producer of the heftiest giants—over 1,000 lbs.— has been Canada's Prince Edward Island. On the North

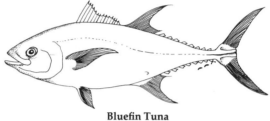

Bluefin Tuna

American Pacific seaboard their overall range is believed to extend from about opposite the Columbia River down to at least Baja California, including California's famous Catalina Island. The North American migratory patterns and distribution are very complex and not yet fully understood. *Note:* Overexploitation of bluefin tuna has brought the species to a precarious state, necessitating international legal protection in the form of catch limits. Such protection may be necessary for many years to come. Check on current sport-fishing regulations. HABITS: (1) The so-called school tuna travel in schools that can be enormous. All members of a given school are about the same size. (2) As they grow older and larger, they travel in progressively smaller schools, then in little groups, and even in pairs or alone. (3) Since they migrate considerable distances in tropical and temperate seas and are swift, active hunters, their diet embraces many kinds of small fishes, along with miscellaneous other tidbits such as squid and shrimp. (4) They tend to prey on smaller fishes that congregate in large, dense schools. That makes food shopping easier. WHERE CAUGHT: Open sea at various levels, surface on down. HOW CAUGHT: When school tuna, by trolling artificials. Bright-colored feather jigs are about the best. Live and dead fish are also trolled in some areas. Whether because of their aggressiveness or curiosity isn't known, but it often helps to attract school tuna by creating bubbly white water right at the boat's transom. This is done by towing an old automobile tire while trolling. The bigger tuna, including the largest giants, are caught by chumming and bait fishing at various levels while at anchor or drifting. BAITS & LURES: Herring, mackerel, menhaden, northern whiting and other fishes, alive or dead, whole or in chunks, also whole squid. Ground-up fish, such as menhaden or herring, are good chum, which can be fortified with small pieces of fish. Trolling artificials include shiny spoons. (I've never tried it myself, but it's reliably reported that school tuna have been hooked on shiny beer can openers to which a hook was soldered. But that's just a novelty.) TACKLE: Bluefin tuna—all sizes—are very strong and fast. School tuna have been taken on spinning tackle and even salt-water fly rods (casting to the fish when near the surface), but conventional tackle is indicated for all sizes and is a must for the larger bluefins. Caliber of weapons is gauged approximately to sizes of the tuna currently in the area and ranges up to 130-lb.-test big-game tackle.

Bluefish

SCIENTIFIC NAME: *Pomatomus saltatrix.* COMMON NAMES: "Blues" is about the only one for the adults; but fishing writers also call 'em "choppers" because the fish can display ferocious

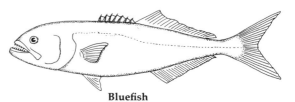

Bluefish

action with their teeth (the blues' teeth, that is, not the fishing writers'). Another name, now rare, is "tailor." Young bluefish, to about a pound, are nicknamed "snappers"; and from over a pound to 2, 2½ lbs., "snapper-blues." An old size label for 3- and 4-pounders is "harbor blues," from their habit at that age of dashing in and out of harbors and bays in pursuit of prey. COLOR: A medium blue, with a greenish cast, on the back and sides, silvery below. SIZE: In the sport fishery, to 14–16 lbs., occasionally to 18 lbs., with a potential to at least 20. World record blues now top 30 lbs. FAMILY: Uniquely, bluefish seem to be the only known members of their family, Pomatomidae. DISTRIBUTION: Overall, New England (in summer) to Florida. Among seasonal centers of abundance are southern Massachusetts, waters all around New York's Long Island, the New Jersey coast—surf on out—and North Carolina's Cape Hatteras region, which produced an IGFA world record, 31¾ lbs. Schools have been reported offshore in the Gulf of Mexico, but have yet to be reported for the Pacific seaboard. HABITS: (1) Blues like fairly warm water; 58–60 ° F. is believed to be about the minimum. Rising and falling water temperatures trigger their mass-commuting between offshore and inshore ocean zones and up and down the coast. Water temperatures can hasten migrations or stall them. (2) Summer heat can drive them into deep water, which is why the best summer bluefishing is often in early morning, in the evening and at night. (3) Bluefish travel in large schools and move fast when searching for food (which is practically all the time). It may require a lot of rapid chumming to hold a school long enough to extract fish from it. (4) Blues are infamous for their so-called cycles, during which they disappear from a region for years, then just as unpredictably return, building to quantities again. Such cycles can alternate between extremes, a complete disappearance, and so many blues that they're a glut. (5) They're savage, insatiable predators, noted for their wholesale destruction of smaller fishes. (It may seem to be just for the love of killing, but more likely it's one of nature's ways of maintaining a balance of life in the sea.) Blues' penchant for such mayhem necessitates the use of wire leaders to protect against their sharp teeth, which cut through fishing line. It also brings about the mutilation of lures and a need for frequent replacement of baits. (6) When hooked, they change direction suddenly. This is to lessen the hook's pressure, and it can create enough slack for the blue to throw the hook. Anglers have to be alert to this maneuver and reel in slack quickly. (7) *Caution:* Bluefish will bite you. Handle them carefully. WHERE CAUGHT: Open ocean, offshore inshore and surf; in inlets, bays, sounds. HOW CAUGHT: Trolling, surface on down (the biggest blues may be deep); casting lures and/or baits in the surf and from boats; jigging at different levels; chumming at anchor or while drifting; salt-water fly casting. Watch for surface disturbances, with sea birds circling, caused by small fish chased to the top by blues. Blues may go deep or move offshore after a severe storm. Blues are warmer-water fish and coastal migrators, so their runs begin progressively later up the seaboard. BAITS & LURES: Small eels, chunks of fish, whole small fish, strips of squid, still other items. Artificials include spoons, all kinds of plugs, assorted jigs, the so-called surgical tube lures, salt-water flies. Ground-up menhaden make good chum, but other fishes can also be ground up. TACKLE: Any kind of gear, matched approximately to procedures and sizes of blues currently running. Be advised that they're very tough opponents.

Blue Marlin

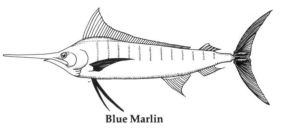

Blue Marlin

SCIENTIFIC NAME: Ichthyologists are not in agreement as to whether the Atlantic Ocean's blue marlin and those in the Pacific are precisely the same species. Externally the residents of both oceans are identical. But internally there are slight anatomical differences that raise questions. Consequently, there are differences in scientific names. Some label the Atlantic blues *Makaira ampla* and give the Pacific version the tag *Makaira mazara*. Other authorities lump both under *Makaira nigricans*, a designation also applied to black marlin. I cite these Latin names because you'll run across them in sport-fishing literature. Don't lose any sleep over them. Fact is, any differences between Atlantic and Pacific blue marlin need concern only technicians. For anglers, the two are identical with the exception of size, so we shall consider them as one species. COMMON NAME: Billfish. COLOR: In life this marlin's color is a beautiful shade of cobalt or steel blue topside, changing to silver and white on the sides and under surface. Sometimes the sides exhibit fleeting splashes of gold. Narrow, lighter-colored bands extend vertically downward from the dorsal surface to the sides. The tail is dark-colored; the first dorsal is midnight blue or purple-blue, occasionally marked with blackish spots or irregular blotches. The body colors and bands fade after death, the shade becoming a gray-bluish. Striped marlin carries a similar color scheme, except that its vertical bands are more pronounced. SIZE: Evidence points to Atlantic blue marlin running smaller than Pacific blues. There have been little guys under 100 lbs., but they're rare. In Atlantic sport-fishing circles a common average is about 250 to 350 lbs. There are much larger fish, however. North Carolina can boast of an 810-pounder caught off Cape Hatteras. Florida and Bahamian waters have surrendered blues up into the 500- and 700-lb. brackets. Based on weigh-ins and sightings, the kings among Atlantic blue marlin appear to be in Virgin Islands waters. An 845-lb. IGFA all-tackle world record was weighed at St. Thomas. And expert skipper-guides will tell you that 1,000-pounders prowl Virgin Islands seas. The largest rod-and-reel blue in northern waters—off eastern Long Island—about which I've heard was one in the 700-lb. class. The weight was only an estimation based on glimpses during a battle that had a sad finale. This blue marlin was hooked at about 1 p.m. of a

Sunday. The fight continued until 2 a.m. Monday morning, 13 hours later, and came to a frustrating conclusion when the big fish simply sank, probably dead from exhaustion. In the Pacific there's an angling range of 250 to 350 lbs., for males, which are smaller than the females. The ladies range up into the 700- and 800-lb. classes and beyond. Hawaii's Kailua-Kona waters also produce such hefties. Tackle-benders going over 1,000 lbs. have been mentioned for Hawaii. FAMILY: With other marlins and the sailfishes, they belong to the family Istiophoridae. DISTRIBUTION: In their U.S. Pacific distribution, Hawaii is *the* place. Those islands are fertile blue marlin territory, and the Kona Coast of the "Big Island," Hawaii, has achieved fame as a hot spot. Although blue marlin occur throughout the tropical and subtropical Pacific, they do not seem to appear regularly in any numbers north of Mexico at about the level of Acapulco. Only occasionally is one boated offshore of southern California, but perhaps there are more than these isolated catches indicate. Baja California, possibly the Gulf of California too, would seem to be a better bet. In its broadest scope their Atlantic range is from about the latitude of far-offshore Georges Bank and southern Massachusetts all the way to Brazil. Regions include Bermuda, the Bahamas, Jamaica, Isla de Cozumel off the Yucatan Peninsula, and the Caribbean in general. Worthy of attention by U.S. anglers are the Virgin Islands and Puerto Rico. In more northerly sections of this range—say, above North Carolina—offshore fishermen contact them only infrequently and then only in summer. However, here again there may be more marlin in those waters than catches suggest. HABITS: (1) Blue marlin are high seas wanderers, and it appears likely that some cover considerable distances. That they do migrate with the seasons is known, as evidenced by their north-bound travels on the East Coast. Probably there are similar movements on the Pacific Coast, but there the pattern is understood even less. (2) Assorted smaller fishes are their main diet, species varying according to local availability. Squid also are a food item. Large blues have an appetite for bonitos and young tunas. (3) Their fight can be spectacular. Long power drives cause line to melt from a reel, alarmingly sometimes. Then there are scorching near-surface runs, proving that blues are among the swiftest marlins. There are combat phases when they bore deep, making the reel's brake run hot, then slow or stop to summon reserve power or to figure out new tactics. Most thrilling of all are the aerial acrobatics when the sea violently disgorges a magnificent blue and silver form leaping toward the sky, then returning to the water in a welter of foam. WHERE CAUGHT: See "Distribution." Occasional blue marlin are raised out toward the inshore edge of the Gulf Stream off Maryland, Virginia and North Carolina in July and August. In Florida productive waters seem to be along the seaward side of the Gulf Stream, which flows closer to the coast there than toward the north, and between that edge and the Bahamas. Late spring and summer are seasons. In the Gulf of Mexico there's a blue marlin sport fishery off Texas and Louisiana. Boats out of Galveston and Corpus Christi, Tex., contact them at intervals. Louisiana's blue marlin searching operates out of Port Eads and Grand Isle on the Gulf. Edges of deep channels, rims of drop-offs and shelves, and the wide theater of open blue-water sea make up blue marlin country. Trolling close to long lines of seaweed formed by winds and currents also produces. Marlin sometimes scout these lines for small fishes seeking cover. This is a technique employed successfully by the New Orleans Big Game Fishing Club in the Gulf of Mexico. HOW CAUGHT, BAITS & LURES: Trolling is the standard procedure, done "blind" with the hope that a natural bait or artificial will raise a blue. Natural offerings include whole balao ("ballyhoo"), squid, mackerel, flying fish, small tuna, barracuda and others, according to locales. Long strip baits, sliced from tuna and other species, also are rigged. Artificials include those of the Knucklehead and Kona Head types, plastic squid and fish, and occasionally feathers. Usually all these come-ons are trolled at a fair clip, up to 8 or 10 knots at times. The faster-towed attractors seem to appeal more to the bigger blues. In the Pacific, some anglers drift live baits—mackerel and other small fishes—for the smaller blues. TACKLE: Conventional-type (revolving-spool reel), generally 80- or 130-lb. test, although some sharpshooters go to 50-lb. tackle. Inexperienced anglers will do well to use the heaviest weapons.

Blue Shark or Great Blue Shark

SCIENTIFIC NAME: *Prionace glauca.* COMMON NAME: I know of only one in the U.S., and it's rarely if ever used any more: blue dog. COLOR: A dark indigo blue on the dorsal surface, a beautiful bright blue on the sides, snow white on the ventral surface. Tips of the pectoral fins and part of the anal fin may be dusky. The colors fade after death, changing to drab gray. SIZE: Sport-caught blues go from about 4 ft. to 7 or 8; weights up to 200 lbs. on the high side. These are slender-bodied sharks. Their weights aren't commensurate with their lengths. Ichthyologists mention long-ago reports of specimens up to 20 ft. long, giants of the species, but the largest for which they have a reliable record is 12 ft. 7 in. Here's an approximate length-weight correlation: 6–7 ft., 65–70 lbs.; 7–8 ft., 100–114 lbs.; 9 ft., 164 lbs. FAMILY: This species belongs to an intrafamily group catalogued as Carcharhinidae, or requiem sharks. Also in this group is the tiger shark. DISTRIBUTION: Range is from Massachusetts on southward in varying numbers. Some, usually strays but occasionally in fair numbers, have been reported offshore as far north as Newfoundland and Nova Scotia in summer. Their southernmost North American limit hasn't been established, but a few have been reported as far south as Uruguay. On the U.S. Pacific Coast: from northern California to Mexico (southernmost limits not known). HABITS: (1) Blue sharks are

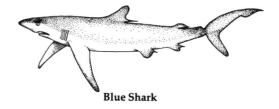

Blue Shark

pelagic, or open-ocean wanderers, cosmopolitan, in tropical, subtropical and warm-temperate seas all over the globe. They're encountered offshore and inshore but not close to beaches. (2) In areas of abundance, such as off Long Island, N.Y., and Block Island, R.I., they're among the more numerous of sharks. (3) In the northern segments of their Atlantic seaboard range they're summer visitors. (4) They scout food at various levels all the way to the bottom but commonly swim very close to the surface, sometimes with the dorsal fin and upper lobe of the tail exposed. They're not especially boat-shy. (5) They devour all kinds of available smaller fishes: herring, mackerels, dogfishes (small sharks) and each other and, when foraging near the bottom, cod, haddock and pollock. They eat squid and eels too. WHERE CAUGHT: Open ocean, at varying distances offshore. HOW CAUGHT: Most productive method is drifting and chumming, with a couple of rigs covering different depths. *Special:* When you sight one near the surface, try dropping some chum to arouse his interest, then cast a fish bait to him. Or, if you like to experiment, a shiny artificial. Blue sharks can be taken on salt-water fly tackle by those who know what they're doing, but it's no adventure for neophytes. BAITS & LURES: As in all shark angling, the most productive method employs only natural baits. Good are live fish like northern whiting, Boston mackerel and the like. Also used: whole small fish, dead; chunk or fillet cut from a larger fish—including a shark; whole squid; live and dead eels; combination bait consisting of fish and a whole squid. Very important: All dead baits should be as fresh as possible. Good chum is menhaden (mossbunkers) ground into mushy pulp "Trash" fishes—commercial fishermens' discards —can also be ground into pulp as shark chum. TACKLE: Blue sharks are caught on spinning tackle. Seasoned hands catch 'em on salt-water fly tackle, but conventional-type weapons are suggested for the less experienced.

Bonefish

SCIENTIFIC NAME: *Albula vulpes* (appropriately, considering this fish's color and wary nature, it means "white fox"). COMMON NAME: Just a shortening to "bone." In angling literature the bonefish has been poetically called "gray ghost of the sand flats," but that's not a commonly used alias. COLOR: A "ghostly white" and gray-silver, often with tinges of light blue or green on the back and sides. The scales have a pearly sheen. Some bones carry indistinct blotches or bars on the back. SIZE: Average run 3 to 5 lbs. Any above 5 lbs. to, say, 8 or 9 are getting into the lunker class, and heavier than that, braggin' sizes. It's believed that the very biggest bones may top 20 lbs., but by how much is unknown as yet. FAMILY: The bonefish is the only living member of his genus in a family

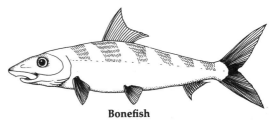
Bonefish

labeled Albulidae. DISTRIBUTION: Overall, from southern Massachusetts (strays) to and including the Florida Keys and on down to Mexico. Bones also are caught in Bermuda, the Bahamas and Puerto Rico. Some of the world's best bonefishing is in the Florida Keys, where the environment for these fish is near perfect. On North America's Pacific Coast bonefish range from Southern California to Panama, and some of the biggest bones are hooked in Hawaii. HABITS: (1) They commonly feed in very shallow water, especially that covering sand bars or mud flats on a rising tide. There they root about the bottom with their snouts for the morsels on which they feed—small crustaceans, worms and other lesser creatures. Sometimes they forage in water so shallow that their dorsal fin and tail are seen. (2) On a falling tide they move off the sand and mud flats to forage on the bottom in somewhat deeper water in intertidal zones along the shores of coral or sandy islands and in quiet coves. (3) *This is very important:* Bonefish are unusually "spooky"—that is, they scare easily. A lure sailing too close over their heads, or even an angler's shadow falling across them when they're in shallow water will stampede them into streaking away. Needless to add, any splashing near them will also send them scampering. (4) With their light coloration they can be difficult to spot, especially if there's any glare on the water, so carry or wear Polaroid sunglasses. (5) They travel variously as loners, in pairs, in pods of half a dozen individuals, and in schools of different sizes. In groups they remain more or less together as they fan out over the flats to feed; but if one fish spooks, the whole bunch takes off. WHERE CAUGHT AND HOW CAUGHT: Most bonefishing is done in very shallow water, where the fish are stalked by wading the flats or intertidal belts or by carefully poling a boat along. Either way, the angler must be extremely quiet. (*Caution:* For wading there should be a firm or hard bottom and reasonably solid footing. Muddy or marly bottoms can be treacherous, with soft spots that plunge the wader into holes.) Casting to the fish is the technique. BAITS & LURES: Bones respond to live baits that match their natural diet—items such as crabs and shrimp. But much bonefishing is done with small fractional-ounce artificials (⅛ to ¼ oz.), including jigs, spinners, assorted spin-fishing models, and salt-water flies. Sometimes baits are more productive than artificials, but often they cannot be placed as close to the fish as lures because of their sight and sound when hitting the water. Of all artificials, flies generally can be cast closest to bones because of their minimum surface disturbance when they hit the water. TACKLE: Fly-casting for bonefish is supreme sport, but is understandably limited by wind conditions in open water. Spinning gear is the most popular tackle, but is getting increasing competition from salt-water fly-fishing equipment. Three details should be remembered: (1) When hooked, bonefish run with dazzling speed. (2) They're surprisingly strong for their size. (3) Don't let 'em get any slack line. It'll cost you fish.

Bonitos

The bonitos are closely allied with tunas and mackerels, to which they bear a marked resemblance. Like their relatives, bonitos possess a mouth of good size, a superbly streamlined body, and carry finlets along the midline of their dorsal and ventral surfaces near the tail. They're fast swimmers of open seas, and they gather in large schools. All are powerful for their sizes and rate as first class game fishes.

Oceanic Bonito

There are several species of bonitos, which accounts for their wide distribution in warmer seas throughout the globe. For sport-fishing purposes, there are four bonitos of interest in North American waters: 1) Atlantic bonito, 2) oceanic bonito, 3) Peruvian or California bonito, and 4) Bonito No. 4. With a few exceptions all four of these bonitos are most commonly caught by oceanic trolling. Natural-feather lures in various color combinations are about the best all-round artificials. Red and white are an old standby. Also used are white and black, green and yellow, tangerine, blue and white, all-white, etc. Since it's never known which combination they might favor on a given day, knowledgeable bonito hunters put out four lines simultaneously, each with a different color combination, then note which elicits a response and change the others accordingly.

Trolling distances astern are according to anglers' own ideas and experience. Bonitos tend to be aggressive and are not especially boat-shy. They have been known to smack lures only 25 or 30 ft. beyond the transom. A good starting arrangement is to have four artificials out—you can experiment with shiny spoons too—at about 20- to 25- ft. intervals, up to 100 ft. or so. Try different trolling speeds too.

Any of the tried-and-true hook patterns are good— O'Shaughnessy, Mustad, Pfleuger-Sobey, Martu, Eagle Claw, etc. Their sizes are gauged approximately to the weights of bonitos currently running. Matching need not be precise. There's leeway because of mouth sizes. The range is from 2/0 through 4/0 or 5/0 for smaller and medium fish, up to 7/0 and 8/0. A 6/0 or 7/0 would be a good compromise if any young tunas are known to be in the area. More important than precise sizes is hook strength. Double-strength (XX), even triple-strength (XXX) hooks are rigged sometimes when large bonitos are involved. They pack a lot of muscle.

Conventional-type gear is recommended over spinning tackle, although the latter will handle these battlers if the wielder knows what he or she is doing. Tackle lightness is up to the anglers' ability and experience. They can go to light weapons, rods rated to handle 10- and 12- lb. lines. Or they can give themselves a margin of safety by using 20- or 30-, even 40-lb. gear. It's wise to consider that heavier tackle if young bluefin or yellowfin tuna are in the area. It costs some action with the smaller bonitos, but is preparation for combat with tunas going to 50 lbs. and more.

Monofilament and braided Dacron lines are fished. The reel should be about a 4/0, spooled with at least 200–250 yds. of line. Suggested for terminal tackle is a leader of wire or monofilament. Eight to 10 ft. will do. Wire can be either stainless steel or the piano type. No. 7 gives a strength range of 69 to 76 lbs. If monofilament is used instead of wire, it should be in somewhat greater strength than the line. *Tip:* Make the connection between line and leader via a snap swivel on the line. It facilitates quick changing of rigs when different artificials or natural baits are tried.

Atlantic Bonito *(Sarda sarda)*

Also known as common bonito. As one of the smaller bonitos, the Atlantic attains weights to 10–12 lbs., but the sport fishing range is more like 3 to 6. At any size it's a fine light-tackle fish, very scrappy. Atlantic bonito is identifiable by its size and color scheme: steel-blue on the back, silvery lower sides and belly, and upper sides carrying 7 to 20 long, narrow, but distinct dark blue—almost black—bars that extend obliquely along the back and upper sides. The body has scales throughout. The color pattern alone is enough to separate it from any tuna frequenting the same waters, and the mouth is proportionately large. But the Atlantic bonito is similar to young bluefin tuna in that it possesses a stout, solid body with streamlining that tapers it to a pointed snout on one end and a very slender tail base on the other. It also is tunalike in having two dorsal fins so close together as to appear confluent. But the triangular first dorsal, which has spines, is proportionately longer than the tuna's, being about one-third as long as the body proper. Atlantic range extends as far north as Nova Scotia, but the southern limits are yet to be determined—some believe down to Florida and the Gulf of Mexico. One of the better developed sport fisheries for this species is the segment of coast from Long Island, N.Y., down along the New Jersey seaboard. Atlantic bonito prey upon quantities of schooling fishes such as mackerel, menhaden and herring. They also consume squid and little fishes such as sand launce (sand eels) and silversides. They can really work over a school of victims, and when feeding at the sea's surface, they can be seen to leap clear of the water. The most popular technique, as mentioned, is trolling of feather lures, but they also are taken on whole small fish and on strip baits. Strips cut from their silvery undersides make fine bait to catch still more bonito. They also respond to shiny spoons. If a school is sighted at the surface, try casting small artificials such as popping plugs. It hasn't been established definitely yet, but Atlantic bonito appear to be all-year residents off Florida and the Gulf of Mexico coast. Off New Jersey and New York they're strictly summer visitors, lingering in decreasing numbers on into September.

Oceanic Bonito *(Katsuwonus pelamis)*

Common handles have included striped bonito, skipjack, skipjack tuna and Arctic bonito. A New York–New Jersey nickname, "watermelon," provides clues to the fish's body shape and markings. Although typically tunalike, the oceanic's

body and markings do suggest a watermelon when one sees
the four to six blue or brownish stripes extending
longitudinally along the lower sides. The body's upper section
is dark blue, while it is white lower down. Other field marks
are a large mouth, extending obliquely backward to about the
middle of the fairly large eyes; absence of body scales (except
along the lateral line and on the trunk's forward and upper
section); two dorsal fins, the first with spines and a noticeably
concave outline, the second much smaller and soft, with rays;
eight finlets between second dorsal and tail, seven finlets on
the underside; and a rather large tail. Strictly oceanic in habit,
they are high seas wanderers noted for extensive travels. In
tropical and near-tropical regions they're all-year residents. To
the north and south of those belts they're late-spring and
summer visitors. Distribution includes the following: offshore
of New York and New Jersey (July, August, early September);
off North Carolina (late April into early November); off
Florida's eastern coast (just about all year); California (from
about August until November); and Hawaii (most of the year).
In California they're generally numerous south of San Diego,
but are also encountered northward to Point Conception and
the Channel Islands. Oceanics appear to be more numerous in
Pacific waters than on the Atlantic side. They're also
widespread throughout the Caribbean. Oceanic bonito
reportedly grow to lengths of 2½ ft., possibly 3, and weights
up to 30 and 40 lbs. are on record. But those are exceptional
fish. Averages in sport fishing takes are under 2 ft., with
weight ranges up to 10 lbs., occasionally to 15 among larger
specimens. On the U.S. East Coast the favored angling method
follows the same general procedure as for Atlantic bonito. In
California they troll with feathers, chromed spoons and bone
lures. Californians also chum for them, rigging live bait that
includes anchovies, sardines, smelt and strips of squid and
fish. Oceanic bonito are swift fish, and trolling speeds can go
up to 8 m.p.h. Tackle wielded for the oceanics should be
somewhat sturdier than that used for the Atlantic bonito.
Oceanic bonito subsist on smaller fishes, squid, and other
forms of high seas life.

Peruvian Bonito (*Sarda chiliensis*)

The Peruvian bonito is also known as California bonito and
Chilean bonito. Its range of distribution runs from Vancouver
Island, British Columbia, south to about Banderas Bay, Mexico.
This species shows up again in the vicinity of Panama, and
ranges from there to off the coast of Chile. They are, however,
seldom found in abundance north of Santa Monica Bay,
California. Summer and fall months are the best seasons in that
state. Maximum sizes are in the vicinity of 3, 3½ ft. and 35 to 40
lbs.; individuals as heavy as 25 lbs. are rare. These bonito are
excellent fighters, and when in a dining frenzy will accept
almost any bait or artificial offered. With a boat at anchor, the
best attractors are live anchovies or sardines. They will also
grab squid and strip baits. Highly recommended for trolling are
red and white feathers, chromed jigs and plastic squid. Light

tackle provides maximum action.

Bonito No. 4, or Atlantic Spotted Bonito

This species' name calls for an explanation. It's one of those species that have undergone periodic name changes, and its exact classification still is a matter for debate. Yale University ichthyologist-oceanographer Edward C. Migdalski prefers the name Atlantic spotted bonito, and that's the one I will use here. Other names in circulation include: false albacore, albacore (universally employed in the New Jersey–New York region), little tuna or little tunny, mackerel tuna, and bonito. Several Latin scientific labels have been applied over the years, but the one that persists as a favorite is *Euthynnus alleteratus*. Their distribution extends along the Atlantic seaboard from the offing of Rhode Island and southern Massachusetts to Brazil, including Bermuda, the Bahama islands, the Caribbean Sea and the Gulf of Mexico. They travel in schools like other bonitos, but their appearances are erratic and unpredictable, as regards both time and quantity, from season to season. The only definite thing about their showings from my own experience in the southern New England and New Jersey region is that they occur in summer, and are at their best—or what passes for same—from July into early September. Some seasons they appear in large schools, but they're not what could be called dependably abundant. In North Carolina they're hooked offshore from April until November and inshore in midsummer and late summer. They're not listed among Florida's top game fishes; yet they're encountered off the Atlantic and Gulf coasts from spring on through summer. In Bermuda, presumably the Bahamas as well, they appear to be available all year but are most numerous from about May into early November. In common with other bonitos, they feed voraciously on smaller schooling fishes and squid. Those boated in sport catches go from about 2 to 4 or 5 lbs., with possibilities up to 8 or 20 lbs.

Cabezone

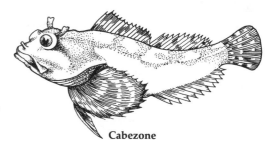

SCIENTIFIC NAME: *Scorpaenichthys marmoratus*. COMMON NAMES: Marble sculpin, giant sculpin, bullhead, blue cod. Forget those last two. "Bullhead" is the name of some fresh-water fishes, and the cabezone is not a cod. COLOR: Body is very variable, according to environment—reddish or reddish-brown through dark brown, tan or grayish, to a shade of green. A lighter mottling on the sides makes the skin look wrinkled. Females tend to be greenish—males, reddish. Belly can be a bright blue, greenish or tan. SIZE: They've been reported up to 2½ ft. long and 20–25 lbs. FAMILY: The scientific family name is Cottidae, or sculpins. It's a very large family with many

Cabezone

representatives along the North American Pacific and Atlantic seaboards. Some 48 different cottids—42 in the sea, six in fresh water—are described for California alone. The cabezone is one of the largest Pacific sculpins, also one of the ugliest and one of the best-eating—but *beware of the roe, which is poisonous.* DISTRIBUTION: From Alaska southward, past British Columbia and all along the California coast, to Baja. HABITS: (1) The cabezone is a bottom feeder, consuming an assortment of items that include crabs (about 50% of their diet), young abalone and mollusks, small fishes. (2) Hooked cabezones often head for the nearest rocks or dense vegetation, where they become difficult, if not impossible, to dislodge. (3) Normally abundant and an all-year resident in many parts of their range. WHERE CAUGHT: Inshore ocean waters and off beaches, notably in rocky areas, around the mouths of coastal rivers, and around gardens of marine vegetation such as kelp beds. HOW CAUGHT: Simple sinker bouncing—bottom fishing. BAITS & LURES: Shrimp, sand crabs, rock crabs, mussels, sea worms, clams, pieces or strips of fish, abalone trimmings. TACKLE: Spinning tackle is the most popular, but light conventional gear is O.K. too. *Special note:* Their meat is naturally bluish-green. It turns white on cooking. *To repeat:* The roe is poisonous. Do not eat it or give it to pets.

Calico Surfperch

SCIENTIFIC NAME: *Amphistichus koelzi.* COMMON NAMES: California pogie and humpback perch. COLOR: Olivaceous or silvery, generously peppered with tiny brownish or reddish specks that form vague, irregular blotches or bars. Often there's a brassy or coppery glint to the sides of the head and belly. The fins, except the pectorals, have dusky tips. SIZE: Maximum is about 12 in. and a pound or so. Despite their smallness, calico surfperches are popular among beach anglers in central and northern California and make up a good 50 percent or more of their catches. FAMILY: One of 20 surfperches, family Embiotocidae—19 in salt water, plus one fresh-water species—found in California. DISTRIBUTION: Overall range of calico surfperch is from just south of Cape Flattery, Wash., to Santo Tomás Point, Baja California, Mexico. HABITS: (1) Lacking positive information, biologists presume that the calico surfperch is similar to the barred variety in habits. If so, the calicos tend to gather in bottom depressions and feed heavily on sand crabs and other small crustaceans, and occasionally on little mollusks. (2) Tagging experiments showed that barred surfperch travel very little, moving less than two miles from an area. Calico surfperch may be similarly localized. Such localization of any species can become bad news if fishing pressures clean out populations in an area. There are no migrations to provide "transfusions," and salt-

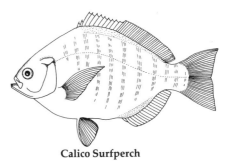

Calico Surfperch

water stocking is often impractical and/or prohibitively expensive. WHERE CAUGHT: Like barred and redtail surfperches, the calicos are common in the surf belt along sandy beaches. Some of the best calico surfperch fishing is along the beaches of Monterey Bay. HOW CAUGHT, LURES & TACKLE: Spinning tackle is good because of the casting and small artificials involved.

California Yellowtail

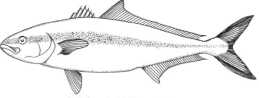

California Yellowtail

SCIENTIFIC NAME: *Seriola dorsalis*. COMMON NAMES: Yellowtail and amberjack. The latter is confusing because there's an Atlantic Coast species by that name. COLOR: A conspicuous yellow or brassy stripe runs from the snout across the eye area to the tail at about the midlevel of the body on each side. Above this stripe the color, when fresh out of the water, is a bright, metallic green, blue, or combination of green and blue. Color below the stripe is silvery. A bright yellow caudal fin or tail gives the species its name. Other fins are dusky green and yellow. SIZE: Most of the yellowtails recorded for California anglers weigh between 10 and 20 lbs. Tournament winners can be in the 50- to 60-lb. bracket. A former world record, caught in Mexico, was logged in at 105 lbs. 12½ oz., and subsequently was topped by a New Zealand fish weighing 111. FAMILY: The yellowtail is one of 12 jacks, members of the family Carangidae, inhabiting California waters.
DISTRIBUTION: From about Point Conception, Calif., including Catalina Island, to Cabo San Lucas, Baja California, Mexico, and the Gulf of California. Yellowtails rate among southern California's top-ranking sport fishes. HABITS: (1) They travel in large schools, which arrive off southern California by May or June or earlier migrating northward from waters offshore of Baja California. In Baja and the Gulf of California they're an all-year species. (2) They dine enthusiastically on whatever foods abound in the areas they happen to be at the time, giving anglers latitude in selection of baits. Items include anchovies, sardines, young mackerels, squid and assorted crabs. (3) They can be unpredictable and erratic, showing abundantly in an area one day, vanishing from that place the very next, coming back again a couple of days later, and so on. (4) Yellowtails are also unpredictable in their responses to baits, playing very hard to get. They also can be boat-shy. WHERE CAUGHT: These jacks are oceanic. Much of the action with them is around offshore islands and banks, and off rocky sections of mainland coast where kelp beds are abundant. HOW CAUGHT: A favored method combines chumming with small live fishes and casting a live bait to the yellowtails after a suitable feeding frenzy has been generated. Trolled artificials also nail yellowtails at times, as does casting natural baits or artificials to surfaced schools encountered by chance. BAITS & LURES: Natural attractors

include anchovies, sardines, small queenfish, smelts, butterfish, other little fishes, alive or dead, plus strips of fish and squid. Artificials include feathers and other jigs, spoons, and even fake squid when yellowtails are real hungry. TACKLE: The choice between conventional and spinning belongs to the angler. The former type might be better for less experienced fishermen, since yellowtails reach respectable sizes and are given to strong power surges. Those details might also influence choosing between light and light-medium gear. In any case, no slack should be allowed to develop when arguing with a yellowtail. Slack provides a chance to throw or spit out the hook. Since they're fast, strong scrappers, they can't be "horsed"—that is, forced in with the rod. That could pull the hook out of the fish's mouth or break the line.

Channel Bass

SCIENTIFIC NAME: *Sciaenops ocellatus.* COMMON NAMES: Generations of Atlantic Coast fishermen have called this fish channel bass, but on the Gulf Coast it is universally called redfish, or simply red. "Red drum" is another name usually reserved for technical discussion and is the best of the three. "Channel bass" is a misnomer because this species is not a bass but a member of the family Sciaenadae, which includes the croakers. Profile resemblances shared by the red drum and black drum (see page 181) include a solid-looking body, rather blunt head, two dorsal fins separated by a deep notch, and a more or less straight-edge tail. But the channel bass is readily distinguished from its relative by a conspicuous black spot on the tail's base. Too, the channel bass lacks the black drum's chin barbels. The black spot accounts for another regional nickname for channel bass, "spot tail." COLOR: The channel bass is a shade of green, with a brassy or bronze tinge, along the back. On the sides its color becomes a red-pink with pearly reflections or a coppery tinge, shading gradually to a white underside. Fin colors are as follows: dorsals and tail, dusky; pectorals, a rusty red; ventrals and anal fin, whitish. SIZE: Their sizes in sport catches vary widely, according to segments of coast and where caught in those segments. In Virginia and North Carolina, for example, where channel bass are popular opponents, boat- and surf-caught fish can range from 10- to 30- and 40-pounders, whereas in the Gulf of Mexico redfish average under 10 lbs. Bay specimens are usually smaller than those extracted from the surf. A world record was an 83-pounder, 4 ft. 4 in. long, taken on 50-lb. line at Cape Charles, Va. FAMILY: See "Common Names." DISTRIBUTION: Southern New Jersey and Delaware southward to Florida, then on to Mexico via the Gulf Coast. Years ago, old-timers say, channel bass were caught occasionally in New York waters,

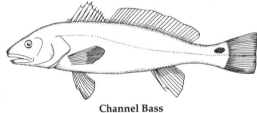

Channel Bass

and strays have been reported as far north as Massachusetts. HABITS: (1) They're bottom feeders. (2) Their principal foods are crabs and shrimp, varied with smaller fishes and mollusks. (3) Available evidence indicates that red drums do not undertake extensive coastwise migrations, but confine their movements to a shift inshore when waters warm in the spring, then back out in autumn's progressively cooler weather. However, in the more northerly sections of their Atlantic seaboard range there may be coastal migrations in spring and fall. (4) Summer is a prime angling season throughout their range. WHERE & HOW CAUGHT: As channel bass, this species has starred primarily as a surf-fishing target, notably on the North Carolina coast. But it is also caught by trolling and bottom fishing, often combined with jigging at anchor. Along the Gulf Coast it is also caught by fly and plug casting from boats. BAITS & LURES: In addition to the artificials just mentioned, it also responds to metal jigs. Natural baits include crabs, squid and mullet. TACKLE: The principal combat stratagem of these fish is a persistent, dogged pull, interspersed with short dashes, and with one of any size the argument is backed by muscle. They are at their sportiest when hooked in a booming surf or caught on spinning gear or a salt-water fly rod.

China Rockfish

SCIENTIFIC NAME: *Sebastodes nebulosus.* COMMON NAMES: Regionally, china fish, black and yellow rockfish, black and yellow rock cod and, uncommonly, *cefalutano.* "China fish" can be confusing because that's also a regional name for the greenspotted rockfish. "Black and yellow rock cod" is a misnomer, since rockfishes are not allied with the cod family. COLOR: Its body form is similar to that of other rockfishes. The color is blue-black above and on the sides, fading to a lighter shade on the belly. Sometimes there are whitish and light blue mottlings. Distinguishing this species from other rockfishes is a pronounced bright yellow stripe that starts at the base of the dorsal fin's spiny section, then curves downward and backward to the tail's base. SIZE: Lengths of 16 in. and weights of a couple of pounds are about maximum. FAMILY: Another affiliate of the rockfish group, some 52 or so different kinds of which are recognized on the U.S. Pacific seaboard. Scorpaenidae is the family name. DISTRIBUTION & WHERE CAUGHT: Their distribution is in ocean waters, shallow out to moderately deep, from about Point Conception, Calif., to southern Alaska. They have also been found on down to northern Baja California, Mexico. HABITS: (1) China rockfish offer lively resistance and pose a challenge by streaking to the nearest rock crevice when seizing a bait or when hooked. (2) All rockfishes seem to be very sensitive to water

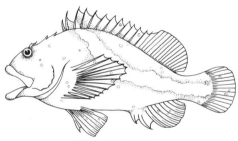

China Rockfish

temperatures and currents. They may be numerous in a given area one day and absent the very next, even though weather and other conditions seem the same. HOW CAUGHT: Fishing near the bottom, at anchor. BAITS & LURES: Shallow-water baits are shrimp, strips of fish or squid, pieces of crab, fresh-dead anchovy. In deeper areas the bait is a strip of squid or fish. TACKLE: The mouth is of fair size, accommodating hooks up to 2/0, 4/0. Equipment, conventional-type and spinning, is light, but should have some "backbone" for arguing the fish away from—or out of—rocky crevices. That goes for all rockfish angling.

Cobia

SCIENTIFIC NAME: *Rachycentron canadus*. COMMON NAMES: Crab-eater, black bonito, lemonfish, cubbyyew (!), cabio, black kingfish, coalfish, black salmon, *bacalao,* and ling in the Gulf of Mexico. Forget 'em all except "cobia"; the other are regional and misleading. COLOR: Body is dark brown above, lighter brown and silvery lower down, whitish on the belly. A blackish lateral stripe, somewhat wider than the eye, extends from the snout to the base of the caudal fin or tail. SIZE: Cobias go to 8, 10, 15 lbs. and, with decreasing frequency, much better. The Gulf of Mexico yields cobias of 30 to 50 lbs. and up to 70. FAMILY: It's believed that the cobia has no close relatives, so he's classified in a family by himself, Rachycentridae. DISTRIBUTION: Southern New Jersey southward, with wide distribution and abundance in the Gulf of Mexico. Also reported common in the West Indies. Extreme limits of the species' range are southern Massachusetts and New York, offshore in summer, and Argentina. The species has not been reported for the Pacific Coast. HABITS: (1) Cobias are warm-water fish, which governs appearances in more northerly parts of their range. (2) They're commonly encountered under or around floating debris, such as patches of seaweed, large pieces of wood and the like, as well as around buoys and even anchored barges. In the Gulf of Mexico they're also found around offshore drilling rigs. Other waters with cobia potential are those around jetties, wrecks and other submerged masses. (3) They're often seen cruising leisurely near the surface, solo or in pairs or small groups, a seeming sluggishness that belies their fighting ability. (4) Young cobias may infiltrate inlets, large bays and sounds, but the older individuals favor the shoaler areas of open sea. They feed extensively on all kinds of available small fishes and crustaceans. WHERE CAUGHT: Primarily in shallower waters of the open Atlantic and Gulf of Mexico. (I should add good summer action has been had with these fish on Chesapeake Bay and in the ocean off Virginia.) Cobias are caught from boats, shores and piers, including those on oceanfronts. HOW CAUGHT, BAITS & LURES:

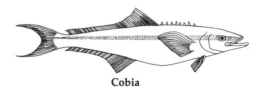

Cobia

(1) Trolling 6-in. shiny spoons on a short leader, from near surface to intermediate levels. (2) Sinker bouncing or bottom fishing with live or cut baits, the boat at anchor or drifting. Live baits include crabs in the shedder state and eels. (3) Letting a live bait drift away from the boat. (4) Casting artificials from boats or shore to cobias near the surface. Effective artificials include plugs about the size of those rigged for striped bass, in blue, silver and mackerel finishes, and 1½- to 3-oz. jigs with white or yellow skirts. Leaders are always used. TACKLE: Spinning or conventional tackle—your choice, but it's suggested that it be able to handle monofilament lines of about 15- to 25-lb. test. Cobias give a good account of themselves.

Corbina

SCIENTIFIC NAME: *Menticirrhus undulatus*. COMMON NAMES: California corbina. COLOR: A dark, metallic blue on the back, fading to lighter sides and a white belly, with dusky fins. SIZE: Sizes go up to 16, 18, 20 in. Weights up to 7 and 8 lbs. are on record, but are exceptional. FAMILY: One of eight kinds of croakers recognized by California's Department of Fish and Game. Ichthyologists catalogue the California corbina with the drums and croakers (Sciaenidae) and ally it in that tribe with the whiting group of the Atlantic. DISTRIBUTION: The corbina is a bottom species distributed along sandy beaches and in shallow bays from about Point Conception, Calif., down to Cabo San Lucas, Baja California, and over into the Gulf of California. HABITS & WHERE CAUGHT: (1) Throughout their range they travel and feed in small groups in shoreside zones in shallow water, from only 1½ or 2 ft. in a surf on out to depths of about 45 ft. Sometimes they cruise or forage in water so shallow that their backs are exposed. (2) About 90 percent of their food is sand crabs. Other crustaceans and clams are of minor importance. Corbinas feed in interesting fashion by scooping up mouthfuls of sand, spitting out fragments of clam shells and other unwanted items, and ejecting the sand through their gills. (3) They're a sedentary species, seldom moving any distance and displaying no migratory patterns. Their only shifts seem to be offshore in winter and to spawn. HOW CAUGHT, BAITS, LURES & TACKLE: Corbinas are popular with beach casters, and a lively surf that churns up food from the sand is likely corbina territory. Although not large, they pose a challenge. They're wary and can be difficult to hook because they mouth or toy with a bait and seldom hit solidly. Rigging is for the bottom, and baits include sand crabs (preferably in the soft-shell state), bloodworms, mussels, clams, pileworms. Hooks are No. 2 or No. 1, and a 3- or 4-ft. leader of low-visibility monofilament is recommended. They're game battlers.

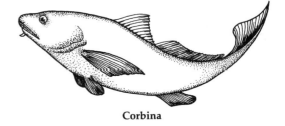

Corbina

Corvinas

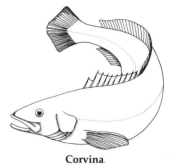

Corvina.

SCIENTIFIC NAME: *Cynoscion spp.* COMMON NAMES: According to species, shortfin corvina, totuava, gulf corvina, white sea bass ("bass" is a misnomer), orangemouth corvina, etc. COLOR: Corvinas are characterized by a lateral line that extends the length of the body and on out to the end of the tail; and, generally, a metallic sheen to the body color, which according to species may be blue, greenish, gray, olive, coppery or brassy, usually with silver below and a white belly. The fins may be black, dusky, orange or yellow. SIZE: Statistics on individual species are scarce. Collectively, their reported sizes range from 15 in. up to 30 in. for the striped corvina *(Cynoscion reticulatus)*, to maximum lengths of 2 ft. for the Gulf corvina *(Cynoscion othonoptherus)* of the Gulf of California and 3 ft. for the yellow corvina *(Cynoscion phoxocephalus)*. A huge relative, the totuava *(Cynoscion macdonaldi)*, a kind of giant weakfish, is confined to the northern and central Gulf of California. Called *totoaba* in Mexico, this king among North American croakers reportedly reaches lengths of 5 and 6 ft. and weights to 200 lbs. FAMILY: Corvinas is a collective name for several species of croakers roaming the Pacific seaboard, and they're among the 150 or so different kinds of fishes making up the Sciaenidae (croaker) family. All told, the Sciaenidae are a diversified tribe. In addition to croakers, they include the drum, weakfish and whiting groups. Close relatives of the Pacific coast's corvinas are the Atlantic Coast's weakfishes, the spotted weakfish *(Cynoscion nebulosus)* and its famed cousin to the north, the battler known simply as the weakfish *(Cynoscion regalis)*. DISTRIBUTION: Some eight kinds of croakers are described for California waters. Under the banner Corvinas, representatives of the family are distributed from Alaska all the way down to Peru. The majority of them are encountered in Mexican waters, including Baja California, and southward. HABITS: Judging by available data, very little is known about corvinas' habits. We can presume, though, that they feed on many kinds of smaller fishes. WHERE CAUGHT: Corvinas are oceanic, inshore (some species) and offshore. Some species, such as the gulf and orangemouth corvinas, are hooked in the Gulf of California. Perhaps the most important Pacific Coast corvina in sport fishery is the misnamed California white sea bass, which isn't a bass. At least one species, the orangemouth corvina, was introduced successfully into southern California's Salton Sea. HOW CAUGHT, BAITS, LURES & TACKLE: As a group they are caught by a variety of methods that include fishing at anchor with live or dead bait and casting and trolling artificials such as shiny spoons, plugs and leadhead jigs. The lightness or heaviness of tackle goes according to fishing methods and the weight of corvinas expected. Some are also caught by salt-water fly-fishing, rigging large streamers.

Crevalle

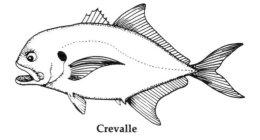

Crevalle

SCIENTIFIC NAME: *Caranx hippos*. COMMON NAMES: Crevalle jack or jack crevalle; sometimes "crevally" in either instance; common jack, cavella and cavalla. COLOR: Variously a dark blue, almost black sometimes, or blue-green or greenish, often with brassy tints along the back and upper sides above the lateral line. Farther down the color becomes silvery, sometimes yellowish. The dorsal fins and tail are dark or dusky. The prominent anal fin often is yellow. A narrow lateral line extends along each side. There's usually a noticeable black spot on the rear edge of each gill cover. SIZE: A 20-pounder is about tops for Florida crevalles, although larger fish to 25 lbs. and better are caught. Maximum size is not really known, but tackle-benders up to 45 lbs. are reported in that state. Even heavier giants have been mentioned. If there's a general range in the sport fishery, it's more like 1 to 10 lbs., with some going up in the teens. FAMILY: One of the Carangidae family (jackfishes or jacks) or carangid fishes. DISTRIBUTION: This species has wide distribution in tropical and subtropical waters in many regions of the world. In U.S. waters it occurs in both the Atlantic and Pacific. The Pacific form is scientifically labeled *Caranx caninus* but is considered practically identical to the Atlantic fish. On the East Coast, crevalle have been reported as far north as Nova Scotia as strays, on down to Uruguay. They're listed for Bermuda (the common name there is horse-eye jack), the Bahamas, the Caribbean and the Gulf of Mexico, and are found along both Florida coasts, usually in good supply. In the Pacific they're caught in Hawaii, and from the Gulf of California to Peru. HABITS: (1) Crevalles are fast, enthusiastic, voracious predators, preying upon smaller fishes such as mullet. Their hunting technique is to herd a school of victims into a compact mass and tear in. (2) Crevalles travel about in schools, with some tendency among older, larger individuals to branch out on their own. WHERE CAUGHT: The bigger crevalles are caught offshore, but the species also frequents inshore areas and fans out over flats at high tide. They're credited with a wide salinity tolerance, from high to low saltiness, which accounts for their being found in brackish water and their excursions into coastal rivers. HOW CAUGHT, BAITS, LURES & TACKLE: Whatever their size, crevalles are topflight sport fish—hard fighters and real dandies on light tackle. Almost any method will take them: fishing at anchor with cut bait or live bait (mullet and pinfish are good), trolling artificials, plugging, spin casting with small lures, and fly casting with streamers. Top-water and deep-running lures are effective, but must be trolled at a lively clip. Plugs also do a job. Ditto streamer flies. A key to success with artificials is to keep them moving briskly, often the faster the better. If a crevalle is seen and doesn't smack an artificial when it lands, it should be retrieved at a speeded-up pace. Sometimes increased retrieve speed will induce hits when the fish can't be seen. As the variety of methods hints, there's a wide choice of tackle—conventional or so-called all-purpose boat type, spinning and fly. The choice is the user's. Action can be fast and furious when a school is contacted, even more so if they happen to be in one of their feeding frenzies. An old Florida stunt when the fish do not show is to locate a school by plug casting, then switch to fly tackle for the hottest kind of sport.

Dolphin

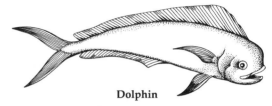

Dolphin

SCIENTIFIC NAME: *Coryphaena hippurus*. COMMON NAMES: *Dorado* in Latin America, *mahi mahi* in Hawaii. COLOR: The fish has been called a "finned rainbow." In the water a dolphin is a vivid blue-green. The large tail is golden yellow. It's when one is reeled aboard that the rainbow effect manifests itself. There occurs a series of color effects that is phenomenal and startling. In succession the fish may become a bright green with ripplings of yellow or iridescent gold, a vivid blue with transient splashes of silver, or a mixture of green and yellow. The color changes are usually most spectacular when the fish is dying. After death the colors disappear quickly, replaced by a drab silver gray or grayish-yellow. SIZE: Florida has yielded bulls in the 60- and 70-lb. classes. Hawaii has produced dolphin up into the 70-lb. bracket. And the Bahamas yielded an IGFA world-record bruiser going 85 lbs. Twenty pounds is about tops, with most fish going less. Generally speaking, it's the smaller dolphin—5 or 6 lbs. to maybe 15—that are encountered inshore, while the brutes are found farther off. FAMILY: The family's scientific name is Coryphaenidae. It has only two known members. The other is the smaller pompano dolphin (*Coryphaena equiselis*). DISTRIBUTION: Dolphins are widely distributed in warm seas, reaching greatest abundance in tropical and subtropical waters but also are encountered—in fewer numbers—in warm-temperate regions during the summer. Off New Jersey and New York, for instance, they appear offshore only in summer. These fish probably travel northward with the tepid Gulf Stream, which provides both transportation and food. Gulf Stream travel also accounts for their being encountered occasionally in southern New England waters and, as stragglers, as far north as Nova Scotia. Their southern Atlantic limits are not defined clearly, but dolphin swim in Bermudian and Bahamian waters, throughout the Caribbean, in the Gulf of Mexico, off Panama, and southward. On the Pacific seaboard their overall range can extend as far north as the U.S. border with Canada—strays, probably summer only. They're not too common north of Catalina Island, Calif., but become increasingly more numerous south of there—toward Baja California and beyond. HABITS: (1) Dolphins are fish of the open sea, although youngsters are found inshore periodically. They travel in small groups or schools of varying size as a general rule, but the bigger individuals tend to move about in pairs or as loners. (2) On the

Atlantic Coast they may be encountered in that zone out to and including the Gulf Stream, where they are often found lurking under or around floating patches of golden sargassum weed. This weed harbors small food fishes and also provides a kind of cover. Dolphins are open-sea rovers along the Pacific Coast too. (3) They're quite catholic in their diet, eating smaller schooling fishes such as mackerel, mullet, anchovies, silversides, triggerfish, sardines, jacks, etc. They will also take squid and crabs. A favorite offshore item is flying fish, which sometimes are caught "on the wing" by zealous dolphins leaping clear of the sea. (4) Dolphins are in fact among the fastest of marine fishes, actively pursuing prey and sometimes being chased themselves. Aerial acrobatics are part of their strategy both in hunting and eluding foes. (5) Dolphins are top drawer as rod-and-reel opponents. They're fast. They hit a bait in a smashing strike. They fight furiously, punctuating their resistance with flashy runs and spectacular jumps. They're surprisingly strong for their size, and their resistance is often heightened by a cute trick of throwing their flattened body broadside to the line's pull. (6) Dolphins have one very odd habit. It's the fact that a hooked dolphin left in the water will keep others hanging around, and often they succumb to hooks too. Knowledgeable dolphin hunters capitalize on this curious habit, even risking a possible loss of the fish already on. WHERE CAUGHT, HOW CAUGHT, BAITS, LURES & TACKLE: Blind trolling for other species—bluefin tuna, sailfish, blue or white marlin—will often raise dolphins. And it's a pulse-pounding sight to see one or more of these beautifully colored speedsters come streaking in out of nowhere in pursuit of a feather, Knucklehead or some other artificial, or a rigged whole mullet or balao ("ballyhoo"). Pacific Coast fishermen also use flying fish and live baits successfully. Anglers wise to the ways of dolphins keep their eyes open for floating patches of weed or other buoyant debris —a wooden crate, perhaps, or a large timber. A dolphin, or maybe a pair, is under that debris. An educated guess is that such cover attracts the small fishes on which they feed, or perhaps it gives some shade from a hot sun. Making passes with a bait or artificial can bring response. Or, for real sport, try light-tackle-casting a popping plug, shiny spoon, or a fly or streamer. Dolphin also seek food along tide and current rips marked by a long line of patches of floating weed. Little food fishes seek haven from the current in these weed lines. Trolling an artificial parallel to the rip can bring response. If a school is encountered, it presents an excellent opportunity for exciting casting. In waters where dolphin are abundant, drifting bait can be effective, notably in the vicinity of reefs. Also in waters where there are good numbers of them, they can be chummed, the boat drifting or at anchor. It's possible to extract several from a given school this way.

Fluke or Summer Flounder

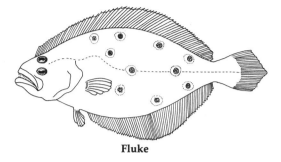

Fluke

SCIENTIFIC NAME: *Paralichthys dentatus*. COMMON NAMES: "Summer flounder" is the common name, but "fluke" is more familiar to the greater number of fishermen. COLOR: The color of this flatfish's pigmented upper surface is governed by the color and nature of the bottom on which it happens to be at a given time. Thus the body color can be a grayish-yellow if the individual is on sand, or a shade of brown, olive, or nearly black if the fish happens to be on mud. Also part of the color scheme, influenced by the bottom, are blotches, along with a scattering of spots that may be either pale or dark. Even the texture of the colors can vary, from uniform, resembling smooth mud, to coarse in a simulation of sand or gravel. This is protective camouflage, making the fish less visible to prey and foes alike, and fluke have an amazing talent for adapting their color pattern at will. As with all flatfishes, the underside, or blind side, of the body is a ghastly white. Fluke are "left-eyed." If a fluke is held, flat body vertical, head pointing away, mouth underneath, the fish's pigmented side and eyes will be on the holder's left. A winter flounder, held in similar fashion, is "right-eyed." SIZE: Range is from 1½ to 2½ lbs. for youngsters, through mediums of 4 to 6 lbs., on up to the "doormats" (a local nickname) of 13 to 16 lbs. Occasionally they go even heavier. Fluke in the 20-lb. class are on record. FAMILY: The catchall name for the tribe that embraces fluke, flounders, soles and halibuts is flatfishes. It's an enormous family. Estimates of the number of its different species go to 300 and more. It's a family with two extremes in sizes, small and large, and nothing much in between. Biggest is the Atlantic halibut (recorded weights up to 600, 700 lbs.). At the other end of the scale is the sand flounder, or windowpane, weighing in at 8 oz. to a pound. Fluke belong to a group within the family with the scientific name Paralichthyidae. DISTRIBUTION: Atlantic Coast from Maine to South Carolina, beyond which state they're replaced by another species, southern fluke or southern flounder *(Paralichthys lethostigmus)*. Centers of greatest abundance include Long Island, N.Y., and New Jersey. HABITS: (1) Fluke are among the most active and aggressive of flatfishes. Unlike many of their smaller cousins, fluke do not believe in sitting around the house waiting for food to come their way. They go out and get it. They're fierce predators. And despite being shaped like a platter, they move with surprising swiftness. All smaller fishes are their prey, but they'll accept almost anything that moves—within reason—and that includes crabs, shrimp, marine worms, squid, and make-them-an-offer. (2) Fluke winter offshore, out on the continental shelf, where they escape hibernal cold in depths from 25 to 60 fathoms. The sport-fishing season begins in mid- or late spring, the initial showings understandably occurring in more southerly parts of their range. Fluke like reasonably warm water. As water temperatures in inshore ocean zones and bays start to inch upward, the fish move toward land, infiltrating inlets and taking up summer residence in bays and channels.

WHERE CAUGHT: Throughout their range they occur from bay shallows out to moderately deep water offshore, according to seasons. Like most flatfishes, they're essentially bottom dwellers. However, they will hunt and pursue food right to the surface if need be. For anglers their habitat is the shallower water of bays and salt-water estuaries. Waters around gardens of eelgrass are often productive, since they harbor food. Gateways to the sea and channels—especially channels adjacent to inlets—are also prime fluke-hunting areas because food is borne along by the tides. HOW CAUGHT, BAITS & LURES: Angling techniques include (1) Drifting. This is best. It covers more territory than still-fishing, thus increasing chances of contacts, and imparts movement to the bait. Tops for drifting is a combination of live killy, 2 or 3 in. long, carefully hooked through the lips, and a strip of squid on the same hook. Let one end of the strip dangle free and split that end up the middle to create two fluttering, eye-catching tails. (2) Chumming is a supplement to drifting when the boat isn't moving too fast. It's best used when the fish are scattered. See Chapter 6. (3) Fishing at anchor. This method, like drifting, calls for a combination of live killy and squid strips. Chumming is also a valuable aid. With or without chum, the bait should be kept in motion by reeling it slowly along the bottom. A good procedure is to let the current carry your rig away from the boat, then retrieve it slowly along the bottom, and repeat. (4) Angling from docks, banks, etc. This is another technique that proves effective. Fluke cruise docks, banks, channels and inlets in search of tide-transported food, but the problem may be in getting the rig into deep enough water. Casting helps but rules out a lip-hooked live killy. Squid strips are effective, or try a combination of squid strips and dead spearing, or a dead sand eel. Affixing two or three small, shiny spinner blades above the hook helps. Keep your rig in motion. On a low or falling tide try deeper parts of channels and shallower areas when the tide is higher. (5) Ocean-front and jetty surf casting. This is one of the least productive fluke-catching methods, but it occasionally produces fish. You have the same problem with live killies here, that is, keeping them on the hook when casting. On jetties the current may carry the rig out, in which case the casting and live-killy problem is eliminated, and the technique is the same as for boat fishing at anchor. A combination of squid strip and dead spearing also works.
(6) Trolling. This method is least popular, but it has drifting's advantage in covering more ground where fluke may be prowling. It accounts for fewer fluke than other techniques, with the possible exception of surf casting, but it also nails some of the bigger ones. A strip of squid in combination with a live or dead killy or dead spearing is a good bait. Shiny spinner blades just ahead of the rig will help. Occasionally bringing the bait or artificial up into intermediate levels can pay off.
TACKLE: Conventional and spinning gear are used. As always, the lighter the tackle, the greater the action; but inexperienced anglers must remember that fluke commonly attain weights to 10 and 12 lbs. and resist with enthusiasm. Also to be kept in mind are the weight of the rig and its sinker, and that on piers

and jetties the fish may have to be lifted several feet from the water. In trolling there is sinker weight and water drag on the line.

Grunts

These are small marine fishes characterized in general by moderately deep bodies, steeply sloping foreheads, small to medium mouths, a continuous dorsal fin about equally divided between spiny and rayed sections, and a well-developed tail with a V indentation on its rear edge. Many species are very colorful. Yellow is common. Among other hues are blues, greens, grays, reds and silver. Among many of them the inside of the mouth is pinkish, red or orange. Overall, weights average from about ½ lb. to 2 lbs., with one species, black margate, largest of the group, recorded up to 10 lbs. in Florida. Grunts are warm-water fishes, widely distributed inshore and offshore in tropical and subtropical waters. Many of them favor coral reefs or rocky bottom. Nocturnal feeding is common among grunts, and natural foods include marine worms, little fishes of various kinds, small crabs, shrimp and assorted invertebrates. Some species are valued for food. Others are used as bait for larger fishes.

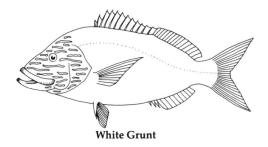

White Grunt

Bluestriped grunt *(Haemulon sciurus)*

U.S. distribution is in southern Florida, both coasts, around reefs and bars and inshore. More abundant on the state's Atlantic side. Also found in Bermuda and the West Indies. Color pattern is gaudy, with yellow and blue lengthwise stripes on the body, brownish or blackish dorsal fin and tail, the latter edged in yellow, mouth bright red inside. Caught by bottom fishing with small pieces of mullet, shrimp, pilchard, etc. Also hits small artificials. Ultra-light tackle is needed, since they usually weigh less than 1 lb. but can go to 2 or 3.

Margate *(Haemulon alubum)*

Distribution is about the same as for blue-striped grunt, and add the Bahamas. Color is gray or pearl-gray. From about its midline upward the body usually carries three dark brown stripes. Taken around outer reefs in fairly deep water. One of the largest grunts, recorded up to 8 lbs. Like other grunts, caught by bottom fishing with cut bait.

French grunt *(Haemulun flavolineatum)*

This grunt is quite common in southern Florida. Distribution also takes in Bermuda, the Bahamas, the West Indies. Color pattern is distinctive: body striped alternately in bright yellow and grayish-blue, with stripes below the body's midline curving upward in the rear section. Fins usually are bright yellow, and inside of mouth is red. A bottom species found inshore in fairly shallow water and also offshore in deeper water around reefs or over rocky bottom. Takes small pieces of bait—shrimp, mullet, pilchard, etc.—readily, but is an ultra-light target because the weight is under a pound.

Sargo *(Anisotremus davidsonii)*

This Pacific Coast species is also known as blue bass, perch, china croaker and black croaker. U.S. distribution is in California, Point Conception southward, whence it extends to Baja California. Body color is an iridescent silver, grayish along back, with black-edged gill covers and a dark ventral band that runs across the back and down each side like a saddle. Body is deep; mouth is small, with thick lips and fine teeth. They're bottom feeders, eating small crabs, shrimp, clams, sea snails. Taken on or near bottom, but bait small hooks (No. 4) with proportionately small pieces of clam, mussel, shrimp or fish. Very light tackle needed. They have been recorded at 20-plus in. and 4 lbs., but average much smaller, more like a maximum of 14 in. and weights to a pound or so.

Porkfish *(Anisotremus virginicus)*

The range is Florida to Brazil, also Bermuda (where it was introduced) and the West Indies. Its distinctive color scheme includes bright yellow and light blue lengthwise stripes, bright yellow fins, silver and yellow head. Also distinctive is a black stripe running diagonally downward from the forehead through the eye to the corner of the mouth. Behind it is another short stripe running from the origin of the dorsal fin to the gill cover. The body is deep; the mouth is small, with thick lips; the large tail is deeply forked. Porkfish feed on shrimp, small crabs and other invertebrates, little fishes, and sea worms. They're bottom dwellers, often feeding at night. They can be caught by bottom-fishing methods and baits used for other grunts, and are ultra-light-tackle game (maximum is about 12–14 in., 1½– 2 lbs.). Florida appears to have its best U.S. distribution.

Black margate *(Anisotremus surinamenis)*

This grunt is about the biggest, but also least common. Average weight is 1 to 2 lbs., reported up to 8 in Florida. Range is from there to Brazil, including the West Indies. Body is deep, with large scales; mouth is small (white inside), with thick lips; tail is large, forked. Body color is a shade of gray, sometimes dusky on top of head and parts of back. Fins are dusky gray or black. Distinctive is a dark vertical band that straddles the back and runs down on either side just forward of the dorsal fin. Bottom fishing with shrimp or pieces of cut fish is the method. Black margates frequent reefs and other areas common to grunts, and come inshore.

White grunt *(Haemulon plumieri)*

This is one of the most common grunts, with an overall range from North Carolina to Brazil. It is said to wander as far north as Chesapeake Bay. Also described for Bermuda (introduced there) and the West Indies. Color scheme includes bluish-gray body color with lateral lines of yellow and bluish, splash of yellow on the head with blue lines on sides of head, blue-gray dorsal fin with yellow edge, red interior of mouth. A bottom dweller, shallow water on out to offshore reefs, the white grunt feeds on sea worms, crustaceans, often at night. It readily takes baits such as shrimp, pieces of mullet and pilchards. The white grunt is a lively fighter on very light tackle. Average weight is under a pound, but is said to reach even 4 lbs. in exceptional specimens.

Gulf Flounder

SCIENTIFIC NAME: *Paralichthys albigutta.* COMMON NAMES: Just "flounder." COLOR: The upper or pigmented surface is grayish or gray-brown mottled with paler blotches. Usually quite distinct are three roundish spots, each with a halo of a lighter color, whose positioning is roughly triangular. The fins may be tinged with yellow. The underside is white. Like fluke, the Gulf flounder is "left-eyed." SIZE: They are among the smallest flounders, with an average maximum length of about 10 in. and a weight of less than a pound. Larger (to 12–15 in.) specimens are reported. FAMILY: Bothidae. The species is closely related to the fluke or summer flounder, *Paralichthys dentatus.* The two resemble each other, but the Gulf flounder is appreciably smaller. DISTRIBUTION: Overall, from North Carolina to Florida, then around the latter state into the Gulf of Mexico and along its rim to Texas. HABITS: (1) Like other flounders and their kinfolk, these flatfish are groundfish, or bottom dwellers. (2) Unlike some other flounders, they favor sandy floors over mud. (3) Their food consists of small crustaceans and invertebrates. WHERE CAUGHT: Gulf flounders are encountered in relatively shallow inshore zones. HOW CAUGHT: Bottom fishing at anchor is the method. BAITS & LURES: Baits include pieces of fish, shrimp and marine worm. TACKLE: Gulf flounders' small size is against them. Tackle should be extra-light.

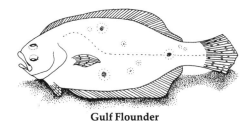
Gulf Flounder

Haddock

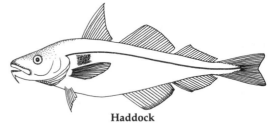

Haddock

SCIENTIFIC NAME: *Melanogrammus aeglefinus*. COMMON NAME: None except haddock. COLOR: Fresh from the water, haddock are about the prettiest colored of the cod family quartet, but that isn't saying much. A notable difference, apart from sizes, is the color of the lateral line. On cod, pollack and tomcod it's white. On the haddock it's black. The back and upper sides above the lateral line are a dark tone of blue- or purple-gray, which becomes silvery below, often with tinges of pink. Most specimens exhibit a sooty patch on the "shoulders" —or where they would be if a haddock had arms. This patch varies in size, shape and distinctness. All members of this group share a distinctive trait—three dorsal fins. The haddock's leading dorsal fin differs from that on the relatives in being appreciably higher than the second and third dorsals, noticeably triangular and coming to a point. SIZE: Haddock run smaller than their cod and pollack cousins. A broad average range is from about 14 to 24 in. and 1⅛ to 5 lbs. The largest reported in commercial catches has ranged from 16½ lbs. to 37. The largest sport-caught specimen isn't known. FAMILY: Haddock are in the cod family, Gadidae, along with codfish and American pollack. DISTRIBUTION: From the Gulf of St. Lawrence and northern Newfoundland to Virginia, with deepwater strays to the offing of Cape Hatteras, N.C. HABITS: (1) Haddock are more exclusively groundfish—bottom dwellers—than cod or pollack, and they're not as actively voracious. (2) They're quite as omnivorous as cod. They do not rely as much on small fishes but compensate in the variety of other creatures they engulf. Mollusks and gastropods (conchs, snails, etc.) are very big items in haddock supermarkets. (One researcher counted 68 different kinds in the stomachs of 1,500 haddock he autopsied.) Worms are also fancied highly. Haddock will devour squid and small crabs as well. To a lesser extent they consume young eels, herring, small mackerel, even baby haddock at times. WHERE CAUGHT: They tend to be more selective than cod in the type of bottom they prefer, and are rarely caught over rocks, ledges or kelp beds, where cod go, or over soft mud. Too, they tend to live in deeper areas than cod for the most part. Haddock become scarce in depths as shallow as 30 to 60 ft., are more likely to be at levels from 150 to 450 ft. Like cod, they're cold-water fish but can't tolerate water temperatures quite as low. HOW CAUGHT: Deep-sea bottom fishing. BAITS & LURES: Skimmer clam, pieces of herring. TACKLE: Conventional tackle suggested. Must have enough "spine" to handle fairly heavy rigs in currents.

Hakes

SCIENTIFIC NAME: The genus *Urophycis*. There are several species of these bottom fishes, collectively encountered with varying ranges along the Atlantic seaboard of North America: white hake, red or squirrel hake, blue hake, spotted hake, long-finned hake, others. They're all relatives of the Atlantic cod and pollack (see pages 172 and 223) but do not resemble them, being much more slender. Among themselves, however, the hakes look much like one another. Shared traits include an elongated body, two dorsal fins, moderately long head with a mouth of fair size, and a rather small tail with a convex trailing edge. Hakes are bottom residents, and their colors are usually a drab shade of brown, reddish-brown, muddy, or near blackish to match the type of ground they frequent. According to species, they're encountered at depths ranging from relatively shallow water on out to depths of 50 fathoms and more. Again according to species, they may be found in temperate and cool-temperate zones, on down to Chesapeake Bay and as far south as the offing of Florida.

Squirrel Hake

Although some kinds are caught by bottom fishermen, we are concerned here with the red or squirrel hake *(Urophycis chuss)*, for it is this species that contributes more than others to catches on party boats. In areas where they are boated most commonly, which is to say the ocean off New Jersey and New York, they're invariably called ling, so we'll shift to that common name. ("Ling" is also another name for the white hake, encountered in the same general region as red hake, but subordinate to them in catches. And it's a Gulf Coast name for cobia (see page 201).

In common with other hakes, ling are bottom dwellers. They devour shrimp and other small crustaceans, as well as squid and a wide variety of small fishes such as alewives, butterfish, eels, smelt, silversides, and the young of neighbors such as mackerel, flounders, menhaden, etc. Ling are small fish. A length of 30 in. and weights to 6 or 7 lbs. are maximum and exceptional. Most of those in sport catches go 1 to 3 lbs.

These ling are typically hakes in body form. They frequent soft bottoms at varying depths out to deep grounds. Most of those taken on hook and line are caught in water of 40 to 80 to 100 ft. Because they frequent dark-colored floors, their matching color scheme is also on the dark side. These ling are brown—reddish, muddy or greenish—and sometimes almost black on the back and upper sides. On some the color is uniform; on others it's mottled. The lateral line is pale. Below it the sides become white, grayish or yellowish, and there may be small dusky dots. Most of the fins are of the same general color as the body, but the ventrals can be a pale pink or yellow.

In normal abundance they accept any kind of bait in pieces: skimmer clam (good), bloodworm, sandworm, mackerel, herring, etc. They bite readily. Another species known locally as whiting responds to the same baits, and the two species frequently contribute to mixed catches on deep-sea party boats from spring into fall. One or two bottom-rigged hooks will catch either or both. Ling do not have a lot going for them sport-wise.

Kelp Bass

SCIENTIFIC NAME: *Paralabrax clathratus*. COMMON NAMES: Locally you may hear them called calico bass, when small, bull bass, when large, rock bass, sand bass (also the common name of another species, *Paralabrax nebulifer*, encountered in approximately the same range), and cabrilla. COLOR: A somber shade of brown or gray-brown. Blotches in a darker hue mottle the upper sides, while the underside is tinged with yellow, as are the fins. SIZE: Kelp bass as heavy as 17–18 lbs. have been reported, but the largest authenticated specimen seems to be a 14½-pounder. Some individuals reach a ripe old age for fishes. California's Department of Fish and Game mentions a 27⅜-in., 14-lb. 9-oz. kelp bass, caught from a Newport Beach jetty, that appeared to be 31 years old. In 1953 California imposed a 10-in. minimum keeping size for conservation. *Note:* Check on current California regulations concerning kelp bass. FAMILY: Kelp bass are grouped with the rock basses, affiliates of the Serranidae family, or marine basses. DISTRIBUTION: Their range is from San Francisco and central California to Cabo San Lucas, Baja California. HABITS: (1) Their food consists of shrimplike crustaceans and assorted little fishes such as anchovies. (2) Growth is slow. A nine-year-old is only about 16½-in. long. (3) In normal supply, kelp bass are considered year-round frequenters of kelp beds, but the best fishing season is from May to October. WHERE CAUGHT: True to their name, their favorite hangouts are around kelp beds, including those not visible at the surface, and they seldom are found very far from such gardens. HOW CAUGHT, BAITS & LURES: The prime method is to fish at or near the surface, in or around kelp gardens, with live anchovies. But they also can be taken on shrimp, pieces or strips of squid, queenfish, anchovy or mackerel, as well as on abalone trimmings. At times they are also hooked near the bottom. Another method is trolling spoons, plugs and streamer flies (yellow and bronze reported to be effective colors) in kelp bed areas, but the problem is to keep artificials from tangling in the kelp. TACKLE: Whether conventional or spinning it should be light. Hooks are small, about No. 1.

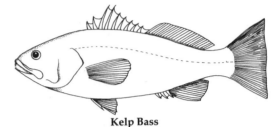

Kelp Bass

King Mackerel

SCIENTIFIC NAME: *Scomberomorus cavalla*. COMMON NAMES: Kingfish, and maybe cavalla. COLOR: On the back and high on the sides a bluish-gray, which abruptly becomes silvery or gray-silver lower down, then white underneath. Lack of markings on the sides separates the king from the cero and Spanish mackerels. A further aid to identification is a lateral line on each side of the body. SIZE: A wide range, as small as 6 lbs. and as heavy as 100. FAMILY: Superb streamlining characterizes all members of the mackerel family, Scombridae. DISTRIBUTION: Overall, from Virginia and North Carolina on down along Florida's eastern coast, over into the Gulf of Mexico to an extent, and on to the West Indies. The Bahamas have them too. HABITS: (1) Speed and a large mouth—with about 40 teeth in each jaw—arm this fellow to prey upon a large assortment of smaller fishes, even swift ones. A prime food item is a species of halfbeak known as balao ("ballyhoo"). The king also likes shrimp and grabs squid when available. (2) King mackerel are a schooling species. Like some of the tunas, notably bluefins, they tend to form groups according to age. Their schools are often larger when the fish are younger, and all the individuals in a given school are more or less the same size. Again like tunas, king mackerel are more likely to travel in groups of decreasing sizes, and finally in little bands or even in pairs or alone as they grow older and bigger. (3) They migrate coastwise. (4) Oddly, they usually do not jump after being hooked, as billfishes do, but when assaulting a bait. It's a dramatic sight to see that long, silvery form explode from the sea, arch in the sun, then, in a display of "pinpoint bombing," come down precisely on a bait with its jaws. Kings also are notorious for barreling in behind a bait and chopping it off short of the hook. WHERE CAUGHT: Schools of juveniles will come inshore, even invade bays periodically, but the adults are oceanic nomads. HOW CAUGHT: Trolling and drift fishing with live and dead baits; casting and trolling of plugs; deep trolling of a mullet or a ballyhoo; jigging baits or lures over a school. BAITS & LURES: Come-ons for king mackerel trolling are whole-rigged ballyhoo (a favored food, remember?) and mullet, as well as long fish strips sliced from the lighter colored undersides of local species. With long strip baits it's wise to rig a second hook (check IGFA regulations if you're record-minded) to take care of larcenous "short-strikers." Jap feathers and shiny spoons also get a share of trolled kings. A wire leader guards against a mouthful of sharp dental armament. TACKLE: Pound for pound, they rate in the upper echelons of battlers. Don't wield tackle lighter than about 20-lb. test unless you know what you're doing.

King Mackerel

Ladyfish and Tenpounder

SCIENTIFIC NAME: *Elops saurus*. COMMON NAMES: The Atlantic seaboard's ladyfish has a counterpart, practically a carbon copy, on the Pacific Coast in the tenpounder. The tenpounder was given a separate scientific name, *Elops affinis*, but is now thought to be the same species. Both fishes are strikingly alike in appearance and size, habits and places they frequent, and share some angling methods. It seems safe to include two for the price of one here. By the way, another common name for the ladyfish or tenpounder, is the big-eye herring. COLOR: Ladyfish and tenpounders are characterized by an elongated, very slender body, silvery on the sides and greenish or bluish, or a mixture of the two, along the back. The fins are dusky. SIZE: Details of both species' life cycles are wanting. Presumably they feed on small fishes and invertebrates. If we can take Florida ladyfish as typical, a sport-fishing average is 1 to 3 lbs., with occasional fish up to 7 lbs. and reportedly reaching 10 lbs. Tenpounders appear to have approximately the same size span. Both species are recorded at lengths up to 3 ft., but these are deceptive because the two fishes are so slender-bodied. FAMILY: Scientists aren't clear on this, but it would seem to be Elopidae. DISTRIBUTION: U.S. Atlantic seaboard from North Carolina to Florida and into the Gulf of Mexico. Ladyfish are most common in the warmer parts of their range, notably in Florida, where they are year-round residents along just about all shores, especially in the southern part of the state. The Bahamas and the Caribbean also are regions of distribution. HABITS: (1) Not uncommonly they forage for food around bridges and piers, and in Florida they are frequently hooked at night in lighted areas. (2) On light tackle ladyfish have been likened to bonefish in the speed and power of their first run. Ladyfish also are noted for their leaping—like scaled-down tarpon, you might say. WHERE CAUGHT: You can look for ladyfish in regions they normally inhabit. This includes shallow waters inshore and in inlets, bays and estuaries. Their schools wander indifferently over mud and sand bottoms at levels ranging anywhere from near the bottom to the surface, depending upon where the most food is at the moment. Tenpounders are encountered in similar areas in California, and they too respond to a similar assortment of artificial and natural baits. HOW CAUGHT, BAITS & LURES: Ladyfish are very good light-tackle battlers. A similar compliment can be paid to the tenpounder. Ladyfish in particular are excellent fly-rod opponents, responding to streamer flies and salt-water bugs. Because they wander through so many levels, several techniques will produce: bottom fishing at anchor drifting, casting from boats, fishing from docks and piers, and, as mentioned, fly casting. They respond to a variety of small artificials in surface or deeper-running models; small spoons, feathers and jigs and small plugs all score. Shrimp, small pieces of fish, and little bait fishes, alive and dead, also account for fish. TACKLE: Hooks are small, about No. 4 to No. 2. A short leader of light wire is

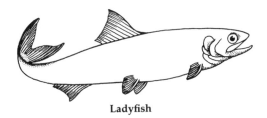

Ladyfish

rigged for ladyfish because their skin is abrasive. Light
spinning or bait-casting tackle is just right for both species.

Mako Shark

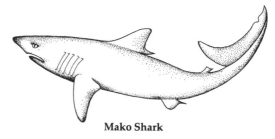

Mako Shark

SCIENTIFIC NAME: *Isurus oxyrhinchus.* COMMON NAMES:
Mackerel shark and sharp-nosed mackerel shark. That latter is
an apt name, since the mako does have a pointed snout and is
very fond of mackerel. COLOR: The mako is one of the most
brilliantly colored sharks. While still alive, this shark's back is a
bright, rich blue, a shade of ultramarine, which grades to a
blue-silver on the sides, all contrasting with a pure white belly.
This vivid coloration lasts for a while after capture, then yields
to a uniform shade of gray with faint blue undertones. Any
color you see on a mounted mako is a taxidermist's art. SIZE:
The author's best, to date, was a 320-pounder, but the potential
goes to at least 500 lbs. Commercial fishing reports mention
monsters to 1,000 lbs. An approximate length-weight scale,
based on sport and commercial catches, goes as follows: 6 ft.,
135 lbs.; 7 ft. 8 in., 230; 8 ft., 300; 9 ft., 700–800; 10½ ft., 1,009
lbs. Note how weights climb sharply after 8 ft. in that scale.
FAMILY: The mako is catalogued with the porbeagle *(Lamna
nasus)* and white shark or man-eater *(Carcharodon carcharias)*
within a group known as mackerel sharks. Makos are
duplicated on the North American Pacific seaboard by a closely
allied form, *Isurus glaucus,* ranging from about Point
Conception, Calif., on down to at least the southernmost
reaches of Baja California. The big beast also is referred to as
"mako" and also has such aliases as bonito shark, mackerel
shark and paloma (which means "dove" in Spanish and is
incongruous, all things considered). DISTRIBUTION: In
tropical, subtropical and warm-temperate parts of the Atlantic,
north and south. Distribution in the Americas is yet to be
mapped fully, but it can be stated that they travel at least as far
north as the offing of Cape Cod, Mass., and as far south as
Brazil. Distribution also takes in the open sea off Bermuda and
the Bahamas, and they are an all-year game in Florida. HABITS:
(1) In northerly segments of their U.S. range they're summer
visitors. Once there are hints of approaching autumn, they
vanish. (2) Water temperatures undoubtedly are a factor, since
makos seldom if ever are caught in waters cooler than about
60 ° F. (3) They're fisheaters. As already noted, they have a
fondness for mackerel, and massive coastwise migrations of
Atlantic mackerel are probably a major factor in luring these
sharks to the north. Herring and other small quantity-
schooling fishes also contribute to their diet; and since they are
fast, active predators, they can also catch tuna. Like humans,
makos have a fondness for swordfish meat, and they may very
well be the broadbills' worst enemy in nature. (4) In addition to
being swift and active, makos are very strong. Their pull has

not been measured, but dynamometer tests on other species showed that a 10-ft. hammerhead registered initial tugs of 1,500 lbs. from a standing start, while a silky shark, weighing no more than 350 lbs., could break a new 12-thread manila rope testing at 1,350 lbs. if given a 20-yd. run. A mako of comparable size should be able to equal, if not exceed, those shows of force. (5) Makos usually hit a bait hard, sometimes torpedoing upward from underneath a bait with such speed and power as to carry them into the air 8 or 10 ft. And makos fight with the same power and swiftness, tearing away on long, powerful runs. These are details that make them the most desirable of sharks in big-game fishing. Another is their display of aerial fireworks. Not every mako will leap. An average is about three out of five. WHERE CAUGHT: Makos are oceanic wanderers, invariably caught offshore. Some may pursue food into large, deep sounds, but I have never heard of any being captured there. HOW CAUGHT, BAITS & LURES: As in all shark fishing, wire leaders are a must. Hooks go to a 12/0. The Martu pattern is good because of its penetration. Although makos are caught by trolling whole-rigged fish in Florida, the best method is drift-chumming. Natural baits include northern whiting (very good), eels, mackerel and other local fishes, rigged whole— and alive whenever possible. Large fillet baits are good too, and they can be cut from any kind of fish, including a shark already caught. Makos will respond to whole squid too, alone or impaled on the same hook with a whole fish or fillet. TACKLE: Weapons must be suitably rugged—80-lb. equipment at the lightest, with a 10/0 reel filled to capacity. If a fisherman isn't sure of himself, 130-lb. tackle is better. Seasoned "light-tackle" anglers try 50-lb. gear. *Caution:* It should go without saying that a mako—or any shark, for that matter—should never be brought into a boat while still alive. See "Big-Game Fishing," Chapter 11.

Mutton Snapper

SCIENTIFIC NAME: *Lutjanus analis*. COMMON NAMES: Mutton-fish. COLOR: The body is typical of snappers—red, mangrove, lane, vermilion, dog, and others—and is quite colorful. The color scheme is subject to variations, but in general is greenish-brown or olive on the back and upper sides. This fades to a lighter shade, with brassy or silvery tints, and becomes reddish along the ventral surface. The dorsal fin goes to a yellow tone with red, orange or pink tints. The tail may be yellow above, reddish below. Other fins have tinges of red or pink. There are usually a few thin blue lines along the lower part of the head from the corners of the mouth. On either side the pectoral fin's tip points to an oval, blackish spot. While still in the water, the body is saddled with half a dozen or more dusky bars, extending down on the sides. These fade away quickly after

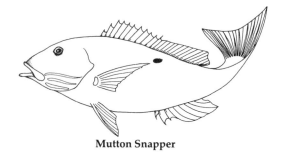

Mutton Snapper

the fish is caught. *Note:* Splashes of red may be more pronounced among some individuals, leading to possible confusion with their cousins the red snappers when sizes are comparable. But the latter species' vivid red or pink-red body color and darkish fins are a guide to separation. There's an oval spot on a mutton snapper's side, barely above the lateral line. The red snapper has a similar spot, but it's at the base of the pectoral fin. SIZE: In sport catches the average size span is approximately 5 to 10 lbs. Fifteen- and 20-pounders also are boated, and in Florida the potential goes to 30. FAMILY: A member of the snapper family, Lutjanidae. DISTRIBUTION: This is a good sport fish, distributed in the southern segments of both coasts of Florida, in the Gulf of Mexico, the Bahamas and the West Indies. HABITS: Studies of stomach contents indicate that mutton snappers feed primarily upon shrimp and other crustaceans, along with miscellaneous smaller fishes. WHERE CAUGHT: Mutton snappers frequent reefs, bars and holes, including the so-called blue holes (circular pits in the sea floor, deeper than the surrounding bottom and therefore detectable by their darker blue water). They come close inshore sometimes, and also are encountered in channels. HOW CAUGHT, BAITS, LURES & TACKLE: Mutton snappers are worthwhile light-tackle opponents. Rigging for the bottom is the basis of methods that include still-fishing and drifting with live shrimp, and slow trolling that bounces an artificial or natural bait along the sea floor. They take both live and dead baits, as well as such lures as jigs (fished on bottom). Around reefs, coral heads and holes they can be chummed to the surface, then cast to with plugs, feathers, etc. Sometimes they show on flats to provide lively spinning and fly-tackle action on small artificials. Deep trolling of strip baits just above the bottom also produces. Rigs usually incorporate a short length of light wire—12 to 14 in.—because of these snappers' teeth and sharp-edged gill covers.

Northern Porgy

SCIENTIFIC NAME: *Stenotomus chrysops* or *versicolor*. COMMON NAMES: "Porgy" and "scup" are used interchangeably. The former is often pronounced "pogy" in waterfront vernacular. The latter is a shortening of the American Indian *scuppaug* or *scuppang*. Other names, rarely heard now, are maiden, fair maid(!), and ironsides (appropriate, considering the fish's tough scales). COLOR: This porgy is only twice as long as it is deep, which gives it an almost oval profile. Larger specimens are consequently nicknamed "dinner plates." The color is pearly gray, with iridescence, somewhat darker on the back. The head is silvery. Some carry dusky, indistinct, longitudinal stripes, occasionally tinged with light blue, on the dorsal surface and upper sides. The belly is white. Dorsal fin, tail and

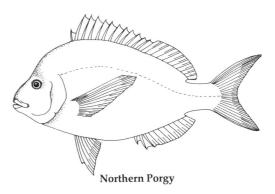

Northern Porgy

anal fin are dusky. The pointed pectorals are a pale color tinged with brown. SIZE: In some regions—Long Island's Peconic Bays are an example—the first spring showings are the larger fish, nicknamed "sea porgies." These weigh 2 to 3 lbs., hang around for a few weeks, then move out somewhere, perhaps to deeper water, and are replaced by the standard summer sizes, ¾ to 1 lb. Also in hot weather, bays and harbors are often infiltrated by swarms of little fellows weighing only ounces and dubbed sand porgies. Adults put them back to grow up, but kids think they're great because of their abundance. FAMILY: Porgies are members of the Sparidae family. DISTRIBUTION: Scup occur from southern Massachusetts to North Carolina, with some straggling beyond to Maine and South Carolina. South of Cape Hatteras they're replaced by the southern porgy (Stenotomus aculeatus), also called scup, which is practically a carbon copy. HABITS: (1) Scups are bottom dwellers, favoring clean, hard-packed sand over rocky areas and "broken ground." (2) Their diet comprises marine worms, small crabs and mollusks, and very small fishes, occasionally with bits of sea vegetation on the side as a salad course. (3) Scups are gregarious and travel in schools, some of them very large. (4) After wintering offshore, they begin moving inshore with spring's climbing thermometer. They like warmer water. (5) Their runs can exhibit radical, unpredictable fluctuations within a given area. They can make an initial appearance in hordes overnight, then fall flat on their little faces a few days later, pick up again, slow down, etc. Based on my experience, I believe that they are unusually sensitive to temperature drops of only a degree or two, and when these occur will move temporarily to deeper water. (6) Under normal conditions, they can be so numerous you literally have to fight them off with clubs. Catching two at a time is commonplace. WHERE CAUGHT: Throughout the summer, porgies support a large sport fishery on bays and the Atlantic. HOW CAUGHT & TACKLE: Hooks must be small. The range is from No. 10 or 9 for the smallest, through a No. 7 or 6, to No. 1 for the so-called sea porgies and dinner plates. It's better that a hook be undersized than too large. Rigging is for the bottom, no leaders needed. A bank-type sinker of only enough weight to hold bottom is tied to the line, for if porgies are small, excess sinker weight detracts from their resistance. Right above that may be tied two hooks by their snells, with or without three-way swivels, according to preference, and just far enough apart to keep from tangling with each other. An alternate arrangement is to tie in the first hook immediately above the sinker, then bridle a second hook to the snell of the first in a Y arrangement. The lightest kind of spinning or conventional tackle and line will do fine. BAITS & LURES: Scups bite readily, even greedily, on pieces of clam—either hard-shell or skimmer—squid, bloodworm, sandworm, shrimp, or a bit of crab in the shedder state. However, baits must be in small pieces because porgies have small mouths.

Pacific Flounders, Soles and Halibuts

The flatfishes, with which these species are catalogued, constitute an enormous, far-flung family with great representation in North American waters. The continent's Pacific seaboard alone harbors an impressive collection. Here's a sampling of species: Arrowtooth halibut (*Atheresthes stomias*), bigmouth sole (*Hippoglossina stomata*), butter sole (*Isopsetta isolepis*), California halibut (*Paralichthys californicus*), C-O turbot (*Pleuronichthys coenosus*), curlfin turbot (*Pleuronichthys decurrens*), diamond turbot (*Hypsopsetta guttulata*), Dover sole (*Microstomus pacificus*), English sole (*Parophrys vetulus*), fantail sole (*Xystreurys liolepis*), hornyhead turbot (*Pleuronichthys verticalis*), longfin sanddab (*Citharichthys xanthostigma*), Pacific halibut (*Hippoglossus stenolepis*), Pacific sanddab (*Citharichthys sordidus*), petrale sole (*Eopsetta jordani*), rex sole (*Glyptocephalus zachirus*), rock sole (*Lepidopsetta bilineata*), sand sole (*Psettichthys melanostictus*), slender sole (*Lyopsetta exilis*), speckled sanddab (*Citharichthys stigmaeus*), spotted turbot (*Pleuronichthys ritteri*), starry flounder (*Platichthys stellatus*). SIZE: Their size span is wide. Among the very smallest are sanddabs under 12 in. long, weight less than a pound. From there the range goes up to the king of the West Coast group, the Pacific halibut, recorded at lengths up to 8½ ft. and weights to 500 lbs. FAMILY: All these species share the universal characteristics of the flatfishes: (1) broad, horizontally flattened bodies; (2) both eyes on the same—upper—side of the head, with "right-eyedness" or "left-eyedness" according to species, and (3) single long continuous fins at the body's two outer edges. Variations occur in such details as sizes, color of pigmentation, mouth development and dentation, etc. DISTRIBUTION: Collectively, the Pacific flatfishes have a distribution extending from Alaska and the Arctic down to Baja California. HABITS: Most flatfishes live on or near the bottom. Some species stay very close to it, hugging it. Others, more aggressive, prowl upper levels and may even pursue food to the surface. WHERE CAUGHT: According to species, they may be encountered in very shallow water just off beaches, through moderate depths, on out to offshore waters, on down to 100 fathoms or 600 ft. The starry flounder, for example, is found in water only inches deep at times. In contrast, Pacific halibut may inhabit depths as great as 100 fathoms, perhaps more. Considering the many different species, it can be said that somewhere on the Pacific Coast, Alaska to southern California, there's at least one kind of flatfish in season at any given time of year. HOW CAUGHT: Because of flatfishes' habits, bottom angling is a more or less universal technique for them. BAITS & LURES: Overall, Pacific Coast species accept a large assortment of natural baits. Strips of fish have wide use as do marine worms, shrimp, and pieces of clam and squid. Small live baits are rigged for some species. Most flatfishes are caught on natural bait, but some of them will respond to small, shiny or bright-colored artificials. Similarly, slow, deep trolling will account for certain kinds at times. Except for the larger representatives, the halibuts, hooks

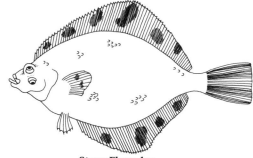

Starry Flounder

usually are small: No. 2 through 1/0 is a general range. TACKLE: Tackle can be light for all except the halibuts. Gear is scaled upward considerably for Pacific halibut, less so for the smaller California halibut.

Pacific Sailfish

SCIENTIFIC NAME: *Istiophoros greyi.* COMMON NAMES: Pacific sail, sail. COLOR: Like the Atlantic sailfish, the Pacific sail is beautifully colored: a dark rich blue or greenish-blue along the back and uppermost sides, becoming silvery or silver-white on the sides and white underneath. The glint as its silver sides catch brilliant sunlight when a sail leaps clear of the sea is one of sport fishing's most breath-catching sights. The big dorsal fin also is a shade of dark rich blue, and may be peppered with black spots. The other fins are dark-bluish or blackish. SIZE: While the East and West Coast sailfishes resemble each other physically and are equally exciting opponents, Pacific sails come in considerably larger packages. Hundred-pounders are not uncommon, and weights can top 200. An IGFA world record, set in the Galapagos Islands, weighed in at 221 lbs. and measured more than 10 ft. FAMILY: Istiophoridae. DISTRIBUTION: Southern California, down along Mexico's Baja California, to Ecuador. They're rare north of southern California, but their distribution includes Hawaii. That state often sees good numbers of them. HABITS: (1) These sails are oceanic wanderers; and they like warm water more than other billfishes. (2) More research is needed on this species. Little is known about its spawning, growth rate, migrational patterns, or life cycle in general. From examination of stomach contents (a smart angling procedure by the way) it has been learned that they feed chiefly on whatever smaller fishes are available in quantity: mullet, mackerel, sardines, and so forth. In common with most billfishes, they eagerly accept squid. WHERE CAUGHT: Open ocean, offshore. HOW CAUGHT, BAITS, LURES & TACKLES: Fishing procedures are basically the same as for their Atlantic Ocean counterparts. See page 176. I need only add that—theoretically, at least—any of the items listed as food for Pacific sails should be effective as bait. Whole squid should be especially good, as all billfishes—swordfish, marlins —go for it.

Pacific Sailfish

Pollock

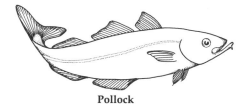

Pollock

SCIENTIFIC NAME: *Pollachius virens*. COMMON NAMES: American pollock, pollack, (with an *a*), Boston bluefish (years ago). COLOR: Color helps set the pollock apart from other Gadidae. It's a shade of green, generally rather dark olive or brownish-green along the back and upper sides, paling to smoky gray or a yellowish-gray below the lateral line, then silver-gray on the underside. A distinct white or pale gray lateral line extends along each side. The dorsal, paired pectoral and anal fins and tail are olive color. The ventral fins are whitish, tinged with red. SIZE: Pollock are the second largest members of their family, topped only by cod. Weights regularly extend up into the 20's, much less frequently to 30 lbs. They are known to reach 3½ ft. and 35 lbs. A world record stood at 43 lbs., a 4-ft. specimen with a 29-in. girth, a product of New Jersey ocean waters. An average range in sport catches is approximately 4 to 15 lbs. FAMILY: Pollock is a member of the cod family, Gadidae. Other relatives are the cod, haddock and tomcod. Note these family trademarks: three distinct dorsal fins and two anal fins. DISTRIBUTION: Their range is in continental waters from the Gulf of St. Lawrence and Nova Scotia to New Jersey, regularly, and as strays to Chesapeake Bay, even more rarely to Cape Lookout, N.C. In the upper extremity of their distribution, small numbers wander to the southern Grand Banks, southeastern Newfoundland, southeastern Labrador, and western Greenland. Centers of abundance lie within that expanse from the gulf of Maine to Long Island, inclusive. HABITS: (1) Unlike cod, pollock will forage for food at any level from sea floor to surface, according to where the best supplies are available. This is a habit of importance to anglers, since it gives latitude in fishing methods. (2) Pollock travel in schools, some of them huge, and they're active predators. (3) As adults they're omnivorous gluttons, devouring almost any kind of fish available, even the young of their cod and haddock cousins. On the list of prey are sand launce, herring, hakes, shrimp, marine worms and, when in a bottom-prowling mood, crabs and other crustaceans. WHERE CAUGHT: Pollock are cold-water fish, found in cool-temperate seas to boreal latitudes. They're ocean fish. Not uncommonly, pollock are encountered on the same grounds as cod. HOW CAUGHT, BAITS, LURES & TACKLE: Much pollock action occurs during bottom fishing for cod. Fishermen prepared for both species rig a low, near-bottom hook for cod, then tie in one or two additional hooks, each on a 2- to 4-ft. leader of monofilament or gut at varying distances above that. Bottom-fishing baits include clam, pieces of herring, smelt, sand launce (sand eel), and pieces of shedder crab. A good all-round attractor is a plump-bellied surf clam or skimmer. It will draw cod too. For my money, the superior pollock action is in trolling. They are sportier than cod, and trolling seems to bring out the best in them. Artificials that attract pollock include Jap feathers in various colors, jigs with long nylon skirts, also in various colors (try yellow), small plugs, bucktails, chromed spoons, streamers, and spinner rigs. Sometimes the attraction of lures is enhanced by garnishing the hook with a piece of pork rind or a strip of squid. A common procedure is to interpose 5 or 6 ft. of No. 6 or No. 7 wire between lure and line, with a snap swivel on the line to facilitate changing of artificials. Trolling at lower levels may be necessary to reach the fish. If the weight of wire line is not enough to take the rig down, then a drail or trolling sinker should be incorporated. Boat casters can get in some licks when a school is sighted at the surface. There's no predicting what offering they might fancy, pieces of natural bait or artificials; but shiny spoons or other bright-colored lures should be effective. Surface action with pollock on light tackle is especially lively. Bottom-fishing tackle has to be sturdy. Rigs are fairly heavy, due to the weights of sinkers often required in currents. Too, the fishing may be in rather deep water, pollock reach a fair size, and there may be some big cod in the same area. For these reasons I recommend conventional tackle over spinning gear—for trolling too. An all-purpose outfit consists of a rod able to handle lines to 30-lb. test.

Pompanos

Under this heading are grouped 10 American species. The pompano group, in turn, makes up one section of a huge and diversified family known scientifically as Carangidae. Four pompanos are described for the Americas' Pacific seaboard, and six for the Atlantic.

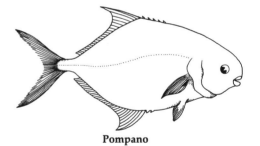
Pompano

All look as though they might have begun as a single set of blueprints, with a few alterations in sizes and colors as time went on and different species developed. The basic form remains, however, so we can draw this composite and call it Your Standard Pompano Model: (1) body shaped like a platter, very deep in proportion to length; (2) back arched and curved in profile; (3) body compressed laterally, rather slab-sided; (4) generally steep forehead and blunt-looking snout; (5) a long second dorsal composed of rays, high in its anterior section and falling away abruptly to low uniform height; (6) relatively small pectoral and ventral fins; (7) large tail, deeply forked; (8) small mouth, low in head. If you've seen the profile of one pompano, you've seen at least enough to recognize a member of the group.

As far as sport fishing goes, there are two main species of interest:

Pompano (*Trachinotus carolinus*)

This superior sport fish is occasionally reported as far north as the offing of Massachusetts, probably as a summer straggler in the Gulf Stream, and ranges on down to Brazil. North Carolina appears to be the northernmost limit for any numbers. Florida is big for pompano, both coasts, and there's distribution all along the rim of the Gulf of Mexico to Texas. Bermuda and the West Indies are also included in its distribution.

Colors aid in identification: back and topmost sides a mixture of blue or green and silver and gray; sides of silver; splashes of yellow on the underside, especially forward, and on the ventral and anal fins; dorsal fin dusky, sometimes with bluish or greenish undertones; tail dusky, tinged with yellow.

This pompano is an important food fish and popular angling target; yet knowledge of his habits is full of holes. He apparently eats various kinds of invertebrates, possibly some small fishes too, when young. Later his diet comprises small fishes, crustaceans and mollusks. He's known to be especially fond of shrimp and the so-called sand fleas.

Pompanos are shallow- and warm-water fish. They're gregarious, traveling in schools, and frequent sandy beaches, inlets, bays, channels and holes in the vicinity of sand flats. A common feeding procedure is to root in sand for crustaceans such as sand fleas. The size range in sport fishing is about 1 to 6 lbs. As often happens, specimens taken in commercial fishing are larger than rod-and-reel fish. In this case netted specimens up to, even exceeding, 20 lbs. have been reported.

Since they come close inshore along sandy beaches, they can be hooked by surf casters, jetty "jockeys," and ocean-front pier fishermen. They're caught from boats also, of course, and are available to bridge fishermen on bays and tidal estuaries. Wherever caught, bottom fishing is the method. Pompano are bottom feeders. And since they have a fondness for sand fleas and shrimp, it naturally follows that these crustaceans are top natural baits. Shrimp can be used alive or dead. Small pieces of clam and fish also are used.

Pompano can also be caught on small nylon jigs—yellow is a favored color—and little spoons, drifted or trolled slowly. Often a shrimp or sand bug is added to the artificial's hook. In any case, the rig must be weighted to keep it on bottom, and this is accomplished with a sinker of standard design or trolling type, according to method. Surf casters rig a pyramid sinker to better hold in sand. (A fish-finder rig is good here.) Round sinkers are better suited to drifting because they tend to roll along the bottom. Jigging the bait or artificial by alternately raising and lowering the rod tip a few inches is more effective than letting the attractor just lie there.

Don't underestimate pompanos because of their size. On light tackle—spinning gear recommended—they're topflight scrappers. They're jittery fish, and they're fast and strong for their size. Moreover, they're unpredictable and full of little tricks, like changing direction suddenly, or turning their flat body against the line's pull to increase resistance. No two fight quite alike.

Palometa (*Trachinotus goodei*)

This fish has the names gafftopsail pompano and longfin pompano, but "palometa" is favored.

The palometa has the typical pompano body, but you can add distinctive characteristics. Most obvious are the elongated anterior portions of the second dorsal and anal fins. The fish's striking color scheme is distinctive and a ready aid to identification. The top of the head and back are blue and silver. The sides are silvery, overlaid by four or five narrow, dusky, vertical bars. Below, the belly is yellow, becoming a bright orange in its forward section. More contrasts are provided by the fins' colors. The elongations of the dorsal and anal fins are blackish, and their other portions are either pale or dusky with bluish edges. The pectoral fins are blue, sometimes flecked with yellow, and the V of the tail is edged in a dark blue, almost black, or dusky shade.

The distribution of palometa is from Florida to Argentina, including Bermuda, the Bahamas and the West Indies. They have a close relative—some ichthyologists believe they may be identical species—in the Pacific gafftopsail pompano, called *pompanito* (Spanish for "little pompano") throughout much of its range, which is from Mexico and Panama to Colombia. Nothing is known about the palometa's life cycle. However, it's a coastal species and presumably parallels the pompano in habitat and feeding.

The best U.S. grounds for palometa are in southeastern Florida. Sometimes they're caught on the Gulf side too. In those waters they're all-year residents, and are caught by bottom fishing from boats or in the surf. Sand fleas are good bait; so are shrimp, alive or dead. They will also hit tiny jigs—try yellow—fished on the bottom. The size range is 2 to 6 lbs.

Red Snapper

SCIENTIFIC NAME: It appears variously as *Lutjanus aya* and *Lutjanus blackfordi*. There has been controversy as to whether the red snapper is a single species or is really two or more related species. But don't let it bother you. Call the fish by its common name and you're safe. COMMON NAMES: Snapper and Pensacola snapper. COLOR: Its claim to distinction is the color that gives it its name, a bright rose-red or cerise, darkest above, becoming lighter on the sides. All the fins are reddish too, but a somewhat paler shade. The trailing edges of the dorsal fin and tail, sometimes that of the anal fin as well, carry a narrow band of black. The only relative with which it might be confused by inexperienced anglers is the mutton snapper (see page 218). SIZE: Red snappers average 5 to 10 lbs. in sport catches, range up to 25 or 30, even 40, and have been reported at 50 lbs. FAMILY: The snappers, Lutjanidae. DISTRIBUTION: Unfortunately for anglers on the Pacific Coast and more northerly parts of the Atlantic seaboard, this excellent sport fish is confined to the tropical and subtropical Atlantic and Gulf of Mexico. In its known extremes, the Atlantic coast range

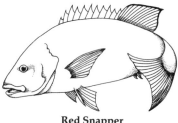

Red Snapper

extends from South Carolina to Brazil, including Bermuda, the Bahama islands and the Caribbean. Red snappers are a major Florida and Gulf Coast sport and commercial species. HABITS: Red snappers are schoolers, foraging a few feet above the sea floor in depths from 100 ft. to 100 fathoms to find crabs, shrimp, other crustaceans, and the little fishes with which they keep body and soul together. WHERE CAUGHT: Deep offshore banks on Florida's Atlantic side and in the Gulf of Mexico are red snapper territory. Strangely, they are uncommon in southeastern Florida. Small ones come inshore along the Gulf Coast, but very seldom on the Atlantic side. HOW CAUGHT, BAITS, LURES & TACKLE: Near-bottom fishing in fairly deep water—120 ft. or more—is the method. Tackle has to be sturdy to handle rigs and fish at those levels, especially when currents are quite strong. This is more an assignment for conventional equipment than spinning gear. Hooks and baits can be of fair size, since red snappers have a large mouth. Cut mullet is good bait. They also will seize shrimp, a piece of squid, and small whole dead fishes.

Rockfishes

SCIENTIFIC & COMMON NAMES; FAMILY: Together with their relatives the scorpionfishes, the rockfishes comprise an enormous marine family containing an estimated 250 species with far-flung distribution in tropical to boreal seas around the globe. In this book we're concerned with those rockfishes encountered along the U.S. Pacific Coast, the group catalogued as the genus *Sebastodes*. Fifty-one species and three close relatives are catalogued under the heading Rockfishes. Many are important in sport fishery or commercially, or both. Among the "first names" of rockfishes contributing to Pacific coast sport and/or commercial catches are kelp, grass, blue, black, orange, China (see page 200) and vermilion. Also included are the bocaccio and chilipepper, along with a rockfish relative, the California scorpionfish *(Scorpaena guttata)*. DISTRIBUTION: In geographic scope they are strung out from Baja California and the Gulf of California all the way up to Alaska. Some inhabit depths down to 600 fathoms and more, and so are beyond the reach of fishermen. Some frequent levels extending from 20 to 50 fathoms. Others are encountered beyond 50 fathoms and down to about 200. Then there are the several kinds found in comparatively shallow water that live up to their name by residing in rocky areas. COLOR & SIZE: Many rockfishes share certain anatomical characteristics, have somewhat similar coloration (what with variations among individual species), and fall within the same general size brackets (up to about 18 to 20, 22 in. for most of them). Among commonly shared traits: a body form resembling that of a typical bass or perch (rockfishes are neither); large mouths, often with varying degrees of

Shortspine Channel Rockfish

protruding lower jaw (which terminates in a small, knoblike process in some species); scales covering the body, a bony structure extending from under the eye out toward the gill cover; spines on the gill covers as well as on the heads, the snouts and anal fins of some species; and a dorsal fin composed of a spiny first section and a rayed, soft portion. HABITS & WHERE CAUGHT: (1) Rockfishes differ from most other marine and fresh-water fishes in that fertilization is internal instead of in the water, and the young are born alive, not hatched from eggs. They share this unusual viviparous (born alive) mode of reproduction with some of the sharks. (2) By and large, they're groundfishes, which is to say that they live and forage for food on or near the sea floor. This does not exclude the upper levels from their travels, and some species approach the surface occasionally, where they have been taken by slow trolling. HOW CAUGHT, BAITS, LURES & TACKLE: Also speaking generally, all can be caught on fresh strip baits. Shrimp and squid also are effective for some species. Tackle runs a gamut of conventional and spinning types from light to moderately heavy. Usually the latter is wielded in really deep water, where heavy sinkers are required, and a common procedure is to rig a 50-lb.-test wire leader and three to six hooks up to sizes 6/0 and 8/0. Here lines go to 30-, 40-, 50-lb. test. Lighter gear does fine in shallower water.

Roosterfish

SCIENTIFIC NAME: *Nematistius pectoralis.* COMMON NAMES: The only common name in English seems to have come from translations of their Spanish labels—*gallo* ("rooster"), *gallo de pez* (literally, "rooster of fish"), and *papagallo* ("daddy rooster"). The roosterfish need nothing more than their exaggerated first dorsal fin for positive identification. It is this "cockscomb" that suggested their name, and they have the curious habit of erecting it when pursuing prey or when they are otherwise excited. COLOR: Except for the towering first dorsal fin, the roosterfish's profile strongly suggests one of the jacks, or Carangidae, and it's believed by some ichthyologists that they may be allied. Their body color is striking. In life the back is a shade of green, and the sides and belly are pearly gray or grayish-white. Dark blue or blackish bands sweep downward from the back onto the sides and curve toward the tail. The undersides of the lower jaw and throat are white. Even the fins are colorful. The tail is green-yellow. The pectoral fins are yellowish-white; the ventral and anal fins, white. Alternate stripes of cream color and blue or green mark the first dorsal, while the second dorsal is gray tinged with green. Atop the head are two dark blue bars extending through the eyes, and there's a black spot on the pectoral fin's front lower edge. SIZE: Roosterfish come in power packages of very respectable size, all muscle. Weights to 40 and 50 lbs. are common.

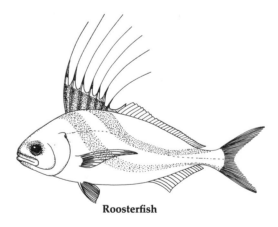

Roosterfish

Maximum is not yet known, but they do reach—and top—100 lbs. Two of the largest on the books so far are a 111-pounder and a 114-pounder. Presumably they grow even bigger. FAMILY: Nematistiidae. DISTRIBUTION: Paradoxically, this unusual-looking battler rates among the finest game fishes yet is one of the least known, sportwise and scientifically. Perhaps its distribution may have something to do with that situation. So far as is known, roosterfish reside only in the eastern Pacific Ocean along the coasts of North, Central and South America. Their distribution is limited in U.S. waters, both in numbers and geographically. Southern California seems to be it, and they're not too common there. Their range appears to be chiefly from Baja California and the Gulf of California down along Mexico's coast and southward. HABITS: (1) They're gregarious, traveling in groups of varying sizes, usually fast. (2) They're also very aggressive, and are seen savagely assaulting schools of small fishes. From this it's gathered that they're primarily fisheaters, concentrating on species that collect in dense schools. (3) Roosters will pursue prey boldly into a surf and in chases frequently exhibit that erect dorsal fin and jump clear of the water. (4) Whatever their size, they hit with a pile-driving wallop, run swiftly, then bore deep for the toughest kind of argument. When a school is contacted, fishing can become pure pandemonium. WHERE CAUGHT: Although occasionally encountered offshore, roosterfish are primarily a coastal species, roaming over sandy bottoms and in rocky places, from the surf on out to moderately deep water. HOW CAUGHT, BAITS, LURES & TACKLE: Since roosters commonly frequent the surf in pursuit of prey, one of the Baja California procedures is to move the boat just off the breakers and cast to them. Chumming with live anchovies intensifies the action. A very good bait down Baja way is a small blue-green-and-silver fish known as a scad (saurel, locally), used alive. Mullet also are bait. Wielded in live-bait roosterfishing are an 8- to 10-ft. conventional or spinning rod and a reel spooling at least 200 yds of 20- to 40-lb. monofilament. Tuna-style hooks are rigged, from No. 1 for small bait such as anchovies on up to 6/0, even 8/0, for scad or mullet. In the smaller sizes, hooks might better be double or triple strength. Roosterfish also can be trolled. Seasoned anglers use 20-lb.-line equipment for maximum sport, but a calculated risk with the heftier rascals. Others go to 30-, 40-, and 50-lb. tackle, according to preference. In Baja waters, where billfishes may also be present, trolling tackle will go to 80-lb. gear, with a suitably strong wire leader. In bottom fishing for roosters, the tackle should be gauged roughly to the sizes of the opponents anticipated, water depths, and weights of sinkers required (currents may necessitate up to 8 oz., possibly more). Both conventional and spinning kinds of tackle are fished, generally in the 30- to 50-lb.-line calibers. Hooks go to 5/0, 6/0. Natural fish bait, especially species with flashing silver bodies, is probably the best roosterfish attractor. Chromed spoons and other artificials in weights from 1¼ to 4 oz. and in various color combinations also have scored. Combinations of blue, purple or black and white, as well as all-white and green-and-yellow, have been successful.

Snook

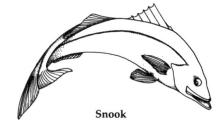

Snook

SCIENTIFIC NAME: *Centropomus undecimalis*. COMMON NAMES: No other except snook. COLOR: Body colors vary to a degree with surroundings. The back runs to a brown, usually with a yellowish or greenish tinge. On the sides this becomes lighter. The lower sides can be silvery, becoming whitish on the belly. A distinctive aid to identification is a narrow but pronounced dark stripe running along each side onto the tail's base. SIZE: A common range is from 2 to 15, 18 and, less frequently, 20 lbs. Numbers of snook in the 25- to 30-lb. bracket are hooked every season in Florida. There are a scattered few even larger. To earn IGFA world-record status you'll have to aim for about 53–55 lbs. FAMILY: Centropomidae. DISTRIBUTION: Although snook are distributed throughout tropical and subtropical zones of U.S. Atlantic and Pacific waters, as well as in the Gulf of Mexico, it's in Florida that they receive their best billing. On the U.S. Atlantic coast they become increasingly few north of Florida, but occasionally stragglers will wander northward with the warm waters of the Gulf Stream to southern New Jersey in summer. Pacific Coast distribution is described as extending from Baja California to Peru. HABITS: (1) Their natural diet consists chiefly of small fishes and crustaceans. (2) Of special interest to anglers is the snook's knife-sharp gill covers. Careless familiarity with these will result in lacerated hands, and they make a wire leader a must in rigging for them. (3) There's often good snook fishing at dusk and at night. Florida regulars capitalize on this from bridges and channel banks. (4) If action is superior at twilight and after dark, it's probably because the fish tend to feed more actively then. WHERE CAUGHT: Snook are substantially coastal residents, staying quite close to shore and seldom wandering any distance to seaward. Their range includes brackish water, and some even venture into near-fresh water in the lowermost sections of streams. Bays, inlets, estuaries, lagoons, channels and canals are also included in their itineraries. Both rocky and sandy coasts can harbor them. Still more areas with snook potential are waters around jetties, piers, bridge abutments and mangrove banks. HOW CAUGHT, BAITS & LURES: They can be taken by trolling plugs and spoons, by live-bait fishing in inlets and from bridges, and by casting jigs, surface plugs and underwater plugs in the surf, around jetties and bars, and in the vicinity of mangrove banks. They'll also grab natural baits—pinfish, finger mullet, shrimp and shiners. Several types of plugs get their share of fish—those that create a bit of surface ruckus as they're retrieved, darters, divers and wobblers, and underwater runners. Ideally, plug colors and finishes should simulate bait fishes accepted by snook. Straight-running plugs can be used too. TACKLE: It's your choice; but if you have a 6–6½-ft. bait-casting outfit or a spinning combination—say, a 7–7½-ft. rod with matching reel, try that. Spin fishing for snook is great sport. Lines range from 10- to 20-lb. test on an average, although some bridge fishermen go to 30-lb. gear on bridges because not infrequently snook have to be worked out from among the pilings.

Spotted Seatrout

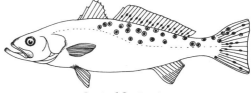

Spotted Seatrout

SCIENTIFIC NAME: *Cynoscion nebulosus*. COMMON NAMES: Regionally, speckled trout (Gulf Coast states and North Carolina), speckles or specs (Louisiana), sea trout (spelled as two words) or just trout in areas where there can be no mistaking the meaning, salmon trout (Virginia), and spotted weakfish (Atlantic coast chiefly). That last is the most appropriate name because the fish is related to the Atlantic coast weakfish *(Cynoscion regalis)* and is not a trout. COLOR: A difference between the two weakfishes is the color scheme (see page 247). The spotted seatrout is a gray or blue-gray along the body's upper half. The sides are silvery, becoming white on the belly. The fins are grayish, sometimes tinged with pale green or yellowish-green. Both species carry black dots, but on the seatrout they tend to be larger, more distinctly round, whereas on *C. regalis* they often merge to form little lines. Black spots are present on the second dorsal fin and tail too (absent on the other weakfish). SIZE: Their size potential approximates the northern weakfish's. An average hook-and-line spread is 1 to 4 lbs., laced with individuals to 6 and 8. A few as hefty as 10 and 12 lbs. are reported. A world record stood at 15 lbs. 6 oz., a Florida product. FAMILY: The two species are in the same family, Sciaenidae (weakfishes, drums and croakers). DISTRIBUTION: Spotted seatrout are among the leading marine sportsters along the entire Gulf Coast, Texas to Alabama, inclusively. The species' distribution also takes in the Atlantic seaboard from about Delaware and the great Chesapeake region shared by Maryland and Virginia, on down past the Carolinas and Georgia to Florida. HABITS:
(1) If waters are warm enough, many populations winter in bays and lagoons to become year-round targets. Like their northern relatives, these weakfish favor warmer water—but not really tropical—and are sensitive to cold. Both species can die in wholesale lots if overtaken in shallow bays by a quickly plummeting thermometer. (2) Spotted seatrout consume grass shrimp and forage fishes such as mullet, silversides and young menhaden. Grass shrimp are just about their favorite, and in this fondness they're again like northern weakfish. WHERE CAUGHT: Spotted seatrout are primarily an inshore breed, occurring along sandy ocean-front beaches and invading bays and their confluent channels via inlets. In this they're like their northern cousins. They're not migrators. Their movements consist mainly of shifting back and forth between inside and

outside waters according to seasons. Areas with promise include shallow, grassy flats, channels and their edges, current-eroded sloughs flanking bars, holes near flats, salt marshes with creeks, and points of land poking out into bays. Spotted seatrout are caught from bridges in many areas. HOW CAUGHT, BAITS & LURES: Spotted seatrout can be contacted at almost any level from bottom to surface, depending upon where they happen to be feeding at the time. When a natural bait is called for, live grass shrimp are indisputably No. 1. However, success isn't limited to that choice. Also used successfully are small live fishes—pinfish are one kind, along with local crabs (preferably in the shedder or peeler state), pieces of fish such as mullet, strips or pieces of squid, bloodworms and clams. Popular all along the Gulf Coast, Florida to Texas, is the "popping cork" technique. Live shrimp are the top choice for this, but those other natural baits work too. The method's basic detail is suspension of a single hook from a float or bobber—trying different levels below the surface if necessary—while drifting. It can be especially effective on shallow, grassy flats. At intervals the float is jounced to create little splashes to attract the fish, hence the "popping cork" name. Bottom fishing with natural baits, at anchor or (better) drifting, is another procedure. So is casting, from boats or shore. The fish respond to a diversified assortment of artificials—plugs of the mirror type and those with a mullet finish, as well as surface and deeper-running models, bucktails, plastic shrimp jigs, streamer flies, popping bugs, shiny spoons. Artificials are also trolled in shallow bays and inlets. TACKLE: Tackle is its user's choice. Spinning gear is ideal. Light conventional tackle—5½- or 6-ft. rod, 1/0 reel—also is fine. For the popping cork method some Gulf fishermen use a simple cane pole without a reel. Fly tackle gives a lot of action. Simplicity of tackle, availability of fish, and a wide choice of methods, baits and artificials are all factors contributing to the widespread popularity of fishing for spotted seatrout. *Note:* Visiting fishermen should inquire locally about the best seasons. They vary regionally.

Striped Bass

SCIENTIFIC NAME: *Roccus saxatilis.* COMMON NAMES: Two that are rarely heard now are "squidhound" and "greenhead." From Delaware Bay to North Carolina you're likely to hear "rockfish" or just "rock." "Linesider" or "linesides" is a nickname occasionally seen in print, notably in fishing columns. "Striped bass," commonly shortened to "striper," is universal. COLOR: The topside is dark olive-greenish, green with tinges of brown, or dark steel-blue, almost black sometimes. There are grayish-brown and grayish-green

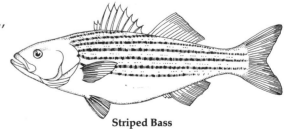

Striped Bass

variations too. This color gradually fades on the sides to become silvery, sometimes with brassy reflections, and white or silver-white on the belly. The dorsal and anal fins, together with the tail, are sooty or dusky. The most important color-pattern detail is the lengthwise lines, the topmost extending from the gill covers to the base of the tail, which give this gamester his common name. These are narrow, soot-colored bands, occasionally broken. SIZE: Most fishermen are satisfied to hook stripers weighing in the teens and 20's, and would be delighted with any in the 30- and 40-lb. classes. World-record stripers now top the 70- to 75-lb. class. FAMILY: Striped bass belong to the Serranidae family, which embraces the marine basses. Another member of this group is the popular black sea bass. DISTRIBUTION: Once indigenous to the Atlantic Coast, striped bass are now as much at home on the Pacific Coast, thanks to their anadromous adaptability, and in fresh water all across the U.S. The original distribution of stripers was confined to the Atlantic seaboard from the lower St. Lawrence River and the Gulf of St. Lawrence to the St. Johns River in Florida. The species also resides in the Gulf of Mexico along its northern rim to Alabama, Mississippi and Louisiana. HABITS: (1) During their first year or two they hang around in small groups. As they grow, they become more fond of togetherness and the groups enlarge. But later they tend to become loners or move around in small groups again. (2) Schooling is most evident during coastwise migrations, when the groups become huge. Studies indicate that schools are cohesive when traveling, but scatter and intermingle in areas where they linger. (3) Striped bass can tolerate a wide range of water temperatures, as evidenced by the extremes of their range, the St. Lawrence River to northern Florida. They cannot stand temperatures much warmer than 70 ° F. for long. This has been proved by mass deaths in estuaries during abnormally hot summers. But it's the rising water temperatures, climbing out of the 40's, that trigger their northward migration on the Atlantic Coast. Warming waters also inspire them to leave their wintering areas in rivers. (4) Striped bass are voracious feeders. They consume whatever smaller fishes may be available, along with quantities of invertebrates. Among items on their shopping list are menhaden, mullet, anchovies, sand launce, eels, killies, silversides, sculpins, hakes, young weakfish, channel bass (red drum), alewives, squid, lobsters, shrimp, several kinds of crabs, sea worms, mussels and soft-shell clams. Their diet on the Pacific Coast is equally varied, including anchovies, herring, blennies, gobies, young salmon, small flatfishes plus sea worms, mollusks, shrimp and assorted crabs. The great range of the species' appetite works to anglers' advantage by allowing considerable latitude in natural baits and artificials. (5) Striped bass tend to feed most actively from sunset to sunrise. This is because many of their prey—eels, sea worms and others—are nocturnally more active. It is a detail to consider in all methods, surf casting to trolling, and in most geographic situations, estuaries to open coast. When stripers are gorging themselves on baitfishes, there can be little or no chance of enticing them with any natural bait or artificial lure.

WHERE CAUGHT: Marine stripers (I'll use "marine" to distinguish them from landlocked bass) are almost exclusively inshore types. There are many places with striped bass potential. No guarantee accompanies any of them, but all are worth a try: (1) Sandy ocean-front beaches, especially at the mouths of inlets. Wise anglers watch for signs of birds working beyond the breakers. If the activity is beyond casting distance, it pays to follow it along the strand on the chance that the fish will come closer. (2) Beaches with rocks and boulders, totally or partially submerged. The rocks attract lesser creatures, which in turn lure stripers. (3) Inlets—inside and outside mouths—the gateway itself, and inside channels flowing into it. Food passes in and out of the inlets with the tides. (4) Points of land where small fishes are swirled about by currents or seek refuge in quieter water. (5) White water in general. It may be in a tide rip or where currents collide. Stripers know that their favorite foods are tumbled about in these agitated areas. For similar reasons a live surf is usually better than a calm one. The only trouble is that an agitated surf, such as after a storm, may be clouded by sand and cluttered with weed, obscuring lures. (6) Rocky jetties, seawalls and waters around bridge abutments. These are productive for the same reason as rock-studded beaches. (7) Mussels and clam beds in enclosed waters and outside. These areas often contain sea worms. (8) Bays and channels with fairly brisk currents are also likely places. (9) Mouths of estuaries and tidal rivers. Bass prey upon smaller fishes passing in and out. Often stripers hold to a side where currents are strongest. (10) Expanses of sedge grass and other marine vegetation in shallow bays, even salt-marsh creeks. These places harbor shrimp, crabs and little fishes. Stripers prowl when a tide is high. (11) Sand bars, or flats, covered by water even at low tide. Small baitfishes lure bass to those areas. Flats may be too shallow for stripers at low tide, so the cue is to wait for high water. HOW CAUGHT, BAITS & LURES: Every striper hunter learns that his quarry is completely unpredictable as regards appearances in given areas and biting moods. One day they will hit, let's say, a plug or bucktail like there's no tomorrow. The very next day they will ignore that, and maybe everything else. Seasons and sizes of the bass can also play parts in feeding patterns, and therefore responses to anglers' offerings. For example, while still migrating along a coast they may favor a natural bait they can grab with ease (travel is work), whereas later on, while they're vacationing in an area, they may be more willing to pursue a surf-worked plug or trolled artificial. Sizes play a role because often the younger bass are more energetic in pursuit of food, hunting in large packs and preying upon schools of smaller fishes. Older, larger stripers often hunt in small groups, or lurk or cruise in likely places. Commonly it's the schoolies that are clobbering baitfish at the surface, while the lunkers are down deep. Such details govern fishing methods. And all these things add up to one big reason for striped bass fishermen to inquire locally. There is absolutely no way that blanket rules can be laid down for these fish. You literally play it by ear from place to place and day to day. Needless to add, it also pays to experiment. Name any basic catching method, and the chances are that it accounts for stripers somewhere. Here are some procedures. Bear in mind that certain methods may be more effective than others in different areas and for different times. (1) Surf casting, ocean fronts and jetties: Metal squids, especially those made to resemble some form of baitfish—sand eels, etc.—on which stripers feed beyond the breakers, are effective. So are plugs of various kinds, including poppers, surface types, deep-runners. A mullet finish is often good, since bass feed on mullet. Natural baits are also cast. These include whole eels or eelskin rigs; live shedder or soft-shell crabs, or large chunks of same (usually secured to the hook with thread or a rubber band for casting); strips of squid or head and tentacles of same (cut strips from the mantle, save the head and appendages for separate bait); sand eels; small whole local fishes—herring, mullet, etc.; "sand bugs" (secured with a few thread wrappings); the head or a chunk of a menhaden or a herring. (2) Bottom fishing in the surf: Here a fish-finder rig is practically standard. Baits include live bloodworms and sandworms, plump-bellied clam, a strip cut from squid or from the lighter underside of a mackerel, mullet or other local fish. Sometimes strip baits are used in combination with worms. (3) Boat casting just off a surf: This is for bass feeding in a surf beyond casting range from shore. Most of the natural baits and artificials mentioned in connection with No. 1 see service here. It's also dangerous, especially in rocky areas. The boat must have a dependable engine and an alert skipper. (4) Trolling: This ranges from near the surface to deep. Wire lines are used; and if that isn't deep enough, a drail or trolling sinker is incorporated in the terminal tackle. Come-ons here include a spinner and worm combination (usually sandworm); two or three sandworms by themselves; shiny spoons—on up to the big bunker spoons (so called because they simulate a mossbunker or menhaden); surgical tubes in red, amber and other colors (these are big in the New York area—and deadly); bucktails; plugs of all kinds, near-surface riders to deep-runners, including darting types and poppers; jigs with long nylon skirts in yellow or red; metal squids, plain or with the hook garnished with a bit of pork rind or squid strip; whole small eels (about 6 in. long), alone or in combination with a spoon or metal squid; plastic eels; and a chunk or the head of a menhaden. It can help to jig the rig with the rod tip while trolling. Trolling is a popular technique for fresh-water stripers. Lures include spoons, lead-head jigs, a spinner and plastic worm combination, and deep-running plugs. (5) Fishing at anchor or drift: Cut or live bait, such as gizzard shad, is effective. (6) Chumming: In recent years on Long Island, N.Y., this has gained increasing popularity in inlet and channel areas, notably around bridges. The procedure is to chum with ground menhaden and bait with a chunk of same. Presumably local species on which stripers feed would work in other regions. (7) Boat casting to surfaced schools: The schools are sighted, either by the commotion they create or by sea birds squawking and swooping over an area. This can be one of the most exciting ways to catch striped bass, especially on light tackle. All sorts of attractors are tried, from natural baits to artificials such as salt-water flies, plugs, spoons, etc. (when bass are working schools of shad at the surface, try casting popping plugs or shiny spoons to them.) (8) Jigging: With shiny jigs—mackerel jigs and others—and salt-water fly casting with large streamer flies. TACKLE: Throughout the striper-fishing arena just about every conceivable kind of tackle —conventional, spinning, bait-casting, surf, and fresh-and salt-water fly equipment—is wielded. There's a similarly wide range of calibers too, from extra-light fly and spinning rods to sturdy boat rods to the more muscular surf sticks. *Note:* Thanks to the species' anadromous habits, great adaptability and general hardiness, a new fresh-water striped bass sport fishery is in the making. Much of the inspiration for establishing striped bass as an inland sport fish comes from South Carolina. The biggest encouragement has come from the huge Santee-Cooper river-reservoir system in that state.

Striped Marlin

Striped Marlin

SCIENTIFIC NAME: Variously, *Makaira mitsukurii, Makaira audax, Tetrapturus audax.* COMMON NAME: Stripes. COLOR: There are distinguishing details in the color scheme. Topside on the head and back the color is a dark shade of rich blue, cobalt or steel-blue. Lower down on the sides this becomes silvery with a pearly sheen and sometimes bronze glints. The belly is white or silver-white. Most distinguishing are the vertical stripes giving the fish its name. Extending downward from the back onto the sides, they number 20 or so and are light blue or lavender. The intensity of their color differs among individuals. Other marlins are not as distinctly marked. On this fish the stripes also persist longer after it has been hauled from the water. SIZE: Striped marlin are believed to grow quite rapidly and can attain a weight of about 100 lbs. in three years, maximum sizes vary widely from region to region. If there's an *average* sport-fishing ceiling for stripes, overall it probably is in the neighborhood of 300 lbs. FAMILY: Striped marlin belong to the family Istiophoridae, along with the blue, white and black marlins. DISTRIBUTION: In the Americas the range is from southern California to southern Chile and includes Hawaii. HABITS: (1) They're migratory, but their travels are not as great as their far-flung distribution would suggest. Instead, populations seem to be more regional, engaging in coastal migrations according to rising water temperatures. Water temperatures below 59 ° F. seem to be the limiting influence in these journeys. (2) Examination of stomach contents shows that they're like other marlins in being primarily piscivorous, with their diet supplemented by squid, crabs and shrimp. They're fast enough to catch such fleet prey as bonitos and mackerels. WHERE CAUGHT: Like other

marlins, "stripes" are ocean rovers. For sport fishermen
they're an offshore coastal species. One of California's
productive areas is from Catalina's eastern end offshore toward
San Clemente Island, then southward in the direction of Los
Coronados islands. HOW CAUGHT, BAITS, LURES & TACKLE: A
favored fishing technique is to sight one at the surface, then
present a trolled bait in the same fashion as for surfaced white
marlin and swordfish (see page 248 and below). Whole-rigged
fishes are standard attractors and include mullet, flying fish,
large sardine and mackerel. Tackle is the angler's choice,
gauged according to the average size span of striped marlin
and personal ability. Adventurous souls will try 12- and 30-lb.
gear. Others go to heavier weapons, through the 80-lb. class.
Inexperienced marlin fishermen might better consider heavier
tackle. And all hands should keep it in mind that larger species
of marlin, requiring gear up to 130-lb. test, may be in the same
waters. At the other extreme, but only for fishermen who
know precisely what they're doing, is salt-water fly tackle.
Famed expert Lee Wulff took a 148-pounder on a 12-lb. tippet,
which was listed as a world record in its tippet class by the Salt
Water Fly Rodders of America, International.

Swordfish

SCIENTIFIC NAME: *Xiphias gladius*. COMMON NAME: Broadbill
swordfish, shortened to broadbill. COLOR: Invariably
broadbills are darker above—gray, brownish or almost bronze,
blue or blue-gray—and on some specimens the color is very
dark. The lowermost sides and belly are an off-white; the fins
are dark. SIZE: They attain awesome size. Commercial fishing
records for Canada's Maritime Provinces and the northeastern
U. S. list several in excess of 500 lbs., and respectable numbers
of specimens up to 13 and 14 ft. long, counting the sword, in
dressed weights of 600–700 lbs. and undressed weights up into
the 800's and 900's. One, harpooned on Georges Bank in 1921
and brought into Boston, weighed 915 lbs. after dressing and
was estimated at 15 ft. and about 1,100 lbs. in life. To date, the
biggest sport-caught broadbills have been found off South
America's Pacific shores. An IGFA all-tackle world record,
1,182 lbs., was caught off Chile. U.S. sport catches are well
below such monsters. The range is more like 150 to 350 lbs., but
larger fish are not ruled out. FAMILY: Swordfish are in a family
by themselves, Xiphiidae. DISTRIBUTION: Distribution is far-
flung in warm and warm-temperate seas throughout the
world. The Atlantic Ocean range is from the southwestern Gulf
of St. Lawrence, southern Newfoundland and Nova Scotia to
as far south as northern Argentina. On the Pacific seaboard the
range is described as extending from southern California to
Chile. This widespread distribution is misleading, because
nowhere—at least so far as recreational fishermen are

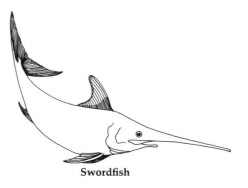

Swordfish

concerned—could broadbills be called numerous. HABITS:
(1) Swordfish are oceanic, high seas wanderers, usually well
offshore, perhaps 10 to 20 miles or more. But they do stray
inshore occasionally. (2) One might be inclined to think of
swordfish as tropical residents, since they are exotic in their
own way. Swordfish do not seem to be overfond of tropical
waters, although some are caught there periodically. It may
well be that there are more in those warmer seas than catches
indicate, with the fish seeking cooler strata in great deeps. In
the main they favor temperate and moderately cool waters, as
evidenced by commercial takes as far north as Nova Scotia.
Fondness for temperate and cooler waters may be the prime
mover in their seasonal migrations along the coasts, although
the routes have yet to be defined clearly. Their northward
Atlantic treks begin sometime in late spring, along about May.
Some broadbills are in evidence throughout the summer, but in
gradually dwindling numbers. Come September, any still
around are a bonus indeed. (3) On the Pacific seaboard a run
builds during summer around California's offshore islands,
peaks in September and lasts into October, with some fish still
around in November. But on the East Coast commercial
fishermen seem to have been more successful than anglers.
(4) Broadbills are fisheaters, to which they will add quantities
of squid whenever available. Bucketfuls of small fishes in great
variety have been found in their stomachs: mackerel,
menhaden, herring, bluefish, whiting, hake, young dolphin
and bonito, etc. They also eat quantities of the so-called
blackfishes, those dark-colored species residing in deeps of 150
fathoms (900 ft.) and more beyond the continental shelf. The
presence of these in swordfish stomachs supports the belief
that the broadbill's eyes are unusually large to better see in the
darkness at such levels. Single prey are simply "inhaled" and
swallowed whole. But when feeding involves schools, as it
often does, the modus operandi is to slash the bill from side to
side to stun or kill the victims, which can then be gobbled at
will. (5) On both seaboards water temperatures starting to
creep downward are a cue to swordfish to get on the move,
and they vanish. Where they go for the winter isn't known for
certain. A strong likelihood is that they travel on a southerly
tangent to deeper areas far offshore, probably to the edges of
continental shelves and their deep canyons. Supporting this
are occasional autumn and winter longline catches in the
Atlantic. WHERE & HOW CAUGHT: At times broadbills will
gather in small groups, but virtually all of those racked up by
sport fishermen are loners, sighted only after scouting square
miles of sea. More often than not, an entire day of cruising is
spent without so much as seeing one. The most I've ever seen
in one day were four, none of which would take a bait even
after repeated passes. An old swordfishing saying has it that
odds are 5:1 that you will not see a broadbill on a given trip, 5:1
against getting it to take a bait, and 5:1 that you won't hook the
fish. The only quarrel is with the odds—they're too low. And
to them should be added other odds. Swordfish reportedly
have been taken by fishing at anchor with live bait. Rarely do
they hit during blind trolling. The standard procedure is to

sight a fish at the surface. Broadbills come to the top periodically to laze in the warm surface layer. Often the best hours in which to look for one are between about 10 a.m. and 12 noon on a sunny day, although they surface on overcast days too. There they betray themselves by exposing the first dorsal fin, perhaps even a part of the back, and the upper tail lobe. Ideal swordfishing conditions call for a calm sea. The fish are hard enough to sight as it is, without dancing waves confusing the picture. All hands aboard should engage in peering throughout a 360 ° arc. Once a target is sighted, it becomes a tricky matter to present the bait—trolling it past him, practically under his nose—and trying to get him to take it. BAITS & LURES: Various small fishes such as mullet, bonito, eels, ballyhoo (balao), flying fish, young dolphin and mackerel are rigged whole, sometimes with two hooks (here care must be exercised so as not to violate IGFA regulations). The best bait I know is a whole, plump-bodied squid weighing about a pound, with a single hook. Whatever the bait, a basic swordfish rig consists of a single hook, size 10/0 to 14/0, ring-eye type, on 15 to 30 ft. of leader. The Martu and Sobey are performance-proven patterns. Walt Drobecker, a charter-skipper friend of mine, had his own method of rigging whole fish. This was his procedure: (1) Remove the backbone by making parallel cuts close alongside it. This leaves a shallow trench. (2) Feed the hook in through the mouth and bring it out at about the start of the trench. (3) Lay the leader in the groove left by the backbone. (4) Bury the hook in the bait's flesh about two-thirds of the way back from the head. (5) Complete the rig by sewing the groove shut (with the leader inside), along with the bait's mouth, using twine or stout thread. All baits should be as fresh as possible, and thawed beforehand for flexibility if frozen. TACKLE: Broadbills have hard, bony jaws, but parts of the mouth are soft and a hook can rip free from them. Veterans set the striking drag of their reels accordingly. Suggested are these: at not more than 20 lbs. for 130-lb.-class tackle, 16 lbs. for 80-lb.-line weapons, and 10–12 for 50-lb. gear. Adjustments of the brake can be made during the fight as needed. Swordfishing tackle is heavy. Favored gear is 130-lb. line, a rod rated to take it and outfitted with roller guides throughout, and a 10/0 or 12/0 reel. Experienced big game fishermen add to the sport by going to 80-lb. equipment, or even 50-lb. tackle. Lighter gear doesn't tire the fish as quickly, so fights are longer. On the debit side, the chances of losing fish are increased.

Tarpon

SCIENTIFIC NAME: *Tarpon atlanticus* and occasionally *Megalops atlantica*. Similarly, the tarpon family name is given variously as Elopidae and Megalopidae. COMMON NAMES: Silver king (used by fishing writers), *sabalo* (rare now), tarpum, big scale.

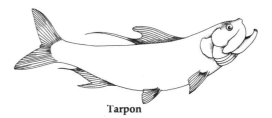

Tarpon

COLOR: Tarpon are distinctive in appearance. Along the back, color is a dark or smoky blue or green, which abruptly becomes a bright silver on the sides and belly. (Brownish variations with brassy glints have been noted for landlocked tarpon.) SIZE: Range is to 100–150 lbs., up to 200 for exceptional fish. There's a 247-pounder on record. FAMILY: Tarpon are allied with the humble herrings and also have a kinship with the ladyfish and the celebrated bonefish (see pages 216 and 191). DISTRIBUTION: Tarpon are encountered on both coasts of Florida and throughout the Gulf of Mexico, as well as in some areas of the Caribbean. They also occur in the Bahama islands and to a lesser extent in Bermuda. Tarpon are warm-water fish, and any found north of Florida would be in summer and in greatly reduced numbers. Ocean pier fishermen in the Carolinas occasionally latch onto one, and strays have been reported as far north as Nova Scotia. Via the Panama Canal, tarpon have infiltrated Central America's Pacific waters, and distribution runs northward perhaps to Baja California and may go farther. HABITS: (1) On their food list are small fishes such as mullet, pinfish (an important tarpon bait), sea catfish and needlefish, along with crabs and shrimp. (2) Tarpon confine themselves to warm water, which is why they frequent sun-heated shallow areas. The lowest point of their temperature tolerance seems to be about 65 ° F. On the low side of their thermal range they become sensitive to temperature drops and can be killed when overtaken by sudden cold snaps. (3) Tarpon can survive in water that is silty or muddy or that contains insufficient oxygen for other species. (4) They are active night feeders. The hours from dusk to darkness are therefore productive for anglers. WHERE CAUGHT: Tarpon, as noted, are shallow-water residents. Although primarily a salt-water species, tarpon have the peculiar habit of entering estuaries and rivers—ascending them for many miles, often ending up in creeks, canals and along mangrove banks—where they adapt readily to changes in salinity. These are not salmonlike spawning expeditions, but probably are prompted by searches for food. HOW CAUGHT, BAITS, LURES & TACKLE: In Florida anglers use a great variety of tackle. Here are several methods that will rack up tarpon there: (1) A technique in passes and harbors along the Gulf shore and Florida Keys is to anchor in the path of incoming schools and bait with live or dead pinfish or live crabs. Here it becomes important to select a proper depth for the rig. Some experimenting is required, and this is when having three or four rigs out at different planes can save time. Once a productive level is found, all rigs are dangled at that depth. (2) Boat fishing at anchor or drifting with live or dead baits— pinfish, crabs, mullet, shrimp—is productive. (3) Trolling spoons and large plugs is another method. (4) In southernmost Florida and through the Keys, a popular method is to fish the flats, of which there are countless miles all the way to Key West. This is called sight casting—that is, spotting the tarpon first, then casting to them. By now you probably have guessed that tarpon are a prime marine fly-fishing objective. They are indeed, but it's obviously action only for the experienced.

Several details are magnified. Right off the bat is an opponent's size potential to 100-plus lbs. Important: Tarpon have very tough jaws, and as tackle is scaled downward in caliber, planting a hook becomes increasingly more difficult, often necessitating repeated striking of the fish, and you may not succeed at that. Long runs seem to become even longer on light tackle. Any control of the fish at all, if such is possible, imposes great demands on skill. Arguing with a tarpon of any bulk on fly tackle can be long, drawn-out combat, and not everyone wants to do battle with giant tarpon. In my opinion, there's a lot to be said for the action with juniors—the 20- to 25-pounders. You'll find they're peers of their big brothers, complete with jumps. Tarpon fly-rodders can be opinionated in choice of effective attractors, with preferences varying from one locale to another. Big streamer flies have proved effective for the larger fish. Rigged for "baby tarpon" (up to 25 lbs.) are wet flies and little bucktails and popping bugs. Other method weapons run a full gamut of conventional and spinning types, influenced by the anticipated sizes of tarpon, methods, and individual angler's ability. Main thing is that the tackle can handle the fairly large plugs, spoons or feathers rigged in trolling, or the natural baits, live and dead, employed in still-fishing and drifting. *Miscellaneous techniques and notes:* (1) Fly-fishing with tiny artificials provides great sport. (2) Sight casting on flats is a real challenge. Favorable depths are about 4 to 6 ft. (3) Also productive is casting to a surface-cruising school. Live bait such as pinfish or mullet is good. One procedure is to let the bait fish swim freely. (4) Many tarpon are caught around bridges, where they lie in wait for food wafted their way by a tide. Two procedures can be tried. One is to anchor on the upcurrent side and drift a live bait toward the bridge; the other is to toss an artificial on the upcurrent side and retrieve it toward the bridge with the tide. (5) A few thoughts about plugs. Large ones are effective in deeper areas when trolled or retrieved slowly. With surface plugs you may have to experiment. (6) Surf casting is not a major Florida technique, but it can be productive in autumn, when there are mullet runs along the state's eastern seaboard. Try natural mullet baits and artificials made to imitate them.

Tautog

SCIENTIFIC NAME: *Tautoga onitis.* COMMON NAMES: "Tautog" stems from the Narragansett Indian *tautauog*, plural of *tautau*, meaning "blackfish," which is another common name. Fact is, that's more common than "tautog" in many areas. Other regional nicknames have passed into disuse: white-chin, oysterfish, moll, black porgy and salt-water chub. COLOR: The body is a drab brownish-black, dark gray, grayish-brown,

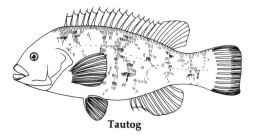

Tautog

greenish-gray or dusky brown. There are blotches, or mottling, sometimes in the form of vague, irregular bars, in a darker shade of the basic color. The belly is a somewhat lighter tone, and there's an off-white patch on the chin (hence the old nickname "white-chin"). Darkness or lightness of body color is influenced by the kind of bottom in an area. The darker the floor, the darker the tautogs. All this is camouflage. SIZE: The size range in sport fishing catches is from 1 lb. up to 6 and 8 on an average, with sprinklings of fish to 10, even 12 lbs. Their size potential goes higher. Rhode Island waters and Long Island Sound grounds have yielded huskies to 16 lbs. An IGFA world record was 21 lbs. 6 oz. Generally speaking, those caught in bays and adjacent channels are the smaller fish, 1 to 6 lbs., while the heavier tautogs are caught around ocean-front jetties, in big open sounds, and on ocean grounds. Rocky areas and artificial reefs are good producers. FAMILY: Tautogs are grouped with the wrasses as Labridae. With 400 to 500 recognized species, the Labridae comprise one of the world's largest fish families. Also in this tribe, closely related to the tautog and a frequent companion on the same grounds, is the cunner, or bergall, a bait-stealing pest. DISTRIBUTION: Tautogs are Atlantic Coast residents, their range extending from Nova Scotia to South Carolina. The greatest abundance is from Cape Cod, Mass., to the Delaware capes. They're strictly coastal, staying mainly within 10–12 miles of shore in waters no deeper than about 68–80 ft. They may be found in somewhat deeper areas when their favorite hangouts—I'll come to them in a second—are present. Throughout their distribution they're caught on ocean grounds and in sounds, inlets, bays and channels. HABITS: (1) Few fishes are as crazy about rocks, wrecks, artificial reefs, jetties, seawalls, and the underpinnings of piers, docks, bridges and trestles. There's no mystery to this one-sided love affair. Long-submerged objects collect blankets of barnacles and mussels, tidbits of which tautogs are inordinately fond. They also devour assorted crabs, sand fleas, shrimp, marine worms, small lobsters and sand dollars. That former name, oysterfish, came from their fondness for mollusks. (2) Tautogs are well equipped for their feeding preferences. Their jaws are strong and armed with sturdy teeth. Those in the front of the mouth are larger than their mates, adapted to nipping and biting off such morsels as barnacles and mussels. In the back of the mouth are flat grinding teeth, just right for crushing shells. At dinner they have an odd rat-a-tat-tat method of feeding, head downward if necessary. (3) They also believe in togetherness at mealtimes, and may feed practically shoulder to shoulder. That brings up a big point: in few other kinds of fishing is it so important to pinpoint the grounds. Tautogs may be feeding by the dozens within a comparatively small area; yet the bottom 15 or 20 ft. away will not have a single fish. Precision anchoring is often required, and this is where a depth sounder comes in handy. (4) Because of their tough lips, trip-hammer manner of feeding, and agility, tautogs are tricky to hook, and they're adept bait thieves. When they take a hook they're surprisingly strong for their size. They will also run for the nearest cover, and if they

can't be controlled, a frayed—broken—line is often the result.
WHERE CAUGHT: Tautogs are caught from rowboats, small
outboards and party boats, from jetties and breakwaters, from
piers and docks on channels. Fishing is done at anchor. Surf
casting in rocky areas also produces, but is not as effective as
boat fishing. There are two major seasons: spring and fall.
There's productive fishing in summer, but only in deeper,
cooler waters, and generally in rocky areas. HOW CAUGHT,
BAITS & LURES: Rigging is for the bottom, using only enough
sinker weight to keep the rig there. Fiddler crabs are excellent
tautog bait. Green crabs are good too, along with pieces of blue
crab. Also used are pieces of sandworm and skimmer clam.
Hooks go from a No. 8 or 7 for small bay fish up to Nos. 2 and 1
and 1/0 for larger tautogs. It's better to have hooks a size too
small than too large. They must be needle-sharp because the
fish have tough, leathery lips. Tautogs seize a bait readily if
they're hungry. They can be very independent when not
hungry. Chumming with cracked mussels can help when
action is slow, but it also attracts the less desirable bait-thieving
bergalls. TACKLE: Tackle can be light or light-medium,
conventional or spinning. But if spinning tackle is considered,
it must be remembered that moderately heavy sinkers may be
required and also that extra strain is put on a rod when tautogs
streak for a rock crevice, wreck or other haven, a frequent
maneuver, and when attempts are made to free a snagged rig.
Line of 10 or 12 lbs. is sufficiently strong, and it can be
monofilament or braided. The former is preferred in rocky
places because it's more resistant to abrasion. Even in ocean
fishing, 100 yds. will suffice. Tautogs are not long runners.

Tripletail

SCIENTIFIC NAME: *Lobotes surinamensis*. COMMON NAMES:
Also called buoy fish, chobie and buoy bass. The name
tripletail was inspired by the fact that the fish's anal fin and the
rear section of the dorsal, which resemble each other in shape
and size, extend rearward so close to the caudal fin as to give
an impression of three tails. Actually, there's only one. The
three-tailed effect is a ready field mark in identification.
COLOR: The tripletail's colors are subject to some variation.
Browns usually predominate, in shades ranging from light to
quite dark, almost blackish sometimes. Occasionally the basic
color is a brown with undertones of green or gray. Yellowish
tinges are reported for some specimens. Lower down on the
sides the color can be tannish, or silver-white. The body is
moderately deep, and there is a continuous dorsal fin
consisting of a section with 12 spines and a rear portion with 16
rays. The head is basslike, with a protruding lower jaw. SIZE:
An average range is 5 to 15 lbs. Lengths to 2½ ft. and weights
of 20 to 25 lbs. are not rare. A Texas state record stood at

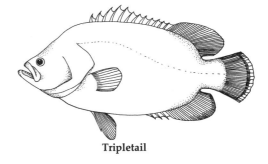

Tripletail

28½ lbs. Their potential is believed to go as high as 50 lbs.
FAMILY: The species is catalogued as a relative of the sea basses
(Serranidae), but it has its own family, Lobotidae. An eastern
Pacific relative is described for waters off Mexico and Panama.
DISTRIBUTION: Principally in the Gulf of Mexico, Texas to
Florida inclusive. From southern Florida, Gulf and Atlantic
sides, the range reaches to the Carolinas. Strays turn up north
of there, reportedly all the way to Cape Cod, Mass., on
infrequent occasions. Any occurring above the Carolinas
would undoubtedly be summer visitors, well offshore, in the
Gulf Stream. At its southern extreme the range extends to
Argentina. Throughout, tripletails are warm-water fish.
HABITS & WHERE CAUGHT: (1) He's primarily an open-sea fish
but also comes inshore, where he may be found along surf
beaches and in bays and estuaries. (2) He's a bottom feeder,
and can occur at depths ranging from shallows on out to 100 ft.
or more. (3) His "buoy fish" and "buoy bass" nicknames were
prompted by a fondness for hanging around buoys and
channel markers. (4) Presumably for a similar need of food,
he's also encountered around rocks, submerged pilings,
wrecks and even floating debris. (5) Tripletails school, but they
also travel in small groups, in pairs or alone. (6) They are fond
of shrimp and other crustaceans, and small fishes also figure in
their diet. HOW CAUGHT, BAITS, LURES & TACKLE: The most
common technique is still-fishing, and good spots are waters
around buoys and other markers. Live shrimp or small live
crab is about the best bait. Pieces of clam and mullet are also
impaled on hooks. Natural baits are tops, but tripletails are also
known to hit small artificials cast to them.

Wahoo

SCIENTIFIC NAME: *Acanthocybium solandri*. COMMON NAMES:
In Hawaii it's *ono*. Local names in the Caribbean area and the
Bahamas are queenfish and peto, respectively. COLOR: The
body is steel-blue, almost blue-black, and sometimes a mixture
of blue and green along the back. The sides are silver or silvery-
gray, becoming white or silver underneath. A wahoo is a rather
brilliant fish when first removed from the water. At the end of
a fight there are rather bright, bluish bars along the body sides,
but these quickly fade. SIZE: Wahoos come in a wide
assortment of packages, according to areas. Hawaii
consistently produces big ones, some up to 70 lbs. and better.
Waters off Cape Hatteras, N.C., have surrendered a
91½-pounder. Florida produces them in the 15- to 50-lb.
range, laced with heftier specimens. FAMILY: Because of its
resemblance to Spanish mackerel and certain other members of
the family, most ichthyologists classify the wahoo with the
mackerel tribe (Scombridae). DISTRIBUTION: The species'
Atlantic range goes at least as far south as Brazil. To the north,

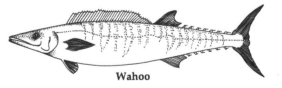
Wahoo

Cape Hatteras, N.C., appears to be the limit. An occasional wahoo is reported trolled far offshore of Long Island, N.Y., in midsummer, strays wandering up the coast with the Gulf Stream. Florida also is wahoo country, as is the Gulf Coast, offshore, all the way around to and including Texas. U.S. Pacific distribution seems mainly concentrated in Hawaiian waters. HABITS: (1) Wahoos are open-ocean wanderers. Although they are reported to school in certain areas and seasons, they do not seem to be as fond of togetherness as other mackerels, and certainly do not travel in groups anywhere near the size of those formed by Atlantic mackerel (see page 174). From my experience it would seem that they are frequently loners. Like Atlantic mackerel, they alternately appear and disappear from areas. This may indicate some sort of migration—no such patterns have been defined yet—or perhaps a cyclic change as yet undetected. In some regions wahoos are more or less year-round residents, but late spring into early autumn seems to be fairly dependable in most areas. (2) This slender gamester—whose name sounds like an Indian war whoop or maybe a Rebel yell—is as speedy as it looks. Vicious strikes, fast runs and the power inherent in a muscular, streamlined species with weights that can go to 50 lbs. and more combine to make the wahoo a highly desirable hook-and-line opponent. A wahoo's hit alone is in a class by itself. WHERE CAUGHT: Wahoos are caught chiefly by offshore trollers, either purposely or incidental to billfishes and tunas. HOW CAUGHT, BAITS, LURES & TACKLE: They will smack artificials, notably feathers (red and white, all white, etc.) set out for tuna, and whole-rigged small fishes such as balao (ballyhoo), mullet, mackerel and the like. They will also hit strip baits. These fast, hard hitters are notorious "short-strikers," which is to say that they're adept at streaking in on a bait, amputating its rear section, and escaping scot free. Whole-rigged fish and long strip baits are especially vulnerable unless the hook is impaled far enough aft. A tail hook rig punishes some of these thieves. One arrangement is to bridle a ring-eye tail hook on the bend of the first and impale the bait on both; or the second hook can be rigged in tandem with the first by a short length of wire. Record-minded anglers using two hooks must be careful to comply with IGFA regulations. Wahoos can also be caught by drifting offshore with live bait. Hook sizes need not be a matter of precision. The scope is from a 1/0 or 2/0 to 5/0 or 6/0, gauged roughly to the sizes of the wahoos anticipated. With large baits for big fish the size is upped to 7/0 and 8/0. Hooks are rigged on wire leaders, 5 or 6 ft. long, in about the same strength as the line or a few pounds heavier. No need to go real heavy. Wahoos will strike any moving thing that interersts them—within reason, of course. Therefore when fishing for them it's a good idea to remove any unnecessary shiny hardware—swivels, spinners, etc.—in the terminal tackle. They have been known to smack swivels, ending a contest right then and there. It's a bit extreme, but tobacco-colored wire can be substituted for potentially distracting shiny leaders. Trolling speeds go to about 6 or 7 knots, and wahoos are not adverse to hitting fairly close astern.

As always, though, it pays to experiment with trolling speeds and distances. Lures and baits can be trolled from outriggers or flat-lined. The only purpose outriggers serve is to keep rigs separated. Wahoos strike so fast that a rigger's drop-back means little or nothing.

Warsaw Grouper

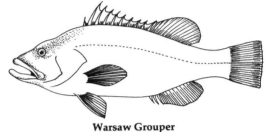

Warsaw Grouper

SCIENTIFIC NAME: *Epinephelus nigritus*. COMMON NAME: Also called black grouper—a bad choice because it's the name of a smaller grouper, *Mycteroperca bonaci*. COLOR: The body color is an almost uniform somber brown, sometimes grayish-brown, or so dark as to look almost black. Although usually fairly uniform throughout, this color occasionally is punctuated by a few whitish spots or small blotches. In addition to color and respectable sizes, aids to identification include: a large mouth with a strong, somewhat projecting lower jaw; a pointed trailing edge on each gill cover; a prominent continuous dorsal fin with spined and rayed sections; large staring eyes, high in the head; and a well-developed tail with a deep base. The dorsal fin's anterior section carries 10 spines (a detail separating this fish from other Atlantic groupers, whose dorsal spines number 8, 9 or 11). The first spine is very short and stout. The second and third spines are the tallest. All are sharp. The dorsal fin's rayed portion has a curving edge. SIZE: For size, a king among the groupers. Most of those sport-caught are in the 50- to 100-lb. bracket, but hefties to 200 are not uncommon, and the potential climbs to 500 lbs. FAMILY: Warsaws are catalogued by some authorities as belonging to the grouper section of Serranidae. DISTRIBUTION: Warsaw groupers live in tropical Atlantic waters and are also encountered in deeper areas of the Gulf of Mexico. They're an all-year sport species in southern Florida. HABITS: They're better battlers, pound for pound, than some other Atlantic groupers. Considering their bulk, depths, etc., bringing them to gaff is a workout. WHERE CAUGHT: All fishing is offshore. HOW CAUGHT: Bottom fishing with natural baits, dead or alive. Fishing for them in Florida is more or less specialized charter-boat angling involving wire line or heavily weighted mono. BAITS & LURES: Warsaws grab live or dead fish baits on large hooks, and occasionally respond to artificials. TACKLE: Their great bulk puts them in the heavier-tackle category, especially since they're caught on or near the bottom in deep water.

Weakfish

Weakfish

SCIENTIFIC NAME: *Cynoscion regalis.* COMMON NAMES: Weak, and for the larger ones, tiderunner. Also, regionally, seatrout, which is not a good choice, as the fish is in no way a trout, gray weakfish and yellowfin. COLOR: On the back and upper body sides is a dark shade of green, green-blue, blue or olive. This gradually fades lower down, where the sides carry glints of green, violet, purple and blue, burnished with gold, silver and copper. Numerous small, vaguely defined spots in dark green, black, and occasionally bronze pepper the back and upper sides. On some individuals the spots run together to give an illusion of irregular lines slanting downward and forward. The dotting usually is confined to the area above the lateral line. The belly is silvery or white. The dorsal fins are smoky or dusky and may carry a yellow tinge. The tail also is a dusky color, or dark olive-greenish, and may be tinged with yellow on its lower edge. The pectoral fins are greenish or a mixture of green and yellow. The "weak" in its name has nothing whatsoever to do with its fighting ability. It refers to the fish's delicate mouth parts, from which a hook can—and often does —tear free. This has prompted an affectionate nickname, "papermouth." SIZE: When weakfish runs are at their best, it's not uncommon to hook scrappers up to 8 and 10 lbs., with late-in-the-season tiderunners going up to 12 and 13. In the 1920s and 1930s Long Island's Peconic Bay system was one of the Atlantic Coast's greatest weakfishing arenas, and 15- to 17-pounders were common. There are unconfirmed reports of weaks up to 30 lbs. in the long ago, presumably netted. FAMILY: Weakfish belong to the family called Sciaenidae, a group that also embraces croakers, drums and whitings. Nearly 150 species make up this large tribe, many of whose members are noted for their ability to produce croaking or drumming sounds. Farther south on the Atlantic seaboard these weakfish are replaced by an equally popular relative, the spotted seatrout or spotted weakfish. DISTRIBUTION: At its greatest, the species' Atlantic Coast range is from Massachusetts to Florida's eastern shores. Given mild water temperatures—weakfish are sensitive to cold—some will straggle northward in New England. For anglers, the main distribution is from Long Island, N.Y., and New Jersey to and including Chesapeake Bay. Weakfish also provide sport in Virginia and North Carolina and are called gray trout in both states. HABITS: (1) They're schooling fish by nature—the groups can be very large when they're young, and are most apt to be found over clean, hard-packed, sandy bottoms. Essentially they're shallow-water, warmer-water fish, but not tropical. (2) Overall, the season can start any time from April on. Warming waters prompt their appearance a bit earlier in more southerly segments—Virginia and North Carolina— while May is the usual month in New Jersey and New York. In southern New England they may not start to show until June. In all regions they peak in late spring, hang around through the summer, after which the run's duration depends upon how soon autumn makes itself felt. Weaks are quite sensitive to cooling waters. Regional water temperatures and weather in general—specifically, a lack of severe storms—are key factors. (3) Weakfish are very adaptable when it comes to food. They will buy whatever is in best supply at the moment. If necessary, they'll forage low over a bottom. Nothing there, they will go higher, through intermediate levels to the surface if necessary. Or they'll haunt the edges of tide rips, where currents buffet and confuse lesser creatures, or prowl a surf just beyond the breakers. Commonly they feed near the bottom in the surf and estuaries, the attractions being crabs, mollusks and marine worms. Added to those items on their food shopping list are squid, shrimp and other invertebrates, killies (mummichogs), spearing or silversides, young porgies (scup), small menhaden, herring, butterfish, or whatever other small fishes are on sale. WHERE CAUGHT: Throughout their range, weaks occur in the ocean-front surf and in inlets, bays, sounds, channels, tide rips, sloughs, holes and tidal creeks. They commonly enter shallow water, even little creeks meandering through salt marshes. Some venture into estuaries too, but this species draws the line at fresh water. Accordingly, they can be caught from boats, shores, bridges, docks, piers and jetties. HOW CAUGHT, BAITS, LURES & TACKLE: Bottom fishing is one method and is usually done at anchor, but also serves in drifting if drifts are not too fast. Natural baits are used. Grass shrimp, strips of squid, and sandworm are good. Rig: a 1/0 or 2/0 hook on an 18- to 24-in. leader of low-visibility mono or other material, attached to the line with or without a swivel, according to preference, 6 in. above the sinker. A sinker of suitable weight is needed to hold bottom—the round type is preferred, since it moves along the bottom better than a bank type. A second hook can be rigged, tied into the line on a similar leader in similar fashion. Although it's not a popular technique, fly rodding for weakfish merits tries. In quantity it's nowhere near as productive as other methods, but for quality —action—it's tops. Battlers up to at least 6 lbs. are taken on fly tackle with such come-ons as streamers, bucktails and shrimp-type flies. Small natural shrimp have possibilities too, as do plastic imitations. Chumming with shrimp should be an aid.

White Marlin

SCIENTIFIC NAME: *Makaira albida* or (more recently) *Tetrapturus albidus*. COMMON NAMES: Marlin, billfish, and occasionally, "whites." COLOR: Along its back above the lateral line the white's color is a rich, bright blue, often with a hint of green. This changes to silver-white lower down on the sides and white underneath. The first dorsal is a shade of medium to darkish-blue, and may be spotted with black or purple-blue. The tail is blackish. Within the marlin group the white is

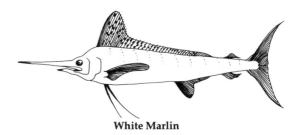

White Marlin

separable from the others in having the tips of its dorsal and
anal fins rounded rather than pointed. Its pectoral fins also
have rounded ends. In still another difference, the body is
shallower, less thick proportionately, and tends more toward
flat sides. SIZE: In sport catches the majority have a weight
ceiling of about 50 to 60 lbs., but there are huskies up into the
70-, 80- and 90-lb. brackets, and they can reach and top 100. (A
world-record white, caught in Florida, weighed 159½ lbs.)
FAMILY: These are the smallest members of the marlin family,
Istiophoridae. DISTRIBUTION: Southeastern U.S. and Gulf of
Mexico sportsmen have their Atlantic sailfish, their northern
brethren have their white marlin. Unfortunately for West Coast
anglers, white marlin are endemic to the western Atlantic
Ocean, with a range extending from the offing of Block Island,
R.I., and Long Island, N.Y., to Venezuela. They also occur off
Bermuda, in the Bahamas, and throughout the Caribbean.
HABITS: (1) Like their bigger relatives, they're chiefly
fisheaters, engulfing young mackerel, herring, anchovies and
other small species. They also enjoy squid. They will feed at
whatever level is the most rewarding at the moment. No fools,
they seek out food concentrated in dense schools, and they're
also fast enough to take care of loners. (2) White marlin are
migratory, but their travel plans have yet to be mapped. One
thing is for sure: they travel northward and more inshore with
the warmer weather of late spring and early summer.
September sees them thinning out and moving farther offshore
in the northern segments. To the south, off Maryland to North
Carolina, some may still be around on into October, barring
storms and unseasonable cold. Then they are gone until the
next year. Maryland, incidentally, has some of the finest white
marlin fishing known. (3) Summer is the fishing season in
northern parts of their range. In Florida and in the Bahamas,
Walker's Cay southward and including Bimini, the best season
is in winter through early spring. WHERE CAUGHT: Like all
marlins, whites are oceanic nomads, generally staying well
offshore. In summer, when they visit northern segments of
their range, they usually appear so far offshore as to be out of
reach of fishing cruisers, then move in toward the coast as
water temperatures climb. HOW CAUGHT: White marlin
always live up to their billing. When they take a bait or
artificial, they do it with enthusiasm. They run like the dickens,
showing their muscle all the way, and punctuate their fight
with leap after leap, often "walking" on their tails on the
surface. Trolling is the method. Sometimes it's done blind. In
other areas—and this is standard off New Jersey, Long Island,
and Block Island—the fish are sighted at the surface first,
where they betray themselves by exposure of the tail's upper
section. The first dorsal may not be seen, since it's more or less
retractable and usually isn't fully erect unless its owner is
alarmed or otherwise aroused. This helps to differentiate at a
distance between a white marlin and a surfaced swordfish or a
shark, both of whose dorsal fins are rigid and exposed. In the
sighting method the boat maneuvers so as to present the bait
practically under the fish's snout without spooking it. The
technique is similar to that used for swordfish (see page 237).

BAITS & LURES: White marlin will hit natural baits and artificials. Among the former are whole-rigged eels, fish (mullet, ballyhoo, etc.) and squid. Fish strips, from bonito and other species, are also rigged but are generally less effective than whole fish. TACKLE: The caliber of weapons is your choice. For maximum sport, seasoned hunters use 20- to 25-lb. tackle. Less experienced fishermen might better go to a happy medium in the 40- or 50-lb. class. Spinning equipment is wielded by light-tackle buffs, but conventional gear is more practical. Needless to say, reels should be filled to capacity. If blue marlin are known to be in the same area, lighter tackle is a calculated risk. Conversely, heavier blue marlin weapons are too heavy for whites, killing them prematurely and discounting a lot of the sport.

Winter Flounder

SCIENTIFIC NAME: *Pseudopleuronectes americanus*. COMMON NAMES: They are commonly called simply flounder, and known regionally as spring flounder and fall flounder because of their seasons of greatest abundance. That "winter" in their name is deceptive; few are caught at that time of year. In fact, the fish usually spend their winters in the mud, inactive. COLOR: In shape of body and in size and position of fins, this flounder is typical of other flatfishes—soles, fluke, dabs, halibuts. As usual, the broad dorsal surface is pigmented, the underside being white. The colored surface is dark, with variations according to the bottom they happen to be on. Usually it's a shade of brown, sometimes greenish or olive, or a reddish-brown, or a dark grayish or dusky brown that is almost black. In contrast, pale shades are seen on those living on sandy floors. The color may be uniform on some specimens but is more likely to be irregularly blotched with darker tones of the body color. Winter flounders are "right-eyed." What that means is this: If a winter flounder is held with his snout pointing away from the holder, width vertical, mouth below, the eyes and pigmented side of the body will be on the holder's right. (*Note:* All flatfishes, a huge family with more than 300 known species, are either "right-eyed" or "left-eyed.") SIZE: Young ones are only a few inches long with weights in ounces (thus nicknamed "postage stamps") to about ½ lb. Average size range in sport catches is from ½ to 1½ lbs. But showings can be laced with larger fish, called sea flounders, weighing 2 to 3½ lbs. They grow even larger in a limited region between Montauk, N.Y., and Block Island, R.I. These king-size flatties are dubbed "snowshoe flounders," and have been known to reach weights of 5 and 6 lbs. FAMILY: They are members of the Pleuronectidae group within the flatfishes family. DISTRIBUTION: The range for winter flounder is from Labrador to South Carolina and Georgia in its extremes. The fish are very

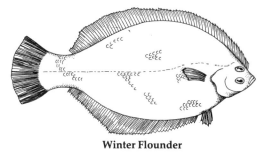

Winter Flounder

common from the Gulf of St. Lawrence and Newfoundland to
Chesapeake Bay, with notable centers of abundance from New
England to southern New Jersey. HABITS: (1) These flounders
usually winter in the mud, out in the ocean or in the deeper
parts of bays and sounds. Periods of unseasonably warm
weather in late February can cause some of them to stir and
prowl for food, at which time eager-beaver anglers catch a few.
But their spring run is more apt to start in March as waters
begin to warm a little. Often the first fish caught still carry dabs
of mud on their upper surface, leading to the nickname
"blackback." A spring peak occurs in April and May. In
deeper, cooler waters they can be caught all summer. Those
living in shallow bays either move out into the ocean or seek
deeper areas. (2) Another run occurs in fall, starting along
about September. It peaks in October and lasts into November
—even December if the weather isn't too cold. Then comes a
winter lull until the next spring showing. (3) Flounders are
cool-water fish, but they can't tolerate extremes in either
direction. Mass kills have occurred in shoal bays during
summer heat and when a sudden cold snap overtakes them.
(4) These flounders are among the most exclusively bottom-
dwelling flatfishes. Seldom do they venture more than a few
inches above bottom, another important angling detail because
it dictates rigging. Further, they are not as aggressive as their
larger cousins the summer flounders or fluke (see page 207),
which often share the same areas. Their lack of aggressiveness
often necessitates looking for them. (5) The natural food of
winter flounders consists of small forms of crustaceans and
mollusks, along with little invertebrates and any young fishes
small enough to wrap a mouth around. Their diet is limited to
items that can be accommodated by their small mouths.
WHERE CAUGHT: Inlets, channels, shallow bays and sounds
are among flounder-fishing areas. In addition, areas with
flounder potential are canals, if not polluted or crowded with
boats, and to a lesser extent, close-inshore ocean zones—for
boats, not surf casters. In hot weather try deeper areas and
holes. Sand flats well covered with water at high tide
sometimes produce. HOW CAUGHT & TACKLE: Rigging is
always for the bottom. The best arrangement is a simple device
called a spreader. This consists of a piece of stiff wire, 10 in. or
so long, with a loop at each end for the hooks. It permits the
use of two hooks and keeps them from tangling. At the top of
the spreader in its middle is a swivel attachment for line.
Directly under it a loop takes a sinker. A bank-type sinker of
suitable weight to hold bottom is tied close to the spreader.
Flounder hooks must be small, and they are attached to a
spreader by their snells—no leaders. A very good flounder
hook is the Chestertown pattern. Its bend is well suited to
small mouths. Flounders have a habit of swallowing a bait
deep in their gullet. The Chestertown's long shank facilitates
removal. Most flounder fishing is done at anchor. Some
drifting is done. It has an advantage of covering more ground
but usually is not as productive. One rig for drifting consists of
two hooks, the first tied to the line by its snell, with or without
a barrel swivel, and the second hook tied in at about the

midpoint of the snell of the first to form a Y-shaped arrangement. Either a bank-type or round sinker can be used, just heavy enough to hold bottom. Each anchoring place should be given a fair chance to produce, then changed if it fails. Chumming always helps. Sometimes flounders are feeding only yards away from a boat. Without chum to draw them they may remain independent. Chumming also aids when fishing is slow. The best device for flounders is a chumpot, a meshed sack filled with cracked mussels sold for that purpose. (See Chapter 6). Lacking chum, you can stir up the bottom with a pole or drag the anchor and thus release tiny shellfish that draw flounders. One of flounder fishing's major attractions, along with quantity catches, is the simplicity of tackle. Any kind of conventional or spinning equipment will do, so long as it's light. Accent lightness because flounders are small fish. The only possible limitation on very light spinning tackle might be its ability to handle sinkers of 5 oz. or so, sometimes required to hold bottom in areas where tidal currents are fairly strong. It's most important that a flounder rig be right on bottom at all times. A rig that is too high will not catch them. Even a few inches can make the difference. Flounders bite lightly, tending to nip at the bait and release it before finally accepting it. The smaller fish nibble so daintily that they may not be felt if the angler has not kept his line taut and remained alert. They do not toy with a bait for very long. The hook should be set quickly. A short upward lift of the rod tip will do it. If setting the hook is delayed, a flounder can strip it of bait. BAITS & LURES: Because of the fish's little mouth, pieces of bait must be small. About the best baits are bloodworm and sandworm. Pieces of clam are also effective. Sometimes a piece of clam gets results when worms will not. Worth trying is a combination bait consisting of small pieces of worm and clam on the same hook. Pieces of mussel can also be used as bait. Bait should be checked periodically. Crabs, sea robins, blowfish and other larcenous souls are adept at stripping hooks. Bait should be replaced at intervals. Worms and clams are soft and do not stand up well. Further, prolonged submersion leaches out their scent and color. Conservation note: Winter flounders are non-migratory. Therefore populations are localized, which means that if an area is cleaned out, that's it. Anglers are urged to return all undersized fish to the water, alive and unharmed. Unhooking must be done very carefully, and the fish handled as little as possible. Sport fishermen also are urged to keep no more flounders than they can use.

Yellowfin Tuna

Yellowfin Tuna

SCIENTIFIC NAME: *Thunnus albacares.* These fish are among species about which ichthyologists have been debating for years. Part of the haggling resulted from indecision as to whether the Pacific and Atlantic forms were identical or closely allied. Accordingly, those in the Pacific were labeled *Thunnus macropterus* and those in the Atlantic were designated *Thunnus albacares.* The argument continues, but a consensus now favors the idea that the two fish are one and the same and groups them under *Thunnus albacares.* Incidentally, you may occasionally see the name *Neothunnus* (literally, "new tuna") *macropterus.* It's the same fish. COMMON NAMES: For many years the name Allison tuna was used on the Atlantic-Caribbean side of the U.S. This too precipitated a debate, as to whether yellowfins and Allison were identical. That argument seems to have been resolved with an agreement that the tuna once called Allison are in reality larger and older yellowfins. Praise be for small favors. COLOR: The yellowfin is perhaps the most gaudily dressed of the tunas. As its name indicates, the fins carry a bright yellow color. In life there's also a yellow band along each upper side from head to tail, but this fades quickly after removal from the water. In contrast are the rich, deep blue of the back and the silver on the sides and belly. There may be spots or irregular markings in white on the lower sides. It is truly a beautiful fish. The body is typically tunalike, although more slender than that of the bluefin. Like all tunas, yellowfins have dorsal and ventral finlets, which are yellow edged with black. As they grow older and larger, they are more readily distinguished from other tunas by their unusually long, sickle-shaped second dorsal and anal fins. SIZE: Their gluttony is probably the reason that they grow rapidly, reaching 50 lbs. at about age two and a half, 100 at four, 150 lbs. at age five, and 200 by their sixth birthday. The range in sport catches is more likely to go up to 40 or 50 lbs. I should add that Hawaii produces them in unusually large packages. Trolling offshore drop-offs has caught brutes up to 250 lbs. There is a 269½-lb. IGFA world record for Hawaii. FAMILY: The tunas, of course. DISTRIBUTION: Yellowfin roam tropical and subtropical seas in many parts of the world. Water temperatures of 60 ° to 80 ° F. seem to be favored. On the U.S. Pacific Coast their range is from about Santa Barbara Channel or Point Conception southward to Baja California, including the Gulf of California, then on down the Mexican seaboard to as far south as Chile. As mentioned, they're a big item for anglers in Hawaii, where a name for them is *ahi.* In the western Atlantic their overall scope is from roughly Maryland to Florida, around into the Gulf of Mexico, then throughout the Caribbean and on to Brazil. HABITS: (1) They do migrate, but what tagging has been done indicates that they do not travel over such great distances as do their cousins the bluefins. Their fondness for warmer water undoubtedly exerts a restricting influence on their migrations. (2) Yellowfins gorge themselves on many kinds of small fishes —whatever species happen to be in good supply at the time.

Many will seize a bait even though their stomachs are already loaded with food. WHERE CAUGHT: Everywhere found, they are open-ocean wanderers. HOW CAUGHT, BAITS, LURES & TACKLE: They're excellent rod and reel opponents at any size, as are all tunas. There's live-bait fishing in some areas, but the favored technique is trolling artificials, usually fairly fast. Among effective lures are the so-called Kona heads from Hawaii, Knuckleheads, feather lures (red and white and all white are noteworthy), spoons and plastic squid. Several kinds of live baits—mackerel, mullet, small reef species—are used whole or in strips. Hooks go up to about 6/0, 8/0 for the heaviest fish and are gauged accordingly. Tackle must be able to take tough combatants like yellowfins. Tackle of the 50-lb. class should handle most of them. Inexperienced anglers might want to wield 80-lb. gear if fish of 100 lbs. or more are a possibility.

15. Shellfish

Most citizens call any fish with a shell attached shellfish, so I use that term here for familiarity among readers. In this section I'll cover some of the popular shellfish—both crustaceans and mollusks—and offer what suggestions I have. Basically, most of these creatures are commercially sought—that is, men do it for a living. But certain crustaceans and mollusks also provide the sport fishermen with effective and inexpensive baits, and we'll look into that, too.

There are three points I want to stress right off the bat:

1. In most areas, shellfishing is strictly controlled by state and local regulations. A license may be necessary for both amateur and professional, and there are certain size limits on hauls or catches. There can be stiff fines for violations.

2. Professional or commercial fishermen often consider certain areas their own territory. They take a dim view of competition, even from amateurs.

3. Along with conservation, pollution is a very serious consideration in shellfishing today. This affects all filter-feeding animals such as the mollusks—your clams, mussels, scallops and oysters. I can't stress often enough that anglers should check with local authorities to find out what waters are on the polluted list. Hepatitis and other gastrointestinal diseases can result from eating seafood caught in polluted water.

American Lobster

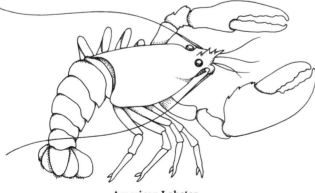

American Lobster

For generations of North Americans, the lobster has been among the most popular—and also one of the most expensive—items on seafood menus. Distribution of this appealing creature is from Canada's Maritime Provinces southward along the Atlantic seaboard to North Carolina. Newfoundland, Nova Scotia and Maine are within the region of greatest abundance.

The lobster is a member of an enormous family of creatures called crustaceans and closely resembles the crayfish, his fresh-water cousin. The big difference, along with the lobster's greater size, is the two large front claws. These are more powerful and formidable in the lobster. The larger one is called the crusher claw. Its mate is called the quick claw since it's fast and is used in seizing and biting. The lobster has 19 pairs of appendages in all including long feelers for touch, jaws and mouth parts. For locomotion he possesses four pairs of walking legs, paddlelike swimmerettes and a fan-shaped tail powered by a strong abdomen. He can swim backward with amazing speed by enlisting the aid of his jointed and flexible abdomen. A lobster's diet consists of a wide assortment of small

255

fishes, worms, crabs, mollusks, sea urchins and any other items he can capture. Lobsters are also cannibalistic, even when young. Like all crustaceans, the body of the lobster is encased in a hard shell that is shed at intervals as its occupant grows inside. Shedding, as it is called, occurs as long as the lobster continues to grow, but with decreased frequency as he becomes older. Those lobsters that survive man's traps and other perils can attain the respectable age of 15 years or more.

Lobstering is a commercial enterprise, although a few hardy amateurs may do it occasionally for pleasure. Commercial fishermen set traps on the ocean bottom in depths ranging from 10 or 20 ft. to as great as 200. They mark the trap positions with buoys. These traps—or pots, as they are commonly called—are usually fashioned from strips of wood or lath. Rectangular at their base, they are often arched above. The important detail is that they have a funnel-shaped opening through which the creatures can enter but which prevents their escape. Stones or bricks serve as anchors to keep the buoyant pots on the sea floor, and they can be baited with practically any kind of fish. Invading the territory of commercial lobstermen where they make a living can be dangerous business, and you had better be prepared to deal with an angry businessman.

Lobsters, as I said before, are primarily for eating purposes. Pretty expensive as bait, don't you think? Many seafood places keep their lobsters alive in tanks on display, where customers select the sizes they want. Mature lobsters are a dark greenish-blue or sometimes a reddish-brown. The smallest are nicknamed chicken lobsters, but it is illegal in most places to keep and sell youngsters weighing less than 1¼ lbs.

Broiled or in such gastronomic delights as lobster thermidor, this crustacean's edibility is too well known to require any further comments.

Clams

In the enormous mollusks division of the animal kingdom, clams are in a class labeled Pelecypoda, which means, literally, "hatchet foot." They have a far-flung distribution in the world's salt waters and are also found in fresh waters.

Clams, like their cousins the oysters, mussels and scallops, are compressed, soft-bodied animals with no head and are enclosed within two hard shells, in this case also called valves (hence they are called bivalves). Their shells are hinged and through contraction or relaxing of muscles are closed tightly or opened at will. Surrounding the clam's soft body is a mantle, or envelope, of protective tissue. It is the materials that are secreted by this mantle that help to form the outer shell. The shell's hinge, or umbo, is its oldest part, and outward from it curve the concentric lines of growth that can be counted to determine the owner's age. Clams are filter feeders and take in water through an incurrent siphon. With it come vital oxygen, planktonic organisms and the minute plants that nourish the creatures. It's because of this feeding system that mollusks can be dangerous in human consumption. They may take in toxic plankton or, in polluted areas, disease-causing agents. Contaminated mollusks have been known to cause hepatitis when eaten raw.

Clams are both eaten and used as bait, and some serve both purposes. Here's a rundown on some of the species commonly found in North America:

Hard clam

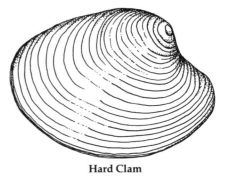

Hard Clam

This mollusk is a highly esteemed citizen of the Atlantic Coast from Maine to Florida, residing in sand and mud bottoms in shoal waters of bays, coves, sounds and other tidal areas. He lives just below the bottom's surface, into which he burrows with his single muscular "foot," in places where hard clams gather in beds or colonies. Hard clams grow faster than soft clams, and their thicker shells (reason for the "hard" in their common name) make them appreciably heavier. Their valves run from a shade of gray to off-white and inside are edged in purple-blue. Those most often seen are up to 3 in. across the longer axis.

Hard clams are harvested commercially by dredges and by hard-working diggers wielding long-handled tongs and rakes. Amateurs collect them in shallow water by scratching bottom with hoes or rakes or by treading—that is, walking slowly in waist-deep water and feeling for the clams with their toes.

At today's prices, fewer and fewer edible hard clams are being employed as bait, especially since another kind of hard-shell clam that I shall also discuss, the skimmer, is available. But hard-shell clams can be impaled on hooks in pieces for many kinds of marine sport fishes including cod, tautog, flounders, pollock, sea bass, scup or porgy, striped bass and croakers.

Hard-shelled clams are delicious eating, raw or cooked (in chowder or such delights as clams casino), but sizes are arbitrarily graded as a guide to table use. Largest are designated as "chowders," meaning that they're a bit too tough for eating raw on the half shell and so are minced for chowder. Next smallest are cherrystones, a size frequently offered on the half shell in restaurants. Next size downward in this flexible grading system is called littleneck. Quite small, these also are eaten raw on the half shell. Some diners favor them over cherrystones believing them to be more tender since they're the younger clams. I've lived by the sea all my life and have eaten clams since I first cut my teeth, but I never can detect any great difference in tenderness. Fact is, I prefer cherrystones because thay have more meat.

Soft or Steamer Clam

Soft or Steamer Clam

Also known as the steamer clam, long clam, nanny nose, long-neck clam, squirt clam and sand clam. The soft-shell is characterized by shells that are more narrowly oval and their long "neck," which is a siphon. The shells are light blue or whitish, and they grow up to 5 in. across their broad axis. They reside a few inches below the surface in sand or mud in intertidal zones. Distribution is from the Arctic Ocean to the latitude of North Carolina on the Atlantic seaboard and from British Columbia to central California on the Pacific Coast. Their prime use is as food.

Soft clams are harvested both commercially and by amateurs working tidal flats exposed at low water. They tend to burrow deeper than hard clams, but hoes or garden forks will excavate them. They can be located by small holes in the surface created by their siphon. Sometimes they betray their presence by squirting a little jet of water upward.

The favored cooking method is steaming, then serving with melted butter. The siphons, or necks, of steamers serve as convenient handles to lift them out of their shells. Greenhorns bite the clam off short of the siphon. This is a waste. The siphon is covered by a blackish skin, but this slips off easier than your socks and provides another tasty morsel.

I have a passion for steamers and have consumed them by the dozens, so it's extremely unlikely that I would use them for bait. Nevertheless, they do come in for that service. Usually the siphon is the part put on a hook because it's tougher than the rest of the clam. Its blackish skin is removed for better visibility. Soft-clam bait will take flounders, eels, tautogs, porgies, and other species that go for clams. They can also be utilized as chum by cracking their shells only enough to let body juices escape. When small, they can be impaled whole on a hook, shells and all, for species that eat shelled mollusks when no other fishes are available. But in my opinion, these are expensive bait and better in my mouth than a fish's.

Surf or Skimmer Clam

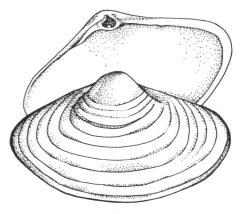

Surf or Skimmer Clam

From a sport fishing standpoint, one of the most important bivalves is the surf clam, more popularly known as the skimmer on the U.S. East Coast. Other aliases are ocean clam, hen clam and sea clam. They dwell a few inches deep in sand beds or colonies anywhere from just beyond a surf's breakers out to depths of 75 ft. Their range is from about Labrador to North Carolina, south of which they are replaced by a smaller cousin. The surf clam resembles the hard clam but grows larger, reaching 7 in. across, and its shell is thicker and heavier. The color is usually a shade of grayish white with tinges of light brown or dirty yellow.

You see the shells on ocean beaches and used as ashtrays.

Skimmers are taken commercially by dredges that dig into the ocean floor and dislodge the clams, passing them back to a collecting bag. As a conservation measure, some states require that a dredge be equipped with water jets, fed by a pump aboard the boat, to wash out the immature seed clams. Sometimes a receding tide after a storm at sea will partly expose some skimmers, but in bulk they're dredged for sale at bait stores. They are too tough to be eaten raw but can be finely minced for chowder, and their prime use is as bait and secondarily as chum. For skimmers' use as bait see "Terminal Tackle," Chapter 2.

Geoduck or "Gooey-duck" Clam

Geoduck or "Gooey-Duck" Clam

This is a Pacific coast bivalve, and it is not only large but also bizarre-looking. Its siphon, when fully extended, can be up to five or six times longer than the shells. Geoducks are basically dug for their edible portions, but pieces can be used as bait too.

Pismo Clam

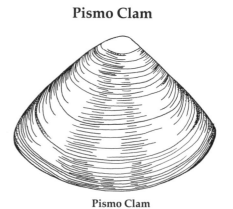

Pismo Clam

Named for California's Pismo Beach, the pismo is another Pacific Coast breed. Distribution is from about the latitude of San Francisco down to Mexico. Pismos resemble the Atlantic surf clam in configuration and also attain fair size, reaching up to 7 in. across the shells. Like skimmers, pismos have thick, heavy shells, although their color is a shade of brown with occasional narrow stripes that form patterns on the shells. They're gathered by various methods, all involving digging into sand beaches exposed at low tide or in waist-deep water. Rakes, hoes and garden forks are among the implements. Pismos are used for both food and bait. Such demands have been imposed upon them by this dual service that the state of California has enacted laws to protect them. State regulations must be consulted before clams are taken. Fines await violators.

Crabs

Crabs belong with the crustaceans, a gigantic zoological class that has thousands of different kinds of representatives in salt water, on land and in fresh water throughout the world. It's conceivable that not even zoologists know precisely how many different kinds of crabs share this planet with us.

Like lobsters, crayfish and other crustaceans, crabs have three rather definite body portions—head, thorax or trunk, and abdomen. The head and thorax are united as one and are covered by a single shell known as a carapace. Crabs, also like their other crusty relatives, wear an exoskeleton—literally, a skeleton on the outside of the body. This skeleton not only keeps body and soul together but also serves as a protective armor. As crabs approach maximum growth, this hard outer covering poses a problem, but nature solves it neatly by a process peculiar to the crustacean class. It's called molting and consists of shedding an outgrown shell and forming a new and larger one. A

crab may molt several times before reaching full growth. During molting, crabs are spoken of as shedders or peelers and while awaiting a new carapace, as soft-shell or softie.

Numerous species of crabs inhabit North American coastal waters, from Canada and Maine southward on the Atlantic seaboard and on around the Gulf Coast, as well as along the Pacific Coast and on up to Alaska. Some are edible and can also be used for bait (but expensive bait at today's prices), and others are just plain bait crabs.

Among the edible species are the giant king crabs of Alaskan waters, which you usually find canned or in frozen food departments or on restaurant menus, the stone crab, found in Florida and other southerly waters, and the famous blue crab, widely distributed from New England all the way down to and in the Gulf of Mexico. (It is reported also in scatterings as far north as Nova Scotia.) The blue is the best known crab in American waters.

Blue Crab

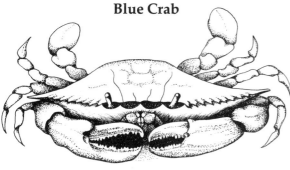

Blue Crab

Blueclaws, as blue crabs are also called, have a large fan club among recreational anglers, small kids to senior citizens. They're easily recognizable by their bluish-green carapace. Since they will accept almost any kind of meat, fish or animal, they can be taken by bottom fishing with a small loop of wire on which is strung the bait. Pieces of fish or beef, or whole small fishes such as silversides or mummichogs (killies) work well as bait. Great care is needed to bring them in, however, because blue crabs are wary and will release their claw hold on a bait if they become suspicious. A more popular and effective way to capture them is with a crab trap. This is a simple, square, cagelike device that is baited with pieces of fish, even fish heads, and lowered to the bottom. Wise bay anglers take along a crab trap and let it do its work while they rod-and-reel for finned game. Other anglers prefer a long-handled dip net that is designed just for crabbing. With careful looking, crabs can be spotted on the bottom in shallow water and sometimes clinging to pilings of bulkheads. Occasionally they are seen gliding with a current. Capturing them with a net isn't easy, as crabs are agile and water refraction is deceiving.

Be careful when you pick them up. Blue crabs are afraid of nothing and that includes you. Given a chance, they will nip you. Timid handlers can pick them up by dangling a piece of cloth in front of them and, when they seize it, quickly transferring them to a container. Veteran handlers grasp them at the rear of the carapace, between the swimmerets, or rear appendages, out of reach of the big front nipping claws.

Blue crabs can live for a time out of water, and keeping them alive assures freshness, flavor and safeness in eating. They must be protected from the sun and heat. A portable ice chest or a shaded box will do it. Ideally, they should be kept cool and moist with layers of wet seaweed or, in a pinch, wet newspapers. Soft-shell crabs should be kept separate to protect them from their hard-shell kin. In no case should they be too crowded, and it won't do any harm to keep the smaller apart from their big brothers. Otherwise the bigger ones may pick on the youngsters and kill them.

Blue crab is a delectable table item. A standard procedure is to put hard-shelled blue crabs in vigorously boiling, salted water and boil for about 20 minutes, covered. Some chefs tell me they add beer to the water, claiming it adds to the crabs' flavor. Personally, I could never taste the difference, but maybe it makes the crabs die happier. After cooking, we cool them and extract the delicately flavored meat with the aid of a nutcracker and pick. Right then and there we eat the meat as it comes from its donors or as the main ingredient of a seafood cocktail or salad.

Soft-shell blue crabs are prepared in an entirely different way. They're cleaned, deep-fried in fat about 375° F., big claws and all, then drained and served up with tartar sauce. Just thinkin' about fried softies makes me slobber.

Conservation note: Egg-bearing females should be returned to the water. They are not appetizing-looking anyway. Undersized crabs also should be released. Check on possible local or state minimum-size limits.

There are numerous crabs that see service as bait. Here are some of the species and their uses:

Lady or Calico Crab

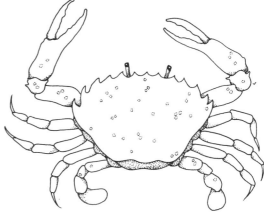

Lady or Calico Crab

These are found along sandy beaches and inlets from southern New England to the Gulf of Mexico. Characterized by an overall yellowish color and peppered with reddish or purple spots, they are best used in the shedder state but may also be rigged in the hard-shell state when small. They are a good surf-fishing bait and can be used in other methods. Lady crabs attract a number of species, including striped bass, tautog, weakfishes, channel bass and cod.

Fiddler Crab

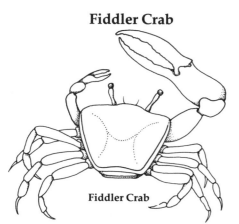

Fiddler Crab

Fiddlers are found on the Pacific and Atlantic coasts and are distinguished by one odd main claw that is grotesquely bigger than its mate. Usually this one big claw is removed, after which the hook is thrust into the opening left. Fiddlers are effective baits for practically any marine fishes whose diet includes crabs.

Hermit Crab

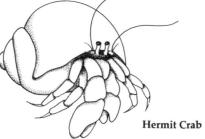

Hermit Crab

Like the fiddler, there are several species of hermits on the Pacific and Atlantic seaboards. They usually inhabit tide pools and shallow waters and often occupy the deserted shells of periwinkles, snails, moon and whelk shells. When used for bait, hermits are removed from their own shells, their large claws are removed, and they are impaled on a hook whole or, if too large, only the abdomen is used. They are effective for an assortment of marine battlers including bonefish, permits, tautogs and any other crab-eating species.

Ghost or Sand Crab

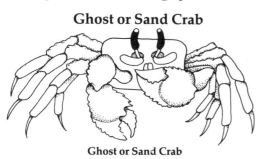

Ghost or Sand Crab

This crab is encountered along sandy beaches from New Jersey southward and can be offered to all fishes that include crab in their diets.

Green Crab

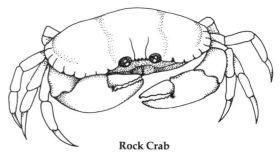

Green Crab

This little crab has a limited distribution, being more or less confined to a segment of the Atlantic Coast from Maine to New Jersey. He can be identified by the dark green color of his shell and is found in shallow water and pools. He's a favored bait for tautogs, preferably in the hard-shell state. Small ones can be impaled whole, large ones are cut into halves or quarters. The claws are generally removed first. The easiest way to get them is at a bait shop; but some anglers gather their own by luring them with chum of either crushed mussels or clams, or by a fish tied to a length of twine, whereupon they can be captured by dip net. In quantity they can be caught in a minnow trap or a similar contrivance of wire mesh with a funnel entrance. Traps can be baited with pieces of fish, whole dead fish, or crushed mussels or clams. Green crabs are hardy and will live out of water in a cool place for several days. As with blue crabs, it's a good idea to separate larger and smaller as well as peelers and hard-shells and for the same reasons.

Rock Crab

Rock Crab

Different species are often included in the general term "rock crabs" along the Atlantic and Pacific coasts. They favor rocky places and sometimes are partially buried in sand. They're also found in deeper waters. They're effective bait with any fish that has crab in his diet.

Crayfish

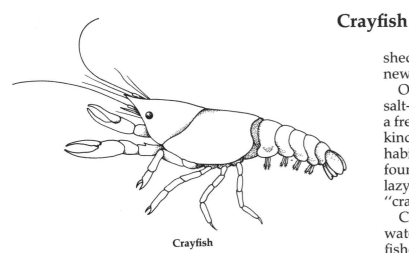

Crayfish

Crayfish belong to the enormous crustacean class, which also includes lobsters, crabs and shrimp. They are smaller but resemble their lobster relatives more than the other class members. Crayfish have only 10 appendages, the foremost pair being well-developed nipping claws. They also have a broad, flattened tail that serves as a sculling oar in locomotion. When they're startled, they seek safety with a rapid flexing of the abdomen, which works the oarlike tail. Like all crustaceans, they shed each growing shell when they need to form a new and larger one.

One big difference between the crayfish and his salt-water cousin, the lobster, is that the crayfish is a fresh-water resident. There are many different kinds of crayfish in North American waters, with habits varying from species to species. They're found in lakes, quiet ponds, moving streams and lazy rivers and have such regional nicknames as "crawdaddy," "crawfish" and "grass crab."

Crayfish are important to the ecology of fresh water by serving as food for several species of fishes, bass and trout among them. They also serve well as bait. Enterprising anglers catch their own. A simple method, but one that requires time and good reflexes, is to prowl a shallow stream, lifting rocks and hand-grabbing any that dart out. They're also hunted at night with a flashlight, since this is the time they feed and are moving about. Funnel-shaped traps baited with raw meat, set in shallow water, are used to catch them in number. Crayfish are good eating, but the problem is finding enough of them in edible sizes.

Mussels

Fishermen should be particularly careful about any mussels they gather for human consumption. To begin with, a mollusk should be of a known edible variety. Also important, they should be taken only from waters known certainly to be pollution-free.

Mussels reside in intertidal zones and, like most other mollusks, they're filter feeders. They take in water through an incurrent siphon, filter out vital oxygen and microscopic plankton food, and then expel the water through an excurrent siphon. Not very exciting but it works. It's this filter-feeding that can make ordinarily edible mollusks dangerous for human consumption. In polluted areas they may also take in any pathogenic or disease-causing organisms that might be in the area, accumulate them, and provide an unpleasant extra for anyone brash or innocent enough to eat them. Serious gastrointestinal disturbances and hepatitis have been traced to mollusks. Some mussels have become unfit to eat through the ingestion of organisms known as dinoflagellates, such as those which cause the so-called red tides that are lethal to fishes.

Mussels do us a couple of favors, which is very generous of them considering that it gets them killed. For marine anglers all along the coasts, they serve as both bait and chum, and for everyone, including anglers, they (the right kinds, that is) also serve as food.

Ribbed (Inedible) Mussel

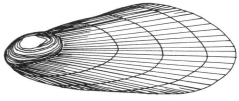

Ribbed (Inedible) Mussel

How can you distinguish between edible and inedible mussels? First of all, those used for bait and chum are considered inedible and usually have a bitter, strong, unpleasant flavor. Second, the shells of bait and chum mussels have ridges that radiate outward, giving them the common name ribbed mussels. Often these mussels are seen growing in clumps of different sizes along the banks of canals and tidal creeks. According to species, their shell colors are described variously as dark brownish, blackish-blue, etc. Some fishermen harvest their own supply; others buy them at bait stations and bayside rowboat liveries.

Edible Mussel

Edible Mussel

In contrast, edible mussels have smooth shells. Usually they are dark blue or violet outside, often bearing a thin layer of a horny substance, while inside they are a pearl color rimmed in dark blue or violet. Here again, enterprising individuals gather their own, twisting them free from their moorings by hand in shallow water or with clam tongs when the tide is up.

I cannot say often enough that amateur gatherers should avoid like the plague those areas where there is even a faint suspicion of pollution. Gatherers should stand warned also against taking mussels from colonies exposed at low tide in hot weather. Some could already be dead and dangerous to eat. Mussels, like clams and oysters, must be alive right up until the time of use, whether eaten raw or cooked. The same test holds for all three: when alive, they close their shells promptly when handled. If shells do not close

tightly, that mussel, clam or oyster is dead and should be discarded. Keep them for bait or chum if you want to but don't ever eat them. Incidentally, if they have been dead any length of time they are not the best bait or chum either, but can be used for crab traps and eelpots.

Three rules for preparation have been suggested for mussels of the edible variety: (1) Scrub each one thoroughly, using a stiff brush and frequent changes of water, to remove any mud, sand, bits of seaweed and other foreign matter clinging to them; (2) trim away any "beard" or fringe around the shells' edges; and (3) cook until their shells open; they're then ready to eat. Further cooking toughens them.

Cooking methods include simple steaming, like soft clams, as well as sauteeing in butter or deep-fat frying (after steaming, in both cases), and some fancier recipes that the French have conceived.

Fresh-water mussels, by the way, are generally considered to be inedible.

The old *r* rule that applies to oyster eating is a guide for edible mussels too. In case you've never heard of the rule, it states that all calendar months with an *r* in their names are good eating times, and that means fall, winter and spring. The reason for the *r* month bit is that these mollusks spawn from late spring into summer, during which time they become watery in consistency, unappetizing in appearance, and at their poorest for quality.

Oysters

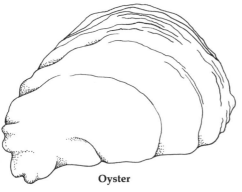

Oyster

The oyster is a bivalve and like its classmates the clams, scallops and mussels, it possesses two hard outer shells that are both home and armor. Other shared bivalve characteristics include a mantle or envelope of tissue enclosing the soft body, gills for breathing, a filter-feeding system to extract nutrients from the sea water, no brain or eyes but a primitive nervous system that reacts to stimuli and

activates the closing of the shell, and simplified versions of vital organs for circulation, digestion and reproduction.

In oysters, it's the mantle that produces those valuable, highly desirable ornaments we call pearls. A pearl begins as a grain of sand, or tiny irritant, that becomes lodged in the mantle or between mantle and outer shell. To counteract the foreign body, the mantle coats it in layer after layer of a pearly substance, actually calcium carbonate, to produce the iridescent gem more valued by humans than by its creator.

There are two marked external differences between oysters and other bivalves. One is in the shape of the shells; the other is in the shell surface. In oysters the shell shape can be described only as a kind of crude teardrop, while the shells of the cousins tend to be more round or oval. As for their surface, that of oysters is rough with an uneven texture, while the shells of most other bivalves are smooth or have small ridges.

The major difference between oysters and other bivalves is in locomotion. Clams move about slowly, and scallops are capable of short swimming excursions; but oysters and mussels stay put, attaching themselves to rocks or other firm surfaces.

The oyster's No. 1 value is as people food, and oystering is a big business. The best known U.S. species is the native eastern oyster, *Ostrea virginica*, found along the Atlantic Coast and rim of the Gulf of Mexico from New England to Texas. On restaurant menus eastern oysters are often referred to by the region from which they come—Blue Point (New York), Chesapeake (Maryland) or Cape Cod (Massachusetts). Also important is the native oyster of the Pacific seaboard, *Ostrea lurida*, or the Olympia oyster. Its overall distribution is from British Columbia to southern California, but its greatest region is Puget Sound in the state of Washington. Other oysters are the transplanted Japanese oyster, found also in U.S. West Coast waters, and the so-called tree oyster, named for its habit of attaching itself to the roots of mangrove trees in the South.

Oysters can be presented in a variety of ways that include delicious oyster stew, fried, poached, minced in fritters, and in creations such as angels on horseback (skewered), soufflé, oysters casino, and croquettes Normandy. With frying and oyster stew as close seconds, the best known presentation is probably on the half shell, raw in their own liquid. However, there are two schools of thought on the latter, the enthusiastic and the no-thank-you plus a few in-betweens. It's all a matter of taste. The legendary eater Diamond Jim Brady reportedly ate a couple of dozen *before* breakfast.

It's a tradition that oysters be eaten only during months with the letter *r* in their name—September through April, in other words. The reasons usually given for sticking to those months is that oysters may be spawning at the other times, and during which period their meat is inferior in flavor and watery-looking.

In any event, oysters should be eaten only when absolutely fresh, and under no circumstances from polluted or doubtful waters.

Oystering is a commercial enterprise, as I've already pointed out, but at times amateurs have gone out to harvest their own. You can extract oysters from their beds by hand or with tongs, but be sure you don't run afoul of the law or an irate oyster farmer. By and large oysters are shallow-water residents occurring at depths ranging from a few feet to perhaps 50. As a group they have a wide tolerance of salinity and water temperatures. They favor bays and sounds for colonization and brackish areas where the saltiness is cut by fresh water from rivers. The locations in which they are harvested have much to do with their flavor and nutritional value. All of this, of course, is the result of diet. In certain locales, if they eat minute plants to excess, they take on the plant color. Mostly the color—green or brown—is confined to the gills, but sometimes the entire body is tinted. It does not render the oyster inedible. What is more of a concern (as it is with other bivalves) is any unseen disease-causing organisms that might be ingested in polluted areas. And make sure your oysters are fresh at all times!

The consumption of oysters is traditionally credited with boosting humans' lovemaking powers, but so far this has been reported exclusively among males, and until supported more substantially, it must be suspected of lying in the realm of imagination or wishful thinking. In any case, it hasn't done the oyster trade any harm.

The question has arisen, "Can oysters be used as bait?" The answer is yes. As such, they have been employed for a number of bottom fishes such as flounders and tautogs. Presumably any species that respond to clam bait would also find oysters tempting. The big drawback to an oyster as bait is that it is fragile and difficult to keep on a hook. Conceivably, oysters could also be used as chum, minced like clams. But that brings up another big drawback. You guessed it—cost. At today's prices it would be unbelievably expensive. So unless you have the ambition and locales for gathering your own, you'd better stay with the likes of mussels and surf skimmer clams.

Scallops

Scallops are represented by species in both the Pacific and Atlantic oceans, and the characteristic shape of their roundish, ridged shells has become a famous decorating design throughout the world.

Scallops are bivalve mollusks (two shells), a characteristic shared by the Pelecypoda class to which they belong, along with clams and oysters. The shells of the scallop are on an elastic hinge and are activated by the muscle. Relaxing the muscle allows the shell to open. Contracting it closes the shells tightly. In the case of scallops, it is this muscle that is a highly prized—and highly priced —item in seafood markets and restaurants. In the case of clams and oysters, there is no such discrimination.

Scallops and their cousins in this zoological class have no heads, but they do possess light-sensitive receptors, or "eyes," around the edge of the membranous envelope that encloses the body.

Bay Scallop

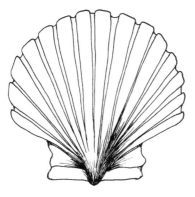

Bay Scallop

Two species of scallop figure prominently in the market. One is the so-called bay scallop, which has a maximum width of about 2 in. and grows in a grayish-tan shell. Its distribution runs from about Cape Cod, Mass., to Cape Hatteras, N.C., and has a small similar relative that is distributed from there on down to Florida.

Sea Scallop

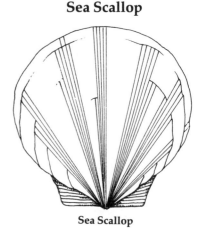

Sea Scallop

The other well-known species is the sea scallop, larger than the bay variety and sometimes attaining dimensions up to 5 in. It inhabits a reddish-brown shell and is found from about opposite the St. Lawrence River to Florida.

Many seafood fanciers favor bay scallops over sea scallops, claiming that they are more tender, more delicately flavored. Maybe so. But I've eaten my weight several times over in both kinds; and while I might favor bay scallops over the other, I could never see a vast difference—at least not enough to merit the marked difference in prices. All are the finest kind of eating.

Scallops probably would be as effective as clams for bait but at their market price, and eatin' quality, never!

Scalloping is a commercial industry. Years ago, individuals (properly licensed where required) used to gather their own scallops, but you rarely, if ever, hear about that anymore.

Shrimps

I respectfully propose that we all rise for a moment in standing tribute to shrimps. As a group, few noted creatures serve man in so many important ways. They unselfishly allow themselves to be devoured by a huge assortment of fishes that in turn provide man with rod-'n'-reel recreation. Shrimps, too, are excellent bait and chum. And they also grace man's dinner table and are delectable seafood—deep-fried, in a curry sauce, in salads, cocktails and sandwiches.

Since few amateurs go after shrimps, I'm going to dwell here on the importance of shrimps as bait.

Zoologists catalogue shrimps with the class of animals labeled Crustacea. With them in this gigantic group are their cousins the prawns, along with crabs, lobsters, crayfish and other forms. There are many kinds of shrimps, both salt- and fresh-water, found all over the world in a range of climes from boreal to tropical. Numerous species are encountered along the North American coast. And, as you might anticipate, they come in a wide span of sizes. In salt water there are little marine forms, collectively called krill, that are less than an inch long and provide food for whales. In contrast are mantis shrimp, which reach lengths of almost 12 ins. There's a similarly wide size range among fresh-water species. Many are very small, but one kind, with the scientific name *Macrobrachium*, grows to about a foot.

Edible Shrimp

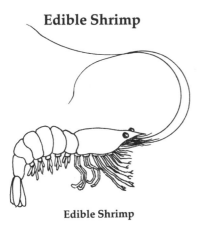

Edible Shrimp

Your standard shrimp consists of two main sections. The front section contains the head, or cephalothorax, along with the eyes and mouth parts and five pairs of walking legs. The second section is the abdomen, commonly called the tail, and it also carries five pairs of walking legs, which gives the shrimp a total of 20 legs in all.

The color varies considerably among different species. There are white shrimp, brown-colored shrimp, and a species known as royal red characterized by a pinkish color and probably familiar to most people. This so-called pink shrimp, for example, varies in color in different regions. It's light brown on the Atlantic Coast, pink in another area, and sometimes yellow in the Gulf of Mexico.

One shrimp used for bait is commonly called grass shrimp and is found in bays along temperate segments of the U.S. Atlantic Coast. These shrimps are too small to eat but are used as bait and chum for such finned game as weakfish. Enterprising anglers seine their own along the shores of bays.

I'd like to say they're not for eating, but maybe I should qualify that with a little story. As a boy, I was hand-seining a bay shore with a friend when a grizzled old bayman approached us and, holding up a grass shrimp, asked, "Ever eat these?" He told us they were good. "Eat 'em alive," he advised, "like this," and with that he seized one and bit it off just behind the head. Not to be "chicken," we followed suit. To this day I don't know whether the elderly stranger was pulling our leg. Those shrimp were nothing but shell, legs and salt.

Sand Shrimp

Sand Shrimp

Small species, such as the so-called grass shrimp and another kind commonly known as sand shrimp, should be impaled whole on a hook. With larger species, the live shrimp should be hooked carefully—there are slender-wire hooks especially designed for live baits. They can be impaled through the hard shell, just behind the head so long as vital organs, which are visible as a small, dark area inside the body, are avoided. Large shrimp can also be cut in half to make two baits. Anglers use dead shrimp sold in packages for that purpose.

When chumming with live shrimp, you'll find a problem in keeping them from scattering. The usual procedure is to pinch them, not enough to kill them, but enough to discourage their straying. If you use frozen shrimp, thaw them beforehand or otherwise ice crystals will make them buoyant and impair their distribution.

Local bait depots, notably around bays, sell small live shrimp for bait and chum. Many anglers prefer the live form because of the added attraction of their movement.

In some bays it may be possible to capture supplies of small shrimp for bait by using a small seine or a dip net in very shallow waters close to the beach. Sometimes night is the best time—with a light, of course.

As pointed out elsewhere when discussing individual species, there are number of fish that respond to shrimp bait, including young bluefish, red drum or channel bass, bonefish, snook, Pacific Coast rockfishes, spotted seatrout, king mackerel, striped bass, ladyfish and crevalles.

16. <u>Secrets of the</u> <u>Culinary Department</u>

I never cease to be surprised at the numbers of anglers who do not eat their catches. In some cases there's a dislike of fish as food. Those fishermen would rather catch 'em than eat 'em. In other instances, though, there are anglers who do not eat their catches simply because they either are not fully aware of the species' edibility or perhaps do not know how to prepare them for the table. What follows is a kind of general guide to both of these details, a lead-in to what I hope will be your exploration of seafood cookbooks.

Cleaning & Cutting

A handy device for scaling, filleting, etc. of small fishes is a fish cutting board. (It resembles an office clipboard.) At one end is a strong, spring-powered clamp that holds the tail securely while "surgery" is performed.

Special general note about fin removal: The tail is amputated after it has served as a convenient handle. The easiest way to remove other fins is to shear or cut them off close to the body, but this leaves some bone in both the dorsal and anal fins. Make a cut on each side of these fins just deep enough so that both fins and bones can be cut free and lifted out.

Scaling

Tip: If you must scale your fish in the house, have the fish underwater in a sink or suitable pan. It will prevent scales from flying all over and decorating ceilings, walls, curtains, etc.

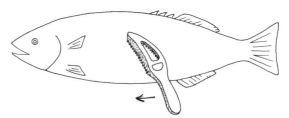

Grasp fish firmly by the tail and work "against the grain" from the tail to head. Be sure to get scales right alongside fins. An inexpensive scaler works well. In a pinch, use a dull knife or a soupspoon. There's also an electric scaler.

Gutting

For an "operating table" lay down several layers of newspapers. These will protect any surface and keep slime and other gunk from getting all over the place. Newspapers also provide ready wrappings for the guts to be discarded

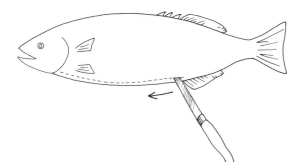

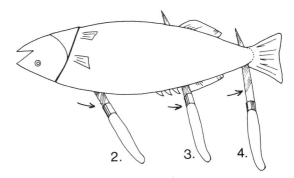

Gutting is simple. More difficult is overcoming the laziness to get at the chore. Surgery consists of making a lengthwise cut with a sharp knife into the body cavity along the midline of the underside. Pull entrails out and discard. Check cavity for pockets of blood, especially along the backbone. Remove them with a knife point. They're potential spoilage sites. Caution: Certain entrails are poisonous to humans and fatal to pets. Play it safe and

Place knife blade more or less flat against backbone. Using a slight sawing motion, cut toward the tail until fillet is freed (Step 4). Remove any fine rib bones remaining on both sides of fillet.

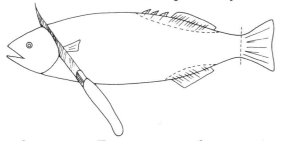

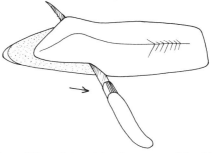

throw them away. To prevent spoilage, gutting is usually the first step in dressing fish for the table, so the head is still on. In warm weather, it's advisable to remove head and gills as spoilage can start there. Note: With some small species, flounders and soles are examples, most of the entrails come free with the head.

To skin: Lay fillet skin side down and hold firmly at tail end. Cut, using same sawing motion as when filleting, between meat and skin as close as possible so as not to waste meat.

Filleting

Gutting and other dressing are unnecessary when filleting. Scaling depends on whether or not skin is to be left on fillets. It is a matter of taste, but on some species the skin should be removed or it will impart an unpleasant flavor.

Steaking

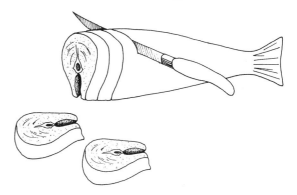

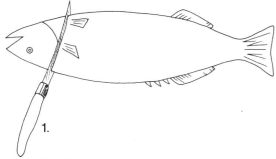

Hold fish firmly. With a sharp knife, cut downward at a slight angle just behind pectoral fin. Cut down to, but not through, backbone.

Some fishes, like salmon, swordfish and halibut, are customarily steaked. Others may be steaked specifically for barbecuing or broiling. Still others are cut into steaks for the reason that they're too damn big to be prepared any other way. Preliminary steps are scaling, gutting and removal of head and fins as previously shown. A steaking knife must be very sharp. Cut through the backbone with it; sometimes a sharp butcher's knife will do it. On some backbones you may need a cleaver or butcher's saw. Cut steak to desired thickness.

Coping with Oily Fish

There are many oily fishes, such as mackerels, bluefish and tuna, and they will spoil rapidly in warm weather. Such catches should be refrigerated as soon as possible. By rights you should also gut oily (and any) fish promptly after bringing them in. This further helps to prevent spoilage. Mates on charter and party boats will do it for you (it earns them a tip), or you can do it yourself on the way back to the dock. While you're at it, remove the head and gills at the same time for the same reason. The gills, especially, can be a site of spoilage.

Diners who find fish oil objectionable can take some of it out during cooking. One method broils the meat to eliminate excessive oil. First cut lengthwise slits on the underside of the fish. Then put the fish on the broiling rack, and the collection pan below the broiler rack will take the oil runoff that comes from the slits in the fish.

Handling Shark Meat

The meat of sharks has never gained popularity on American plates. Shark meat is good eating, in my opinion, so I have to assume that the fear of sharks and a widespread but erroneous belief that practically all of them are man-eaters have prevented any real consumption of shark meat in the U.S.

Sharks are a vast, largely untapped source of food. The meat is white, firm and devoid of bones. Best of all, it can be turned into palate-pleasing concoctions by any of several methods—baking, broiling or barbecuing as steaks, in chowder, fish cakes, fried, as fish sticks, in fish 'n' chips, smoked, and as the main ingredient of a seafood cocktail or salad.

At present, only a comparatively few species are known to be edible. Among those are the blue shark, mako, porbeagle, thresher, some species of dogfishes (mistakenly called "sand sharks") and the terrible-tempered white shark.

Some important tips on transporting shark meat:

1. If the carcass's skin is left intact, shark meat generally will keep throughout a fishing day back to the dock.

2. Once a shark is butchered, the meat must go under some kind of refrigeration as soon as possible. If not, it will spoil quickly. Avoid rough handling that might bruise the meat, which can also contribute to spoilage.

3. For car trips from the dock to home it should be carried in iced bags. Large plastic bags are sold on many coastal sport fishing docks. Put one inside the other. Place the shark meat in the inside bag, then pack shaved ice around it in the outer bag. That way the water from the melting ice won't soak the meat.

4. Don't carry the bags in a car trunk, where temperatures can reach 130 ° F. in summer.

5. Get extra ice, if needed, on the trip home.

6. At home immediately transfer the meat to an electric refrigerator or freezer.

7. Shark meat should be eaten as soon as possible after catching, for optimum texture, flavor and safety.

I've eaten shark meat many times—makos, principally, because they're the best, and I make it a rule to keep it under ordinary refrigeration no longer than one day or two after catching, no more than a day in the case of blue shark. In a refrigerator's frozen-food compartment shark meat—except that from blue sharks and similarly quick-spoiling species—might last safely for several days, and much longer if properly wrapped and placed in a regular deep-freeze unit. Fact is, not enough shark meat has been consumed yet to amass sufficient data on the maximum length of time it can be stored safely. Meanwhile, play it safe and eat it no more than one or two days after catching, and don't ever store it in metal containers.

If shark meat starts to go bad, you'll know all about it by the scent. Because it contains a lot of nitrogen, shark flesh develops an ammonia smell when it's spoiling, and it can be strong enough to make your necktie go up and down like a shade. As with any kinds of fish, if you're ever in doubt about the state of shark meat, throw it out.

Edibility & Tips on Preparation

The following comments cover the edibility of the popular salt- and fresh-water species profiled in this volume. I've also added some tips on preparation.

Amberjack

Amberjacks are edible, have even been called tasty, but are not commonly eaten by U.S. fishermen.

American Eel

Eels are good eating when fried, smoked, pickled in aspic, or as a base for fish chowder.

American Shad

A good shad run provides a fine opportunity to stock the home larder. Although the roe is a great delicacy when fried and more publicized than the meat, the latter is very tasty too. As often criticized, shad are indeed bony, but that's a small price to pay for delectable eating.

Arctic Char

A good eating fish. Smoked, it's a gourmet item.

Atlantic Cod

There are several tasty fish dishes that a cook can fashion from the humble cod. They can be filleted or cut into steaks, then broiled or baked with or without sauces. Codfish cakes, finnan haddie and fish chowder are three other delicious dishes, and creamed codfish on toast is a delight. My wife sometimes simmers or poaches the fish, then flakes it after it is cool and serves it on a bed of lettuce as a seafood cocktail. Small cod, called scrod, are good eating as well. For some reason New Englanders gave small cod the nickname scrod, and as such you'll find them listed on menus and in markets. They usually weigh about 5 to 6 lbs. Scrod can be baked whole—after dressing, of course.

Atlantic Croaker

Their meat is white, firm and flavorful. There are numerous species of croakers on the Atlantic, Gulf and Pacific seaboards, all of them considered edible. They're mostly small and usually are scaled and prepared as panfishes. Larger ones are filleted or prepared whole for baking. Methods also include broiling.

Atlantic Mackerel

Atlantic mackerel are a fine food fish if you like the oily type. Diners who find oil objectionable can render out much of it during broiling by cutting lengthwise slits on the underside and placing a collecting pan underneath. Like other oily fish, mackerel will spoil rapidly in warm weather if not kept iced during transport and promptly refrigerated. They scale easily, and fin removal is no problem.

Atlantic Permit

This fish is a pompano, and pompanos are rated as good food fishes. Permits usually are filleted and skinned and any dark meat is trimmed away. The fish is variously baked, broiled or fried, according to tastes.

Atlantic Sailfish

I've heard it said that fresh-caught sailfish can be prepared like other fishes, but I've also heard that it's inferior to other fishes when prepared. Generally, it's smoked.

Atlantic Salmon

Like the Pacific salmons, this superb game fish is very good eating. According to sizes, they can be filleted or steaked and cooked by various methods which include poaching and broiling.

Barracudas

The question of eating barracudas in general is a controversial one. Many local fishermen flatly state that they're poisonous and won't touch them with fork and knife. Others eat them freely. I've never been able to get a definite answer from anglers and skippers in areas where 'cudas are caught extensively. There's a dietary theory that appears to have substance. It's known that at times in certain areas barracudas devour quantities of reef species —puffers, triggerfish, parrotfish and others— whose internal organs, notably liver and gonads, contain poisonous substances. The theory suggests that these toxins may accumulate in barracuda flesh. If true, the larger the 'cuda, the greater the danger from fish poisoning. Only trouble there's no external sign to warn of it. So much for the red side of the ledger. I've eaten barracuda on several occasions in seafood restaurants in Key West, Fla. It was delicious. Once, while trolling for marlin off Puerto Rico, a 'cuda attacked one of our fish baits. The mate, a *Puertoriqueño*, reeled in the attacker, disappeared below with it under his arm, and emerged with paper plates heaped with small steaks grilled in the galley. It was some of the most delicious fish I've ever enjoyed.

Black Drum

The smallest ones up to 12 or 15 lbs. are favored for the table. The meat tends to become coarser and less flavorful with the larger size. Note: Black drums have a reputation for being infested with parasites. These organisms are believed to be harmless to humans, and thorough cooking should kill them. But, if in doubt, don't eat the fish.

Black Bullhead

Very tasty on a plate. See notes on preparations of catfishes.

Black Marlin

In Japan marlins are an ingredient in "fish sausage." I'm told that the meat is white and delectable, either cooked or raw. I've fished for black marlin out of Cairns, Australia, but residents there don't seem to eat the fish.

Black Perch or Black Surfperch

These Pacific Coast fish have more meat for their size than others in the surfperch family and are good eating. Large ones should be filleted. Small ones are delicious cleaned, scaled and pan-fried.

Black Sea Bass

Black sea bass are delicious, up among the best finned seafood in my opinion. The meat is white, firm, delicately flavored. Small sea bass are best prepared for cooking by gutting, skinning and removal of head and fins. Shear off the fins close to the body. The dorsal fin can be removed by "running," that is, by making two parallel cuts, one on either side, close, then lifting out the dorsal fin and

its attached bones and cutting them free. Dress larger fish in a smiliar manner. Whole sea bass can be baked, and the larger ones also can be filleted and cooked by any method you like. Some people grumble about the number of bones, but this is a minor complaint considering the good eating. Besides, after yanking the poor fish out of his happy home and carving him up for the table, it's not nice to begrudge your victim a skeleton. In any case, sea bass are a gastronomic delight. I personally like them baked whole, served with a boiled potato and plenty of salt and pepper.

Blue Catfish

For years fishermen tended to disdain the blue cats and catfishes in general. It's suspected that this was largely due to the critters' appearance, especially those fleshy whiskers decorating the snout, chin and corners of the mouth. There's also the fact that they're scaleless, so feel more slimy to touch. That aversion is abating. As Southerners and Midwesterners knew all along, catfishes are among the finest eating of fresh-water produce. Blue catfish in a stew or fried is very good indeed.

Bluefin Tuna

Bluefin tuna are edible and are prepared in various ways by home chefs. I prefer to leave cooking and canning to professionals. Any home-canned tuna that I've eaten was too strong for my taste, probably because the dark meat was left in.

Bluefish

Blues are a natural for the table, but be advised they're an oily fish. If this is objectionable, you might try the oil-draining cooking method suggested for mackerel. They can be prepared by any of the standard seafood cooking procedures. Baking whole is a favorite of mine; some home chefs add stuffing. Blues can also be cooked as fillets or steaks. I happen to favor blues of about 2 to 5 lbs. for dining because the larger ones are apt to have a somewhat stronger flavor. Best of all, in my opinion, are pan-fried baby blues, or "snappers," as they're called, fresh out of the water. They make an excellent beach barbecue, cooked over a charcoal or driftwood fire.

Bluegill

The popular bluegill, a fresh-water sunfish, is among those species classified as panfishes because their sizes readily lend them to frying-pan cookery. See Panfishes, page 275.

Blue Marlin

Blue marlin are eaten in some foreign countries including Peru and Chile. The Japanese reportedly make sausage from them. But they haven't found acceptance as a table item in the U.S. Anglers who have chomped on blue marlin steaks have pronounced them delicious. I can't vouch for that, but it's suspected that know-how in preparation is a must. If the meat were to be smoked and turn out as good as smoked white marlin, it would be a delicacy. There's an experiment for you! All you have to do is catch a blue marlin.

Blue Shark

These sharks are edible, but the threat of spoilage is greater than among other species. Once a carcass has been opened, butchering must be completed and the meat placed under refrigeration as soon as possible. That includes icing down for any transport.

Bonefish

Bonefish usually are considered inedible because of their numerous bones. Actually the meat is firm and flavorful although it contains fat and many small bones after filleting.

Bonito

Bonitos are bloody fishes, like their relatives the tunas, and this contributes to a stronger taste in home preparation. Commercial canning not only produces white meat but also establishes a mild flavor. If a strong fish taste is objectionable, it can be lessened in home preparation a bit by gutting and bleeding soon after catching. Some home chefs bleach the meat by soaking in salted water, even milk. Light rinsing in salted water for a few minutes also helps, it's said.

For those anglers who like a gamy fish taste, here are two methods of preparation. The first comes from Gertrude Marinaccio, wife of charter skipper Carm Marinaccio. Her formula is to gut the fish and remove the scales, after which it can be steaked (cut crosswise into slabs of desired thickness) or filleted. If it's to be steaked, remove all fins. As much blood as possible should be removed before cooking by placing the steaks or fillets in cold salted water with a piece of ice for at least three hours to bleach them. When removed, drain and blot any excess water, after which they can be baked or pressure-cooked. Gertrude does the latter for 45 minutes, then cools the meat, breaks it into small pieces for salad, and stores in containers in the deep freeze.

The second recipe comes from my friend Ed Migdalski and can be adapted to any bonito. Ed eviscerates the fish, lops off its head, removes the skin. Then he fillets it, placing the pieces in a clean pail or dishpan with plenty of salt and tap water. Let fish stand for an hour or two while the solution bleaches out the blood. Remove from brine, drain, take up excess moisture with a damp cloth, sprinkle thoroughly with table salt, let stand overnight. Broil well, basting the fillets with melted butter and lemon or hot bacon fat. Decorate with bacon strips and baste with melted butter.

Brook Trout

They're a fine table fish and can be cooked by any of the standard methods of preparing seafood. They're also good as a main ingredient in a chowder and are a delicacy when smoked. See Rainbow Trout, page 275.

Brown Bullhead

Hot from a frying pan, brown bullheads are really good eating! Bullheads are in the catfish family, and like catfishes, should be skinned before cooking.

Brown Trout

It's a matter of taste, but for edibility brownies are usually farther down on the list than other trouts. Small brownies can be gutted and beheaded (be sure to remove gills, too), and then they can be pan-fried, baked or poached. Brown trout also can be split and broiled. The bigger brown trout can be filleted or steaked, then baked, broiled or poached.

Cabezone

Fresh cabezone meat has a startling bluish-green appearance that turns white on cooking and belies the fact that this is an excellent food fish. Chiefly it is prepared by skinning, filleting and frying in deep fat, since the meat has a tendency to fall apart when baked or broiled. *Warning:* Do not—repeat *do not*—eat the roe of cabezone. It's poisonous and will cause violent illness.

Calico Surfperch

See Black Perch or Black Surfperch (page 270) for culinary suggestions.

California Yellowtail

Yellowtails are good eating, fresh or smoked. When preparing for frying or broiling, a West Coast friend of mine suggests that the flavor is improved by removing a fairly thick layer of dark oily meat lying just under the skin along the middle of each side. I agree but I must add for some diners this is a matter of taste.

Carp

Carp have been a highly fancied table fish for centuries in Europe. Cassiodorus, a sixth century Roman writer, observed: "The ordinary man may eat what opportunity affords him; on the princely table belong such rare delicacies as the carp which lives in the Danube." Carp have never attained such table popularity in the U.S., however, although quantities are sold in large metropolitan areas. Small ones are favored and can be prepared for the table in a variety of ways. Skinning is suggested. Larger carp tend to be coarse, but their meat is used for fish cakes and fish chowder.

Chain Pickerel

The meat of chain pickerel is fine grained, flavorful. The chief objection is the bones. Baking, with skinning beforehand, is one culinary procedure. In another method the fish is filleted and the skin left on.

Channel Bass (Red Drum, Redfish)

They're edible, but the meat becomes coarser and less palatable in larger drums. They're at their best for eating when weighing no more than 7 or 8 lbs., to 12 lbs. tops; and the smaller the better. The larger redfish are edible only as fish cakes or in a chowder.

Channel Catfish

When I was fishing a South Carolina river once at lunchtime, our guide produced a skillet and fixin's. He got a fire started, then deftly cleaned, skinned and filleted a couple of "cats." Let it be said that few fishes, before or since, have tasted as good as that fried catfish! All catfish should be skinned.

Catfishes can be filleted and baked and Southern catfish stew is out of this world!

China Rockfish

They bring good prices in fresh-fish markets, which is testimony to their edibility.

Chinook or King Salmon

According to fishes' sizes and consumers' tastes, chinook salmon are filleted or steaked and broiled, poached or baked.

Ciscoes

Ciscoes are good eating, fresh or smoked.

Cobias

Cobias are a fine food fish, known for their delicate flavor, when prepared by any of the standard culinary methods. Cobias must be skinned. They can be filleted or steaked, fried, broiled or baked. They're good smoked, too.

Coho Salmon

Cohos are excellent eating. They're at their very best when ocean-caught and eaten fresh, broiled, baked or barbecued. Cohos can also be smoked. They're also put in cans, but canned coho isn't in the same league with fresh fish.

Corbina

Grouped with the whitings, the California corbina (with a *b*) is rated as a high-quality table fish. The meat is light, finely grained and mildly flavored. Deep-fried corbina fillets rate with the best of finned fish on a plate.

Corvinas

If you like weakfish, you'll probably enjoy this relative. Their flesh is white, mild, fine-textured. Preparations include scaling and filleting or baking whole. In South America they pickle corvinas.

Crappies

Their meat is sweet and flaky, I'm told, but tends to become soft in hot weather.

Crevalle

Many anglers pronounce these jacks unfit for eating, criticizing the meat for its dark streaks or as being coarse and without flavor. Others call the smaller specimens passable, but take a raincheck on the larger ones. Bleeding immediately after capture—amputating the tail is one procedure—is said to help the flavor. Suggested preparation: (1) Fillet and skin; (2) Cut fillets into halves, lengthwise; (3) Remove streaks of red meat and any remaining bones. Broil or fry fillets or boil and cool for seafood salad.

Cutthroat Trout

They're a fine table fish, readily prepared by any of the standard methods—frying, baking, broiling, etc. Smoked, they're a delicacy.

Dolly Varden

Many anglers enjoy the added bonus of the good flavor of this char, a Western relative of the trouts. I've never tried them myself, but the pink to reddish flesh is said to be very tasty when prepared by any of the trout recipes.

Dolphin

For years I caught dolphin and heard about their edibility but just didn't get around to sampling it. Some said it was out of this world. Finally I did get to eat dolphin. It was very good but not the "best eating fish in the sea," as some fanciers have exclaimed. Maybe the dolphin couldn't live up to its billing—in my opinion.

Flathead Catfish

Very edible indeed. See notes on other species of "cats" and bullheads.

Fluke or Summer Flounder

Nature doesn't offer much better seafood dining than fresh—repeat—*fresh* fluke. The meat is snow-white, firm, sweet, deliciously flavored—with no strong fishy taste. Filleting is the usual preparation, which eliminates gutting, beheading and fin removal. The skin can be left after scaling on the fillets or removed, according to taste, after which the slabs of meat can be fried, baked or broiled. Small fluke, too thin to be filleted, can be cooked whole after dressing by frying or baking. Like all flatfishes, fluke have many thin bones, but on a plate most of the skeletal system can be lifted free with a fork.

Fresh-Water Basses

Basses' flesh is usually white, firm, without excessive fat and variously fine to coarse-grained, depending upon species and ages. Small ones are scaled, cleaned and pan-fried. Larger ones are scaled and baked whole, or filleted and skinned. *Note:* Some of the bigger basses, notably largemouths, have an objectionable flavor described as being "like mud" (whatever that tastes like). It's believed that any objectional taste is related to environment and can be eliminated by skinning.

Grass and Redfin Pickerels

Pickerel meat is white, finely textured and very tasty, but their seemingly endless supply of small bones discourages many diners. Angling writer Vic Dunaway suggests this procedure: (1) Fillet the fish, leaving the skin on (scales are small and difficult to remove; veteran anglers usually skip scaling, unless they have one of those electric scalers). (2) Place the fillets on a cutting board, skin side down and slash each one several times from end to end with a sharp knife. The idea is to cut the bones into even smaller pieces. Avoid cutting through the skin, otherwise the fillets will fall apart. (3) Fillets then can be cut into serving-size pieces and deep-fried.

Green Sunfish

Some folks like this panfish; others don't. You have to be the judge. See Bluegill, page 270, for some notes.

Grunts

Grunts are small fishes. They rate as tasty panfish. Some are cleaned, scaled and pan-fried whole. Larger ones are scaled and filleted or baked whole.

Gulf Flounder

The smaller Gulf flounder tastes like its kissing cousins, southern and summer flounders, which I find delicious. See notes under Fluke or Summer Flounder.

Haddock

Smoked haddock is better known as the ingredient of finnan haddie. To those who really relish seafood, haddock is among the favorites.

Hakes

They're quite edible. Some anglers pronounce them good. They're perhaps best in fish cakes, since the meat is soft. For the same reason, they have poor keeping quality.

Hickory Shad

Hickories are edible although said to be inferior to American shad. They can be cooked fresh or can be smoked or pickled.

Kelp Bass

These sporty little fish are good on a plate too. They can be filleted and skinned for frying, broiling or barbecuing, be the main ingredient in fish chowder, or be dressed for baking whole.

King Mackerel

They're rated as good to excellent eating, depending upon who's doing the munching. As in all mackerels, the meat is oily. The largest are usually steaked. Small ones can be cooked in the same way as other mackerels.

Kokanee

This salmon rates high in edibility; but since their flesh tends to be oily, they can spoil very quickly without refrigeration.

Ladyfish and Tenpounder

Numerous bones dent this fish's popularity.

Lake Trout

Lake trout are excellent eating and can be prepared by any of the standard fish cookery methods as well as by smoking.

Lake Whitefish

Along with cousins lake cisco and mountain whitefish, this fish is very good eating. Scaled, whitefish are pan-fried, broiled, baked and smoked. They can be filleted.

Landlocked Salmon (Quananiche)

Landlocked salmon have a high rating as a table fish. They can be filleted, then poached or broiled.

Mako Shark

Mako meat is good eating. It's firm, white and not at all gamy. In my opinion, broiled mako steaks are the equal of swordfish, if not better. (All sharks, lacking bones, are easy to butcher and cut into steaks.) Smoked mako is a treat. As with all shark meat destined for table use, mako should be placed under refrigeration immediately after butchering.

Mountain Whitefish

They're rated passable to good when eaten fried, and according to tastes. But most eaters agree that they are very tasty indeed when smoked. See Lake Whitefish.

Muskellunge

Muskies are considered good eating by regulars. Preparations include: scaling, skinning (optional), filleting, steaking and cutting into chunks. Baking is a popular cooking method.

Mutton Snapper

With their white, firm meat, mutton snappers are excellent eating—baked, broiled or cooked, by whatever method.

Northern Pike

Northern pike can be prepared in the same ways as Pickerels, see page 273, but it is very bony.

Northern Porgy (Scup)

Porgy meat is excellent. Only trouble is, they're tough to scale. (Don't ever try to give undressed porgies to anyone who knows them.) Porgies must be scaled or skinned. Dipping them briefly in boiling water beforehand helps a bit in scaling. In the long run, you'll be doing yourself and conservation a favor if you return any small fish to the water, alive and unhurt. The bigger porgies are better for home consumption because they can be filleted and skinned, which is easier than scaling.

Pacific Flounders, Soles and Halibuts

All members of this group are highly edible. Their meat is white, delicately flavored and quite firm. Only sizes and boniness rule out some of the smaller species, too little to fillet or steak or too bony to cook whole. They can be pan-fried, baked or broiled.

Pacific Sailfish

Butchering a game fish as magnificent as this one for the table seems almost sacrilegious, especially when there are so many smaller, more edible species for the taking. I haven't eaten Pacific sailfish. Reportedly the meat is tough and generally unpalatable when cooked, but it is said to be good when smoked. With anglers liking trophy mounts the way they do, it seems unlikely that many of these billfish, when sport-caught (as opposed to, say, commercial Japanese longlines), can be sentenced to a cook pot or smokehouse.

Panfishes

Grouped under this heading are many fresh-water species, nicknamed panfishes because their sizes suit them to frying-pan cookery. Among them are bluegills, other sunfishes, crappies and yellow perch. "Panfish" isn't a widely used term in salt-water angling, but it can be applied to small marine species, such as some of the flatfishes, small pompanos, etc. To prepare panfishes for the table: (1) Scale the fish. (2) Amputate the head, being sure to remove the gills. The pectoral fins can also be removed with the head, but unless they're close to the head this may waste some meat. They can be sheared off. (3) On some species part or most of the viscera may come away with the head. When it doesn't, you'll have to gut the fish. (4) Remove the dorsal fin and other remaining fins. Easiest, but not the most professional, way to do this is to simply shear them off as close to the body as possible; but it must be remembered that this will leave some bones in the fish. Cutting off the tail isn't absolutely necessary, but it will make for more room in the frying pan. (5) Rinse the fish in tap water or wipe with a wet cloth that has been soaked in salted water.

Pollock

Better than his cousin the cod to catch but not quite as good eating. See Atlantic cod, page 269, for preparation and cooking suggestions.

Pompano

Pompano are probably known to more people on dinner plates than on hook and line. As seafood goes, they're a kind of *pièce de résistance* and star on menus in Florida and all along the Gulf Coast. I have consumed pompano in eateries from Miami to famed Antoine's in New Orleans. They're a gas-tronomic delight. If there's a criticism, it's personal. They're just a bit too rich for me to want to eat them often.

Pumpkinseed

See Panfishes, opposite, for preparation and culinary notes.

Rainbow Trout

Some anglers call it the tastiest of the trouts. See general notes under Brook Trout, page 271.

Redbreast Sunfish (Bream)

Check Panfishes, opposite, for different ways of preparing for the table.

Redear Sunfish

See culinary hints for Panfishes, opposite.

Red Snapper

In seafood restaurants, red snapper is *haute cuisine*. Some connoisseurs say it's the finest eating of all fishes. I wouldn't go that far, but it is mighty good. Red snapper fillets invariably are sold in markets with their red skin still on, a guarantee against some other species being sold as red snapper (which occurs). Wise home cooks like the fish whole so that they can get a bonus in the form of small, extra delicately flavored morsels of meat at the inside of the throat. The snapper heads also can be used for stock for fish chowder or bouillabaisse.

Rockfish Family

Rockfishes comprise a big Pacific Coast family, all of which are considered good eating. After filleting and skinning they can be cooked by any of the standard methods.

Roosterfish

Roosterfish are marketed in Mexico and Central America but are still little known in the U.S. or Canada. They're described as palatable. Usual preparations for cooking are filleting, skinning and trimming away of dark meat which might otherwise impart a strong flavor.

Sauger

Sauger meat is white, firm and good. Saugers can be scaled and filleted without skinning, then broiled or fried. Dressed, they can also be baked whole.

Snook

They're as pleasing on a plate as they are on a hook.

Spotted Seatrout

These sporty opponents are good eating. They are not trout but are in the drums tribe, related to Croakers and Weakfish. See notes on the latter opposite.

Striped Bass

Striped bass are an excellent table fish, among the best. They can be prepared by any of the standard fish-cooking formulas, served plain or with sauces or garnishes. Large ones may be steaked and broiled, the smaller ones baked whole after beheading and dressing. Various sizes are skinned and filleted or scaled and filleted. It's a personal matter, but stripers about 4 to 6 lbs. are usually preferred for eating. This by no means rules out heavier candidates, however. This fish, prepared by a good cook, is one of the finest fish dishes of all when planked (a whole small fish baked on a wooden plank). *Magnifique!*

Striped Marlin

Opinions of the edibility of striped marlin, baked or broiled, differ radically, from dry and tasteless to good. I've caught it but never eaten it, so I can't testify. If it's anything like white marlin when smoked, it's a delicacy.

Swordfish

The edibility of swordfish is too well known to need elaboration here. But there's this advice: If at all possible, get your steaks from a fresh-caught fish. As an excellent substitute, try a mako steak. In my opinion, it's just as good, maybe better. Fact is, you may have already eaten mako without realizing it. A long-standing rumor is that less ethical restaurants have fobbed it off as swordfish. Frozen swordfish is passable, not in the same league with the fresh meat.

Tarpon

It can't be proved by me, but I've been told that tarpon are edible. The reports are that the flesh is coarse, stringy or very soft and generally unpalatable. All those I've caught were released. I figured I had my sport, which was what I wanted mainly. I like to think I contributed a little something to conservation. Besides, I'm not big for trophies.

Tautog (Blackfish)

Tautogs are good eating, with white, firm meat. They can be cooked by any of the standard procedures. With small ones cooked whole (gutted and dressed first of course), bones are a bit of a nuisance but a minor price for flavorful seafood. Larger tautogs can be filleted. In any case, they're usually skinned prior to cooking.

Tripletail

Their eating quality is in the mouth of the chewer. Opinions range from good to excellent. Customary preparations are filleting and skinning. Cooks may bake, broil or fry.

Wahoo

Wahoo meat is white, firm and good eating. It has been likened to that of the King Mackerel, a relative. (See page 274.) It's good when smoked and reportedly is good when steaked and broiled.

Walleye

Walleye is a fine eating fish, prized by fresh-water commercial fishermen.

Warsaw Grouper

The Warsaw and other members of the grouper family rate quite high in the dining department, but the skin should be removed because it's tough and has a strong taste. The meat is white and firm, excellent when deep fried as fillets or fish sticks. Baking is a popular culinary technique. Groupers are also good in fish chowder and fish stew.

Weakfish

Weakfish are an excellent table fish. Their meat is white and delicately flavored. If the skin is to be left on (some diners believe it adds flavor, but that's a moot point), the fish must be scaled. After gutting and dressing, they can be baked or broiled. They're delicious either way. Weakfish have bones, but these lift out easily with a fork after the fish is cooked.

White Bass

These fresh-water kin of striped bass are good eating. Those extracted from cool, clear waters usually have better flavor than those taken from warm or muddy areas. See Striped Bass, page 276.

White Catfish

If you haven't eaten fried catfish or catfish stew— or better yet, both, and still better, in the South—a small piece of your life is missing. See both Blue Catfish and Channel Catfish, pages 270 and 272.

White Marlin

White marlin are not considered candidates for cooking by any of the usual methods. However, I have eaten white marlin smoked and found it tasty.

Winter Flounder

Flounders are excellent eating. When fresh, their meat is white, firm, delicately flavored. (Don't judge it by some of the near-mushy fillets sold frozen in packages in supermarkets.) The only quarrel is with the bones. However, larger flounders can be filleted. Those too small to be filleted are cleaned and dressed and cooked whole, after which the bones can be lifted out easily with a fork. Flounders are variously scaled or skinned, as desired. Frying, broiling and baking are popular methods.

Yellow Bass

Like the meat of white bass, the flesh is white, flaky and very tasty. You'll find suggestions for preparation under Striped Bass, page 276.

Yellowfin Tuna

Yellowfin tuna are an important cannery contribution. Their meat is also said to be good when prepared at home. When cooked, the color of the meat is a happy medium between the whiteness of albacore and the darker shade of some other tunas. A home culinary procedure is to fillet the fish, skinning the fillets and cutting them into smaller pieces, if desired, then boiling them. Cooled, the meat makes a good seafood salad.

Yellow Perch

They're delicious. My friend Ed Migdalski, an epicure as well as an expert fisherman and icthyologist, recommends frying them without the skin. See other ideas under Panfishes, page 275.

17. How to Smoke Fish & Build Your Own Smokehouse

When properly smoked, fish has a delectable flavor. What's more, smoking fish greatly increases its range of uses as food. Still further, certain species that normally are discarded or overlooked can be smoked to produce a taste sensation equal—maybe even superior—to that of some top-rated fishes prepared by standard methods. Home fish smoking is not difficult, and it becomes even easier if a few anglers get together to share the work. With appropriate liquid refreshments it can be turned into a little social event, producing delicacies not readily obtainable elsewhere—and often expensive when obtainable.

There are small, portable fish and game smokers on the market, and they do a job. But many anglers and hunters like to build their own, perhaps for greater capacity.

The smokehut pictured here was designed by Lou Mussler, a Florida fisherman. He has used it to create palate-pleasing delicacies by smoking just about anything that swims—short of whales, porpoises, seals and humans. Their list includes many kinds of finned fishes along with crabs, oysters, shrimp, and spiny lobsters. Its design is simple and efficient, and it's easy to construct.

A word of caution. It is advised to follow direc-

How to Build a Fish Smokehouse

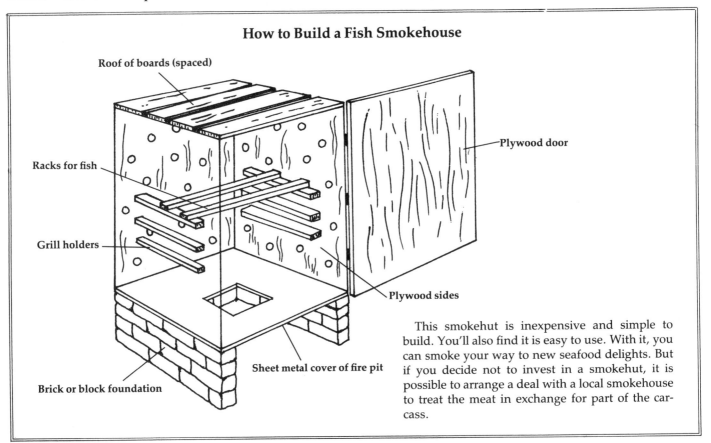

Roof of boards (spaced)

Plywood door

Racks for fish

Grill holders

Plywood sides

Brick or block foundation

Sheet metal cover of fire pit

This smokehut is inexpensive and simple to build. You'll also find it is easy to use. With it, you can smoke your way to new seafood delights. But if you decide not to invest in a smokehut, it is possible to arrange a deal with a local smokehouse to treat the meat in exchange for part of the carcass.

tions carefully and with common sense since this smoke house involves an open fire. In addition, in urban, suburban and other well-populated areas there may be ordinances either prohibiting a smokehut or setting minimum distances between it and other structures. Check beforehand.

Building a Smokehouse

Materials Needed

Gather the following to build a smokehouse: (1) four pieces of exterior plywood, 4 ft. wide by 5 ft. high by ¾ in. thick; (2) some wooden slats about 2 in. wide and 1 in. or so thick for smoking racks and grill holders (see illustration); these can be cut to suitable lengths to fit inside; (3) some random-width boards for the roof; they can be almost any thickness—say, 1 in. or thereabouts—but for appearances' sake should be more or less the same thickness; (4) a piece of heavy, galvanized sheet metal, 4 ft. square; (5) bricks or foundation building blocks; (6) a few screws or nails; (7) three small hinges; (8) a hook and eye to keep the door closed. *Note:* You can use a square of plywood, same thickness as the others, for a roof instead of the random-width boards, but if you do, you'll have to drill holes in it so that the smoke can escape.

Tools

A hammer, saw, screwdriver, tinsmith's shears, a brace and 1-in. bit, and a shovel.

Construction

(1) Using your shovel, if necessary, clear a level space large enough to accommodate the smoke-hut's fire pit or foundation. With the bricks or cement blocks, fashion a three-sided fire pit about 16 in. high with inside dimensions of 32 in. by 32 in. Make this fire pit as level as possible. (2) Cut a hole about 24 in. square in your sheet metal. Lay the sheet squarely on the fire pit. The purpose of this, of course, is to help protect the hut's wooden edges against fire. (3) Before putting up the plywood sides and back, nail or screw lengths of the slats to each of the two sides, as shown. Secure the lowermost slat on each side about 6 in. apart above the first. These slats should be as level as possible, and those on one side should be even with those on the other. These strips on the smokehut walls will support the racks, also cut from slats, on which the fish are smoked. (4) Nail or screw the plywood sides and back together. If a disassembly feature is desired, use screws. (5) If random-width boards are used for the roof, space them with a gap of about ⅛ in. between them for escape of smoke. If you substitute a piece of plywood for the boards, drill eight 1-in. holes at random so the smoke can get out. (6) Drill 10 1-in. holes in each side and in the back—but none in the door. These holes allow the smoke to linger inside long enough to do its work before escaping. (7) Cut grill slats to fit inside the smokehut. These will rest on those racks you fastened earlier. You'll need about five slats per shelf. Do not fasten them to the slat racks. They will rest loosely on the racks, an equal distance apart. NOTE: An alternative to the slat racks is to fashion a grill from ½-in. hardware cloth, which is nailed to the grill holders like a shelf.

Woods to Be Used in Smoking

Smokehut owners develop their own preferences for a certain kind of wood or a blend. You can use any wood of a kind that produces a good non-acrid smoke. Good smoking materials include green or dry apple tree wood, birch, cedar bark, hickory, and corn cobs. Caution: Do *not* use evergreens or resinous woods such as pine or fir.

Note: Do not paint the smokehut.

Preparation of Fish for Smoking

Lou Mussler recommends the following procedure: First off, certain species to be smoked—tunas, albacores, bonitos, crevalle jacks and the like—should be bled immediately after catching. (1) Remove head and tail. Don't forget the gills. (2) Clip off fins close to the body. (3) Leave skin and scales on. (4) Split fish along backbone on both sides, being careful to follow the bone structures to the entrail cavity. (5) "Unfold" the fish and remove bones and insides. (6) Larger fish to be smoked should be cut into fillet sections not more than 1 in. thick. Leave the skin on.

All moisture must be removed from fish before smoking. Failure to do this will result in poorly smoked meat. Here's how you go about it: (1) Make a "salt pickle"—1 lb. of salt to 1 gal. of water. (2) Soak fish for 24 hours, then remove from brine and let stand in a pail of *unsalted* water for one hour. (3) Remove fish from the fresh water, dry with a clean cloth; let them air-dry in a cool place. (4) While they're drying, protect against flies and other insects by covering with netting or a screen. (5) When thoroughly dried, place fish on the smokehut's racks and proceed as follows.

Smoking Process

(1) Make a small pilot fire, building up its flame until the smoking material begins to burn. (2) Heap on enough wood to ensure long, slow burning. (3) Smudge with wood chips or moist leaves. (4) Stir the coals occasionally. (5) Continue the smoking for about eight hours. Inspect the fish periodically for an even, dark brown color throughout the process.

Cooking Fish

I inject this here because it becomes involved in the smoking procedures that follow. Smoking does not actually cook fish. To cook them you must turn the fish over on the grill slats so that the skin side is down.

Make a cooking fire in the smokehut by using dry hardwood that will burn with sufficient heat to draw out the fish oil. But do *not* make the fire too hot, because this should be a slow-cooking process. Test the fish at intervals with a long-handled fork by turning the flesh away from the skin. Fish on the lowermost grill will be done first. Remove and replace with fish from the upper grills for faster cooking.

Smoking Shellfish and Eels

The Mussler smokehut comes highly recommended for smoking oysters, clams, eels, lobsters, crawfish and shrimp. For best results with these, Lou says, use a grill of hardware cloth.

Lobsters and Crawfish

Split lengthwise and crack claws. Remove such inedible portions as "lungs" and stomach. Place on grill, unopened portion of shell down, and smoke in the same manner as fish. Turn them over when thoroughly smoked, then cook (see above).

Shrimp

Cut off heads, wash, dry, place on grill. Smoke until light brown, then cook. Turn them over three or four times during cooking period. Shrimp are done when the meat has shrunk in the shell.

Caution: Do not keep smoked lobster, crawfish or shrimp longer than a week.

Oysters and Clams

Here Lou follows a reverse procedure. Wash the shells clean, place on grill. Cook until shells are open. Lower the fire to a smoking stage, then smoke the clams or oysters for about two hours. Eat immediately. Oysters and clams are served on the half shell, dunked in melted butter, seasoned to taste with pepper and salt.

Eels

It has been Lou Mussler's experience that it doesn't pay to work up a sweat over whether eels should be smoked while hanging or while lying flat. Either way is O.K., he says. You can hang them while smoking, he adds, but lay them skin side down when cooking.

Storing Smoked Fish

"Smoked fish may be kept for short periods of time provided they're wrapped in aluminum foil and kept in a cool or cold location," Lou advises. *In warm weather smoked fish should be considered perishable.*

Final Tips

Lou Mussler wrote his instructions for building a smokehut and smoking fish so that they would be simple to follow. "There's no need to make a big production out of them," he comments. "However, preparing fish for smoking and the actual smoking and cooking processes take time. Don't try any shortcuts; you'll only ruin the entire project. As for the use of fancy and exotic herbs—well, that's up to you. But if you want smoked fish to taste like smoked fish, then smoke 'em, don't disguise 'em."

18. <u>What Have You Got There?</u>

(Curious & Unusual Fishes)

Long before my time, some unidentified sage—it may have been old Whatsisname—commented that the only thing usual in fishing is the unusual. That's stretching facts a mite; yet it contains more truth than poetry, as the saying goes.

And the same holds for the underwater kingdom's finned citizens. Salt and fresh waters house many unusual fishes. In our "aquarium" here is but a sampling.

Alligator Gars

Alligator Gar

Fierce-looking and armor-plated in his own fashion, this beast is one of North America's largest fresh-water fishes, exceeded only by some of the sturgeons. Matching his fearsome appearance is what could be called an actively antisocial attitude toward anglers. Backing this belligerency are strong jaws armed with teeth. Even accidental contact with the fangs can cause painful, even severe, punctures. And when alligators have malice in mind it can be dangerous to bring one of any size into a boat. Anglers aware of potential mayhem can discourage a gar's rude behavior with sharp raps on the noggin when landing it.

Old, unauthenticated reports handed down from one generation of fishermen to another tell about alligator gars reaching lengths of 12 to 14 ft., even longer, with weights up to 400 lbs. These monsters supposedly prowled the backwaters of Arkansas, Louisiana and Mississippi many years ago and may have grown in the telling. On record is a specimen 9 ft. 8½ in. long, 302 lbs. Catches of 100-pounders, and occasionally one approaching 200 lbs., are not rare; but a 7-ft. alligator gar tipping the scales at 150 lbs. rates as a lunker.

As for this fellow's personal appearance, he is the largest of the gar family (*Lepisosteus spatula*) and has the long, slender body typical of his relatives. His single dorsal fin and rounded anal fin are positioned far back on the body, one above the other, and the tail is well-developed, with a rounded trailing edge. The upper jaw of the alligator gar carries a double row of teeth, whereas that of other gars has a single row. The gar's color scheme is an olive-green above, fading to a lighter shade below, then to an off-white on the belly. There is a generous sprinkling of blackish spots along the sides and on the dorsal, caudal and anal fins, although these markings may lessen on older fish.

Alligator gars are found up the Mississippi River as far north as St. Louis, Mo., through large tributaries of the Gulf of Mexico, and in northern Mexico. They've also been reported in the Ohio River and on into Kentucky.

Anglerfishes

Anglerfish

There are several species of anglerfishes in seas throughout the world, but the one we're concerned with is the most common North American kind, the American angler, *Lophius americanus*. It's also known as the American goosefish and goosefish, as well as by a collection of regional aliases—some 32 by one count—that include monkfish, frogfish, allmouth, bellyfish and molligut.

He's a grotesque creature, even in a water world populated by odd-looking characters, a fact that accounts for the variety of colorful nicknames.

Viewed from above, the body's shape bears a passing resemblance to a broad paddle with a short, stubby handle. In profile the body is squatly arched. All the fins, including the tail, are rather small in proportion to their owner's size. The pectorals are noteworthy. Positioned ahead of the gill openings, a reverse of the standard form, the pectorals have a thick, fleshy "arm" at their base, presumably as an aid in getting around on the bottom.

But the most interesting fin is the first dorsal. This is the appendage that puts the "angler" in the fish's name. The first spine of this fin is specialized —elongated, flexible, movable and strategically located immediately behind the mouth. At its end is a fleshy tab. Together the spine and tab constitute a "fishing rod" and "lure." This is the equipment that gives its owner the name anglerfish.

Being sluggish and awkward in movement, the angler relies mainly on his clever fishing rod to capture prey. He accomplishes his food shopping neatly by lying quietly on the bottom, where his color blends in admirably. The body's upper surface is a dark, nondescript brown, variously mottled with lighter and darker brown shades. Instead of pursuing prey, this angler secures it by waving his tiny "lure" with his fishing rod, drawing little fishes within range of his cavernous mouth.

Other characteristics of the American goosefish are equally unusual. His head occupies a sizable portion of total length. The mouth is enormous, extending across the front of the head and is armed generously with small, needle-sharp teeth. His eyes are small and surmounted by horny protuberances. The skin has no scales but is profusely covered with a mucous coating.

All members of the angler family share grotesqueness, some to such a degree as to be nightmarish. One member lives at levels where no sunlight penetrates. Not only does he have a stout fishing rod, but also a line outfitted with horny hooks. What's more, the lure takes the form of a little bulb that can be made luminous at will in the dark.

Another family member, labeled *Photocorynus spininceps*, is involved in the most extraordinary male-female relationship in all the underwater world. The females of this species are giants in size in comparison to the male. Since they are sluggish and solitary, the chances of females and males getting together in the Stygian vastness would seem to be slim. Nature compensates. Soon after they hatch, the males—only a fraction of an inch long— seek out females. How they locate them isn't known. When a female is found, the tiny suitor attaches himself to her body and remains affixed for life. The male grips the female's skin with mouth and teeth, after which, and in time, all the male's organs, except those involved in reproduction, disappear completely. The parasitic male is supplied with oxygen and nourishment by the female host, and their blood systems merge. No slipping away to play poker with the boys!

The males remain lifetime dwarfs. In one pair captured near Iceland, the female was 40 in. long and the male 4. Attachment can be anywhere, and sometimes more than one male is attached to the same lady.

Rod-and-reelers occasionally hook American goosefish and bring them in only as a curiosity. Knowledgeable fishermen will tell you that portions of this unbeautiful creature are edible

Burbots

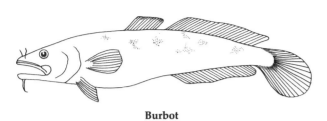

Burbot

The burbot (*Lota lota*) is such a strangely shaped fish that it looks as though the manufacturer changed blueprints during building. His body's forward section is codlike, then becomes shallower and flattened from side to side in its stern section. The head is fairly long, has a good-sized mouth with many tiny teeth, and carries a barbel, or "whiskers," on its chin and two more atop its snout. The burbot's fins also are distinctive. There are two dorsals, equal in height, but the first is shorter and the second, in the rear half of the body, is matched by an anal fin underneath. The caudal fin is unusual, being oval, and fine scales cover the body. The burbot is drab in coloration. The uppermost sides are dark olive-green, yellow-brownish or black mottlings cover the sides, and the color below is grayish.

In addition to his odd shape, the burbot's other special claim to fame is that he's the only fresh-water member of the codfish family.

Burbots are also a controversial species. In some areas they are given status as a sport species, and in other areas they're looked upon as bait-stealing trash fit only for discard or for grinding up as chum. They certainly have the appetite of the cod. In the stomach of one specimen were found 135 young sunfish and in another's belly were 101 small yellow perch.

Flying Fishes

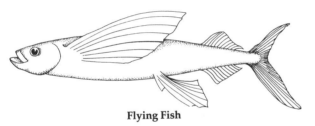

Flying Fish

These unique creatures, with the family Latin handle *Exocoetidae*, have been reported on the U.S. East Coast as far north as Massachusetts; and other species have been described on the Pacific Coast from southern California down to Mexico. Largely, however, flying fishes are found in tropical regions all around the world.

The spectacle of an echelon of these fish suddenly erupting from the sea and flying in formation over waves is one of the great free shows put on by the sea. Strictly speaking, they do not fly in the sense that birds do; that is, there is no flapping of wings. In the case of the fish, the "wings" are elongated pectoral fins, extending almost to the tail of some species, that have been adapted for a special function: to escape enemies. In the air these fins are extended but, like those of an airplane, are held rigid in flight. So it would be more appropriate to call them "soaring fishes." They're an amazing example of adaptation in nature.

Their flying, or soaring, is accomplished in this

manner: Power for take-off is supplied by the tail. While gaining take-off speed, the fish keeps his pectoral fins tightly against his sides for minimum water resistance. At the precise instant of breaking water, the pectorals are extended as wings. For a second or two before becoming airborne, the fish may taxi a few feet at the surface, the elongated lower lobe of the tail serving as a rudder to steer just before take-off. Once airborne, the fins provide lift. When the flight is ended, the fish's slender, streamlined body re-enters the water with ease, and its owner swims about his business— unless danger reappears, in which case, the fish takes off again.

Two basic types of "fish-aircraft" species are recognized. The one just described relies solely on the pectoral fins for lift and soaring. The other type has the pectoral fins plus a pair of well-developed pelvic fins, which supply added lift and also function like an airplane's ailerons, enabling the fish to nose upward for climbing or to head downward and bank in turns. In both power systems the pectoral fins are the principal lifting surfaces, and the tail is the source of power for take off. Once the fish is airborne, there is no source of power.

Flights vary in nature and duration according to whatever disturbs the fish. Some flights are only a few yards. Others carry the fish 300 ft. or more: A Pacific Coast species has been observed in flights of 1,000 ft. The general flight pattern is in one direction, although the fish can touch down, submerge, gain speed again, and take off in another direction. It's reported that they can soar to heights of 25 or 30 ft. as they ride puffs of breeze. It appears that when there's wind they can take off into it without gaining flying speed with their tail. The wind, of course, supplies the lift. How the fish know of a breeze, much less its force and direction, is open to speculation, but a theory is that wave motion under the surface gives them this bit of flying-weather information.

The little rascals rarely collide with boats in day flights, but at night they're attracted by lights, which can cause fatal blunders. Flying fishes serve mainly as bait for large gamesters like dolphins and marlins, but they are said to be good eating; and some fishermen set up nets at night on their boats to capture the fish in flight.

Grunions

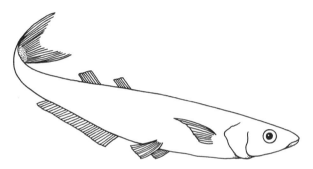

Grunion

Grunions are a phenomenon in more ways than one. To begin with, they're not hook-and-line fish; yet they're caught in wholesale lots by California anglers. Moreover, they also have drawn flocks of equally enthusiastic non-fishermen to that state's beaches.

The phenomenal aspect is in spawning and it's amazing. All fishes that you're familiar with spawn in water, right? Not grunions. They go ashore to breed, which is roughly equivalent to dogs buildings nests in trees to whelp. Even more amazing is the time precision required, and how the fish adhere rigidly to a schedule without a calendar, a watch, a tide table—or newspapers, radio or TV.

Spawning begins in late February or early March and lasts into August or early September. Within that span grunions spawn only on three or four nights, following each full or new moon and within a one- to three-hour interval immediately after high tide.

When the urging tells them it's reproduction time, they come ashore on ocean-front beaches, each female escorted by one to eight males. She deposits herself high enough on the apron of the high tide; then the female digs herself into the sand, tail first, with vigorous body movements, and buries herself up to her pectoral fins. She then discharges her eggs. The males get as close as they can to the female and release their spermatic fluid so that it flows down around the body of each female and fertilizes the eggs. Spawning accomplished, the males and females flip themselves back into the water. Actual spawning consumes about 30 seconds, but the fish may be out of water several minutes. Females will spawn four to eight times during a season.

After the eggs are buried in their incubator of moist sand for about 10 days, they're ready to hatch. This again is timed nicely with the high tide so that it washes them out of the sand and the eggs are then carried to sea by the waves. If something goes awry, and the first series of high tides doesn't release the eggs from the sand, there's no need to panic, because the eggs can remain buried in the sand for another two weeks and still will hatch if washed free.

Grunion spawning is so regular and so predictable that the California Department of Fish and Game has announced the dates and hours in advance. It's during this season that anglers and non-anglers capitalize on the free windfall of fish, catching them by hand as they flip around the beach. If this seems like a dirty trick to the fish, consider the great numbers captured in commercial nets.

Several southern California beaches are productive areas, but prospective participants must check on the latest regulations. In the past there have been closed seasons and restrictions on gear, and a valid state fishing license has been required. (Incidentally, grunions are good eating when broiled or fried in deep fat after rolling in a batter of the cook's choice.)

The Latin handle for these fish is *Leuresthes tenuis*, but they are sometimes misnamed "smelt" and "little smelt." Identification details: (1) slender body, grayish green down to a thin blue and silver stripe along the side, silver below; (2) deep-V tail; (3) small mouth, no teeth; and (4) sizes run only 6 to 7 in. maximum.

Hagfish

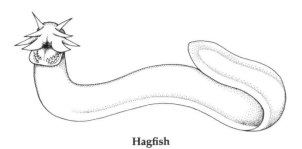

Hagfish

The poor devil can't help it, but the hagfish is one of the most loathsome sea residents.

The hag belongs to the *Myxinidae* family and is zoologically classed as cyclostome, which means "round-mouthed." Hags are eellike in form and, like sharks, are primitive fish with a skeleton that is cartilaginous. They have no scales and lack paired fins. What passes for a fin is a fold of skin that runs continuously around the tail section. The mouth of the hag is one of its most unusual features. It has no lips, no jaw or teeth as such. But the hag has a sharp tongue, studded with filelike

"teeth" which the fish uses as a coarse rasp to drill his way into other fishes' flesh. Although blind, hags locate food by means of highly sensitive appendages around the mouth and on the head and by a specialized olfactory apparatus.

As if its appearance isn't repellent enough, even more loathsome is the slime that profusely pours out from mucus sacs along its body sides. Production of this slime is out of proportion to the hag's average 1½- to 2-ft. size. A single hag can easily fill a 2-gal. pail.

But then hagfish weren't put on earth to drive away or entertain us humans. Like crabs, sharks and other scavengers, they are part of the sea's Department of Sanitation. We can only guess at what the sea would be like if disintegration by water were the only means of disposing of all the dead creatures through the ages.

Hagfish are bottom residents, vary in color from blue to brown to gray, and favor cool and cold waters. They're found along the North Atlantic coast from Arctic areas south to North Carolina.

Hammerhead Sharks

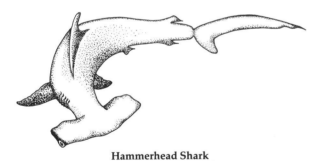

Hammerhead Shark

These odd-looking members of the very ancient shark tribe (Sphyrnidae group within the family) are widely distributed throughout the world. They occur in all the warm-temperate and tropical seas, including the Atlantic, the Pacific, the Gulf of Mexico, the Caribbean and the waters around Hawaii.

One thing about hammerheads is that they can't be confused with other ocean residents or even other sharks. The reason, of course, is the anatomical oddity that gives them their name. Their head does indeed suggest a hammer. No other fish anywhere in the world shares that distinction.

In all members of the family group the cartilaginous skeleton of the head has been modified to

form two blunt-edged extensions, one on either side, with a common anterior edge. On some species, like that big brute the great hammerhead, this leading edge is nearly straight. More often, on others, it's curved. On one species the curvature is so pronounced, and the head so wide front to back, as to cause a departure from the name hammerhead.

As if this strange head formation were not enough, the eyes are located at the very ends of the "hammer," and the nostrils are near them. Why Dame Nature singled out hammerheads for this unique arrangement can only be surmised. An educated guess is that it's a form adaptation that probably evolved millions of years ago through a certain manner of feeding. Its advantages, if any, are not understood, but it has been theorized that wide separation of eyes and nostrils better enables their owners to zero in on prey.

Hammerheads have always had an unsavory reputation; much of which may be attributed to their odd appearance. But in recent years, on record, are numerous attacks on swimmers, some of them fatal. So should you ever see one of these odd creatures, remember that hammerheads can be dangerous.

Needlefishes

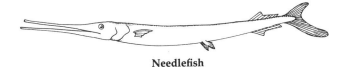

Needlefish

Needlefishes are pretty strange and unfriendly-looking creatures. No one knows how many species of these unique sea denizens exist. The family name is Belonidae.

As for appearance, can you imagine a javelin with fins? Some people see a passing resemblance to the fierce and ugly alligator gar, but they are not related. Needlefishes' bodies, if anything, are more shallow than the gars', and needlefishes are all characterized by long, skinny jaws that become pointed and beaklike on the ends. The lower jaw projects somewhat beyond the top one, and both are armed with sharp teeth.

The body is elongated and extremely slender. It's said that some needlefish "tail-walk." They jump and skitter along the water surface when they want to escape larger fish.

One species, nicknamed garfish, is found in California, and another larger species in North American waters is found in Florida and the Bahamas and is called houndfish. There is a special interest in the houndfish because of his danger to man. It applies to night angling in any tropical waters where they are found. Fishing lights startle these fish, and they often become alarmed by them. This can send the fish into a series of long leaps clear of the water, and the jumps can be in any direction, even toward a boat. An airborne needlefish is like a thrown spear. Serious injuries —some of them fatal—have been reported. Night anglers using boat lights have been advised to protect themselves with shields.

Needlefishes respond to natural baits and to lures and are eaten, but their green-colored bones discourage some diners.

Northern Barracudas

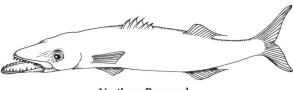

Northern Barracuda

Some years ago I happened to mention to non-fishing friends that there are barracudas—or northern sennets, as they are also called—in the waters of Long Island, N.Y. As you probably know, most people think of barracudas as tropical fish. Well, the consequent raising of eyebrows in my living room was almost audible. My listeners were much relieved to learn that northern barracudas seldom reach lengths greater than 12 to 14 in., if that. They're considered harmless.

These northern sennets, however, are full-fledged barracudas. The profile and the toothy mouth are unmistakable. The color is a greenish or olive along the back, white farther down on the sides, without spots or blotches. The dorsal fins are dusky and the tail is blackish.

Northern barracudas are found on the Atlantic Coast from New England southward. They travel in schools, usually quite close inshore, and probably infiltrate bays via inlets.

Paddlefish

Paddlefish

There's no mistaking this finned curiosity. He has an elongated snout that is both broad and flat, suggesting the blade of a spatula—a point reflected in the fish's Latin name, *Polyodon spathula.*

This is the only field mark needed, but here are other species details. The paddlefish has a moderately stout body about a third of the way back. There are no scales. The eyes are very small and contrast sharply with the fish's roomy mouth. The gill covers appear to be very long and taper narrowly on their free end. There is a single dorsal fin of modest size positioned well back on the body. The large tail has been likened to a shark's fin. Color scheme is a shade of gray, slate or bluish, fading on the sides, giving way to a white belly. Sizes range up to about 80–90 lbs.

The paddlefish is thought to be a survivor from a long-gone group of ancient fish. Interestingly, its skeleton is like a shark's in that it is composed of cartilage instead of bone. Another odd detail is that the young paddlefish have numerous teeth in their jaws, but when they mature their mouths become toothless, probably because of change of diet. Adult paddlefish—with no teeth—are plankton feeders, and in common with other plankton consumers, cruise with their large mouths open, like animated vacuum cleaners, funneling in quantities of organisms filtered from the water by their numerous long gill rakers.

Paddlefish are distributed throughout the Mississippi River system all the way from the Missouri River into Montana, on to the Ohio River and south into Louisiana, Mississippi and Texas. In different areas you hear them referred to as spoonbill, flatbill, shovelnose cat, boneless cat or spoonbill sturgeon. All are poor nicknames, since the paddlefish is neither a catfish nor a sturgeon. So far, its only known relative is in China.

Torpedoes, Rays & Skates

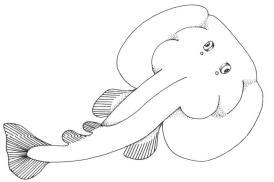

Torpedo (Electric Ray)

These three curious creatures, members of the order Batoidei, are often hooked accidentally by fishermen, but they do put up resistance. For the most part they're discarded, although anglers in some parts of the world eat the wings of the rays and skates.

In my opinion the torpedoes, known as electric rays, are the most fascinating of the three. They're characterized by round, thick bodies and a short, stout, almost sharklike tail. (They are distant, long-ago relatives of sharks.) And, like rays and skates, they have an anatomical peculiarity—their pectoral fins thin out so as to form, in effect, "wings," but these are thicker than those that appear on rays and skates. Electric rays are sluggish and spend much time buried in mud or sand. They swim feebly, with sculling motions of the tail. Their thick wings are of little use in propulsion, which brings up the most interesting detail of these animals.

It's an adaptation to compensate for the fish's poor swimming talent. Within the wings sections are located an ingenious electricity-generating apparatus. These electrical organs are developed to the extent that they can make up as much as one-sixth of a torpedo's total weight, which is more impressive if you consider that specimens up to 100–150 lbs. are on record. These electrical organs consist of thousands of disks piled in columns. With them, the torpedo can deliver shocks of 8 to 220 volts, depending on species and size. A shock is made up of 12 to 100 separate pulses, each lasting about 1/300 of a second. The shock power is considered less than that of some of the truly dangerous electric eels. Still, it's enough to knock down and temporarily disable a man—or at least clear his sinuses. That's why the creature's other nicknames include "numbfish" and "crampfish."

The North American range is from Nova Scotia to North Carolina.

Unlike torpedoes, other rays make good use of their wings and, by undulating them, are able to gracefully fly through the sea. Other rays also differ from torpedoes in their slim tail structure. The upper surface of the body is pigmented, each species with its own color and markings. By harmonizing with the sea bottom, the color scheme is excellent camouflage against foes.

Some rays are huge. The mantas, also called devilfish, are known to have reached widths of 23 ft. and weights of 3,500 lbs. Another unusual member of the ray family is the sting ray, a less active, rounder and smaller species running 2 to 3 ft. across the wings. Sting rays bear one or more sharp poison spines on their tail and can deliver a nasty jagged wound that can be highly toxic to a victim when they lash out their tails. Wounds are not necessarily fatal to humans or serious, but the potential results are not fun and games: severe pain, swelling, cramps, inflammation, infection and even gangrene. The ray only wields his tail in defense, but the problem is that rays lie concealed at the bottom in shallow water and may be stepped on accidentally.

The last member of this curious related trio is the skate, and he is very similar to the ray in that he makes good use of his wings for locomotion. Skates also have the same broad body of the rays, lack an anal fin, and possess the same pointed teeth. The skin of the skate differs, however, in that most species carry thorns or prickles. While not as active as rays, skates do leave the bottom and venture upward even to the surface. But when alarmed, skates hug the sea floor, and it's thought that a suction may be created which makes it difficult for predators to dislodge them.

Skates range in size from 1 ft. to 4 or 5 ft. One of the largest is the barndoor skate, believed to reach widths of 6 ft. and weights to 60 lbs.

Exclusively salt-water residents, skates are found in latitudes ranging from tropical to sub-polar but are most numerous in temperate zones.

Sawfish

Sawfish

With their long, broad, flat, bony extension of the snout, armed with a row of sawlike teeth along each side, sawfish can hardly be confused with any other species. (Their family name is Pristidae.) These odd creatures are considered rays and are also similar to their remote kin the sharks. Interestingly, they combine some of the features of both: broad body, sharklike gill slits and fins. Like some sharks, too, the babies develop as eggs inside the mother but are born alive. In case you're worried, the saw of a baby about to be delivered is covered by a sheath to protect Mama. (Dame Nature thinks of everything!)

As for color and size, sawfish are commonly grayish-brown with a whitish underside. They reach great size: lengths of up to 16 ft. and weights to 700 are quite common. The beasts can grow to 20 ft. and weigh in as high as 1,000 lbs. It's comforting to know that they're sedentary in habit, loaf around the bottom, and rise only long enough to attack schools of small fish. In these forays they slash their saws vigorously from side to side to kill the prey. They also use the saw sometimes to poke the sea bottom for other tidbits.

Sawfish favor warm waters, and their greatest North American abundance is in Florida and the Gulf of Mexico.

Contrary to myth, they do not attack whales, although they occasionally take on a larger fish. So far as is known, sawfish do not attack humans without provocation, but even the small ones should be treated with respect.

Sea Robins

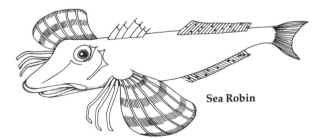

Sea Robin

These fellows are the bane of fishermen. Not only are they ugly-looking, with birdlike wings, but they are also inveterate bait stealers. They'll take anything offered as bait and often drive away desirable species.

To get down to their curious aspect, I'll deal with two species you are most apt to encounter. Both are found in the Atlantic from New England to the Carolinas.

These two are the common and the striped sea robins, and they resemble each other so closely that to describe one is to describe the other. The head is large and enclosed in a bony plate, the mouth is low in the head, the large eyes are high, and the fanlike pectoral fins suggest birds' wings, hence the fishes' name. The body is slender and out of proportion to the big head. There are two dorsal fins, the second of which is about the same size as the anal fin under it. Three developed rays, or bony rods, are separate from each of the pectoral fins and serve as independent feelers with which sea robins appear to walk along the bottom.

The common sea robin is reddish, sometimes grayish-brown above with four or five blotches across the back. The underneath color is pale yellow to dirty white. His dorsals are gray and the pectorals are yellow-orange. The ventral fins are yellow or brown. The striped sea robin's color scheme is similar, with these exceptions: the pectorals have pale edges and lack crossbars, and there is a dusky brown stripe lengthwise below the lateral line.

As I mentioned, sea robins spend most of their time on the sea floor and are pests fishermen learn to live with. They're small fishes. An average for the sea robin and the larger striped sea robin is under 12 in. Robins are quite edible—tasty, in fact; extracting the meat requires effort, but it's worth it.

Spearfishes

Longbill Spearfish

Spearfishes are seldom seen by anglers and are boated even more infrequently. This is strange, since they are found in both the Pacific and the Atlantic. Maybe more are caught than reported, but even so, they're a once-in-a-blue-moon prize. I've seen only one caught—in the Caribbean Sea off Mexico. On that trip the Woods Hole, Mass., Oceanographic Institution had asked that any spearfish boated be kept for study, but the angler didn't know this and released his catch, thinking it was an anemic sailfish. It's said that most of the spearfish captured are taken on commercial lines in the central and western Pacific.

The term spearfish has been used collectively for billfishes—e.g., marlins, swordfish and sailfishes—because they have a spearlike projection of the snout. But this is an incorrect label. There's a distinct species within the billfish family known by

the name spearfish, and let it be understood that it is this species I am spotlighting here.

Ichthyologists recognize three spearfish species—the Atlantic longbill (*Tetrapturus pfleugeri*) the Atlantic shortbill (*Tetrapturus belone*) and the Pacific shortbill (*Tetrapturus augustirostris*).

The family trademark is a bill or spear. That spear on the longbill is more in proportion to the fish's length than the weapons of the other two. Their spears are, in fact, quite short. All have very slender bodies, even more so than sailfish, and are pretty skinny. To give you an idea, the 6½-ft. specimen I saw weighed only 33 lbs.

Spearfishes share several characteristics with marlins and sails. The first dorsal fin is very long; the second is relatively tiny, and under it is an equally small anal fin. They all share two longitudinal keels on either side of the tail base along with a large, crescent-shaped, caudal fin and two long, skinny pelvic fins.

In general the spearfishes' color scheme is like this: a dark or metallic blue, sometimes with a greenish tinge, on the back and uppermost sides, shading to grayish or white lower down on the sides, and finally becoming a white or silvery on the belly.

Sturgeons

White Sturgeon

To anyone interested in fishes, angler or not, sturgeons present an unusual and fascinating picture. They're primitive animals, relatively unchanged from their ancestors of remote geological times. In other words, the sturgeons we see today are the sturgeons of a million years ago.

These fish have many primitive characteristics. The skeleton is not ossified and consists largely of

cartilage. They don't have a spinal column, but a forerunner called a notochord. Other holdovers from prehistoric days are the plates of bony armor covering the head, along with the rows of bony plates on the body. The tail shape goes back to that of primitive fishes.

As for family features, the sturgeon has a long snout, rather pointed or cone-shaped. The mouth is located well back and is fleshy and protrusible, ideally adapted to the sturgeons' manner of sucking in food along the bottom like a vacuum cleaner. Just ahead of the mouth are four barbels, or "whiskers," fleshy appendages which aid owners in finding food. Another detail is the single dorsal fin and the anal fin underneath it.

Mightiest of all the sturgeons—indeed, the largest fresh-water fish—is the beluga sturgeon, encountered in Eastern European waters. Weights on record run to 2,000–2,500 lbs. Its roe commands very fancy prices as beluga caviar. Of the 16 species seven occur in the U.S.: white, lake, green, Atlantic, pallid, shovelnose and shortnose. Heftiest of these is the white sturgeon with reported weights up to 1,800 lbs.

Thresher Shark

Thresher Shark

Threshers are unique among all fish—instantly identifiable because of their tail's great upper lobe, which resembles a scythe blade. In all, the tail occupies about half of the total body and is used to obtain food. This is the procedure, as reported to me by a group of commercial fishermen: A group of threshers surround a school of fish, such as blues or mackerel; then they whip their tails to agitate the water and drive the fish into a panicked mass, all the while swimming in gradually narrowing circles around the school. Once the fish are herded together, the sharks barrel into the mass, swinging their "scythes" from side to side, killing or stunning fish by the dozens. A grisly testimony to the power of a thresher's tail was relayed to me by a charter skipper friend. His mate leaned over the gunnel to look at one brought alongside, and at that precise moment the shark went berserk; its tail came high out of the water and slashed downward, decapitating the mate.

When you consider that common threshers can reach 20-plus ft. with a corresponding bulk coming close to 1,000 lbs., the tail becomes a formidable weapon indeed.

Except for this grotesque tail, threshers look like any other shark.

As for their range, their wanderings take them as far north as Nova Scotia and the Gulf of St. Lawrence and as far south as northern Argentina. In the Pacific they have been reported for the Hawaiian Islands area and from Oregon south to Chile. They have a fondness for warm water and, oddly, there are more reports of threshers off Rhode Island and its satellite Block Island than elsewhere on the U.S. East Coast.

Whale Shark

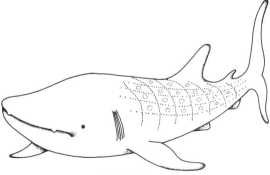

Whale Shark

The "whale" in this leviathan's name is an oblique reference to its size and doesn't indicate any relationship between its owner and whales. The whale shark is a gill-breathing fish in good standing, while whales, as you probably know, are lung-breathing mammals.

But this fish's name is most appropriate. The whale shark is the largest known fish anywhere in the world. (Its closest competitor *in fresh water* is the previously mentioned beluga sturgeon.) There are records of whale sharks at 50 ft., reports at 60 ft., and conceivably they might reach 70 ft. Unfortunately such monsters are usually not weighed, scales strong enough not being available.

Anatomically the whale shark is a creature of incongruities. He has a stout trunk section but is graceful-looking aft, and his fins are disproportionately small for so large a creature. His tail is distinctively large, its upper lobe being about 20 percent of the shark's total length. In comparison with the large head, the eyes are tiny. The mouth is at the very front of the head instead of being underslung, like that of most sharks. You'd expect this behemoth to possess huge teeth. Instead, they're minute, their lengths measured in millimeters. They occur in rows—about 310 of them—but only 10 to 15 are in use at any one time. The other rows are standby replacements. One 18-footer was credited with 3,600 teeth!

The monster's habits also are a study in contrasts. Depsite his power, a whale shark is almost lethargic, enough so to be accidentally rammed by a steamer on occasion.

Whale sharks also appear to be oblivious to small craft, which they have been known to nudge or attack. It's conceivable that they were after tuna being played by anglers and bumped into the boats by mistake.

Whale sharks wander open tropical seas throughout the world, including the Gulf of California, the Gulf of Mexico and the Caribbean. On the Atlantic Coast they have been spotted as far north as Long Island, N.Y., on down to Florida, and offshore Bermuda.

On the basis of recorded performances, the beasts do not seem to be inclined by temperament toward assaults on people, but the smart procedure is to observe a whale shark and leave it alone.

19. Bill's Fish Chowder

Here's a concoction we've cooked up from odds 'n' ends kickin' around the place . . . some fishing lore, a little philosophy, human interest stories and here and there a touch of humor. Eat slowly and enjoy.

A fishing rod is a stick with a hook at one end and a fool at the other.

—Samuel Johnson

George's Fantastic Fluke: A Fabulous But Fanciful Fake

One of the most devout fishermen I've ever known was an octogenarian named George who lived on Long Island. Last I heard, George was still toting an elderly, asthmatic outboard motor around with him in his car and renting rowboats at fishing stations all over the island. George credited fishing with his being so mobile in his eighties. Maybe it was fishing that also gave him a splendid sense of humor and inspired a very funny practical joke.

Like thousands of other bay and inlet fishermen throughout the great New York–New Jersey angling arena, George's favorite quarry was the fluke, a flatfish closely related to the even more popular flounder. Fluke are aggressive predators. They hit a rig hard, put up a lively fight; and with a size potential that goes up as high as 17 lbs., they're fine opponents on light tackle. Those bigger fluke are nicknamed "doormats" because of their roughly oval shape and size. Old George had boated his share of doormats, including a couple up to about 16 lbs.; and as he drifted in search of even heftier ones he wondered if it would ever be his good fortune to catch a world-record fluke, which at that time would have had to weigh something better than 20 lbs.

That wasn't to be, but George's wistful thinking was translated into some delightful whimsy.

At home George swiped some of his wife's oil-cloth and got some kapok stuffing from an old life jacket, along with a little paint. From his cellar workshop there emerged the world's largest "fluke," a specimen that would have weighed maybe 40 to 50 lbs. in real life and was the size of a young halibut. And it sure looked real, even to the fish's pigmented surface. For added realism George painted two streaks of red around the gills to look like dripping blood. He took the fake with him in his outboard.

Came the hour in the afternoon when fluke-fishing party boats returned to port. George carefully anchored his craft off to one side of where they would pass, close enough so that their passengers could see that this thing he held up was a fluke, yet not so close that they could detect that it was a fake. As each party boat passed, George held up the dummy on the end of a straight gaff. "Some of those guys' eyes came out on stalks," George chuckled.

He pulled that stunt for years, and most likely he is still doing it wherever he is now.

Codfish Aristocracy

In New England many years ago, this term was a derogatory label affixed to newly rich folks who didn't handle their money too gracefully—high-hatting or snubbing former friends and going in for ostentatious displays of wealth.

Shark

This term is said to have originated in England shortly after a slave trader by name of John Hawkins displayed the first shark creature seen in Britain around the year 1564. Word of the malevolent, greedy-looking creature spread rapidly throughout England, and before long the word shark was being used to describe those who gouged and swindled the have-nots. In that context it's still very much in use today.

Pool Shark

A guy whose major interest is playing pool for money, preferably with someone much less experienced than himself.

We have other fish to fry.

—Rabelais

Getting a Bang Out of Fishing, or, A Boom in Hammerhead Sharks

Two highly experienced big-game anglers* were trying to attract a blue marlin while trolling off the island of Bimini in the Bahamas when a great hammerhead, the largest of five species of hammerhead sharks in the western Atlantic, cruised into their scene and showed interest in their bait. Now the two fishermen had themselves a problem. If there were any blue marlin around, this big interloper could scare them into the next county. Or, if they happened to hook a marlin while he was around he could dismantle the billfish. They had to get rid of that shark, but they didn't want to go to the trouble of hooking and dispatching the monster.

It was never explained how their boat happened to have sticks of dynamite aboard, but she did. Our two heroes conceived the bright idea of shoving a stick of the explosive inside a baitfish, lighting the fuse, and tossing this loaded hors d'oeuvre to the hammerhead. And they did it.

The hungry hammerhead gulped the tidbit and then, in what has to be one of the most diabolical bits of timing on record, swam under the boat just as the dynamite took off—*KAPOW.* The blast lifted the sport fishing cruiser's stern section right out of

---

* They shall remain nameless, mercifully. I think they suffered enough needling at the time.

the water and sprang virtually every seam in her very expensive wooden hull. The two fishermen had to pump like crazy as they raced for port with wide-open throttles. As it was, they barely made very shallow water before the poor boat sank.

Fishwife

A term believed to have originated in England (*The Oxford Universal Dictionary* traces it back to 1523) and originally was applied to women who peddled fish in the streets. Since those female peddlers developed shrill and grating voices and often used very coarse language, the term came to be applied to women who talk in that manner. (An aside: What're we going to call 'em today, fish*persons?*)

Dead as a Mackerel

The expression means as dead as anything can get, as though there were degrees of deadness. I don't know why the mackerel was singled out as the criterion. A mackerel doesn't get any more or less dead than anything else.

Fishing for an Answer

An old expression meaning to try to get information, or an answer to a question, by inquiring in a roundabout manner.

I am no fisherman, and hope I never get lazy enough to take it up.

—Will Rogers

Colorful Characters I Have Known

Because it embraces so many people (upwards of 60 million Americans, according to one estimate) of all ages, all economic levels and all degrees of intelligence, sport fishing probably has a greater quota of colorful characters than almost any other participator sport. I've crossed paths with quite a few myself.

Among the oddest was a waterfront habitué I knew many years ago. I don't believe I ever heard his real name. Everyone called him by his nickname, which is unprintable. ''Boobie'' will do here. Boobie was one of those people whose age you can't determine—know what I mean? He might've been an older-looking young man or a young-looking older man. Boobie had very few serious moments. He was an imp at heart, and his roundish face was invariably cracked in a silly grin. If he'd had curly hair he'd have looked something like Harpo Marx. You didn't have to be around Boobie more than half an hour to realize that he wasn't playing with a full deck.

No one seemed to know what Boobie did for a living, if anything. Someone said he had inherited a lot of money, which could've been true because he had an awful lot of time in which to hang around the docks and go fishing. The only work I ever saw him do—and I don't know if he was paid for it—was to serve as a combination mate and deckhand on a big, luxurious, privately owned fishing cruiser called the *Joyanna,* owned by a rich sportsman named Carl (this and the boat's name are fictitious here for anonymity). Carl and Boobie met on the waterfront, probably in a gin mill, and subsequently became fast friends. It was a relationship reminiscent of that between George and Lennie in John Steinbeck's *Of Mice and Men.* Boobie worshiped Carl and would do just about anything he asked, especially if he (Boobie) thought it would get a laugh. I suspect that Carl kept Boobie around as a kind of court jester. I know that Carl put him up to a lot of his stunts.

Boobie's clowning had no limits. A favorite stunt of his on the *Joyanna* was reserved for fellow passengers prone to seasickness. It's a wonder it didn't get him killed. In full view of anyone who was seasick, or who was beginning to turn green around the gills, he would lay out two slices of bread and butter them. On one slice he'd stretch out half a dozen fat, wiggling bloodworms and make a sandwich. If his victim wasn't leaning over the rail by then, Boobie cut the sandwich in half diagonally and lifted a bloody half to his mouth. That did it.

There was a little of the sadist in Boobie or Carl, or both.

Another of Boobie's gastronomic stunts was to eat chum on a dare. In this case the chum was a ground-up, oily, blood-streaked, vile-smelling pulp created by shoving menhaden through a meat grinder. When dared, Boobie would dip a dirty old ladle into a big can of that gop, scoop up a big mouthful, and swallow it. It's a wonder that didn't kill him, now that I think of it.

Boobie's finest hour as a court jester came at a huge marina in Florida. It was on a busy weekend afternoon. All the boats were back in the marina, and their people were sitting around drinking and talking. Here comes the 52-ft. *Joyanna,* an eye-grabber in herself, gliding slowly into the full sunlit view of hundreds of people. Standing right up in her bow, on one leg, the other extended in back of him like a ballet dancer's pose, is Boobie—stark naked.

Carl and the *Joyanna* are long gone. I don't know what happened to Boobie; he dropped from sight. Wherever he is, though, I'm sure he's still the happy clown.

Crab

A person who's grouchy—usually a chronic grouch. Based on the fact that many crabs, notably the blueclaw, or blue crab, are feisty and belligerent. Blueclaw crabs are not even afraid of humans. They'll take you on as quick as they'll look at you—maybe quicker.

Slippery as an Eel

It's self-explanatory if you've ever tried to hold on to a live eel with your bare hands.

Cockles of the Heart

The derivation of this expression goes back to the Latin phrase *cochleae cordis,* meaning "ventricles of the heart." The English must have thought that the bivalve mollusks that are so popular there were so heart-warming and delicious that they tagged them cockles. Today you may hear the statement, "You've warmed the cockles of my heart,"—meaning that one's innermost depths of emotion have been touched.

No human being, however great, or powerful, was ever so free as a fish.

—John Ruskin

Eels in the Plumbing

Some years ago certain apartment houses in The Bronx developed stoppages in their water supply. Plumbers searched for causes and discovered—of all things—eels in the pipes. They were like so many corks. It goes without saying that even the plumbers were mystified by this strange state of affairs. So scientific aid was enlisted. Dr. Edward Gudger, curator emeritus of fishes at New York's famed Museum of Natural History, turned detective temporarily and came up with an explanation:

When young eels approach the U.S. coast from their natal grounds in the great deeps in that region of the Atlantic Ocean down around the Sargasso Sea, they swing inshore. While the males generally stay behind in bays and coastal creeks, the females invade rivers, where they will spend much if not most of their lives. Numbers of females enter New York's Hudson River, Dr. Gudger knew. He reasoned that some of these girls entered the tributary Croton River with the idea of traveling upstream. Soon they encountered Croton Dam, which forms Croton Reservoir, a supplier of New York City's water. This would pose no insurmountable hurdle to eels, Dr. Gudger figured. Eels can live quite a while out of water, and on a dewy-damp or rainy night, aided by the mucus lubrication of their skin, they could slither up the wet, glassy slope on either side of the dam (what a sight for some guy driving home from a local tavern with a snootful!), then down grassy slopes on the other side and back into the Croton River.

After a while they came to the viaduct leading into Croton Reservoir. Here they encountered another obstacle: two sets of screens designed to filter out leaves, dead fish and other debris from water flowing into the reservoir. Periodically the screens were raised for cleaning, whereupon the eels said, ''Let's go, ladies!'' and swam into the reservoir. From there, Dr. Gudger concluded, they found their way into feeder lines and eventually into apartment house plumbing, where they became tightly wedged like so many corks.

When I mentioned the Bronx affair in a magazine article about the American eel, the owner of a New York City plumbing supply firm wrote me a letter saying that municipal water department workers and plumbers had told him about finding eels, carp and other fresh-water fishes in water mains and plumbing in the very heart of Manhattan. There have even been reports of very small fishes issuing from faucets in some city areas.

Card Shark

Applies to a professional gambler always on a hunt for victims. Usually he isn't above certain techniques that help assure his winning—like dealing from the bottom of the deck, aces up his sleeves, and so forth.

Crawfish

As a verb this word's slang meaning is to renege on a deal or duck responsibility.

Lobster Shift

A term used for years by those in the press to refer to staffers who came to work after the main edition of a newspaper had been put to bed, usually in the wee hours of the morning. Some say it was coined by New England newspapermen who went to work at the hour lobstermen were going out in their boats; others claim it describes the lobster-red complexions of hard-drinking editors assigned to work the early morning shift.

Your bait of falsehood takes this carp of truth.
—Shakespeare: *Hamlet*

Madison Avenue Salmon

Traditionally in American taste, canned salmon meat should be an orange-pink. That of the chum salmon is not as much so as the meat of other Pacific salmons, which brings up this true story:

A U.S. cannery was stuck with hundreds of cases of canned salmon that didn't move off store shelves after customers discovered that the fish was more white than pink. There was absolutely nothing wrong with it. It was just that the meat was white instead of pink. A marketing troubleshooter was called in. His solution was simple but ingenious: A sign on the shelves that read ''This Salmon Guaranteed Not to Turn Pink in the Can.'' The cannery's entire supply was sold out.

Violence in Vermont

Old-time residents of Vermont are famous for their stringent economy of words. ''Yep'' and ''nope'' suffice as replies in most instances. They can be similarly frugal in their actions when so inclined.

One balmy spring afternoon two oldsters were out fishing on Lake Bomoseen. For hours they sat in silence and as immobile as statues, neither getting so much as a nibble. Finally one of them shifted his feet slightly, barely noticeable. His buddy transfixed him with an angry glare. ''What didja come out here fer,'' he growled, ''to fish or practice yer dancin'!''

''. . . Or Would You Rather Be a Fish?''

Most people think this rejoinder springs from a popular song of the mid-1940s. It is in reality an elaboration of the 1920s "flapper day" expression "What shall we do? Go fishing?" The connotation here, as you might guess, is that fishing was the "pits," or last thing any high-stepping flapper figure wanted to do. To them it was a great quip. Times have sure changed.

Chowderhead

This expression doesn't refer to a kind of clam but means a stupid dolt or blockhead.

Eel's Hips

Reportedly a 1920s term for anything commanding admiration for one reason or another, similar to the '20s expression "cat's meow," meaning the same thing. (That's a little historical culture we're throwing in for nothing.)

Next to prayer, fishing is the most personal relationship of man.

—Herbert Hoover

An American Lobster Tale

This is an old joke, with apologies to mothers-in-law.

Seems a New England commercial fisherman was vacationing in Florida when he received a telegram from his associate: YOUR MOTHER-IN-LAW'S BODY FOUND IN HARBOR BEING EATEN BY LOBSTERS. ADVISE. The vacationing fisherman hastily fired back this reply: SHIP THE LOBSTERS TO MARKET AND SET THE OLD GIRL OUT AGAIN.

Fishball

An old, uncommon term for an unpleasant, cheap or generally despicable person.

Loaded to the Gills—Drinks Like a Fish

While fish take in water in order to receive oxygen, a person who is said to be "loaded to the gills" or who "drinks like a fish" has consumed an inordinate amount of alcohol for another purpose entirely. Unlike the fish, however, the inebriated reveler can't expel any liquid out the gills.

Hooker

A street-walking prostitute. Not known if it's a spin-off from "getting hooked on."

No man is born an artist nor an angler.

—Izaak Walton

A Drop in the Bucket

Ever hear of a bucketfish? It's an invention, not a species. It was spawned way back by an unidentified practical joker who got sick and tired of anglers who (1) hog a boat's fighting chair and don't give others a chance, or (2) who fall asleep in a fighting chair when they should be alert for a fish's strike. It's a fun stunt that also works on unsuspecting beginners.

A bucketfish is easy to make. It consists of an ordinary metal pail to which is tied a couple of feet of stout twine. At the twine's free end is secured a snap swivel.

When the patsy—I mean the occupant of the fighting chair—dozes off or is looking elsewhere, the bucketfish's snap swivel is snapped on his line (or hers—women have equal rights), and the pail is eased overboard. Then all the conspirators stand by for the lively tableau that is sure to follow. What happens is that the pail rapidly travels downward on the fishing line, sped by the boat's forward motion. It fetches up against the victim's rig with an abruptness and force that causes line to suddenly peel off the reel at a great rate. With the reel's ratchet screeching in protest, it's a good simulation of a hard strike. (Be sure to see a note of caution at the end of this item.)

Instantly the patsy comes to life and grabs the rod out of its holder on the fighting chair, yelling that he has a strike. The bucketfish starts to "fight" right away, like a fish of respectable size trying to get away. By maintaining some seaway and varying her speed, the boat can cause the pail to resist with differing degrees of energy, even make some "runs." The victim's companions cheer him on.

The illusion can be maintained for a considerable time. Finally he's urged to reel his fish in, and the boat slows to make it easier (as though the fish finally tired). At this point it adds realism if someone stands at the transom with a big flying gaff, being careful to block out the catch until the last minute. He might even make a swipe or two in the water with the gaff, the others all enthusing about the size of the fish. Then comes the grand finale, when the gaffer turns and reveals the bucketfish. Sometimes there's a little added touch for hotheads: the bucket of water is dumped in his lap.

There's a version that I think I like more, but it requires a special item instead of a pail. This item is a metal disk, brass or aluminum. Its dimensions vary, but any I've come across have been about 12 to 15 in. or so in diameter and perhaps a quarter-inch in thickness. Otherwise the rig is the same as for a bucketfish. The sashaying of the disk in the water is very realistic. And the grand finale has an added touch. On the disk in large red letters is this legend: DID I HURT YOU, HONEY?

Be advised that either version of the stunt evokes variable, sometimes unpredictable, reactions from its victims. Mostly they take it good-naturedly, even pretend to be amused. A few sulk and won't talk to anyone the rest of the day.

I have to tell you about a time the bucketfish gag backfired.

It was on a charter boat off Long Island. This fellow kept going asleep in the fighting chair, and finally the skipper suggested the bucketfish treatment, to which the patsy's companions agreed enthusiastically. Yanked out of a snooze by the sound of his reel's ratchet, he hastily lifted the rod from its fighting chair holder and began battling his fish. And quite a battle it was, the bucketfish resisting mightily and pulling line yardage from the reel in power runs. After a while the boat's captain and mate began to exchange puzzled glances. The fight continued for another half-hour, the angler seemingly unable to reel in the bucketfish. Standing at the transom, flying gaff at the ready, the mate looked up at the skipper on the flying bridge and shrugged his shoulders, as much as to say, "You've got *me*, Cap." A few minutes later they peered into the water and saw something that dumbfounded them. Instead of a bucketfish, the angler had been fighting a mako shark. What had happened was that the mako, attracted to the bait, rubbed against the bucklefish's line, and his sandpaperlike hide severed it, freeing the pail. Then the shark grabbed the bait.

The patsy said he knew all the time he was fighting a shark. He never did believe his buddies' story about the bucketfish.

Caution: There's a certain risk in losing tackle in the bucketfish stunt. My advice is that you don't play it unless the angler's outfit is securely in the

fighting chair's rod holder or attached to the patsy by means of a harness. You can imagine what could happen if he were holding the rod loosely while asleep.

Fish or Cut Bait

This famous old command originated as a reprimand to the lazy angler aboard. We hear it all around us to remind someone to "make yourself useful," or, "don't just sit there; do something!"

Red Herring

In days of old the British would drag a red herring across the trail of a fox to destroy its scent and thereby divert hunting dogs. The meaning remains much the same today: anything to distract attention from the real issue. President Harry Truman used the term to characterize the congressional hearings on communism in government in the early 1950s.

Ye Gods and Little Fishes

A remark of contempt that originated with the lower classes in the late 19th century. Later it became a general exclamation of derision or amazement.

For you catch your next fish with a piece of the last.
—Oliver Wendell Holmes

Touché!

It was during a running of the great United States Atlantic Tuna Tournament out of Galilee (Point Judith), R.I. Another contest day was over, and the tourney fleet was returning to its base of operations to weigh the catches of those boats lucky enough to have whipped a giant bluefin tuna. I was aboard the tournament's press boat along with four or five other scribblers and photographers.

We were only about a mile from the jetty flanking the entrance to the harbor when someone on our boat's flying bridge yipped "Swordfish!" and excitedly pointed off to starboard. We were electrified and looked where he pointed. Swordfish are among the most prestigious of all game fishes. Out there, sure enough, could be seen the dorsal fin and upper lope of the crescentic tail of a broadbill swordfish, lazing along at the surface as those regal billfish often do on sunny summer days. Judging by the distance between the dorsal fin and tail, this broadbill was estimated to be in the 300- to 400-lb. class.

There was only a slight breeze chop on the water, not enough for the waves to play tricks on the eyes, as they sometimes do. This looked like a swordfish sure enough, yet there was a nagging suspicion ringing a bell in the back of my skull. One, it was too late in the summer for swordfish, but this could've been a stray. Two, what made me even more suspicious, I think, was the closeness of this one to shore, now less than a mile. The nearest I'd ever heard of one coming was about three or four miles, and that was close. This situation just didn't add up, as the saying goes.

Since other boats were beginning to group around the swordfish, we didn't stop. Later I confirmed my suspicions. That "swordfish" was a fake created by a Montauk charter captain friend of mine, Frank Mundus. Frank had nailed the dorsal fin and tail of a broadbill to a suitably long plank—a four-by-four, as I recall. On the way in that afternoon, he unobtrusively slid that dummy in the water. From any distance it was realistic, I can tell you. Some of the USATT boats paused long enough to investigate, then moved on, saying nothing and leaving the hoax in the water to fool others. I heard tell that one boat actually hurled a harpoon at the "fish."

Getting Hooked on . . .

Nowadays this expression has a drug addiction meaning, but an older, more innocent meaning was to be overly fond of something.

Fishy

This adjective is attributed to Benjamin Disraeli, the British statesman and writer who used the expression in his 1844 work *Coningsby*. It still remains a label for anything of a suspicious nature.

Happy as a Clam at High Tide

The happy clam is a safe clam. Clams can be best harvested when their beds are in very shallow water or at low tide. We use this old adage in modern times to connote "feeling secure and happy."

A sly old fish, too cunning for the hook.
—George Crabbe

Codfish Are Collectors (of a Sort)

Cod have incredible appetites. "Glutton" becomes a weak word when applied to them. Get a load of these items found in the stomachs of cod along with their normal diet (which includes smaller fishes and any other creatures their mouths can accommodate): electric light bulbs, nuts, bolts and other small items of hardware; empty beer cans, pieces of wood, cloth and tar paper; and lengths of rope. One fisherman found a whiskey bottle—empty, worse luck.

And another sinker bouncer actually found something of value. All excited, he telephoned me to report that in the stomach of a cod he had caught that afternoon was a woman's necklace. The bauble had probably been lost overboard from some vessel, or possibly had been accidentally thrown out with some garbage that was jettisoned at sea. One thing for sure, that cod hadn't eaten the lady. Last I heard, he was going to have it appraised. I never learned how he made out.

Needless to say, cod are not a dependable source of free jewelry. But over the years conchologists—shell collectors—have looked to cod for specimens of shells otherwise unavailable. Some collectors used to haunt large wholesale fish markets, like New York City's famous Fulton Market, where cod were cleaned in quantity.

There was sound logic in this procedure. Cod, being bottom feeders, eat a lot of mollusks. They devour them shells and all. In the fish's gut the meat is digested out and the shells are stacked for elimination. Only catch is, collectors have to get there before cod go to the bathroom.

There Are Plenty More Fish in the Sea

This popular 20th century proverb and cliché is addressed to someone whose romance has come to an end.

Loan Shark

A description of a man who lends money at usurious interest and employs harsh methods—like breaking the kneecaps—to collect delinquent accounts.

Clambake

A party or social get-together. In the 1950s it also was applied to a swing musician's jam session.

There are as good fish in the sea that ever came out of it.

—Sir Walter Scott

What Price Glory?

When I was an editor on the staff of a national sport fishing magazine, a press release came to me from an East Coast angling club announcing the winners of its annual contest for members. As my eyes scanned the list of eligible species and winning weights, they came to a screeching halt at one figure, 8½ lbs., for a black sea bass. That figure jumped right off the paper at me because the existing International Game Fish Association world record for black sea bass stood at 8 lbs. even. Here was a new world record. I wondered if the club and the angler realized it.

I telephoned the contest's chairman to check. "Is that weight, 8½ lbs., correct?" I asked.

"Yep," replied the chairman. He said that he and others had witnessed the weighing.

"Do you realize that's a new world record?" I asked.

Something in the silence at the other end of the wire told me he didn't.

I asked him if he knew what had happened to the fish. Sometimes fishermen keep their prized catches on ice for a few days for bragging purposes.

Again, silence at the other end. "What happened to that fish?" I nudged him.

"The guy ate it," said the contest chairman.

Logic in Reverse

A grandfather was introducing his five-year-old descendant to fishing and had decided that there was no time like the present for the kid to learn how to dig his own worms. So the two of them had at it. For a while the boy was real enthusiastic, but then the novelty wore off and it became work. Finally he stopped altogether. "Hey, Grampa," he said, "how come you buried these worms out here in the first place?"

Pretty Kettle of Fish

This phrase originated from a custom that was common along the Scottish seacoast. At the start of the salmon runs each year, groups of Scots would picnic along the banks of the river, and the "main course" of that picnic meal would be boiled over a fire and eaten in a catch-as-catch-can fashion. In modern usage, the expression describes a predicament. If you listen carefully to your memory, you might hear comedian Oliver Hardy upbraid his timid buddy Stan Laurel with: "A fine kettle of fish you've got us in!"

Fish Eye

An expressionless glance, or maybe a questioning or suspicious stare.

Fishtailing

A way of describing the side-to-side movement of a vehicle's rear section. Aircraft sometimes fishtail in turbulence.

The gods do not subtract from the allotted span of men's lives the hours spent in fishing.

—Unknown source

D.O.A. ("Dead Or Acting")

Sharks are primitive fishes, which is why they're capable of weird actions when they're supposed to be dead.

The eeriest example ever witnessed by me occurred during one of my many offshore shark fishing trips. A blue shark that had been caught, and was as dead as he would ever be, was butchered in preparation for the table—gutted and head cut off. This done, the skipper cradled the carcass in his arms and was carrying it aft for storage on ice when the boat suddenly rolled, throwing him off balance. Out of his arms and overboard slid the blue shark's headless, gutless carcass. No sooner did it hit the water than it sluggishly swam away. This was purely a post-mortem involuntary nervous action. The fish was dead, but his nerves and muscles weren't—yet.

That could've made an uninformed spectator nervous too.

The post-mortem nervous reactions of dead sharks are varied. Take warning: *Some are sudden, violent and dangerous.* Witness: One day a skipper friend of mine had a good payload of customers on his party boat for a day of mackerel fishing. Action was excellent; everyone aboard was cranking in mackerel. Then, abruptly, the activity ceased as though turned off by a faucet. To the captain that meant only one thing. A shark had moved in; and because the species has a great fondness for mackerel, he suspected that the raider was a mako. But species was unimportant. They had to get rid of this shark. He had ruined the fishing. A heavy-duty rod and reel were kept ready for this purpose. Hastily the mate baited a 12/0 hook with a whole mackerel.

The mate caught the shark, and it was a mako, close to 400 lbs., it turned out later. But now the skipper had another problem. He would never bring a live shark of any kind, much less a very lively brute such as the mako, into the boat; but the rifle with which he ordinarily dispatched sharks was back on shore being repaired. He decided to hoist the mako out of the water by the tail and gut him while he hung there outside the boat.

This mako had to be dead, the skipper figured, so it was safe to swing the carcass inboard. And that's what he did. As the corpse was being lowered to the deck its snout came in contact with one of the boat's rail supports, a three-inch-thick piece of seasoned oak. Instantly the jaws seized on that support and broke off splinters. You can imagine what it would have been like if that support had been some angler's leg.

I know of a case in which an angler's leg was involved. It happened in South Africa. Over there they have a species of shark which I maintain makes our white shark or man-eater look like a Sunday-school teacher. It's the Zambezi shark, which reaches lengths of up to 10 ft. and weights to 400 lbs. and is especially dangerous because of (1) a chronically vicious disposition, (2) greater aggressiveness than the white shark and (3) ventures into shallow coastal waters and even journeys many miles up rivers.

Anyway, an angler named J.J. Rickert, who should have known better, was boat fishing at a place called St. Lucia Inlet on South Africa's Indian Ocean coast when he caught a young Zambezi, only 4 ft. long, 42 lbs. and very foolishly brought the shark into his boat. For a while the shark lay quiet and seemed to have expired. Suddenly, explosively, the "dead" Zambezi came to life and attacked Rickert, clamping his jaws on the angler's leg above the ankle. Only by beating the shark on the head for many excruciatingly painful minutes was Rickert able to make him let go. By then the injury to his leg was severe, and the victim had weeks in a hospital to reflect on the folly of bringing a live shark into a boat.

How can you be sure a shark is dead? There's only one reasonably reliable way to find out.

Nudge him in the eye with a suitably long stick or pole. If there's any movement of that eye whatsoever (it may be so slight as to almost escape notice), look out!

On Your Own Hook

This saying is credited to New England fishermen who were paid according to the size of their catch. In the old days of hook and line fishing this meant that the day's wage was dependent on what each angler caught on his own hook. In modern parlance it means "You're on your own."

Having Other Fish to Fry

Means having something else, usually something better, to do at the time.

Neither Fish nor Fowl nor Good Red Herring

This is a medieval saying based on the culinary distinctions of class: fish for the clergy, fowl for common folk and red herring for the destitute. The phrase, loosely translated, meant that the thing in question would be unsuitable for anyone. In the 20th century this catch statement—at least the "neither fish nor fowl" part—is used to describe a vague idea or an item that doesn't fit a definite design.

Like a fish out of water.

—Attributed to a Pope Eugenius

She Couldn't Rob the Cradle

(Foreword: Since this item contains adult material —sexy stuff—parental guidance for all readers under age six is advised.)

Did you know that there are three different modes of reproduction among sharks? Aha, I thought you didn't!

Unlike the standard procedure among other fishes, in which fertilization takes place in the water, fertilization among sharks is—you should pardon the expression—inside the female, which is much more fun, I would imagine. Reproduction then takes one of the three forms, according to species.

Most sharks are ovoviviparous, which is a Latin-scientific way of saying that the young start out as eggs but complete their development as fetuses in the oviducts, all inside the mother. Some sharks are oviparous, which means that the females lay eggs, inside which the infants develop. (Eggs of the oviparous whale shark are a foot long, in case anyone asks you.) And some species of sharks are viviparous, which means that the babies develop in mama's uterus and are born alive, fully equipped and ready to go. Certain species of sharks are noted for the sizes of their litters. The blue shark, for instance, can turn loose anywhere from about 28 to as many as 54 kids at one clip.

Among the champion litter producers is the tiger shark. One large female had 82. This species' prolificacy cost a lady angler a world record. The anglerette was Dolly Dyer of Australia, a noted big-game fisherperson and holder, at one time or another, of several official shark world records. One day, as she was ending a battle with a large female tiger, the shark gave birth to a sizable litter of pups. The weight of those offspring, it was estimated later, cost Dolly another record.

A Fluke

The common name of a species of flatfish is used to indicate something that happened but wasn't supposed to happen or a strange twist of fate.

Tight as a Clam or Clamming Up

Keeping one's mouth shut so as not to betray a secret, or spill the beans.

Hooked

Modern day utterance that means one is caught. Often used in disparaging romantic connotations: "She hooked a husband. . . ." "The poor guy's hooked now."

Leap they like a flounder out of a frying pan into the fire . . .
— Sir Thomas More

Pride & Prejudice

One glorious March afternoon when we were 11 years old, my friend Roger and I sat on the bayside remains of an abandoned ferryboat dock and caught flounders like they had been declared illegal. Our tackle left plenty to be desired. It consisted of mismatched rods and reels that had been retired by our elders because of corroded parts in the reels, missing guides on the rods, and other infirmities. I suspect that our line was in an unhealthy condition too. It was so old that neither of us knew what strength it was. All things considered, it was fortunate that flounders are small fish.

One thing we did know, and that was how to fish for flounders.

By and by an old gent came out on the wharf and without so much as a nodded greeting to us took up a station about 10 ft. away. He was well dressed, although not exactly for flounder fishing from the decaying remains of a wharf. What caught our eyes was his fishing outfit. Roger and I knew enough about tackle to recognize an expensive rod and reel when we saw them. We turned back to our reeling in flounders, and pretty soon our wordless neighbor was fishing too. But with one difference. He wasn't catching anything. And when Roger and I left a few hours—and two dozen flounders—later, he was still scoreless and he still hadn't opened his mouth to us. Obviously he was doing something wrong, expensive tackle notwithstanding, but he never gave us a chance to find out what it was. Had he opened his mouth we probably could have helped him.

The story has a moral: never be afraid to admit your ignorance and ask questions of more experienced anglers, even if they happen to be kids. That's the way we all learn, and none of us learn it all.

Hook, Line and Sinker

This great old saying was born in the Old West. An Easterner who believed a frontier tall tale was compared to a hungry fish who swallowed bait "hook, line and sinker." By the mid-19th century this colorful depiction of a gullible listener was popular all across the U.S.

Mackerel Snatcher (Snapper)

A derogatory term, popular some decades ago, for anyone who belonged to the Roman Catholic faith. The expression refers to the fact that a good many Catholics, who were forbidden to eat meat on Fridays and fasting days, preferred inexpensive mackerel to other food substitutes.

Small Fry

A name often given to kids or children, from the fishing word fry, indicating baby fishes.

Guests and fish stink after three days.

—Benjamin Franklin

"Here's My Card . . ."

Shark-fishing skipper-guide Frank Mundus of Montauk, N.Y., tells this story about one of his customers.

Back at the dock after a day of shark hunting offshore, a member of the party that had chartered Frank's *Cricket II* that day was busily butchering a mako carcass. Out of curiosity he cut open the shark's stomach to see what the monster had been feeding on. The stomach was full of chum—ground-up menhaden—that had led to the mako's downfall, and right on top of the mess was Captain Frank Mundus's business card.

Needless to say, the angler was puzzled. Then he grinned. He called Frank over. "Hey, Cap," he said, "when did you sneak your business card into my mako's stomach? That's gotta be somethin' new in advertising!"

Frank denied he had placed the card in the shark's stomach when the fisherman wasn't looking; but the more he protested that he didn't do it, the more his customer was convinced that he did, as a gag.

It was neither a gag nor a mystery. Frank is in the habit of preparing large quantities of shark chum in advance and storing the stuff in a local fish market's refrigerated storeroom until needed. To show who owns it, he lays one of his business cards atop the pulp in each can. In this instance the card had been ladled overboard with the chum, whereupon the mako gulped it down.

But the fisherman was never convinced that it wasn't a joke.

That reminds me of a similar incident, also involving Captain Frank Mundus.

Again one of Frank's clients was performing an "autopsy" on a shark he had caught that day. In the fish's stomach this angler found the carcass of a rabbit. At this the circle of spectators watching the surgery oohed and aahed, and the fisherman himself was amazed. This shark had been caught well offshore, a place not known for its rabbits. A lot of dockside rubberneckers went back to the city that afternoon talking about how a shark had captured a bunny, way out in the ocean. The fisherman himself talked about his astounding find for weeks afterward.

I don't think Frank ever put him wise to what had happened, which was this: On the way to the dock that morning Frank paused long enough to pick up the carcass of a bunny that had lost an argument with a car. Just for laughs he'd bait a shark hook with that dead rabbit and see what happened. That's what he did, except that no one saw him do it. In due course a shark was attracted by the boat's chum and grabbed the bunny bait.

Holy Mackerel!

According to *I Hear America Talking, An Illustrated History of American Words and Phrases*, this expression, like "Holy Cats," is a holdover from pre-Victorian days when blasphemy (coupling "holy" with other words) was considered naughty, and shocking.

Catch a Crab

This expression is common to oarsmen, especially on rowing crews. You can "catch a crab" one of two ways: by failing to dip an oar into the water while making a stroke, or by neglecting to lift an oar completely free of the water while making a recovery from a stroke. Either way the rowing is thrown offbeat.

Fish Tale or Fish Story

Any story that sounds exaggerated or untrue.

Index